TAFT AND ROOSEVELT

KENNIKAT PRESS SCHOLARLY REPRINTS
Dr. Ralph Adams Brown, Senior Editor

Series in
AMERICAN HISTORY AND CULTURE
IN THE TWENTIETH CENTURY
Under the General Editorial Supervision of
Dr. Donald R. McCoy
Professor of History, University of Kansas

MAJOR ARCHIBALD WILLINGHAM BUTT

*"After I heard that part of the ship's company had gone down," said
President Taft after the sinking of the TITANIC, "I gave up hope for
the rescue of Major Butt. I knew that he would remain until every
duty had been performed and every sacrifice made."*

TAFT
AND
ROOSEVELT

THE INTIMATE LETTERS OF ARCHIE BUTT

MILITARY AIDE

VOLUME ONE

KENNIKAT PRESS
Port Washington, N. Y./London

109463

TAFT AND ROOSEVELT

First published in 1930
Reissued in 1971 by Kennikat Press
Library of Congress Catalog Card No: 71-137968
ISBN 0-8046-1425-3

Manufactured by Taylor Publishing Company   Dallas, Texas

KENNIKAT SERIES ON AMERICAN HISTORY AND
CULTURE IN THE TWENTIETH CENTURY

CONTENTS

VOLUME ONE

INTRODUCTION

WHEN the steamship *Titanic* sank in the Atlantic on the night of April 14, 1912, one of the brave men who stayed on her deck watching the lifeboats carry women and children to safety, was Archibald Willingham Butt, major in the United States Army, military aide at the White House since 1908, and friend of two Presidents, Theodore Roosevelt and William Howard Taft.

"After I heard that part of the ship's company had gone down," said President Taft, "I gave up hope for the rescue of Major Butt, unless by accident. I knew that he would certainly remain on the ship's deck until every duty had been performed and every sacrifice made that properly fell on one charged, as he would feel himself charged, with responsibility for the rescue of others."

Archie Butt, as he was popularly known the country over, wrote letters home, first to his mother and then to his sister-in-law, almost every day while he was the aide and constant companion of Presidents Roosevelt and Taft. His letters of the Roosevelt period were published in 1924. In the further letters now opened to the public he tells the story of the Taft administration as he saw it—the political problems and social life of the White House, the important happenings as well as the less important gossip of the national capital, and, most striking of all, the gradual development of the historic Taft-Roosevelt controversy.

Of that controversy the country has heard explanations without number. Partisan versions of its causes and results have filled columns in the newspapers and pages in many books. The narrative of Major Butt, including as it does a wealth of incidents and anecdotes hitherto unreported, cannot fail to illuminate a discussion which has held so much interest for two generations.

Lawrence F. Abbott, in his introduction to the volume of earlier letters, wrote of Archie Butt:

"He is gossipy without being trifling; truthful without being bitter; and indulges in humor without infringing upon good taste."

Concerning the unpublished letters, now presented, Mr. Abbott said: "One of the striking manifestations of the fine grain of Captain Butt's nature is that he was able to serve two such divergent masters without sacrificing any of his absorbing admiration for the first or of his sincere personal attachment to the second. He saw both men in an official and personal relationship of unique intimacy. The two Presidents whom he served were totally different in temperament. They approached life from different angles. Their qualities were complementary. President Roosevelt was quick, active, decisive; President Taft was deliberate. President Roosevelt believed, as he himself once said, that aggressive fighting for the right is the noblest sport that the world affords; pugnacity of any kind was distasteful to President Taft. President Roosevelt was born with the temperament of an advocate; President Taft with the temperament of a judge.

"Toward the close of President Taft's administration, when Roosevelt and Taft came into political conflict that developed into a bitter struggle, Captain Butt found himself in a difficult position. His personal devotion to Roosevelt had not in the least waned. He felt himself drawn, as so many others have been, to his first chief by a spiritual affinity, if I may use that term, which time, distance, and admitted mistakes or defects could not destroy. But the engaging personality of his second chief had also enlisted his affection. Moreover, he had that high sense of honor which we like to think, and rightly think, is characteristic of the best type of military officer.

"Here was a dilemma. How could he preserve his sense of loyalty to both friends without taking sides with either? His unpublished letters, without directly referring to the struggle which was going on in his own mind, without comparing the two men, without disparagement of either, without expressing a judgment as to the rights or the wrongs of the conflict, indicate clearly by implication that he found the situation a very harassing one. This was not because anyone or either side asked him to declare himself. Indeed, there was no official reason why he should have declared himself, for his position was not a political one, nor did it involve any political duties or responsibilities. But apparently he felt that his own spiritual self-respect would sooner or later call for a decision, even if a private one. He felt, it would seem, that he must either throw himself with whole-hearted sympathy on the side of Mr. Taft, thus breaking with the Roosevelt family, which had entwined itself with the deepest and most intimate feelings of his life; or he must resign his position as presidential aide, in connection with which he had very high ideals and which he regarded as a place of public trust.

"To the casual reader who looks upon the position of a military aide as that of a mere social functionary this may all seem very grandiloquent, but Archie Butt was much more than a social functionary. He was a simple, straightforward, honorable gentleman, and a psychological problem such as he was facing is much more profound and perplexing to a simple and straightforward soul than to the shrewd and calculating man of affairs. Whether my analysis is correct or not, it is a fact that in the spring of 1912 Archie Butt's superb physical health began to show signs of deterioration. He suffered from depression and fatigue, which the kindly eye of President Taft observed, and at the suggestion of the President he planned a trip to Europe for recuperation."

After a month in Europe, Major Butt sailed homeward on his last voyage aboard the *Titanic*.

Born in Augusta, Georgia, on September 26, 1865, Archie Butt was graduated in 1888 from the University of the South, Sewanee, Tennessee. He was a reporter in Louisville, Kentucky, and Macon, Georgia; then correspondent in Washington for a group of Southern newspapers. After enlisting for the Spanish-American War, he became quartermaster captain of volunteers in 1900 and later received his commission in the regular army. Service in the Philippines and Cuba was followed by his appointment as military aide at the White House. In that capacity he was a constant companion of Mr. Roosevelt and Mr. Taft, both of whom bore witness afterward that he had won their friendship as well as their appreciation for extraordinary service.

Nearly all the letters he wrote in the Taft administration were addressed to his sister-in-law, "Dear Clara," Mrs. Lewis F. Butt, of Augusta, Georgia, who authorizes this publication in accordance with his expressed wish that they be made public after a lapse of time.

A WHO'S WHO

OF PEOPLE MENTIONED BUT NOT FULLY DESCRIBED
OR IDENTIFIED IN THE TEXT OF THE LETTERS.

ABRUZZI, DUKE OF THE: A member of the Royal House of Savoy whose attention to, and reported engagement with, Miss Katherine Elkins, daughter of Senator Elkins of West Virginia, was one of the social sensations of the day.

ADAMS, MAUDE: The well known actress.

ADEE, ALVEY AUGUSTUS: For many years Second Assistant Secretary of State. The "Elder Statesman" of the Department..

AINSWORTH, FREDERICK CRAYTON: Army surgeon and for many years Adjutant General of the army. His clash with Leonard Wood, an army surgeon who was also transferred to the Line, was one of the most vexatious incidents of the Administration.

ALDRICH, NELSON WILMARTH: Long Senator from Rhode Island. High tariff apostle. Author of the Tariff bill which was given his name.

ALESHIRE, JAMES BUCHANAN: Popular army officer, Major General and Quartermaster General of the army during the Taft Administration.

AMES, ADELBERT: A veteran of the Civil War. He played a prominent rôle in the Southern states during the Reconstruction period.

ANDERSON, CHANDLER: Counselor of the State Department under Knox. Since a distinguished international lawyer.

ANDERSON, LARZ: Member of the diplomatic service for many years, Ambassador to Japan in the Taft Administration.

ANDREW, PIATT: Assistant Secretary of the Treasury, later member of Congress from Massachusetts.

ASTOR, NANCY LANGHORNE, VISCOUNTESS ASTOR: A daughter of Virginia who married the head of the English branch of the Astor family. Member of Parliament from Plymouth. Wit and politician.

BACON, AUGUSTUS O.: Senator from Georgia, a great constitutional lawyer. For many years leader of the Democrats in the Senate.

BACON, ROBERT: A classmate of Roosevelt at Harvard, Assistant Secretary of State under Taft. Ambassador to France during the Roosevelt visit to Paris. On the staff of General Pershing during the Great War.

BAILEY, JOSEPH WELDON: Senator from Texas. Widely known for his reluctance to wear evening clothes—which later he overcame.

BAKHMETEFF, GEORGE: Ambassador from Russia to the United States. The last under the Imperial régime. His wife, a daughter of General Beale, the Pathfinder of California, was a social leader in Washington for many years.

BALLINGER, RICHARD ACHILLES: Secretary of the Interior in the cabinet of Taft. The storm center of the struggle between the conservationists and the anti-conservationists which disrupted the Administration.

BANNARD, OTTO TREMONT: Banker, lawyer. President of the New York Trust Company. Defeated candidate for Mayor of New York on the Republican ticket, 1909. Fellow of the Corporation of Yale University. Close friend and adviser of President Taft.

BARRY, THOMAS HENRY: Major General U. S. Army. Veteran of the China Expedition and the Philippine campaigns. Close friend and adviser of President Taft in 1909, when he commanded the American forces during the Second Occupation of Cuba.

BELL, J. FRANKLIN: Major General and Chief of Staff U. S. Army. An officer who did distinguished service in the Philippines.

BELMONT, MR. and MRS. PERRY: Social leaders. Mr. Belmont was a former minister to Spain and Congressman from New York City.

BENEDICT, E. C.: New York banker and broker. Intimate friend and frequent host of President Cleveland.

BERNSTORFF, COUNT JOHANN VON: A German diplomat who came to Washington as Ambassador in 1908. His rôle during the Great War is well known. He advised the German Emperor against submarine warfare and fell into disgrace. To-day one of the leaders of the Democratic party in Germany and representative of the Reich in the Council of the League of Nations.

BEVERIDGE, ALBERT JEREMIAH: Senator from Indiana, Progressive. One of the leaders of the Bull Moose campaign. Later the author of the *Life of John Marshall.*

BIGELOW, JOHN: Diplomat and historian. Minister to France during the Civil War. Adviser and executor of Samuel J. Tilden.

BLAINE, MRS. JAMES G.: Widow of the former Secretary of State and Republican leader. Prominent figure in Washington society for many years after the death of her husband.

BLAIR, GIST: Son of Montgomery Blair, Postmaster General in the cabinet of Lincoln. Social figure in Washington and St. Louis.

BLISS, TASKER HOWARD: Army officer and authority on international law. Collector of Customs during the first American occupation of Cuba. Chief of Staff of the Army. American member of the Supreme War Council during the Great War. Member of the Commission to Negotiate Peace, by appointment of President Wilson, 1918.

BLYTHE, SAMUEL GEORGE: The well known correspondent and author.

BOARDMAN, MISS MABEL: Formerly of Cleveland, an intimate of the Taft family. Distinguished socially and for Red Cross work.

BORAH, WILLIAM EDGAR: Elected Senator from Idaho, 1907, and has remained in the Senate ever since. Famous campaign orator. Now chairman of the Senate Foreign Relations Committee.

BOURNE, JONATHAN, JR.: Senator from Oregon. A prominent figure in the pre-convention struggle between Taft and Roosevelt.

BOUTELL, HENRY SHERMAN: Member of Congress from Illinois and Minister to Switzerland and Portugal. Adviser to President Taft in labor disputes.

BRADLEY, WILLIAM O'CONNELL: Distinguished Senator from Kentucky.

BRAGG, BRAXTON: General in the Confederate army.

BRANDEGEE, FRANK BOSWORTH: Senator from Connecticut. Member of the Foreign Relations Committee and outstanding opponent of Wilson's policies. He committed suicide as a result of unwise real estate speculations in Washington.

BRISTOW, JOSEPH LITTLE: Senator from Kansas, 1909–1915. A leading dry of the earliest vintage.

BROWN, WALTER FOLGER: A lawyer from Ohio. Leader in the Bull Moose party. Assistant Secretary of Commerce under President Hoover.

BRYAN, WILLIAM JENNINGS: Democratic leader and perennial candidate for the Presidency.

BRYCE, JAMES: Ambassador from England in Washington many years. Author of *The American Commonwealth.*

BURTON, THEODORE ELIJAH: Long a leading member of Congress both in the House and the Senate. A strong advocate of the International Parliamentary Union and a representative of the United States Government at many conferences on arbitration and international peace. An advocate of the extension of national waterways.

BUTT, MRS. LEWIS F. B.: Sister-in-law of the writer of the letters. The "Dear Clara" of the correspondence.

CANNON, JOSEPH G.: Member of Congress from Illinois from 1873 to 1917 with but one interval of two years. Speaker of the House, 1903–1911. Received sixty-eight votes for the Presidential nomination in the Republican Convention of 1908. A thorn in the side of both Roosevelt and Taft. His power in the party was deplored by both.

CARNEGIE, ANDREW: The iron and steel manufacturer of Pittsburgh, later famous for his benefactions in many fields. At this period he furnished the ground and the funds for the construction of the famous Pan-American building.

CARPENTER, FRED WARNER: Went with Mr. Taft as secretary to the Philippines in 1901, and remained with him as private secretary until 1910, when he was appointed United States Minister to Morocco.

CARTER, WILLIAM HARDING: Major General, U. S. Army. Famous for his campaigns against the Indians, for which he was awarded the Congressional Medal of Honor. A great horseman and a writer of many remarkable papers on army subjects.

CHAFFEE, ADNA ROMANZA: Lieutenant General U. S. Army and Chief of Staff. He commanded the American contingent on the march to Peking during the Boxer War and a year later turned over the chief command in the Philippines to the first civil Governor, who was Mr. Taft.

CLARK, CHAMP: Congressman from Missouri and Speaker of the House during the 62d, 63d, and 64th congresses. He had a small majority of the votes in the Democratic Convention for the Presidency in 1912 during several days' balloting, but was ultimately defeated by Woodrow Wilson.

CLEWS, HENRY: Famous Wall Street man, banker and broker. Mrs. Clews, who was a grandniece of President Madison, was a frequent visitor to Washington and an attractive figure in society.

COCKRAN, BOURKE: Democratic politician and Congressman, famous for his eloquence. His marriage to Miss Anne Ide in 1910, the daughter of Henry Clay Ide, who had been so closely associated with Mr. Taft in the Philippines, brought him into close social contact with the Administration.

COMER, BRAXTON BRAGG: Governor of Alabama and host of President Taft on several occasions. A farmer on a large scale in his home state; also the owner of famous orange groves in Florida.

CORBIN, HENRY: For many years Adjutant General of the army. He married one of the famous Patton sisters of Washington. Upon his retirement he was selected by President Taft for a European embassy but died before entering upon his duties.

COWLES, WILLIAM SHEFFIELD: Naval aide to President Roosevelt and married his sister. Retired as Rear Admiral.

CRANE, MURRAY: Senator from Massachusetts during the Taft Administration. Influential member of the Republican National Committee for thirty years. A president maker.

CROSBY, HERBERT BALL: Major General U. S. Army and Chief of Cavalry by appointment of President Coolidge. After his retirement in 1930 he was appointed Commissioner in the District of Columbia by President Hoover.

CROZIER, WILLIAM: Brigadier General U. S. Army and Chief of Ordnance for many years. Inventor of many now recognized ordnance devices.

DALZELL, JOHN: Congressman from Pittsburgh for thirty years. A stalwart standpatter. A silent member, most important in committee.

DE CHAMBRUN: Count and military attaché of the French Embassy. His marriage with Miss Longworth, sister of the Congressman, brought him into close social relations with the Roosevelts and the Tafts. He was attached to the American Army upon our entrance into the war.

DE KOVEN, MR. AND MRS. REGINALD: Mr. De Koven, a popular composer; his wife, an authoress. Prominent in Washington throughout the Taft Administration.

DE LA BARRA: Minister of Foreign Affairs in Mexico at the end of the Diaz régime and provisional President of Mexico awaiting the election which brought in the ill-fated Madero Administration.

DEPEW, CHAUNCEY: The celebrated raconteur and after-dinner speaker. Also famous lobbyist. Senator from New York, 1899–1911. Frequently a candidate in the Republican National conventions for the Presidency.

DIMOCK, MRS. SUSAN: A famous Washington hostess. Sister of William C. Whitney, Secretary of the Navy under Cleveland.

DWIGHT, JOHN W.: Congressman from New York. Prominent figure in the Aldrich-Tawney tariff fight.

EDWARDS, CLARENCE: Major General, U. S. Army. Aide to General Lawton when the latter was killed in battle near Manila. For many years Chief of the Insular Bureau which brought him into close contact with Taft both as Secretary of War and President. In World War he commanded the 26th ("Yankee") Division.

ELIOT, CHARLES WILLIAM: The famous educator. President of Harvard University and publicist. Declined the offer of the embassy in London when made by Taft, the Yale President.

ELKINS, MISS KATHERINE: Daughter of Senator Stephen Elkins of West Virginia. The attention to her of the Duke of the Abruzzi, of the Royal House of Savoy, was the outstanding international romance of the period. Later married to the son of Congressman Hitt of Indiana.

EMORY, MISS: Daughter of Rear Admiral William H. Emory, U. S. Navy, widely known as "the Swell of the Ocean." Married Mr. Ovey of the British Embassy.

FAIRBANKS, CHARLES WARREN: Long in the Senate from Indiana. Vice President during the Roosevelt Administration.

FITZGERALD, JOHN J.: Congressman from Brooklyn district. When Democrats secured control of House, became chairman of the influential Committee on Appropriations.

FORAKER, JOSEPH B.: Senator from Ohio. Nominated McKinley for the Presidency. Forceful opponent of Roosevelt and Taft in Ohio and in national politics.

FRICK, HENRY CLAY: Manufacturer of steel, and coke magnate. An associate of Andrew Carnegie. Shot by a striker in the famous Homestead riots. A famous collector of paintings.

FULLER, MELVILLE W.: Made Chief Justice of the United States in 1888 by President Cleveland. A Democrat, he had been active for some years in politics. In the Democratic National Convention of 1876 he made the nominating speech of Thomas A. Hendricks for the Presidency.

FUSHIMI, PRINCE AND PRINCESS: Prominent members of the Imperial Family of Japan.

GARDNER, AUGUSTUS PEABODY: Congressman from Massachusetts. Married Constance, daughter of Senator Henry Cabot Lodge. Resigned to enter the army. Died in training camp on the eve of departure for France.

GARFIELD, JAMES R.: Son of the twentieth President. Secretary of the Interior under Roosevelt. An ardent "Bull Mooser." Failure to retain him in his cabinet was one of Roosevelt's grievances against Taft.

GARY, ELBERT H.: Lawyer. Chairman of the U. S. Steel Corporation. Intimately connected with the Trust battles throughout the terms of Roosevelt and Taft.

GERRY, PETER GOELET: Congressman and later Senator from Rhode Island. He married Mathilde Townsend, daughter of Mrs. Richard Townsend. Mother and daughter figure prominently in the Letters. The Peter Goelets were divorced in 1928.

GIBBONS, CARDINAL JAMES: Archbishop of Baltimore. Primate of the Roman Catholic Church in America until his death. A close friend of Mr. Taft.

GIBSON, MR. and MRS. CHARLES DANA: The famous illustrator and his wife, Irene Gibson, the original "Gibson girl," and sister of Lady Astor.

GLOVER, CHARLES CARROLL: President of Riggs National Bank. Long social, political, and financial figure in Washington. Father of the Washington Park System. A close friend of President Taft.

GOETHALS, GEORGE W.: Famous army engineer. Chief engineer of Panama Canal. First Civil Governor of the Panama Canal Zone.

GOMEZ, GENERAL JOSÉ MIGUEL: Leader in the Revolution against Spain. Second President of the Cuban Republic.

GORE, THOMAS PRYOR: The Blind Senator from Oklahoma.

GRANT, ROBERT: Massachusetts judge. Overseer of Harvard University. Writer of fiction and social studies. Popular figure in Boston.

GRISCOM, LLOYD C.: Minister to Japan under Roosevelt. Later United States Ambassador to Italy. He figured largely in the Roosevelt-Taft controversy.

HADLEY, ARTHUR TWINING: President of Yale University many years. Expert on railway transportation. An intimate of President Taft.

HADLEY, HERBERT S.: Governor of Missouri. Ardent friend of Theodore Roosevelt. Successful prosecutor of the Standard Oil and Harvester Trust cases.

HAGNER, BELLE: Daughter of Washington physician. Social secretary to Mrs. Roosevelt.

HALE, CHANDLER: Assistant Secretary of State. Married Rachel, daughter of Senator Don Cameron of Pa.

HALE, EUGENE: Father of above. Senator from Maine many years. Chairman Naval Committee. Bitter opponent of President McKinley's policy of intervention in Cuba.

HAMMOND, JOHN HAYS: Mining engineer. Man of great wealth and worldwide business interests. Carried out many special diplomatic missions for President Taft. Served as special ambassador from the United States at the Coronation of King George V of England.

HANNA, MARCUS A.: Senator from Ohio. President Maker. Warm friend of President McKinley. Warm enemy of Roosevelt. Father of Ruth Hanna McCormick, widow of Senator Medill McCormick.

HARDING, WARREN G.: Editor. Defeated by Governor Harmon in the gubernatorial campaign in Ohio in 1910. Elected to the Senate in 1915. Elected President in 1920.

HARMON, JUDSON: Attorney General in Cleveland's Cabinet. Governor of Ohio. Prominent candidate for Presidential nomination in several Democratic national conventions.

HARRIMAN, E. H.: Railway magnate to whom Roosevelt wrote his "We are practical men" letter. His mergers formed the storm center of railway legislation during the Roosevelt and Taft administrations.

HARRIMAN, FLORENCE JAFFRAY: Wife of J. Borden Harriman, New York broker. Social leader and political worker.

HARRISON, BENJAMIN: President, 1888–1892. Defeated for reëlection by Cleveland. Tariff dissensions figured in the battle much as in Taft's defeat in 1912.

HARRISON, FRANCIS BURTON: Congressman from New York City many
terms. Member of Ways and Means Committee. Governor General of
the Philippines for eight years under President Wilson.

HARVEY, GEORGE: Editor of *Harper's Weekly*. Democrat, but left the party
owing to differences with President Wilson. United States Ambassador to
Great Britain by appointment of Harding.

HAY, JAMES: Many years congressman from Virginia. Chairman of the
Committee on Military Affairs at the outbreak of the Great War.

HEDGES, JOB ELMER: Secretary to Mayor Strong of New York. Prominent
lawyer and politician.

HEMPHILL, JAMES C.: Many years editor of the *Charleston News and Courier*.
Influential Democratic editor in the South.

HENGELMÜLLER, BARON AND BARONESS: Long presided over the Austro-
Hungarian Embassy in Washington. Social figures.

HILL, DAVID JAYNE: Diplomat and educator. President of the University of
Rochester. American representative in Switzerland, the Netherlands, and
Germany.

HILL, JAMES J.: Builder of the Great Northern Railway system. A man of
many interests and great influence in the Northwest. Opponent of the
Roosevelt railway policies.

HILL, JOHN WESLEY: Chaplain of the Republican National Convention, 1908.
Ardent Republican. Lecturer in favor of International Peace.

HILLES, CHARLES DEWEY: Chairman of the Republican National Committee,
1912–1916. Influential in New York politics.

HITCHCOCK, FRANK H.: Postmaster General in the Taft cabinet. Manager of
the Taft campaign, 1908. Shepherd of Negro delegates from the Southern
states.

HITCHCOCK, GILBERT M.: Editor. Senator from Nebraska. Author of the
Hitchcock reservations to the Covenant of the League of Nations which
Wilson supported.

HOBSON, RICHMOND P.: Naval officer. Hero of the *Merrimac* episode during
the Spanish War. Member of Congress, 1907–1915. Lecturer in favor of
Prohibition and World Peace.

HOLMES, OLIVER WENDELL: Son of the distinguished writer. Appointed to the
Supreme Court by Roosevelt in 1902. Since then a prominent figure in
Washington.

HOLT, MISS WINIFRED: Sculptress. Founded the Lighthouse and other work-
shops for the blind. Famous for work among the blind of the Great War.

HOOVER, ISAAC, better known as "Uncle Ike": Chief usher at the White
House since time immemorial. The remembrancer of many administrations.

HOWELL, CLARK: Editor of the *Atlanta Constitution*. Successor to the talented
Henry M. Grady. Member of the Democratic National Committee.

HOYT, HENRY M.: Solicitor General under Taft. Father of Eleanor Hoyt
Wylie, the talented writer.

HUGHES, CHARLES EVANS: Jurist statesman. Investigator of life insurance
conditions. Governor of New York, 1906. Would have received Re-

publican presidential nomination in 1908 had he endorsed the Roosevelt policies. Narrowly defeated by Wilson in 1916. Secretary of State under Harding. Successor of Taft as Chief Justice by appointment of President Hoover.

IRELAND, JOHN: Archbishop of St. Paul. Prominent in the "Dear Maria" correspondence between President Roosevelt and Mrs. Storer. Prominent in the Americanism movement within the Roman Catholic Church.

JACKSON, MRS. STONEWALL: Widow of the great Confederate General. Hostess of the Taft party in Charlotte, N. C.

JUSSERAND, JULES: French Ambassador in Washington for twenty years. As in duty bound, he attempted to be on good terms with both Roosevelt and Taft after the break. Able representative of France during Great War.

KEEP, MRS. FLORENCE: Sister of Miss Mabel Boardman. One of the famous Washington hostesses of the period.

KELLOGG, FRANK BILLINGS: Counsel for the United States in Standard Oil cases and Harriman Railway mergers. Senator from Minnesota. Ambassador to England and Secretary of State under Coolidge. Co-author of the Kellogg-Briand Peace Pact.

KERN, JOHN WORTH: Democratic Senator from Indiana. Nominee for Vice-President on the Democratic Ticket in 1908. Long Democratic floor leader in the Senate.

KNOX, PHILANDER CHASE: Attorney General in the cabinets of McKinley and Roosevelt. Senator from Pennsylvania. Resigned to become Secretary of State under Taft. Frequent Presidential candidate. Profound lawyer. Opponent of Wilson on League of Nations question.

KOHLSAAT, H. H.: Merchant and editor of Chicago papers. The friend and intimate of Presidents from Hayes to Coolidge.

LA FOLLETTE, ROBERT MARION: Senator from Wisconsin. Prominent in railway rate legislation. Frequent candidate for the Presidency. Nominated and polled a large Third Party vote in 1924.

LAMAR, JOSEPH RUCKER: Federal judge in the South by appointment of President Taft.

LAWRENCE, WILLIAM: Protestant Episcopal Bishop of Massachusetts. Close friend of President Taft.

LEITER, MRS. MARY CARVER: Wife of Levi Leiter, Chicago merchant. Mother of Lady Curzon, wife of the English statesman and of Joseph Leiter of Chicago wheat-corner fame. Her home on Dupont Circle is a social center.

LESLIE, SHANE: Irish poet and writer who married a daughter of Governor General Ide of the Philippines.

LEWIS, ALFRED HENRY: Author of Western stories who in this period became a widely read Washington Correspondent.

LI, LORD: Son of the celebrated Li Hung Chang. Chinese diplomat who represented his country on many missions in the days of the Manchus.

LITTAUER, L. N.: Congressman from New York. Glove manufacturer. Interested and prominent in tariff matters.

LITTLETON, MARTIN W.: Congressman from New York. Made the nominating speech for Alton B. Parker in the Democratic National Convention, 1904.

LODGE, HENRY CABOT: Long Senator from Massachusetts. Intimate of Theodore Roosevelt. He remained "regular" when the split between Taft and Roosevelt came. In the opinion of President Wilson, his reservations defeated the purpose of the Covenant of the League of Nations.

LODGE, MRS. H. CABOT: Daughter of Admiral Davis. A woman of rare intelligence and great social and political influence in Washington when she chose to exert it.

LOEB, WILLIAM, JR.: Secretary to Roosevelt for many years. Collector of the Port of New York during the Taft Administration.

LONGWORTH, NICHOLAS: Representative from Ohio. Husband of Alice, daughter of President Roosevelt by his first marriage. Later Speaker of House.

LORIMER, WILLIAM: Member of Congress from Illinois. Elected to the Senate in 1909. His election was invalidated by vote of the Senate because of alleged corrupt practices.

LOW, SETH: Educator. President of Columbia College, New York, 1889. Reformer. Republican. Mayor of New York, 1907.

LURTON, HORACE HARMON: Associate Justice of the Supreme Court. Intimate friend of President Taft.

LYON, CECIL: A wealthy lumberman from Texas. Leader of the Republican party in that state.

McCAULEY, CHARLES: Colonel in Marine Corps. Prominent socially. Cotillion leader.

McCLELLAN, GEORGE B.: Son of "little Mac." Civil War leader. Newspaper man. Member of Congress and Mayor of New York. Professor of Economic History at Princeton University, 1912,

McCUMBER, PORTER JAMES: Republican Senator from North Dakota. Prominent in tariff legislation. Advocate of the League of Nations. Voted for it in all the forms in which it was presented to the Senate.

McKIM, RANDOLPH: Protestant clergyman. Rector of the Church of the Epiphany, Washington. Veteran of the Confederate army. Friend of President Taft. Biographer of his old commander, General Robert E. Lee.

McKINLEY, WILLIAM B.: No relation to the Ohio President. Congressman and Senator from Ill. High tariff man and standpatter.

McLEAN, EDWARD: Son of John McLean, owner of the Washington *Post*. A lavish but not discriminating host of the period. He was involved in an unfortunate way in the Fall-Doheny oil cases.

MACVEAGH, FRANKLIN: Wealthy merchant of Chicago. Secretary of the Treasury in President Taft's cabinet.

MACVEAGH, WAYNE: Brother of the foregoing. Attorney General in the cabinet of Garfield. United States Ambassador to Italy. Famous international lawyer.

MANN, JAMES R.: Member of Congress from Illinois for many years. Republican leader of the House. Prominent in tariff debates.

MEYER, GEORGE VON LENGERKE: Ambassador to Russia. Postmaster General under Roosevelt. Secretary of the Navy under Taft.

MILES, NELSON A.: Lieutenant General U. S. Army. Veteran of the Civil, Indian, and Spanish wars. Prominent figure in Washington during many administrations.

MILLET, FRANK: War correspondent and painter. Intimate friend of Major Butt. Popular figure in the inner Taft circle. He was a fellow passenger with Major Butt on the *Titanic* and was lost with him.

MITCHELL, WEIR: Famous brain specialist of Philadelphia. Later the author of notable fiction.

MOLTKE, COUNT C. P. O.: Of the Danish branch of this famous family. Danish minister in Washington during the Taft Administration. The Countess was Miss Thayer of Boston.

MOODY, WILLIAM H.: Member of Congress from Massachusetts. Secretary of the Navy and Attorney General under Roosevelt. Associate Justice of the Supreme Court, 1906–1910, until compelled to retire because of illness, which Major Butt describes.

MORE, LOUIS TRENCHARD: Educator. Married Eleanor Herron, sister of Mrs. Taft. Frequent hostess of the White House during the illness of the First Lady.

MORGAN, PIERPONT, JR.: Son of the famous banker. Financial agent of the Allies during the Great War. A sound chip of the old block.

MOTT, THOMAS BENTLEY: Colonel, U. S. Army. Served as military attaché in St. Petersburg and Paris for many years. Aided Ambassador Herrick in preparing his Memoirs. Social figure in Washington and Paris.

NABUCO, BARON: For many years Ambassador to the United States from Brazil. He apparently had known Lincoln more closely than any public man in Washington during the Taft Administration. His first post had been as Secretary of Legation in Washington during the Civil War days.

NAGEL, CHARLES: Congressman from Missouri. Secretary of Commerce and Labor in Taft's cabinet.

NEW, HARRY S.: Editor of the Indianapolis *Journal*. Chairman of the Republican National Committee. Postmaster General in the Coolidge cabinet.

NORTON, CHARLES D.: Assistant Secretary of the Treasury. Private secretary of President Taft, 1910–1911.

O'CONNELL, WILLIAM HENRY: Archbishop of Boston. Elevated to the Cardinalate in 1911.

O'LAUGHLIN, JOHN CALLAN: A newspaper friend of Theodore Roosevelt. Assistant Secretary of State for a short time at the end of the Roosevelt Administration. An ardent Bull Mooser.

OLIVER, ROBERT SHAW: Civil War veteran. Assistant Secretary of War under Presidents Roosevelt and Taft.

OULAHAN, RICHARD: Prominent Washington correspondent of the New York *Sun* and later of the New York *Times*.

OVERMAN, LEE SLATER: Democratic Senator from North Carolina for more than thirty years. Still a leading figure in the Senate.

PAGE, THOMAS NELSON: Author and social figure in Washington. United States Ambassador to Italy by appointment of President Wilson during the Great War.

PARSONS, HERBERT: Married Elsie Clews, daughter of the banker, Henry Clews. Member of Congress, 1905–1911, from New York. Prominent political and social figure.

PAYNE, SERENO: Congressman active in all high tariff measures.

PENROSE, BOIES: Senator and Old Guard leader from Pennsylvania.

PERCY, LORD EUSTACE: Son of the Earl of Northumberland. For many years attached to the English Embassy in Washington. Minister of Education in the Stanley Baldwin cabinet.

PHILLIPS, LEE: Geographer of the Library of Congress and Historian of Maps. Social figure.

PINCHOT, GIFFORD: Pioneer forester in the United States. In the forefront of the fight against Secretary Ballinger which disrupted the Taft Administration. He was dismissed by President Taft. Later Governor of Pennsylvania.

PLUNKETT, SIR HORACE: Irish economist and statesman. Frequent visitor to Washington. Apostle of Farm Coöperatives which transformed Ireland.

POINDEXTER, MILES: Congressman and later Senator from Washington. Frequently candidate for the Presidential nomination in the Republican conventions. Mrs. Poindexter wrote articles in the press regarding official Washington which did not meet with universal favor. Later ambassador to Peru.

PORTER, JOHN ADDISON: Yale man. For some time secretary to President McKinley.

PROUTY, GEORGE HERBERT: Republican Governor of Vermont, 1908. Friend and adviser of Taft.

REID, WHITELAW: Long editor of New York *Tribune*. Ambassador to France and later to England. Influential in Republican party councils.

RIXEY, PRESLEY MARION: Physician to the White House during the days of McKinley and Taft. Chief Surgeon of the Navy until his retirement in 1909.

ROBINSON, DOUGLAS: New York real estate broker. Married President Roosevelt's sister Corinne.

ROOSEVELT, MRS. THEODORE: Second wife of the President and mother of all his children except Alice, the daughter of the first wife, Miss Lee of Boston. Since the death of the President she has become a great traveler.

ROOT, ELIHU: Secretary of War and State under Roosevelt. Senator from New York during the Taft Administration. His plan for the entrance of the United States into the World Court of the League of Nations, approved by President Hoover, is now (June, 1930) before the Senate for ratification.

SCHEFF, FRITZI: Viennese actress and song bird. At this time she was married to John Fox, Jr., the writer, a figure in Washington society.

SCHIFF, JACOB H.: International banker and philanthropist. Prominent in finance and Red Cross activities during the Great War.

SHELDON, GEORGE: Banker of New York. Member of the Republican National Committee. Prominent in the 1912 campaign.

SHERMAN, JAMES SCHOOLCRAFT: Member of Congress from New York. Elected Vice President on ticket with Taft, 1908.

SHERRILL, CHARLES H.: New York lawyer and writer. United States Minister to the Argentine during the Taft Administration.

SLOAN, JAMES: Secret service agent attached to the White House. His political prophecies as recorded by Major Butt have proved remarkably accurate.

SLOAN, RICHARD E.: Pioneer Governor of Arizona.

SMITH, FRANK HOPKINSON: The versatile engineer, painter, and writer.

SOROLLA Y BASTIDA, JOAQUÍN: The great Spanish artist and portrait painter. A frequent visitor to America.

STAFFORD, WENDELL PHILIPS: Vermonter. Long Justice of the Supreme Court of the District of Columbia. Able writer and speaker.

STIMSON, HENRY L.: Secretary of War under President Taft. Defeated in the New York gubernatorial election in 1910. Governor General of the Philippines under President Coolidge. Secretary of State under President Hoover. Head of the American delegation to the Naval Conference in London, 1930.

STORER, BELLAMY: Cincinnati lawyer, United States Minister to Spain and Austria. Husband of Maria Longworth Storer, heroine of the famous correspondence with President Roosevelt.

STOVALL, PLEASANT: Leading Democratic editor of Savannah, Ga. United States Minister to Switzerland during the Great War.

TAFT, CHARLES PHELPS: Newspaper owner and financier. Elder half brother of the President. Married Miss Sinton of Cincinnati, a great heiress. He financed the President's political campaigns.

TAFT, HENRY: Leading New York lawyer and partner of George Wickersham, who became Attorney General in the Taft cabinet.

TAFT, HORACE D.: Educator. Head master of the Taft School which President Taft remembered in his will.

TAFT, MRS. W. H.: Wife of the President. She was Miss Helen Herron, daughter of a Cincinnati capitalist. An amiable hostess whose stay in the White House was plagued by constant ill health.

TAWNEY, JAMES A.: In Congress from Minnesota. Apostle of high tariff. Taft's Winona speech in favor of Tawney's reëlection split the Republican party and contributed to Taft's defeat in 1912.

TAYLOR, "BOB": The Fiddling Senator from Tennessee. Famous for his fiddle and his anecdotes.

TILLMAN, BENJAMIN RYAN: First Senator from South Carolina since the Reconstruction period who did not belong to the Bourbon class. After many episodes such as are here described, he became a most useful and admired member of the Senate.

TOGO, ADMIRAL: Commander of the Imperial Japanese fleet in the war with Russia.

UCHIDA, BARON: Imperial Japanese Ambassador in Washington. Later Minister of Foreign Affairs.

UNDERWOOD, OSCAR W.: Congressman and Senator from Alabama for many years. Chairman of the Ways and Means Committee in the House. Co-author of the Underwood Tariff bill. Leading contender for the Democratic Presidential nomination in the conventions of 1920 and 1924.

UPHAM, F. W.: Merchant of Chicago. Prominent in the Taft campaigns for the Presidency, 1908 and 1912.

VILLALOBAR, RODRIGO DE SAAVEDRA, MARQUIS OF: Spanish Minister to the United States during the Taft Administration and a great favorite in Washington and at the White House. He was a member of the Veragua family who are descended from Columbus. Spanish Ambassador to Belgium during the Great War.

WADSWORTH, JAMES W., JR.: Speaker of New York Assembly. Married Alice Hay, daughter of John Hay, Secretary of State. Afterwards Senator from New York. After defeat for reëlection he became leader of the national movement for the repeal of the Eighteenth Amendment.

WAINWRIGHT, RICHARD: Rear Admiral, U. S. Navy. Executive officer of the *Maine* when she was blown up in Havana Harbor. Commanded with distinction the little *Gloucester* in the engagement with Cervera's fleet off Santiago, July, 1898.

WARREN, FRANCIS E.: Long silent Senator from Wyoming. Sat from 1890 to his death in 1929. Very influential in committees. Father-in-law of General Pershing.

WASHINGTON, BOOKER: The famous Negro educator. Head of the Tuskegee school. Reference is made by Major Butt to the political consequences that flowed from the fact that Roosevelt had Washington to lunch with his family in the White House.

WATSON, JAMES E.: Congressman from Indiana. One of the Stalwarts. Now Senator and leader of the Republicans, the "regulars" in the Senate.

WATTERSON, HENRY: Famous Democratic editor from Kentucky.

WETMORE, THE MISSES EDITH AND MAUDE: Daughters of George Peabody Wetmore, long Senator from Rhode Island. Socially and politically prominent.

WHITE, EDWARD D.: Long Democratic Senator from Louisiana. Made Chief Justice of the United States by President Taft. Highly valued as a jurist, and a very plain-spoken friend, by both President Taft and President Wilson.

WICKERSHAM, GEORGE W.: A Philadelphia lawyer who moved to New York and became a leader of the bar. Attorney General in the cabinet of

President Taft. Chairman of the Law Enforcement Commission by appointment of President Hoover in 1929.

WILEY, H. W.: Chemist, long in the Department of Agriculture. One of the leaders of the Pure Food crusade.

WILKIE, JOHN E.: Chief of the United States Secret Service from 1897 to 1912. Very active in counter-espionage work during the Spanish-American War.

WILSON, HENRY LANE: Minister to Chile, to Belgium, and Ambassador to Mexico during the stormy days of the Madero Revolution. Very active during the "tragic week" in protecting the lives of Americans and foreigners. Not approving the Bryan policies in Mexico, he was removed by President Wilson.

WILSON, HUNTINGTON: Assistant Secretary of State under Knox and frequently Acting Secretary during the prolonged absences of his chief. Mrs. Wilson was one of the famous hostesses of the period.

WILSON, WOODROW: President of the United States, 1912–1920.

WINTHROP, BEEKMAN: Private secretary of Taft in the Philippines. Later Governor of Porto Rico and Assistant Secretary of the navy. Banker in New York.

WOOD, LEONARD: Army surgeon at the White House during the McKinley Administration. Close friend of Roosevelt and became Colonel of the Rough Riders at Roosevelt's suggestion. Was made brigadier general in the Army for service in Cuba. Later Chief of Staff of the Army and Governor General of the Philippines. For many ballots leading candidate for the Republican presidential nomination at the Chicago Convention of 1920.

WRIGHT, THE BROTHERS ORVILLE AND WILBUR: While by no means their first flight, the exhibition before President Taft at Fort Meyer attracted for the first time world-wide attention.

WU, DR. (DR. WU TING FANG): The witty Chinese minister who achieved a position of great influence in Washington. The present minister, Dr. Wu, is his son.

TAFT AND ROOSEVELT

CHAPTER I

MR. TAFT'S EARLY DAYS AS PRESIDENT

Washington, D. C.
Sunday, March 7, 1909.

DEAR CLARA:

If anything could be worse than the end of one administration, it is the beginning of another. Crowds gather about the White House and office all day, and even to-day, Sunday, there have been hundreds of persons assembled at the gates and in front of the North Portico nearly all the afternoon, waiting to get a glimpse of the President and some member of his family.

Yesterday I presented over three thousand persons by name to the President and Mrs. Taft, and she, by the way, acted like a trump in receiving this heterogeneous mass of out-of-town folk. He had an engagement at eleven to receive a lot of organizations in the East Room, and at that time I went to the executive office for him.

When I got there, there were at least a thousand people waiting to see him. Most of them were Senators and Representatives from the West with large numbers of their constituents to present. I saw that he would never be able to see them and keep his engagement at the White House; yet he said he had to see the members of Congress who had come to see him on business. I hit upon a very novel plan to get rid of most of them, and, without apprising him of my intention, I went among them and told them that the President was going to receive in the East Room of the White House in fifteen minutes and that

1

Mrs. Taft would receive with him. All who desired to meet her, I said, had better go there. Of course, they all took the bait and started in a mad rush for the East Door of the White House.

After I had cleared the office I told him what I had done and suggested that he come over to the White House at once, as the Lieutenant Governor of New York and large delegations had already been waiting for him for over an hour. He commended my scheme and told me he would leave me to handle Mrs. Taft. I saw her, and she was really a brick in accepting the situation. I then went for him, and in a half hour we had the crowd appeased by beginning the presentations. After receiving upward of three thousand, most of whom were pretty rough-looking characters, she began to feel sick and left the East Room. Until the crowds leave she will receive with him in the East Room for one hour a day, and in another week I hope the White House will get back into its regular routine.

The President took his first ride this afternoon. I was peacefully sleeping after lunch when I was aroused by a telephone message that the President desired me to ride with him from the South Portico of the White House at half-past three. I must say I felt some disgust, for I had been accustomed to ride with Mr. Roosevelt, and I felt it to be a great come-down to jog along with Mr. Taft. I was mistaken in my man, however, for he was out for exercise, and he gave me as much as I wanted.

During the ride he asked me about the appointment of an aide again, and said that General Bell had recommended some officer in place of Bromwell. I tried to squelch this idea, for I am sure no good can come of it. General Bell merely wants someone there as a constant representative, and moreover this place ought to go to the Engineers, who have the disbursements of the funds for the White House. The President leans to Crosby, and I shall try to get him named. He asked me if I knew Crosby and if I liked him, as he did not want to name anyone whom I did not like. This is the first direct intimation that I am to be retained.

I don't know Crosby well, but I am sure he will serve the President and not be a spy on him for any one department or set of men. I want to keep out of it all, but one gets into intrigue in spite of one's wishes in the matter. Clarence Edwards, who rode a part of the time with us, is anxious to have Tibby Mott named as chief aide, and this does not suit me at all, for I am sure we would clash, as our ambitions lie too close together and our natures are too far apart.

Good-night.
ARCHIE.

New Ways in the White House

Washington, D. C.
March 10, 1909.

MY DEAR CLARA:

I am not in a philosophic mood to-night, and I am far from being capable of drawing conclusions from a few facts as I see them now. But of one thing I am reasonably certain: If the President continues to transact business as he is transacting it now, he will be about three years behind when the fourth of March, 1913, rolls around. If he has no idea of money, he certainly has none of time. He moves very slowly, and I defy anyone in the world to hurry him. He makes engagements of which no one, not even his secretary, has any notion, and yet he expects everybody about him to be cognizant of the fact and to have everything in readiness for him.

For instance, yesterday morning he made an engagement to receive the Supreme Court at eleven o'clock, the same hour at which he had summoned the Cabinet to assemble. I had gone to the White House in the morning, interviewed Mrs. Taft, and had received her request to purchase a cow for the household and left feeling that there was nothing else to be done for the day. I was far behind in my personal affairs and had gone to the Lemon Building to write out some checks and to answer a few letters, when suddenly I was summoned to the phone and was informed by Mr. Carpenter that the Supreme Court had arrived and was even then waiting for the President in the Blue Room. I hastened over and, as was natural to suppose, was ten minutes late, for he was already in the Blue Room discussing legal appointments with the learned doctors of the Supreme Court.

Just as I got there I heard Justice White saying that there was nothing of greater importance than the proper appointments of the Judiciary.

"And, Mr. President," he said, "listen to the voice of· the Bar Associations and you can't go very far wrong."

"Yes," said the President in his most persuasive voice, "but I have often seen the entire bar association of a city misled, and one often finds the legal profession in a city recommend some man for judge who is merely popular or else who needs a good legal appointment."

"That is true," said the Justice, "but the bar associations are not as apt to go wrong as the average politicians, even when they occupy pretty high places."

Everyone stood a-gasp for a minute, thinking the President might take the remark to himself, but he evidently did not, for he added:

"I have five lawyers in my cabinet and before they recommend the appointment of a judge they will be pretty certain that the man is worthy of the place."

After the adjournment of the Court, as it were, I went upstairs to have a talk with Mrs. Taft, and it was then that she asked me if she might not purchase a cow out of the funds allotted to the White House. I agreed to try to get on the track of one and suggested that I consult Admiral, or otherwise Dr., Rixey, who owned a dairy farm in Virginia. She said she preferred that I would not, as the President had received a letter from the goodly admiral which they regarded as extremely impudent, to say the least.

It seems the admiral had written a letter asking the President whether he desired him to continue to act as the surgeon for the White House, and the President had construed this into being some sort of threat and had answered that he did not; that when he wanted a physician he would call in an army surgeon, as he had been accustomed to do in the past. The admiral had told me that he felt it to be his duty to give the incoming President an opportunity to get rid of him, but he hardly expected to have his offer construed as an insult.

I took Kitty Boggs to Chevy Chase to lunch with a friend of hers, and on my return I found a telephone message that the White House wanted to speak to me. It was a message from Mrs. Taft to the effect that she and the President were going to the theater to hear Emma Eames in concert at four-thirty and desired me to meet them there.

The Presidential party was late in arriving, and when it came the President was not in it. Mrs. Taft explained that the President was busy and asked me to return in the motor and to say that she had written Madame Eames that he would be present and to beg him not to disappoint her. I returned and found that Gussie Gardner, with some Representatives, was closeted with the President. They were there to get his assistance in the fight they were making against Cannon for a change of rules.

I had heard the President say a few nights before that

the House ought to be allowed to elect its own committee on rules, and I presumed that he would at least remain neutral in the matter. Not so. He rather denounced the efforts of the insurgents, as they are called, and told them frankly that they wanted to get his aid to turn over the House to a coalition of a minority of Republicans and Democrats. He had evidently brought Cannon to his way of thinking on the subject of the tariff and was not in a mood to jeopardize the pact by taking sides with his enemies.

While some might think this a little juggling, I cannot see that he was at fault, for what they wanted him to do was to make effective the very rules which he might need to put through the House the very reforms to which he stood pledged. He raised his voice and denounced his visitors in a way I thought would lead to a rupture, but after he had taken this means to decide the matter he laughed, Taft-like, and told them that he did not feel any animosity toward them and would not hold up the fight they were making against Cannon against them in the future.

This was thoroughly the Taft process. He first gives a blow and then smiles and makes friends. At the bottom of all may be expediency, but he conceals it very well under what he would term the public weal. I told Mrs. Taft what a difficulty we had to make him keep his engagements and that I hoped he would be broken into better training soon, but she merely laughed and said:

"You will never break him into that. He cannot be hurried, and he does not mind whom he keeps waiting or how long they have to wait. He likes to go when he wishes and where he wishes, and he does not mind breaking engagements."

I have found this to be a fact, for once when I reminded him of an engagement he merely said:

"Well, I will go with you, but I give you warning that the day is near when I will do just as I please and will not be bullied."

While this slowness of action may be disconcerting to those about him or to those who have been accustomed to the energetic ways of Mr. Roosevelt, yet it may be part of the character which makes for conservatism and wisdom and which after all has made him a force to be relied on as sane and safe.

It was half-past five before I got him away from the office. Brooks had brought a white tie and frock coat for him to wear to the concert, but he refused to put them on and decided to go in his cutaway, which, by the way, is much more becoming to him than the long Prince Alberts which he is accustomed to wear. He came in late and received a moderate applause, which argues nothing, as the audience was a high well bred one; but after the first number I went on the stage to say that after the next number the President would come back of the scenes and meet the diva.

"Does he like music?" she asked.

"No, he hates it," I responded.

"Then I will sing him something from *Don Giovanni* and cut out the duet from *The Gondoliers*."

I felt sorry that I had spoken, for while he might recognize the well known duet from *Giovanni*, it was mere tune and acting, while the duet from *The Gondoliers* was music. Still, he liked it and thanked her when he went behind the scenes. She said to him:

"I hear you do not like music. Well, I can't blame you, for I am tired of it myself."

Mrs. Taft likes to have aides about her, and I am inclined to think that she will always have one whenever he appears. He can afford to adopt this program, for it is well known that the military does not appeal to him—

as it does to Mr. Roosevelt, for instance. Mr. Roosevelt was always afraid to go about accompanied by an aide, but the President can have as many as he wishes and no criticism will be offered.

ARCHIBALD.

CHAPTER II

PRECEDENTS FROM THE ROOSEVELTS

Washington, D. C.
March 11, 1909.

DEAR CLARA:

I find that Mrs. Taft does not hesitate to adopt some of her predecessor's methods as better than any which have been followed in other administrations. For instance, on the question of receiving reporters, she said:

"Mrs. Roosevelt adopted the custom of never seeing newspaper people, and I think it is a good precedent to follow. When I have anything to give out I shall do as she did and simply have my secretary send the facts to the papers."

And again, when the question of receiving callers came up, she said in my presence:

"Mrs. Roosevelt never received promiscuous callers, and neither shall I. I think the system adopted by her is a good one to continue, and I will only receive those who write and ask me to set a time for them to come."

I find she has little vanity, although she is perfectly aware of her ability to manage her own household, which she does with considerable ability, I must confess. She has made one decided departure, which I must say has given me quite a new light on her character. While I was with her this morning, I suggested to her, as she was going to New York next week, that she might look into the question of china for the White House. She said very directly:

"I have given that question a good deal of thought, and I have made up my mind to continue with the Roosevelt china, as it is called. I shall try to make it the White House china. It is perfectly absurd to change the china with each new administration. The consequence of this custom is that the closets are loaded up with a mass of china most of which is hideous and ordinary and which I would not use on my private table. Mrs. Roosevelt, evidently, gave this question of china a great deal of consideration, and her choice in design and quality was in excellent taste and the best which I have seen here. She told me once that it was Minton, but it is not. It is Wedgwood, and moreover her contract with the manufactory makes it impossible for them to put it on the market, and none can be used anywhere else. I shall do all in my power to make it the china of the White House. The Hayes and the McKinley china is too awful for words."

If she carries out her declared intention, there will be no distinctive Taft china, and I think it indicates an absence of vanity to reach this conclusion.

I went riding with him this afternoon. Bourke Cockran, who was riding on the speedway, joined us at his invitation. As he rode up, he said:

"Well, Mr. President, how do you like it?"

"I hardly know yet," said the President. "When I hear someone say Mr. President, I look around expecting to see Roosevelt, and when I read in the headlines of the morning papers that the President and Senator Aldrich and Speaker Cannon have had a conference, my first thought is, 'I wonder what they talked about.' So you can see that I have not gone very far yet."

"You have gone far enough to have a nasty question to

decide. I refer to the fight against the rule of Cannon in the House."

The President said that no one realized it more than he, and that, while he had a good deal of sympathy for the insurgents, as those opposed to Cannon are called,

"I do not think it a good time to meddle. I may have to use the very machinery they are denouncing to pass a tariff bill. And a tariff bill must be passed. The business interests of the country demand that much, now that the question of revision has come up at all. The moment it was mentioned it became imperative to act and to act as promptly as possible. I think you will appreciate the humor of the situation. I asked Madison if the action of the insurgents was not a little revolutionary. He denied that it was, but Gussie Gardner came forward with the statement that it was not only revolutionary but revolution itself. 'Then, gentlemen, how can you expect me, the head of an orderly state, to join a revolution?' But this did not stop them, and they are still hammering on me to secure the sympathy for their cause."

"If I told them," he said afterwards, when Cockran had ridden off, "how much sympathy I have for them in their fight against Cannon, they might have had reason to feel encouraged."

Little Charlie is a great bookworm and spends most of his time curled up on the sofa, reading. His mother told me that on Inauguration Day he took with him to the Senate *Treasure Island*—to read, he said, in case his father's address bored him.

When I reach the White House in the morning I send up a message that I am there and ask if she desires to see me. She usually does, and I sit bolt upright in one chair and she in another. I have come to the conclusion that a lot of her apparent coldness comes from embarrassment. She says that when I am not there she thinks of a lot of things which she forgets as soon as I come. I find the same thing with myself. Yet I am sure she is kind and good and, if it be possible, I shall find it out—that is, if I remain long enough. She has gratitude. I see all the time an endeavor to recognize some friend who has done some kindness in the past.

Good-night, O receiver of gossip.

ARCHIBALD.

Tentative memorandum of precedence at a dinner in the house of a private American citizen who has no connection with the public service of the United States or a state of the Union, or of any foreign government, and when the dinner is not given in honor of any particular individual or of any corps or organization:

The President
The Vice President
Foreign ambassadors accredited to the United States
The Secretary of State
Foreign envoys plenipotentiary
The Chief Justice
The President *pro tem* of the Senate
The Speaker of the House
Cabinet secretaries other than the Secretary of State
Foreign ministers resident
Associate justices of the Supreme Court
The Admiral of the Navy
Senators
Governors of states
Representatives in Congress
The Chief of Staff of the Army
Foreign chargés d'affaires
Major generals of the army
Rear admirals
Foreign secretaries of Embassy and Legation

Assistant secretaries of the executive departments
Judges of the Court of Claims
Secretary of the Smithsonian Institution
District commissioners
District Court of Appeals
District Supreme Court
Brigadier generals
Captains in the navy
Director of the Bureau of American Republics
Army and navy officers below army brigadiers and
    navy captains
Foreign guests in private life, untitled
American guests in private life

Notes. 1. Foreign representatives take rank among themselves in the order of their audience of credence. (See State Department Foreign List, issued monthly.)

2. Cabinet officers rank in the order of the creation of their respective departments. (See Congressional Directory.)

3. Associate justices rank according to date of commission. (See Congressional Directory.)

4. Senators and Representatives rank according to length of service in their respective Houses. (See Congressional Directory.)

5. Army and navy officers rank respectively according to their number in the army and navy lists, which see.

6. District commissioners rank according to date of appointment. (See Congressional Directory.)

7. Judges of Court of Claims rank by date of commission. (Congressional Directory gives their precedence.)

8. It is not possible to frame an order of precedence for foreign guests who hold office or title under their own governments. In regard to such it would be well to consult informally the diplomatic representative of their country.

9. American guests, being in the diplomatic service of the United States abroad, and being at home on leave, do not take precedence according to their rank, i. e., the American ambassador to a foreign court does not rank, in an American private house, with a foreign ambassador accredited to the United States. He is a distinguished citizen and may be placed according to convenience, but not above the Representatives of Congress.

10. Ex-officers do not retain any right of precedence by reason of past service; but an exception is generally made in favor of an ex-President, who may be placed, by courtesy, next after foreign ambassadors.

11. The wives of guests rank in the same order as their husbands. An unmarried daughter, if actual head of her father's household, comes after married ladies of the same category. If not the head of a household she is ranked as a private citizen, after unmarried ladies.

12. If the usual arrangement of the guests, in alternate succession right and left of the host and hostess, should bring husband and wife together at table, it is customary to shift the lady to the corresponding place on the other side of the host or hostess, as the case may be.

At Dinner with the Tafts

Washington, D. C.
March 16, 1909.

DEAR CLARA:

I have just returned from dinner at the White House, the first time I have dined there since the Roosevelts left. It was a nice cosy evening, and the dinner was not unlike those we had during the last administration, when the family dined alone or with only a few friends. I could not get the Roosevelts out of my mind. The conversation was natural, and the atmosphere was homelike, but there was something missing. It was like being at the White House with the President absent. I thought of President Taft as a fellow guest, a charming man, but I kept looking around for the President. I think he feels the same way. It is my honest belief that he misses the President more than any of us do. He always speaks of him as "the President." Mrs. Taft corrected him once and said:

"You mean the ex-President, Will."

"I suppose I do, dear; but he will always be the President to me, and I can never think of him as anything else."

It was the first dinner party they have had since coming to the White House, and the only thing I can remember now is that they did not have oysters, and I thought at the time that the Roosevelts never had oysters. Somehow I expected oysters for this very reason.

The President did not monopolize the conversation as President Roosevelt would have done. This is not a reflection on Roosevelt, for he never tried to monopolize conversation, but he just naturally did. The moment he spoke everybody was wont to stop and try to catch what he was saying. When the President talked to-night we all went on talking just the same, and the conversation was very general and, I must say, very natural. There was always a feeling after dining or lunching at the White House with President Roosevelt that one must try to treasure up what he had heard the President say.

I was conscious of being bored somewhat and of thinking the dinner very long, yet I was not bored at all. I simply missed the marvelous wit and personality of Roosevelt and the sweet charm of his wife. It is natural to feel this way, I suppose, and I will continue to miss them for quite a time yet, so it is still unfair to compare the White House as it is to the White House as it was. I am forced to confess that certain changes have been for the improvement.

The house is very orderly and quiet. One never hears

any noise at all, and all the domestics seem to be afraid to whisper. After dinner we went into the Red Room, where we had coffee. Mrs. Roosevelt always had coffee served in the library on the second floor. Mrs. Taft has the fire lighted in the Red Room every evening, and the family do not go to the second floor until they go to bed. I think this idea of using the lower floor an excellent one. The Tafts have made it their living quarters as much as the second floor.

To economize has become a fixed habit with Mrs. Taft, and she is fighting against it, I can see, but it is hard for her to overcome it. It is the women who have to grow hard and narrow under adversity, and it is the men always who criticize them after making drudges of them. She was very gracious to-night.

I went riding with the President this afternoon and had a most delightful ride. He was in a good humor and talked of many things, but of few that were worth noting. I find that he does not give out himself as Mr. Roosevelt did. He is very reserved in many ways and especially among individuals. When discussing any general subject he is very free and open. For instance, in speaking of his ambition to elevate the Judiciary, he said:

"The Judiciary has fallen into a very low state in this country. I think your part of the country has suffered especially. The federal judges of the South are a disgrace to any country, and I'll be damned if I put any man on the bench of whose character and ability there is the least doubt."

We passed several persons he knew, but he did not ask any of them to join him.

Congress opened yesterday, and I went with Mrs. Taft and her two sisters to the House and occupied the first row in the Executive Gallery. Mrs. Taft was keenly interested in every move. She wanted to see Speaker Cannon defeated for Speaker but did not want to see the rules changed. She said she thought it was silly to elect the Speaker and then fight against the rules. Since the Speaker was the author of the rules and was in so many other ways objectionable, she thought they should make every effort to defeat him and change the rules later, if necessary. For, after all, it was more the way the rules were enforced by the Speaker than the rules themselves which were objectionable. She was quite excited and did not want to take time to go to the House café for lunch.

The reception of the diplomats, last Friday, was very well done, and both the President and Mrs. Taft looked well and seemed very much at ease. The diplomats are asking why he received them wearing gloves. I noticed it at the time, but failed to think it important. I suggested that he remembered the East, where men wear gloves to protect themselves from various diseases, but I did not think such a reason was a valid one here. There is considerable speculation as to the cause of this departure, but I really think that as he left the room his valet gave them to him and he slipped them on merely without thinking.

Good-night. I have written to-night only to forge a link in the chain, and the work has tired me.

ARCHIE.

CHAPTER III

Mr. Taft Introduces New Methods

Washington, D. C.
March 21, 1909.

DEAR CLARA:

I remember that in one of the comedies of Plautus, if my recollection of my classics be not at fault, one man speaks of a woman as being a good one, the other one says:

"Don't say any woman is good, but only that one is worse than the other."

That is the way I am beginning to feel about Presidents as regards the demands they make on one. In less than a week I have been to New York or vicinity twice, and both trips have been nasty ones from the standpoint of fatigue.

I had looked forward this week to a good rest when the President and Mrs. Taft would be away much as a schoolboy looks forward to the absence of a teacher; but on Wednesday, after riding with the President, he asked me what Mr. Roosevelt usually did regarding aides on trips of an official character. I told him that sometimes he took them and oftentimes did not, but that Mr. Roosevelt was afraid always of the cry of militarism, and while he liked to have his military aides near him, he often requested them to go in citizen's clothes in order to avoid criticism. President Taft said he thought his well known theory, that the military should always be secondary to the civilian, would free him from criticism of this nature, and whenever I accompanied him to wear my uniform, and to so inform his newly appointed senior aide, Colonel Crosby. He then said he wanted me to accompany him to New York on the following morning, and as the train was to leave at eight o'clock there was little time for me to break a score of engagements.

You may have kept track of him, and incidentally of me, through the press, but no newspaper accounts could convey to you the fatigue of those two days. He has marvelous powers of physical endurance, and he keeps one engagement after another with wonderful promptitude and with little evidence of wear on the nervous tissue.

He has the faculty of sleeping sitting up, and while this may indicate some trouble somewhere in his great bulk, I am inclined to think it indicative rather of a phlegmatic temperament. It certainly comes to his assistance just now, when he has little opportunity to rest save as he can catch these little cat naps on trains and between interviews. He went fast asleep sitting at the White House last night while Speaker Cannon was talking to him, and this, too, when the Speaker was leaning over his chair and talking most earnestly on behalf of Jim Watson.

From the minute we left Washington I began to miss excitement, which always attended President Roosevelt on these trips. Even before we left Washington, President Taft took no notice of the crowd—it was not a large one—which had assembled at the depot. He entered his car and never came out to wave a good-bye, and I think even the depot employees missed the "Good-bye, good-luck" of the ex-President. There was a large crowd at Baltimore, and the President never went even to the platform to wave his hand—and so it was all the way to New York. Of course, I am committed to the Roosevelt school of policy and think that the people have a right to expect some return attention from the President when it assembles anywhere to see him pass. But I do not think Mr. Taft will ever care a hang about this form of popularity, although I wish he would, for it reads well all over the country that the President was met by a crowd here and a throng there, who demanded a speech. Mr. Roosevelt always said he was a poor campaigner and that he could only be made to speak when some vital issue was at stake.

At the depot in Jersey City and on the New York side there was a great lot of people gathered, but we were so surrounded by police and secret service men that we had little trouble in reaching our motor. We took the closed motor in Jersey City and never got out of it until we reached Mr. Henry Taft's house in New York. The President did not even look out of the window to respond to the *banzai* of the people of the street. Jimmie Sloan, the secret service man, whispered to me:

"What an opportunity he is missing! For God's sake, captain, get him to lift his hat when the people yell, for if he don't they will stop yelling when he will want them most."

"It's all right, Jimmie," I said. "He will get shaken down after a while, and things will all come right."

"Never," he said. "The other man has educated the public to know what to expect, and this one will be a dead card if he don't change."

It was no use to argue with Jimmie. He, too, had been too long under the magic wand of Roosevelt to see things in any other way.

As we approached New York I still wore my dress uniform, which is merely a modest, neat blue blouse. I said that I should change it for my full-dress uniform, but hesitated to do so, as the other was conspicuous for a New York audience such as we would see at the Grover Cleveland memorial exercises in Carnegie Hall.

"It makes no difference to me," said the President, "but you can't put on too much to please Mrs. Taft."

"It seems to me," she said, "that you are the one who likes the gold lace about. I find that you miss it when it is not there."

"I believe I do," laughed the President, "but I find that things go smoother when I have an officer with me. Somehow they seem to know how to do things without asking me to decide every time."

I think that it is so, for I have noticed that when I ask him, for instance, if he wants to see the newspaper men, he will say "No," but if I bring them to him he receives them and I think is glad to do so.

He wrote his speech on Cleveland, going to New York. He had not thought of it until he got on the train, and soon after leaving Baltimore he sent for his stenographer and dictated it in less than an hour. I know it was finished by the time he reached Philadelphia. In speaking of his habit to delay this class of work he said that it came from laziness chiefly; that he always put off writing a speech as long as possible, while Mr. Roosevelt always had to give expression to what he thought as soon as he thought it.

"If Roosevelt accepted an invitation to make a speech he would begin to think what he would say after the first hour, and the second he would have outlined his speech, and before the twenty-four were over he would have written it in full. Then he would read it to those whose judgment he valued and often would make changes here and there, but this method resulted in splendid productions."

President Roosevelt once told me that he nearly always outlined his speeches on horseback and would dictate them that same night.

Sometimes the method of President Taft works to his detriment. For instance, he had accepted an invitation of the Yale graduates for a dinner at the Waldorf on Friday evening, and he expected to write his speech on the way to New Haven, where he went Friday morning and where he was to attend a meeting of the Corporation Board at noon. After the meeting we went to a luncheon at President Hadley's, and coming back in the train the President went to one room to dictate his speech, but was tired and slept most of the way back, sitting upright, and in consequence his speech at the dinner was a failure; in fact, it was no speech at all, and he felt himself that it was not up to the occasion. There were over sixteen hundred men at this dinner, and the scene beggars description. It was one of the most wonderful personal tributes ever paid a man, I imagine, and the speeches of Sheffield and Hadley were masterpieces of their kind. The only thing lacking was one from the President corresponding in dignity of humor or eloquence to those which had preceded his, but again to quote Jimmie Sloan:

"He fell down."

But it made no difference to those splendid enthusiastic graduates, for they are so loyal to this son of Yale that, had he said nothing at all, it would have pleased them as well. The spirit of the Yale men is splendid. They seem to have accepted the unwritten resolution among themselves to ask for nothing but to give support and loyalty and to feel love and pride in him, the first Yale man to reach the Presidency. At the Carnegie Hall Mayor McClellan said to me:

"I shall feel greatly relieved when I get him out of my town. I do not think there is anything going to happen, but we have received many warnings since he decided to come to New York."

Chief Wilkie told me in Washington that he was surprised at the number of threats which had come to their knowledge. He said the personality of Roosevelt kept away cranks and frightened away anarchists, but the personality of Mr. Taft was that which always seems to invite attacks. "I thought we received a great many letters during the Roosevelt Administration, but they were nothing compared to what come through the mails daily."

I found something of the truth in this while I was with the President in New York. Mrs. Henry Taft gave into my keeping a handful of threatening letters, and Mr. Henry Taft did the same, and neither one knew that the other had done so, as they had not wanted to frighten each other with such matters.

As we reached the Taft house there was a line of photographers ready to snap us as we entered, and they remained about the place the entire time we were there. When we got in the house the President took Miss Boardman and went dancing about the room like a schoolboy. He dances well and is as nimble on his feet as a cat. I have found out three things he does well. He dances well, he curses well, and he laughs well.

I heard him ask his brother, who was urging him to appoint some judge in Ohio:

"Do you recommend him or does someone else?"

"I do not know him," said Mr. Henry Taft, "but Colonel —— asked me to say to you——"

"Well, you have said it, and now, Harry, I want you to tell them, anyone who comes to you, that I am determined to raise the Judiciary of this country to a higher level. I'll be damned if I appoint to the Bench anyone who is not a great lawyer. I am getting —— —— tired of men recommending others for the Bench whom they would not employ themselves where two dollars was involved."

While we were at lunch the question of renting the summer home came up, and Mrs. Taft said she would not decide at once if she found a house which suited her, her reason being that if the President went to Alaska in July it would be a waste of money to rent a house on the North Shore for such a short time as would remain.

"It makes no difference whether I go to Alaska or not, my dear; take the house for four years."

'I will not do it," said Mrs. Taft. "You will have to remain in Washington as long as Congress is in session."

"No, I won't," said the President.

Everyone laughed, and even Mrs. Taft enjoyed the sally, but she said:

"How can one argue with him? Do you wonder that we have only saved in all this time five thousand dollars?— and we should not have that now, had not I worried over every expenditure.

"Yes," she said to Mrs. Henry Taft, who looked a-skance at this statement, "that is every cent we have over and above the President's salary, now."

"My dear," said the President kindly, "how much do you think you have added to our income by worry and trouble?"

"I fear nothing," she said, "but I have made ends

meet, and you have been able to make moves when they were necessary without borrowing money. You might have been sued and arrested for debt, who can tell?" she added.

"Nellie, that is true, and I had not thought of it in that way before, but I want you to stop worrying now, for if I die there is enough to keep the wolf away from you and the children, and as long as I live I will be able to earn enough to keep us going, thanks to the American people."

Good-night.
Affectionately,
ARCHIBALD.

Cannon and the President Dance

Washington, D. C.
Sunday, March 21, 1909.

DEAR CLARA:

I dined at the White House last night. There were only four of us, the President, the Speaker of the House, General Clarence Edwards, and I. We had a good dinner and did not get up from the table until nine o'clock. The Tafts have changed the dinner hour from eight to half-past seven, so if they want to go to the theater they can do so without upsetting all arrangements.

Senator Bradley called by appointment at ten, at which time it was thought Speaker Cannon would have gone, but he had no such idea.

General Edwards and I, after Bradley had left, put on the *Merry Widow* record with Sembrich singing the waltz. The President and Speaker Cannon were talking, standing, when the music began. The President at once began to waltz around the room by himself, and I was astonished to see the ease and grace with which he did it. Uncle Joe, the Evil One, promptly began doing the same thing; though he knew no waltz step, he simply capered around in a sort of ragtime shuffle. But he did it well, and General Edwards and I looked on feeling that, were we to do it, we would not do it either as gracefully or as easily as did these two distinguished figures.

Before going the Speaker made a special plea to the President to appoint Jim Watson of Indiana to some job, and said as a prelude:

"Now, Mr. President, let me look you straight in the eye and ask a favor."

"Look me in the eye always, for it makes it easier to deny you anything."

Whatsoever it was he was asking, the President finally refused, saying that he had promised Beveridge not to do this very thing and he was unwilling to precipitate a row with the Senator from Indiana.

I am going to Clarence Moore's to dinner this evening to meet a Lady Paget.

Mathilde Townsend is still in Florida, so it really makes little difference where I dine. I fear it is becoming another case of "What's this dull town to me?"

Good-night again.

ARCHIBALD.

A Friendly Message to Colonel Roosevelt

Washington, D. C.
March 22, 1909.

DEAR CLARA:

I am leaving to-night for New York. It had been my intention all along to go, but the trip now is made imperative for the reason that the President has asked me to deliver a gift of some kind and a letter to Mr. Roosevelt. I do not think he would have thought of doing this had I not suggested to him that his predecessor would appreciate some word at parting. What I really said, by insinuation, was that it would be the politic

thing to do and that it would be highly gratifying to the
friends of Mr. Roosevelt. It would never have done for
him not to have sent some word or present. Yet I am sure
he would not have thought of it, and I do not say this in
criticism of him, but rather be it to his credit that the
politics of the thing did not appeal to him at all until it
had been put up to him in this way. He simply does not
see the small things and the need to do them, and he cannot play a petty part—of that I am becoming more convinced every day, and if the people expect him to do so he
will be very unpopular with them until they readjust
themselves to his attitude.

At any rate, I am glad to take his message and gift over.
I selected several pieces of gold at Galt's this morning and
took them to him to select one. One was a gold pencil,
the other a gold case for his eyeglasses; and the last—
which when I had found I looked no further, for it seems to
fill the bill to a nicety—was a gold ruler which could be
drawn out to a foot or to a third or two thirds of a foot
and in one end was a pencil. It was handsome enough to
send, and then it had the advantage of being small and
would not take up any room. The President suggested a
traveling case with silver articles, but I tabooed this, as
I knew Mr. Roosevelt would not be bothered to take
anything with him which weighed anything at all. He
thought the cost, $35, too little, but I rather convinced
him that it would not be the intrinsic value which would
appeal to Mr. Roosevelt, but the gift itself. While he was
laboring with some inscription to have engraved on it I
simply wrote the two lines,

THEODORE ROOSEVELT FROM WILLIAM HOWARD TAFT,
Good-bye—Good luck

—the latter being Mr. Roosevelt's great expression at
parting with anyone. The President added the line "and a

safe return." The inches and feet are on one side, so the three lines come well on the other sides.

I lunched with Al Lewis to-day, and he tried to tell me that the press was getting very angry with President Taft for withholding news from it and its members. I told him frankly that the press, with the rest of the country, would have to readjust itself to the new conditions just as the people would have to do later. It is impossible for Mr. Taft to do as Mr. Roosevelt did and to keep the press fed with news every hour of the day. It would be unnatural for him to try to do it.

The whole government has been at concert pitch for the past seven years, and there had got to be a retuning and readjusting. As I told Lewis, the household and the aides have had to be readjusted, and the office was the next, and then the reporters who hang about the office, and finally the entire press of the country, and then lastly the country itself. While I was riding with him, however, I told him just what Lewis said, and his answer was on the same line with my ideas just expressed. He said:

"The people of this country elected me, I believe, and, damn it, I am going to give it to them whether they like it or not."

There is the whole thing in a nutshell. He then told me what he had written to Mr. Roosevelt in the letter which I was to take over.

"I have told him frankly that I could not talk to the newspaper men as he did and that possibly they would try to make it appear that the wheels were all being turned back, but that I would accomplish or try to accomplish just as much without any noise. I think the President's methods were the only methods which could be used to accomplish certain things and to get the conscience aroused, but now is the time for affirmative legislation, and I shall use everything in my power to enact into law those things for which he stood. I have so written him, and I do not want him to misjudge me by what the press are going to say."

I laughed and told Lewis when he was talking about Taft this and that:

"It is just such rot as this which drives me to be a Taft man, for I see how unjust the criticism is going to be."

You can see yourself, Clara, how hard it has been for me to readjust myself to conditions, but the realization that such a readjustment was necessary, if I was to be able to serve him at all, has given me the proper line on which to work and to talk. The sooner others see him in this way, the better it will be.

I shall have another letter to write about my dear other chief when I get back. I feel all caught up in the whirl now and feel already his magnetism. Isn't it strange how he keeps the public mind fired up? There is more about him in the press now than about the President.

This reminds me of someone else who has got to do a little readjustment too, and it is the President. I don't think he realizes yet that for seven years he has been living on the steam of Theodore Roosevelt and that the latter has been his motive power and the things he has accomplished have been largely under the high pressure of Mr. Roosevelt. With Roosevelt out of the country, the President will find, and I think has already found, that his steam has been cut off. He will have to find his own fuel now, and, like a child, will have to learn to walk alone. There is not the slightest doubt in my mind that he will learn to walk alone and will walk possibly all the better, but it is going to be a readjustment all the same.

Good-night.

ARCHIBALD.

CHAPTER IV

Roosevelt Starts for Africa

Washington, D. C.

March 24, 1909.

Dear Clara:

We had a wonderful day in New York. It seems to me that Theodore Roosevelt fills our minds more than did President Roosevelt. Every precaution was taken to have his departure as quiet as possible, but New York was as excited over the event as if it had been another inauguration. I have never seen such a demonstration over anyone. The people were more frenzied in their anxiety to get a glimpse of him than ever before. They literally fought their way to the steamer's side even when there was no chance to see him at all.

Finally I got near enough to him to be seen, and reaching out for me he pulled me to him, exclaiming, just as it was carried by the Associated Press:

"By George, it is good to see you again, Archie," and then asked me a number of hurried questions, not about politics or the situation at Washington, but about people at the White House and office, if they were retained, and had I been able to keep the old crowd together. He mentioned a dozen by name, and I thought: "How can he remember these matters with such greater ones in his mind?"

"Will Forster remain?"

"How's good old Jimmie Sloan?"

"Is Major Loeffler satisfied?"

"Is Charlie Lee still at the stables?"

He appreciated the President's message and present, and sent his love. He did not have time to open the letter, but said he would do so at sea. The crowd was getting unmanageable, so he wrung my hand and added:

"Try to see Mrs. Roosevelt to-day," and I had parted from him. A moment later I heard him yell out:
"Is Dave Goodrich in this crowd?" and the voice came back:
"Present and accounted for, Colonel," and they reached hands across the sea of heads, and then he called out:
"Let all Rough Riders hold up their hands so I can find them," and he began fighting his way to each one.

I got hold of Kermit for a minute to ask about Mrs. Roosevelt, and he told me that she was perfectly calm and self-possessed when they had left, but that he felt her heart was almost broken.

I took the midnight train back to Washington. I called on the President at half-past nine. After he had made several inquiries, I told him of the success of my mission and the appreciation of the gift and message by the President. There it is again. I cannot think of him as anything else. I spoke of him as "the President" the other day, riding with President Taft. I explained by saying:

"I am afraid I am falling into your habit of calling him the President."

"Well, never mind, he is my President, and we will have him as our President still, you and I, even if he is nobody else's President."

He laughed, and so we continue to refer to him as the President.

Good-bye, dear girl.
ARCHIBALD.

President Taft and the Newspapers

Washington, D. C.
March 28, 1909.

DEAR CLARA:

What is worrying me now is all this newspaper notoriety. President Roosevelt had the faculty of having things printed as he wanted them, but the President does not understand the art of giving out news, and therefore the papers print news as they hear it and without any regard to the facts.

Mr. Roosevelt understood the necessity of guiding the press to suit one's own ends; President Taft has no conception of the press as an adjunct to his office. President Roosevelt, for instance, would never permit any news to be given out from his office except as he authorized it or else gave it out himself. If he saw something which had occurred in which he was in any way connected in the papers he would at once begin an investigation as to how it got there, and if he could locate the author of the leak he would dismiss him or else have him transferred to some other department. He was his own press agent, and he had a splendid comprehension of news and its value. He saw the newspaper men freely, but they understood that they were only to print what he authorized them to use, and if they did anything else he would not allow them near the White House or office, and he has been known to have them dismissed from their papers. When there was anything which he himself did not want to put out especially, he permitted it to go out through Mr. Loeb. But the important thing was that nothing went out from the White House except as the President wanted it. After it was printed once he could not control what followed, but the news as first given out was always in accord with the wishes of the President or his secretary.

I heard Sam Blythe of the New York *World* say the other day that, had Mr. Roosevelt been a newspaper man instead of a statesman, he would have been the greatest editor of the "yellow" type of newspaper in the world. He went on to say, and I have heard it from others also, that Mr. Roosevelt had the keenest nose for news of any public man they had ever met. By instinct he knew what would be of interest to the public and what would not be; and frequently, when he was talking with them, he would make suggestions along certain lines for the correspondents to follow which showed him to be what they would call a creative city editor, one who kept the assignment book filled every minute with his own ideas. In his day no one ever gave a hint of the movements of the Executive. When he wanted a thing printed he saw that it was done, but he could make all sorts of excursions and do many things without any fear of their ever getting into print. The same thing is not true now, and that is what is troubling me.

There are a good many leaks about the White House. Neither the President nor his secretary gives out anything of any real interest, nor do they understand the art of giving out news. In consequence the papers seek their information from whatever source they can find and therefore print rumors which, if printed a month ago, would have resulted in a clean sweep of reporters from the executive offices. Not able to find out much of the political intentions of the President or his cabinet, they are turning their attention to the class of news known as bedroom politics. They keep a tab on me, and my goings and comings form an important item almost every day now. The same is true of General Edwards or anyone else they know to be an associate of the President. By keeping tab on me, they can get some news of the movement of the President, and this is where danger comes to me. Presidents do not like to see their aides or associates filling too much space in the papers, and very rightly so, but just how to choke it off is a difficult thing to do, especially as I am so well known to all of them, and they look to me as a friend in need.

I have just finished reading the morning papers and, what is worse, the Sunday papers, and not one has less than a column on a game of golf which the President, the

Vice President, and General Edwards and I played at
Chevy Chase yesterday. How they got wind of the game
at all I cannot imagine, unless it was through a fault of mine.
As I came out of the President's office Jimmie Sloan, the
detective, asked:

"Ride this afternoon?"

And I answered in passing:

"No, golf."

I presume the remark was overheard, and that was all
that was needed for a wide-awake reporter. At any rate,
when we came out of the White House in the big motor
there was a camera man at the gate and a crowd around
to see the President pass.

I led the individual score, but largely by accident, as
the President had the misfortune to go into every wrong
place on the fifth hole and in consequence took over ten
to make it. But for this series of mishaps he would have
led the individual score. It was the first time I had seen
him play, and I was interested myself in watching him,
and, I must confess, greatly surprised by his playing. He
plays a better game of golf than Mr. Roosevelt plays tennis,
although I think if Mr. Roosevelt had taken to golf he
would have been a crack player.

The Tafts gave their first big dinner last Friday, and
it was interesting for many reasons. In the first place it
was a queerly assorted dinner. The President makes it a
rule never to pay any atttention to personal squabbles and
differences, and invites his guests regardless of their views
of each other. It was this way in the Philippines, and it is
evidently going to be the same now.

The newspapers describe the dinner as a "Harmony
Dinner," whereas it had no such motive (Can a dinner have
a motive?), but the guests were merely the logical ones
for a first dinner at the White House during a Tariff
session. There were Senator Aldrich and his wife, Senator

Hale and Mrs. Hale, and Representative Payne, chairman of the Ways and Means Committee, and Champ Clark, leader of the minority, and with him was Fitzgerald, the Democrat whose bolt from Clark's caucus made it possible to effect a working organization in the House. Then there was Gussie Gardner, who led the so-called "Insurgents" in the Republican ranks; the Longworths, and Senator Overman, and a few others from the Democratic side. Mrs. Taft invited me to dine also, but I suggested to her, with some degree of regret, I must confess, that I thought it would be better if she invited Colonel Crosby, the newly appointed senior aide, instead of me.

Mrs. Taft should have allowed the President to enter first, instead of which she bolted in ahead of him and was almost halfway round their guests before he had finished shaking hands with the first couple. The Vice President and his wife had not remained put, and when the President and Mrs. Taft entered they were across the room gossiping with someone else instead of being at the head of the column where they belonged. By the time Mrs. Taft had spoken to everyone except the Vice President and his wife, the President was only midway down the line and simply devouring time with each person. This makes him greatly beloved by everyone with whom he takes the time to talk, so no objection ought to be made to it, even though it makes one of the aides late to dinner elsewhere.

I was going to Count Moltke's to dinner at eight and had planned to hustle in the White House guests, and by taking a motor, which I had waiting for me in front, to be at the Danish Legation before the last of their guests had arrived. The President rather upset my plans, however, by lingering over each of his guests. Mrs. Sherman bustled over to Mrs. Taft with all sorts of apologies for being out of her place and made Mrs. Taft more nervous and upset by saying:

"I thought you would enter with trumpets and the band going, instead of which you came in like anybody else."

I must acknowledge that I have to take Mrs. Taft's word for it that she was nervous, for I did not notice it myself; but it seems that not only she, but the President also was very nervous. When I went to the White House yesterday morning I said how nicely everything went off, but Mrs. Taft said:

"I could hardly tell. I was never so nervous and upset in my life. You can imagine how much so when I went ahead of Mr. Taft and rather assumed his place as host, but I was not more so than he was, for he talked all night in his sleep and this morning told me that he did nothing but dream of that dinner the entire night."

I thought she was rather exaggerating the matter until he told me yesterday that he was never as upset in his life as he was just before the dinner.

"Confound it, had anyone told me that such a thing as a dinner could make me nervous, I would have laughed at it, but I assure you I was as nervous as a young girl of sixteen. The fact of the matter is, the White House is a bigger proposition than one imagines. The moment you enter it you realize how necessary it is to have every detail go off in perfect order. One or two breaks and you become a laughing stock. Then, too, the aides being with us and uniforms and the music—all makes one nervous. It is the first time in my life I have ever felt stampeded. I was not nearly so nervous the day I took the oath of office."

This was rather interesting to me, for I thought the President and his wife were not inclined to take the White House as seriously as I thought they should, but this one dinner has given them its proper proportion. Mrs. Taft, especially, felt that she could walk in and do it all, I fear; and they are both realizing that they may be at the head,

but after all, they are only a part of the machinery and
cannot interfere with it beyond a given point.

Affectionately ARCHIE.

A Little Game of Elihu Root

Washington, D. C.
March 30, 1909.

DEAR CLARA:

I went with the President last night to the Harvard
dinner at the Raleigh Hotel, in honor of Dr. Eliot, who has
just retired from its [Harvard's] presidency. By the way,
in his speech he paid a most glowing tribute to the South
and said that the Southern states were improving more
rapidly in the matter of general education than any section of this country, and that when the South woke to its
possibilities in a literary way it would be the best exponent
of the Anglo-American thought.

But what I wanted to relate was the manner the President was caught napping in the matter of the appointment of Eliot to the embassy in England.

Senator Lodge and others have been urging him [Eliot]
for St. James's ever since Mr. Taft was elected, but up to
yesterday he has said nothing more definite on the subject
than he said at the Harry Tafts', when he was there for
the Cleveland memorial exercises. Only yesterday afternoon, when we were riding, he spoke of this dinner and
said that he had not offered the place to Dr. Eliot, but was
seriously considering it. So when he went to the dinner
nothing had been intimated to Dr. Eliot.

Several speeches were made, the best of which was that
of Senator Root. It was classical and evidently had been
prepared with great care. At least, so thought the President, for he said coming home that if it was going to be
the custom to write every after-dinner speech in Washing-

ton, either he had to begin to prepare his or else remain away from such banquets. At the close of Mr. Root's remarks he spoke of Dr. Eliot with great fervor and said that he hoped his tranquil life would yet be an ornament in the courts of Europe, and suggested with what pride all Americans would view this splendid type of American manhood in the first court of Europe.

When President Taft rose to his feet everyone expected to hear him say that Dr. Eliot had been offered the appointment and that he had either accepted or else had declined. Not so, however; he made no reference to the embassy at London until his closing sentence, when he merely said that with Senator Root he also hoped to see Dr. Eliot's usefulness extended and continued. As soon as he had concluded his remarks I passed to his seat to escort him out, and as he passed Root he stopped to whisper in his ear. As we got into the automobile he said:

"Did you hear what I said to Root?"

"No, sir, I did not," I replied.

"I hope he will not take offense at it, for I said to him as I passed, 'Well, I like your damn cheek.' I had made up my mind to tender the embassy to Eliot, but as I had never spoken to him on the subject it was rather rubbing it into me to refer to it as Root did in my presence. However, I asked the old fellow to see me to-morrow morning, and I will offer it to him then."

This morning when I went to the White House he was still closeted with the sage of Boston, but whether he prevailed on him to accept the post I am not certain. I think Dr. Eliot rather likes the pseudonym of "the foremost American citizen not in office."

I like the outside work, the riding, the golfing, and the trips away from Washington, but I do not care to pose as a lay figure about the White House when a lot of women are hanging around gossiping. I see a good many breakers

ahead and some complications, and when the time comes
for finding fault I want to be a safe distance from the
female breastworks.

ARCHIE.

CHAPTER V

MR. TAFT GETS INTO THE TARIFF FIGHT

Washington, D. C.
April 4, 1909.

DEAR CLARA:

Mr. Roosevelt made engagements for two-thirty for
the reason that he always came over to lunch, and as soon
as he got up from the table he would go into the East
Room. But Mr. Taft does not eat lunch, and so there is
no occasion for him to go to the White House at that hour,
and it is therefore foolish to make engagements for him
then. He eats a hearty breakfast and invariably remains
in his office from eight-thirty until five, when he goes
riding or walking. Sometimes he breaks his fast by eating
an apple, but seldom anything more. I don't think this
fast does him any good, for he eats a correspondingly
larger dinner. He has a tremendous appetite and does not
control it as did his predecessor.

I could not help laughing at him one evening at dinner.
He had finished dinner, and we were sitting around the
table, smoking. There was a large bonbon dish of candied
fruit before him, and every now and then he would take
a piece, apparently unconscious that he was doing it, and
before we arose from the table he had eaten every piece
there was in the dish. He never smokes and in consequence
has to do something, I suppose, to break the monotony
of sitting still.

He is going to stand a lot of work, and his work is going to tell. He is very deliberate, and his method is appalling to the average public man who came in contact with Mr. Roosevelt. One never gets his promise, the first time, to do anything. He will say he will take it under advisement, and that is about the most he will do. He will hear a Congressman at length—as long as the Congressman wants to talk, in fact—but it does them no more good than if they stated their case clearly and then got out. They are beginning to understand his methods, and I hope in time they will find out that it is better policy to submit their case to him in writing.

If a public man can deduce any facts he will listen and act accordingly, but he is not swayed in the least against one merely because someone else is prejudiced. But when he takes a dislike to anyone it is for some reason known to himself, and he does not easily forgive. He is persistent in his antipathies. Mr. Roosevelt once said that Mr. Taft was one of the best haters he had ever known, and I have found this to be true. He does not say much, but it is ever before him at the right time. He does not show his dislike, or rather he does not waste his dislike when there is no need for it, and those whom he dislikes never suspect it until the crucial moment.

He might be taking the heartiest dislike to me now, each day we are together, and I am free to confess that I would not know it until he was ready to part company. I think he likes me, but to what extent I have no idea. The more I see of him, the better equipped I think him for the office he holds; but the more I see of him the more certain I am that his administration is not going to be a popular one. But I may be all wrong, and the very traits of character which fit him, in my estimation, for the office of President, may seep in the public mind and make him one of our most popular Chief Executives in history.

I certainly have opportunity enough to study him. I ride with him every day or else play golf with him. It seems to me that I do nothing else. It never occurs to him to ask me if I have an engagement, or if it is convenient to do this or that, but he takes it for granted that I will want to be with him. I believe he has the right idea of the duties of an aide, moreover, for he uses them in this impersonal way; and while the intercourse may be the less flattering to the aide, it must be of far greater convenience to him.

This afternoon we ride again. It is Sunday, and I have been to church and feel so much better for it. Sometimes I feel compelled to go to church. I do not know whether it is superstition, fear of something to come, or merely to keep in touch with what I have been associated with so long, or merely that the atmosphere of the Church brings me in closer touch with Mother. I know I never think of her without thinking of her faith and her church and her desire to have us keep in touch with it. Isn't it wonderful how the wishes of a good woman survive so strongly after she has gone?

I went to the White House Wednesday last and found a message from Mrs. Taft asking me to come up at once, as she had something to say to me. I found her quite excited. She said that the thought had come to her to try to make the speedway in the Potomac Park what the Luneta was to Manila, the Malecon to Havana, and Hyde Park to London. She asked me what I thought of it, and I said quite frankly that I was surprised that no one had ever thought of it before. She was unwilling to discuss the matter with anyone else, but ordered the automobile and together we drove to the Speedway, and in less than one hour she had chosen the place for the bandstand, fixed upon the day to inaugurate the scheme, which is to be the fourteenth of April, and settled upon Wednesdays and

Saturdays as the two days of the week for the concert. By noon I had given the orders from the President to Colonel Crosby to have the bandstand erected, and to the Secretary of the Navy for the Marine Band, and I undertook to popularize the idea through the press.

In consequence, everyone is looking forward to the opening of the Speedway for this purpose, and while the President gets most of the credit for the idea, it is entirely hers, and the method of putting it into effect also is hers. The President will ride horseback on this day, and Mrs. Taft will appear in the motor car. This alone will guarantee its success, but the President and Mrs. Taft as yet do not know the prestige their presence will give to any entertainment, and she is now quite worried for fear the band will be there with no one to hear it save the President, herself, and those who accompany him on horseback. My only fear is that the crowd will be so large as to be unmanageable. There is an element of danger to him, but he seems unconscious of it. The secret police are as nervous as can be over his declared statement that he intends to appear each day of the concert.

He is still busy with the tariff makers and begins to show considerable anxiety over the situation. While riding Thursday, we were joined by Secretary of the Navy Meyer, and he opened the conversation with the statement that he had begun to fear Aldrich was going to make trouble. The President does not hesitate to tell each person he meets that he does not fear to veto a bill which does not suit him. I think he is giving it out this way so as to frighten the high tariff people, but the feeling is pretty well abroad that he will not dare to veto any bill. I doubt myself whether he would have the grit to hand a veto to Congress. It takes a nerve of a special kind to do this, and even President Cleveland, with all his courage, did not find a sufficient amount to enable him to do it. He seemed to be perfectly sincere, however, when he said to Secretary Meyer:

"I am not very anxious for a second term as it is, and I certainly will not make any compromises to secure one. I fear Aldrich is ready to sacrifice the party, and I will not permit it."

Yesterday in the motor, he and the Vice President talked tariff at length. The Vice President has much the same view of Congress that Mr. Roosevelt had. He said:

"Mr. President, you can't cajole those people. You have to hit them with a club. My advice is to begin to hit. I would send for Hitchcock and shut off the appointments of postmasters until the bill is passed."

"I have already sent for Hitchcock for this very purpose," said the President, "but I only want to use this lever on the members and Senators who are recalcitrant."

"You had better send for him again," said the Vice President, "and shut them all off so that the innocent can get to work on the guilty and it can all be done without any personal threat. Simply have it announced that the party is committed to this reform bill and that everything must give way before it, and that any person who tries to defeat the party wishes must necessarily be considered as hostile to the national party and his opinion will not govern with the government."

The President said:

"I hate to use the patronage as a club unless I have to."

"It is your only club," said the wily V. P. "You have other weapons, but the appointing power is your only club."

Enough of politics. Good-bye. With love,

ARCHIE.

The President and the Favor-Seekers

Washington, D. C.
April 8, 1909.

DEAR CLARA:

The President continues to ride daily and for the past week he seldom asks anyone to accompany him save myself. When he meets other statesmen, or alleged statesmen, on the speedway or in the park, he does not ask them to join him but salutes them with a cheery, "How do you do, Senator" (if it is Smith of Michigan), or "Good-morning, General" (if it is Miles), and he has even let some of the Cabinet pass by without an invitation to join him. Last Sunday he invited General Bell to accompany us, and I think the general was perceptibly disappointed when he saw me, for he felt that this ride would give him the chance of his life to secure authorities for pet schemes and approval of certain appointments which he wants made.

As we returned from the ride and the general rode off, the President said:

"Whew! Did you ever hear anyone talk like Bell! I am really fond of Bell when I am away from him, but after listening for an hour or more to his constant repetitions I am utterly exhausted."

And then I added, with malice, I fear:

"Yes, Mr. President, the good effects of the ride are entirely counterbalanced by this constant shop talk. Why can't people enjoy riding with you without trying to work all sorts of schemes?"

It is just that, Clara. Every man who comes into the presence of a President seems to think that this is the one opportunity he may have to gain some petty advantage over some rival or to advance himself a point or two. One could work upon Mr. Roosevelt at times and get him committed on some proposition or to the advantage or disadvantage of some person, but it is largely a waste of time to try to inflame the prejudices of the President in one diatribe. He listens, and when that person is out of sight he dismisses the whole matter just by some such remark as he made after General Bell rode away.

I would not attempt to deceive President Taft even if I wanted to do so, for I am perfectly certain that he would see through the deception and I would only succeed in weakening myself.

When I am with him by myself, I never talk of the day's business to him. I tell him of any amusing story I happen to have heard and talk of people in whom I know he is interested. He loves to talk about people. He sees clearly the foibles of those about him and laughs immoderately over them, especially when he himself is holding them up for ridicule. His ridicule is seldom malicious. It is good-natured. The fact that he sees the little pretenses of Clarence Edwards and refers with humor to his alleged omniscience does not indicate that he likes Edwards the less. He is extremely fond of Edwards. He takes Clarence seriously, too, where serious matters are concerned, and has great reliance in his judgment. He not only enjoys his society, but has confidence in his ability and implicit faith in his honesty.

The President and Mrs. Taft gave a dinner of thirty-two covers on Tuesday evening to the Japanese commissioners, Mr. Wada and Mr. Sakai.

They passed among their guests both easily and gracefully, and as Crosby and I took station to form the march the band struck up a march which filled the entire White House. I remained to dinner and sat between Swager Sherley of Louisville and Mrs. O'Loughlin.

It was a pleasure to see Senator Bacon at the White

House, and he was as pleased as a boy at being there. He called me up by phone in the afternoon to ask how to get into the White House and, after laughing about the matter, he told me he had not been in for over seven years. After dinner he told me that he had never been invited by the Roosevelts to dinner and that he could not understand it. I asked him if he had ever called and he said he had not.

"Then," I said, "you have the reason. Mrs. Roosevelt would not invite you to dinner if you were the Vice President himself if you had not called."

He was perfectly astonished and said that he thought it was from some more sinister reason, but I convinced him that the fault was his own. It is so often the case. Public men had grown accustomed to the thought that the White House was a sort of public tavern, and I am glad to say that on account of the system established by Mrs. Roosevelt, and strictly adhered to by her, they think quite differently about it now.

When the line was formed for dinner I had told the leading commissioner from Japan that he would go out with the wife of Senator Brown immediately after the President.

"But the ambassador," said the commissioner.

"Oh," I said, by way of explanation, "in this country the hostess always goes out last and that is the place of honor."

Imagine, therefore, my surprise, as the line passed to see Mrs. Taft and the Japanese ambassador the second couple in line. I had urged her to follow this custom as being the one least liable to bring about complications, but she said she preferred the other, and while I was trying to manufacture reasons for her doing so, she had assumed the place in line where she rightly belonged. Even if she should feel that her place was at the end of the line, there could be no doubt where the ranking guest whom she takes out belongs. I am very glad she has reverted to this program.

The only change which I heartily approve is that of greeting her guests. It makes a prettier picture, and, after all, is far more formal and more in accord with the custom of European courts than the manner in which the President and Mrs. Roosevelt received their guests. I am not in favor of following the precedences established by courts abroad, but I have found out since I have been at the White House that the more formal entertainments are, the easier they are to handle and the less liable to grotesque blunders.

The next thing that we can expect is some official decision on rank and precedence to be followed. Many ways have seen suggested to reach some definite ruling in this matter, but the one which appeals to me most strongly is a printed circular from the White House signed by the President himself. It has been urged from time to time that a commission formed of a member of the Supreme Court, a member of the House and another from the Senate, and the Secretary of State, named by the President, be appointed to establish some order of rank for our government, but this would result in a lot of bad feeling, I fear, and then might not meet with success. Whereas if the President would announce his own regulations in the matter, while his successor might change it, still it would always be a precedent to refer to when most needed.

I will not close this letter, as I may want to add a line when I come in from my ride.

We had a delightful ride, though the horse proved rather an inferior animal and I fear he will not be able to carry the President's weight. He has too long a barrel to be a weight carrier. I rode him for a quarter of an hour before the President appeared so as to be certain that he had no vicious tricks and to take some of the ginger out of him in case he had too much spirit. But the opposite proved to be the case, and he has not as much life in him as the President demands in a mount.

He talked a great deal about his Cabinet and seems to take as much pride in them as a college man will take in a good fraternity. He said:

"After one year you will see that as a whole the Cabinet will stand out as one of the strongest ever appointed by any President. Wickersham is a marvel. Already he has handed out enough decisions to make him a record to be proud of."

I then told him a remark of Mr. Roosevelt's which seemed to please him very much. It was made at the time when the newspapers were very critical over the frequent changes.

"My Cabinet is one of the best in history," said President Roosevelt one day to me. "With Root and Taft I will challenge comparison with any Cabinet in history. I place the others where I can get the best work from them. They are a part of the executive machinery and as such they do an immense amount of work."

I did not add the rest of the remark, to wit that a Cabinet made up of Roots and Tafts solely would pretty soon wreck the government, or else split it in pieces.

I met Katherine Elkins to-day, and when she asked me why I never called I made some evasive excuse, such as I felt that there was no place for me near her, that she had become such a celebrity as to seem almost out of reach.

"You little know how lonely I am as a celebrity," she said rather sadly. "The only person who has a right to be near me is far away and we can never meet, so it is a kindness for my old friends to come to see me."

She referred, of course, to Abruzzi, and it is the first

time I have heard of her making any reference to him since the estrangement.

It is now "Good-night," dear Clara.
> With love to the old man, as ever,
> Your affectionate brother,
> ARCHIBALD.

Sorolla Paints Mr. Taft's Portrait

> Washington, D. C.
> April 9, 1909.

DEAR CLARA:

The President is having his portrait painted, and we are having a great time getting him to sit still long enough to have it done. When once we get him in the chair he is a perfect study in still life, but the difficulty is to get him in the chair. The artist is a Spaniard, by name Joaquin Sorolla y Bastida, and he carries an interpreter with him, as he neither understands nor speaks English. He told me yesterday in Spanish that the President was very hard to paint for the reason that there was little expression save joviality and that it was not the expression to paint on great men. He said, too, that which I have long known to be true, that when in perfect repose his face is hard and almost sinister, and that any portrait with this expression would be disliked.

> Good-bye, ARCHIBALD.

Society and Politics in Washington

> Washington, D. C.
> April 13, 1909.

DEAR CLARA:

I went to church at half-past seven o'clock, St. John's, and the quaint old edifice was packed. The membership of St. John's is about twice as large as its seating capacity and on such festivals as Easter all its services are fully attended.

At nine I got a car and motored out to the Alexandria High School, taking with me Belle Hagner and Mrs. Longworth to pay an Easter visit to Quentin, who still remains at school there. We went laden with boxes and bags of candy, fruit, and cake which his mother had sent us to carry over to him. Each of us added something, and Alice, contrary to orders and agreement with the family, slipped two dollars in his hand, so his Easter was made happy.

On our return we went to one of those intolerable crushes at the McLeans' country place, "Friendship," for breakfast. The McLeans are very hospitable, but their entertainments are the most casual and incidental and remind me very much of the entertainments the Slocums used to give in Havana when the major would telephone me to come to a supper he was giving—and, as he did not know the English community, would I please bring any of them whom I might care to invite. Every woman who had a good-looking hat was there, and every man who wanted to see some woman went, and in consequence the place was overcrowded and we were at the table nearly two hours, most of the time waiting for food which never came.

Society is laughing its head over a passing remark of mine, and I fear it is not one of which I am very proud. It has gone the rounds and every woman seems to be repeating it. When Lady Paget was here, and after she had told me several racy stories, she asked me about my trip to England. I told her how I liked it, but that I was greatly disappointed in not seeing two things which I had every reason to expect to see, from the many accounts of them which I had read in various English novels. When pressed to tell her what these two things were I confessed to my disappointment in this way:

"I motored through Kent and Wales and yet when I
returned I had not seen Lady Imogen Maude feeding the
peacocks on the terrace, nor had I got a glimpse of the
Young Squire deceiving a gamekeeper's daughter down
by the rhododendrons."

One hears references to rhododendrons now on every
side, and when last week Miss Emory announced her engagement to Ovey of the British Embassy, Mrs. Longworth sent her a potted rhododendron with "Love and
best wishes for Lady Imogen Maude from the gamekeeper's daughter."

It is turned in a hundred different ways, and last night
at the Bourke Cockrans' ghost dance everyone seemed to
be vying with the other in shaping some witticism to this
remark. It was a great dance last night. I did not get there
until after midnight, as I had gone to dinner, theater, and
supper with the James Wadsworths, but when I reached
the house it presented the scene of the maddest revel. It
was supposed to be a sheet-and-pillowcase dance, but a
number of persons were in fancy costumes and all well
gotten up. Billy Hitt, who is small and rather good-looking,
was faultlessly gowned in one of Katherine Elkins's
beautiful Paris dresses. He wore a dark red wig and a
Merry Widow hat. Oden Hoerstmann was dressed as a
ballet dancer in pink tulle, and when I tell you he weighs
two hundred and fifty pounds and is shaped like a barrel
you can imagine what he looked like. We did not leave
until half-past four, and to-day I feel as if I had been
born in some year B. C. and was aged when I looked upon
the world.

Everybody did some specialty in the way of a dance or
song, and one of the hits of the evening was young Baron
von Stumm, who caught the spirit of the occasion and gave
us a really splendid performance of a Cossack dance.
Margerie Ide and I, with sheets as scarfs, danced and

gave one of those weird Samoan songs which brings the East so close to one, while Nick Longworth remained almost constantly at the piano and filled in all the gaps, when the Filipino orchestra was not playing, with skits and music of his own. The Ides go next week to Spain, where the father has been appointed minister, and the Cockrans are leaving in a few days for England, where they will remain all summer and fall.

Someone described it as the most hectic party of the season and one that will give food for gossip for some time if the facts leak out. At one time everyone acted intoxicated and imitated the last scene in the *Merry Widow*, which is laid at Maxim's. At another time I threw a sheet over the head of Eleanor Terry and, throwing her across my shoulder, abducted her in brigandish fashion to the kitchen, where I left her on the kitchen table. The whole evening was one of mad revel, and yet I did not see a thing done for which a woman might blush.

In its way it was wholesome, but it indicates how the customs of the best society can change so as to admit of such an entertainment and be countenanced. It was in strong contrast to the dinner at the Townsends' the night before, which was composed almost entirely of those who were present last night. That was a dinner of thirty and was as beautiful and as dignified as any entertainment I have ever seen. Mrs. Townsend gave the dinner to invite criticism of portraits of herself and Mathilde which had just been painted by Fleming, the famous French artist now in this country. They are wonderful likenesses, but do not compare to the work of Sorolla, who has just finished the portrait of the President. They appear to me to be chromoish, and while they possess the merit of being likenesses, they miss all the fire and vim, for instance, of the Sargent portrait of Mathilde.

Everybody is pleased with the Sorolla. He has got one

of the rare fleeting expressions of the President, and I marvel to see where he found time to get it. It is an expression which sometimes comes to him when he is thinking of something humorous but has not said it and while his lips are just parting to give it utterance. It is not a smile, there is a total absence of the smirk, yet it lights up his face with rare intelligence and good humor. He himself says he never expects to get another such likeness painted and looks at it and laughs like a boy over it.

I am often much amused by the President's methods of securing some bit of legislation which he wants and which he does not like to ask for too pointedly. It is becoming the custom for statesmen to ride on the Speedway and at about the same hour, too, as when the President usually appears. Some of them use odd means to join him, but I notice that when he asks any one of them he has some purpose in view. Before the ride is over they manage to get in some little request, but usually before they part, he has obtained their voluntary promise to push through certain little plans of his own. I notice that he never makes any promise himself. Yesterday, for instance, he saw Senator Penrose on the Speedway, and only a minute before he had said to me:

"Archie, I think we will not take anyone with us when we ride. I think we get on better without them."

Yet, as he saw Penrose coming to him on a huge cart horse, he stopped, asked him how he was, and casually suggested to him that he join us. I saw Penrose slowly and adroitly leading the conversation in certain lines and then at the right moment put forward some well laid plan for some appointment.

The President said little, beyond encouraging Penrose to talk, and when he had finished he said:

"Penrose, what a beautiful park the army engineers have made of this old bottom. I only wish Congress would be a little more generous and give to the Superintendent of Public Buildings and Grounds more money for the improvements."

"I can see that this is done," said Penrose. "Would you like to have it in the extra session, as there will be an urgent deficiency bill?"

"Yes," said Mr. Taft, "I think it would be a good idea to put about twenty-five thousand for this purpose," and Penrose, who is on the Finance Committee of the Senate, became enthusiastic over the prospect of beautifying Potomac Park.

Just before he left Penrose at the gate of the White House, he spoke to him of the necessity of the government's purchasing the land which lies between the new Union Station and the Capitol.

"There is only one way to get land in Washington," said the President, "and that is to appropriate a sum for the executive to spend as he sees fit, but I doubt if you could procure such a provision."

"We can get it through without any trouble if I can only give some idea of what you need."

"I should say five million would be a goodly sum, but one that would not be too large if any valuable land is to be acquired."

And so Penrose rode away pledged to put five million in the hands of Mr. Taft to spend for land—and Mr. Taft did not tell all the plans he had in view, either. He and Congress are getting along well together, and there is little he can ask now which Congress would not give. He knows this is the time to put through any pet schemes he may have in mind, for there is never any telling when the President and Congress may be divorced. He remembers the experience of his predecessor.

Congress allowed President Roosevelt to do anything he wanted to for the first two years and voted money to him to do with as he pleased, and even permitted him to disembowel the White House and remodel the entire structure with no other supervision than his own. The days of strife came later, when he could not get an appropriation for an additional clerk. President Taft is a keen politician in his way and knows men and how to handle them for his own ends. He may be able to go through his administration and remain on good terms with Congress, but I doubt it. I doubt Congress rather than the President, for when it sees that his smile is not all that it seems and the pat on the back does not mean complacency, it may readjust itself and try to force where it could not wheedle.

Presidential Aides and Entertaining at the White House

Wednesday morning.

Helen Taft is a nice girl and very intelligent without being a prude, and I think she is going to develop along good lines. I was very much pleased with her frankness and appreciation of what was done for her. She said to each aide of her father's as they said "Good-night":

"I cannot tell you how grateful I am for all you have done. I feel it would have been a failure had the aides not taken hold as they did."

Rather nice for a young girl, who is not yet out, to say! The aides did do well. Most of them understood their business, for they had their training in the last administration, yet they did not have much heart in the party last night at the beginning. They still are homesick for the Roosevelts, and it is very funny to see these young subalterns grow sentimental when they pass Mrs. Roosevelt's picture in the lower hall.

Mrs. Taft said to me while watching the dancers:

"How easy it is to entertain here and how beautifully everything goes off! There seems to be no trouble connected with it all."

I refrained from pointing out to her the details of even this entertainment which went to make it a success, and how, if one person had failed in his part, it would have been easy to mar the whole. By the way, you have no idea how lovely she can look when handsomely gowned and with her hair done well. She really looks ten years younger since she entered the White House, and I think she has become more gracious and kinder toward all the world. She has always had a struggle, and she possesses a nature which I think is going to unfold and enlarge itself as it adjusts itself to new and broader surroundings.

Well, we are off at twelve and it is now ten. Weigh not the merits of this letter, but pardon its offences.

ARCHIBALD.

The President Weeps Over a Play

Washington, D. C.
April 15, 1909.

MY DEAR CLARA:

Just the President and I returned from New York to-day. Mrs. Taft remained over there until this morning. In spite of the fact that I was in uniform all the time, the trip was a most pleasant one. We left Wednesday, spent Wednesday night at the Harry Tafts', saw Sothern in *If I Were King*, went to New Haven Thursday morning, where the President attended a board meeting, and returned to New York last night, going to the old Empire Theater where we laughed and cried through four acts with Maude Adams in *What Every Woman Knows*, and took the midnight train back to Washington. So you see we have had a busy time of it. The President enjoyed himself hugely. He refused to take a secretary with him and therefore attended to no business while away.

The President sniffled the first night, but he had to use his handkerchief at the second performance. I was the only one in the box who did not weep a little. I seldom weep, but I choke up—a most uncomfortable act as it makes me red in the face and generally uncomfortable. The President acknowledges openly that he never can control himself at such times, and it was really funny to see the curtain come down and the lights go up and watch him turn his back to the audience until he got his eyes clear of water. His brother Harry, a large, big type also, is no better, and it has been a joke among them for a long time as to which one sniffles first over sentimental scenes. They both agree that their other brother Charlie is more soft-hearted than either.

Mrs. Taft has a contempt for herself for the same weakness and invariably tries to collect herself by laughing at the absurdity of showing feeling over mere play acting.

When President Roosevelt had an engagement, all I had to do was to appear and simply stand for a minute. He at once got nervous under this system and would promptly get up from whatever he was doing and come. It is not so with President Taft. When it is time for him to take a train or keep an engagement my mere presence has no effect on him at all. I could stand within a foot of his elbow for an hour, and it would not worry him in the least or make him nervous. I am forced not only to remind him of the train or the engagement, whatever it may be, but I am usually forced to interrupt him several times before he can be got to move.

From the little I have seen of him I should say that optimism was his prevailing trait of character. He seems to see the best in everything, especially in big movements. While I was riding with him the last time, he made the remark which I took the trouble to write on my cuff as soon as I left him. We had been talking of the unfortunate wrangle between President Roosevelt and Congress. He said after a few minutes of silence:

"I hope I shall not be called upon ever to say anything in disparagement of Senators and members of the House. I have no desire to belittle them. The people can do no better thing than to trust Congress, and Congress can do no worse thing than to betray the trust."

Opening of Speedway

Saturday, April 17, 1909.

I went to a luncheon to-day at Assistant Secretary Oliver's. The luncheon was given to Miss Choate, whom I met in Cuba last year—or was it two years ago? She is very charming, possesses a good deal of style of an English type, and is a bit amusing, as our cousins across the water would say.

The Speedway, or as it is officially designated, the Potomac Drive, was formally opened this afternoon, and a terrible crush it was, too. Mrs. Taft has worried herself almost sick over the possibility of failure. I knew it would be a success but I did not anticipate the crush there would be. It was the result of her own idea and she has really provided a long-felt need here in the Capitol City.

The Duke and the Lady

Saturday midnight, April 17, 1909.

The dinner at the McLeans' was too funny for words. The house is a perfect palace, and the large table surrounded with small tables, in the oak-paneled dining room with its lofty ceiling, was wonderful in gold and rare china. But the dinner itself was the oddest I have ever seen, and everyone is talking of it and wondering if Mr. McLean at the last moment ordered two of the courses left out. It seemed to consist of several salad courses and a sweet. I know I kept passing course after course of dishes which were queer and indigestible-looking, thinking that something would come on soon which might appeal to the palate. The anticipation was never realized and when I really began to get hungry I went ahead into the ice course and the dinner was over.

I sat next to Miss Elkins and enjoyed the time we were talking, which was all during the meal. As she sat down she said, looking at the card of the man on her left:

"You will have to talk all the time to me, for I do not speak to this man."

It was a Count Montiglione, as near as I can get it, and he belongs to the papal party in Rome, and it seems since he has been on his visit to this country he has passed certain criticisms on the ambitions of Abruzzi.

Young Ned McLean and his wife, who was Evelyn Walsh, sat at the head of the table. They eloped and were married last spring, although the parents of both were keen for the match and there was no opposition from anyone. They are so madly in love they will not accept any invitations to dinner unless they are permitted to sit next to one another. So they sat together last night while several engaged couples were separated by the length and breadth of the room. There was a large number of guests invited to the cotillion later, and while there were over two hundred in all I should say the rooms did not appear to be even crowded. I enjoyed the evening for the reason that I sat in a window with Mathilde Townsend all the time and drove home with her later. Truly she is the most beautiful woman I have ever seen.

I cannot make out what is the status between Miss Elkins and the duke. She wears an antique bracelet of very ancient workmanship and his picture in the locket which forms the center of the ornament. I admired the bracelet and she showed me the likeness and, with a sigh, said:

"The saddest part is that I can never have the mate to it."

She talked a great deal of Billy Hitt and it seemed to me her eyes followed him a great deal of the time. He is most persistent in his attention and my belief is that some day he will console her for the loss of the duke.

Good-night, with love,
ARCHIBALD.

CHAPTER VI
THE PRESIDENT MAKES A DINNER LIST

Washington, D. C.
April 19, 1909.

DEAR CLARA:

The baseball season has opened and when I went to the White House this morning it was with the avowed purpose to persuade the President to go to the ball park this afternoon. When I suggested it to him he seemed eager to go, but later said he could not forego his horseback ride. I thought it would be a popular thing for him to appear at one of the opening games. I did not give this as my reason, but urged his health, as I thought it was just as necessary to get his mind off business as it was to exercise. He agreed to go if I would ride with him at two o'clock. He was caught in his office by Senator Beveridge, who kept him until nearly three o'clock, and when he came out he was wilted. As he walked over, he said:

"Beveridge is such an honest and able man, I often wonder what makes him such a selfish pig. He never talks. He only preaches."

We rode for an hour and a quarter. He then changed his clothes and we took the big touring car for the ball park. I had gone out earlier in the morning with Tom Noyes to select a box and then later to buy a big chair for him to use. We had trouble in finding one large enough but finally secured one at Moses'. The immense throng gave us a rousing reception, but his presence, I fear, rattled the home team, for it played worse than it is wont to do, and it never plays exceptionally well. . . .

April 24, 1909.

I fear there is going to be some criticism of his desire to have his aides always appear with him in uniform. I see good-natured flings at him occasionally in the press and some ridicule of us, but we have to take the bitter with the sweet. In time the press will become accustomed to the uniforms with him and let up.

It is one of the disagreeable features of being with him always, as I am. As the playmate or companion of a President one has to accept notoriety, but it seems to me that I get more than my share and I confess it is extremely distasteful to me to have my photograph constantly in the papers and every time I turn around or don a new suit of clothes to find it chronicled in the weeklies. They love to write about those whom they describe as managing affairs at the White House and to whom they delight to refer as powers behind the throne, members of the golf or tennis cabinets, and so on and on, until one wearies of the sight of one's name in print. But it is all a part of the system of our times and the methods of the press of this period. I told the President yesterday that dear friends—like the ——es, I thought—were behind the criticism. I know that both are jealous of me, but just why I cannot imagine. The President's remark, when I told him of the criticism, was:

"Well, Archie, I had once a dear old grandmother and one of her most frequent remarks to my mother was, 'My child, it is much better to be envi-i-ed than to be piti-i-ed.'"

Beginning with to-night and extending through the next month, the President is going to give six dinners and four garden parties. I say the President is going to give them, because that is what is going to happen. Mrs. Taft is opposed to them and prefers to wait until next fall to begin general entertainments, but he wants these dinners for some special reason and has prepared the list of those to be invited in the most careful and painstaking way.

Every morning when I have gone to his office for the past week he has been sitting there, writing out names and erasing others and changing lists. This morning he read me the results of his labors and seemed pleased to have concluded.

"Archie, I am rather proud of these lists. I do not believe there were given six dinners at the White House where more thought has been expended than on these six. The White House is a big political asset when used wisely."

He went on writing for a few minutes and then looked up, his whole face beaming with some unspoken thought, just such an expression as the Spanish artist caught on his canvas. He began to chuckle, gurgle I should say rather than chuckle, and added:

"I should like to hear the comments of some of these men when they receive their invitations. Some of them will be mystified as to why they have been invited. They may suspect later, but I am inclined to think their vanity will prevent them from guessing the truth."

He read out several names and said:

"I presume these people have never been invited to the White House before and seldom to a dinner anywhere. It is real joy to ask these. There is no motive behind their invitations save to give them pleasure, but that is what some of the others will not be able to comprehend, and in wondering how these simple people got here they will overlook the real reason which lies behind their own invitations."

This was one of the longest speeches he ever made to me and it seemed to be the culmination of some thoughts, funny and otherwise, which had been in his mind ever since he began to make out the dinner lists.

ARCHIBALD.

The President Discusses Feminine Discretion

Washington, D. C.
April 27, 1909.

DEAR CLARA:

General Edwards was with us, and after leaving the Newlands' we went zigzag over the country and had a very delightful afternoon of it. By the way, I have had a very satisfactory talk with General Edwards. Mutual friends had begun to say little things to me about him and I know they must be doing the same thing to him. Nothing very malicious, but sufficient to break up our friendship if either became suspicious of the other. I had begun to feel that he was getting jealous of my constant companionship with the President and persons were hinting to him, possibly, that I was coming between the two of them. As I had written you before, the President is devoted to General Edwards and I would not for the world say the slightest word of harm to him. In fact, the President would resent anything of the kind. However, I told the general just what I had heard and that I was on my guard never to be led into saying a word to which he could object, so with this assurance he could be on his guard, if he thought he need be.

Where Washington gossips are interested, it behooves everyone to be on guard. The President goes with hardly anyone else save me and General Edwards, and he does this so as to avoid the one thing which brought to President Roosevelt so many troubles through personal jealousies and cliques. He does not have to offer apologies for his association with either Clarence or myself, for he has always traveled with him and he is an acknowledged intime, while I am his personal and official aide, and when I appear with him it is as an aide and should not arouse any antagonisms or jealousies.

Persons, many of them important in the social and political world, are constantly scheming to ride with him or to play golf with him, but he manages to shift out of it or to be perfectly oblivious to their machinations. It is interesting to watch him grow absent-minded when he wants to do so and pass people by with a wave of the hand and a smile when they are looking for so much.

Mrs. Taft says the dinner last Saturday was very doleful. I knew it would be when I saw the list of guests. They were almost exclusively political persons, many of whom are not talkative in a society way, and others were so impressed by being at the White House for the first time that they were awed into silence.

I was much interested to see Senator Bailey of Texas in a dress suit. You may remember the first time he was invited to the White House to dine, it was in the time of McKinley I think, he sent his regrets for the reason that he did not have a dress suit and that he would never belittle himself by appearing in one. His position caused much amusement at the time and prevented him from ever being invited there again. He has evidently changed his mind, for he was not only conventionally clothed the other evening, but he was the trimmest-looking man in the room. He loses the heavy, bulky look when in evening clothes, and I was quite proud of him as a Southern senator. His wife was most beautifully gowned and had a wonderful set of pearls.

The fact that Bailey was asked to this dinner shows very clearly the attitude of the Tafts to public men. It has been less than a month since Senator Bailey declared that Mr. Taft was less fitted to be President than any man who had ever held office. He said nothing against his character, but hit him pretty hard generally.

The President intends, as I pointed out before, to use the White House as a means to an end. President Roosevelt used it entirely as a reward of merit and to pay for favors already performed and loyalty which had been proven. In fact, sometimes his invitations to dinner would follow so closely on a defense of him in the House as to shock the sensibilities of Mrs. Roosevelt.

I was much amused yesterday while riding with President Taft, when he suddenly turned to me and, apropos of nothing, said:

"Archie, how can you make a woman discreet?"

"You can't, sir," I answered, "unless she is so by nature."

"Well, I believe that to be true."

I knew what he was thinking about. At dinner only a few evenings ago someone mentioned the President, that is Col. Roosevelt, and spoke of an editorial in the *Sun* on his alleged interview in Naples with a fresh correspondent, in which he had been made to say that he had had Taft elected to carry out his policies and that if he faltered he would return and put him aside, or something to that effect. Knowing that the President never said such a thing, I remarked:

"It was made out of whole cloth, and everyone knows he never said any such thing or even hinted at such a thing."

Mrs. Taft broke the silence which followed my defense of the great man, by saying:

"Oh, I don't know. It sounded just like him. It is just

as well to recognize what has got to come sooner or later, and let people and papers like the *Sun* take sides."

She is very decided in her opinions and there is no side-tracking her when her mind is made up. He is the only one who can get her to change her mind.

I sat next to Mrs. McKee the other evening at the Lee Phillips'. Mrs. McKee is a daughter of President Harrison and the mother of the much-advertised Baby McKee. She gave me to understand that although she had left her card she had not received an invitation to the White House. The next morning I said to Mrs. Taft that Mrs. McKee was in the city and staying at Mrs. Arthur Lee's home.

"Well," she said, and waited for me to go on. Whenever she says, "Well," like that, I know she is getting on the defensive.

"I thought you might not know she was here and would like to have her to dinner."

"No, I do not want her to dinner and I am under no obligations at all to her. She was never even polite to me in the past and I have not forgotten it."

When I saw the President I told him Mrs. McKee was in the city and of my conversation with Mrs. Taft, at which he laughed immoderately.

Sunday afternoon when we were out he said:

"Did you notice, Archie, that McKee was at lunch to-day?"

"I did, sir."

"Well," he said, "always keep me informed in these matters."

I cannot but admire Mrs. Taft's honesty and directness. She is uncompromising in all matters of honesty and where principle is involved, and never deceives herself, and in consequence never tries to deceive anyone else. I am beginning to believe that I am going to get along with her simply by adapting myself to her straightforward method and direct mode of thought. I am sorry that I have given you the impression that I am still, unblushingly, flying the Roosevelt colors. I do not think any people can ever take the place in my affectionate regard of President and Mrs. Roosevelt, and I shall always love them as I shall always believe in him, but I admire President Taft very much and see so much in Mrs. Taft to like that I had hoped I was giving you an unbiased impression of them as they appear to me. They cannot be compared to the Roosevelts, for there is simply nothing in common—their life, their mode of thought, their pedestals, their education, and above all their natures are absolutely at variance and as widely separated as the East is from the West, as Augusta, Georgia, is from Augusta, Maine.

With love always,
ARCHIE.

A Speech Is Written in Three Minutes

Washington, D. C.
April 27, 1909.

DEAR CLARA:

The Philadelphia trip proved to be very interesting. The only other person besides the President and his entourage was Wayne MacVeagh, a brother of Secretary MacVeagh, a gentleman of the old school, one who has seen as much of public life and public men as any man possibly who has lived during the past half century.

The President thought to write his speech going over on the train, but by the time he had reached Baltimore he gave up that idea and naïvely remarked that he would make another failure rather than spend the remaining time of the trip locked in a stateroom with a stenographer. He talked with Mr. MacVeagh about Grant a good deal, and while so talking hit on the rather novel expression that had the South followed Lee and the North followed Grant there would have been complete reconciliation long before it really came about. Suddenly he stopped and took out his notebook and wrote on it for certainly less than three minutes, and when he had finished he said:

"There, I have written my speech and I believe it will not be a failure. I have just what I want, and had I thought for days I could not have done better than to elaborate that idea."

He was so pleased with himself that he really grew talkative for the next hour and then turned in and slept until we reached Philadelphia.

The President made the best speech I ever heard him make. He was greatly in earnest and his plea for the South to come more in harmony with more advanced political thought was intertwined with loving tributes to it and its people and the highest praise for its steadfastness to principle and creed.

The dinner Wednesday, which Mrs. Taft called her society dinner, was particularly pleasant and as pretty a dinner as I have ever seen at the White House. We have been accustomed to arrange the guests as they arrive in the order of their precedence and rank around the Blue Room, so that the President could go from one to the other with the greater facility. Just before it was time for them to arrive, the President and Mrs. Taft sent for me to come upstairs and asked that the guests be not so arranged. They thought it better to let them take their positions naturally and without any great form. The President also asked that the band play a march instead of the Star-Spangled Banner. The effect was prettier and far less stiff than at the dinners where we have segregated the guests according to precedence.

The President took out Miss Cannon, and the old rugged

Speaker escorted Mrs. Taft. Just as the line was forming, the Speaker said to the President:

"I suppose Mrs. Taft and I come last."

"No," said the President. "Mrs. Taft always comes after me."

Both Palmer and I were much pleased, for we have never known whether the first decision of Mrs. Taft, namely that she would end the line, or that of the President, that she should follow the example of the Roosevelts and take her place second, would stand. But the President was so emphatic that I think the question as to the relative position of Mrs. Taft is fixed now and for all the time they are in the White House.

Yesterday we went riding as usual, except that we were accompanied by Secretary Meyer. We had a delightful afternoon. We explored the lower end of the island below the bridge, going almost as far as Washington Barracks and were only turned back by the high tide, which made the ground unstable for the President's horse.

About midway along the island we saw a little black boy fishing. His whole attitude seemed to amuse the President and as we rode up to him he said:

"Have you caught any fish?"

"Not any yet," answered the urchin.

"Then what are you fishing for?" said the President, his whole face enveloped in a smile.

Without answering, the boy turned round and, after looking quizzically at the President for a moment, said:

"Is you Mr. Taft?"

"Yes," said the President.

"Well, then I'm just a-fishing to be a-fishing," and went at his work again.

The President laughed immoderately at this reply and said to Secretary Meyer:

"George, I guess that is the way with most of us. 'Just a-fishing to be a-fishing.'"

Several times he laughed over this and kept repeating it as if it amused him way down to the depths.

When I went to the White House Thursday, Mrs. Taft said that the President did not want to ride on the driveway during the concerts any more, that he was becoming sensitive.

"And this worries me, too, for he has never been sensitive and I think he looks well on horseback. Did you notice people laughing at him?" she asked me. "For he seemed to think he caused amusement."

I could say faithfully I had not and I feared he mistook the natural stare and beaming of the people on him for fun making.

People do stare at him in a most ill-mannered way, especially when he rides among them, but he has no reason to get sensitive. I would be quick to note any ridicule. There seems to be nothing but good nature and a certain amount of affection. I have noticed, as the days go by, that this feeling, affection, is more manifest. I think he is creating his own atmosphere, as it were. People are forgetting that he is the residuary legatee, and his smile, good nature, and evenness of temper are winning hearts to him, and, of course, the longer he is President and the more his name is in the paper, the more curiosity there is to see him and the more eager are people to tell others that they have seen him and describe the way he appears, how he is dressed, and how he greets one.

I have seen Mrs. Robeson this year and she has aged very much since I saw her last, though her daughter does not seem to see it, or, if she does, she will not admit it. How well I know that feeling! But the heartache is there, all the same.

Mrs. Robeson was a brilliant woman in her day and her home was a salon for the great and the wicked, even from her own witty accounts. I was entertained this evening by her accounts of Blaine, whom she knew well. The subject came up on account of letters of Mrs. Blaine, which have just been published, in which are many references to Mrs. Robeson. Mrs. Robeson says she could not but reflect how little any woman knows a man, for while Mrs. Blaine was writing to her daughters one thing, Mrs. Robeson says she happened to know the contrary to be true. She has much of her charm left, and what she has lost she still contributes to the world through her daughter. She wrote some exquisite songs in the dim past somewhere. I imagine they were considered quite improper at the time, for they are not all they might be even in the present decadent period. She lives them all over, playing the accompaniments while Miss Ethel sings them with as much passion as ever she did, if Senator Hale's recollection of her voice is to be relied upon. I was much amused and considerably touched to watch her close her eyes and repeat the words as her daughter sang them. All is gone save the memories they recall to her, and she sees herself again in Grant's Cabinet, where her husband was a minister and she was the center of the fashionable world at that time.

ARCHIE.

CHAPTER VII

MR. TAFT TAKES TO HIS BED

Washington, D. C.
May 1, 1909.

DEAR CLARA:

﹥ This is the first day off I have had since the sixth of March, when the President began to ride or to exercise in

some form every day. I do not know what to do with it
now, so accustomed have I grown to report for duty every
afternoon at the White House. I do not like the cause for
my holiday, however. The President is quite unwell. When
I reported at his office this morning he looked up very
languidly and said:

"I am afraid I am not fit to play this afternoon, Archie.
I never felt so sick before. There is some work I must do,
but I am going to bed as soon after as I can and will remain there until I am better."

He really looked all tuckered out and as pale as a ghost.
When he started for Alexandria yesterday he was feeling
done up and asked me to feel his pulse. He did not seem
to have any fever and he thought possibly he had only
taken cold. But to-day he is decidedly sick.

Good-bye, as ever,

Your devoted brother,
ARCHIE.

At Dinner with Ambassador Bryce

Washington, D. C.
May 2, 1909
Sunday.

My DEAR CLARA:

The President is still sick. I think he is quite knocked
out. I went to the White House this morning to see him
and found him in the study, sitting before a big blazing
fire, looking thoroughly worn and tuckered out. When he
gets sick he looks it. I felt very much alarmed, seeing his
great form utterly relaxed, his eyes heavy, and his skin
very white. He could hardly articulate, his throat is so
swollen. When I asked him if he felt well enough to go out,
he said he did not.

"Take a holiday, Archie, and enjoy yourself," he said
with a wan smile.

This is the first time he has ever intimated to me that he realized he was keeping me pretty well on the go. I have been so accustomed to make plans to fit into his that I seemed for a while to be at a loss as to what to do with the day.

As I left him I told him that I was going to lunch with the Newlands.

"Give her my love and say I wish I was going too."

I went out on horseback and enjoyed the time there very much. She was in a splendid mood, witty and charming. Von Brado gave me a wonderful Swiss hunting knife which he brought over to me; something I have long needed. Representative Parsons of New York and his wife were there and several persons rather in the unidentified class, though I think they were all wealthy and had fine motors. Mrs. Parsons, who is the daughter of Henry Clews, is a Southerner by birth, I think, but holds the most extraordinary views even were she a New Englander. As a young girl she wrote a book on socialism advocating all sorts of doctrines and quite startled Newport with her views. She never fails to try to arouse me to argument by advocating some preposterous theories on the Negro problem. She succeeded once, and since then I have refused to take her seriously. She is really very clever and very pretty. She would.have no standing army and told me once that so opposed was she to anything military that she would have the prayer for the Church Militant left out of the Prayer Book, and that she would not send her children to Sunday school if the rector permitted the singing of "Onward, Christian Soldiers."

I left the Newlands' and rode about the country by myself until seven o'clock and enjoyed the absence of everything living. Do you ever get so that the sight of a human being gets on your nerves? There is nothing so good for it as a solitary horseback ride.

The dinner last night at the Bryces' was a heavy, solid, British affair, if I ever saw one.

I was sorry I was not sufficiently late to miss the soup course, but unfortunately I arrived just in time to be nearly poisoned by it. The embassy dinners are served always on silver dishes; plates, platters, and dessert saucers are all solid silver. It looks ornate, but when taken in conjunction with the distance of the kitchen from the dining room, one never has a hot course and seldom a warm one.

After dinner Mrs. Cowles, Mrs. Bryce, and I hobnobbed in the corner, and Mrs. Bryce gave us an account of some of the anonymous letters which she received. When her husband is away she opens all his mail and separates what is private from that which she sends to the chancery. Last week she said she received a letter addressed to him from a man in Baltimore where he had delivered the week previous a lecture on John Calvin. In the letter the writer said that he had been struck with the clearness of Mr. Bryce's phraseology and the depth of his thought and, if it was no trouble to the ambassador, would he tell him where he had acquired these things, as the writer had a son whom he was educating and would like to know just how one made an orator of just the ambassador's type. Mrs. Bryce seemed very much amused at this letter and said that she had written to him that Bryces were born, not made, and moreover,

"I added," she said, "that he had to be born part Irish and part Scotch."

The man wrote back most seriously and regretted that it would be impossible to produce just such a combination, as unfortunately his wife was Swiss.

Mrs. Bryce looked better than I have ever seen her. She worships her husband and he seems to be equally devoted to her. He looks twice her age and quite unlike all

Britishers I have met in the public service. I recall President Roosevelt's description of him, which did not strike me to be very applicable at the time, but the more I see of him and the more I hear him talk the truer the witticism seems to be.

It was after one of the tennis games, when the French ambassador, Secretary Garfield, and some others were having tea in the office. Mr. Bryce was under discussion and his nationality seemed to be in doubt. Someone said he was all Irish, and another thought him Scotch and Irish. President Roosevelt said:

"I should say he was simply a prodigious memory with a lot of hair on it."

I never see him now without thinking of this description.

I heard that Mathilde was to be at this dinner, and I was very cross when she failed to appear.

Good-bye.

> With love,
> ARCHIE.

> May 3, 1909,
> Monday.

The President is slightly better this morning. He came over to the office for a while, but returned early to the house to bury himself in his study. He balked at the last moment last night and did not go to the Cowles' to dinner, and Mrs. Taft had to go without him.

A Pretty Artist Has Her Troubles

> Washington, D. C.
> May 4, 1909.

DEAR CLARA:

I am glad to say the President is decidedly better and last night went to the dinner given in his honor at the handsome new home of Secretary Meyer on Scott Circle.

It was a lugubrious dinner at best; nearly everybody at the table was suffering some kind of malady save myself and Miss Boardman. Mrs. Winthrop was present, in spite of the fact that her face was all swollen out of proportions by an ulcerated tooth, but such is an invitation to dine with the President that the average woman would permit nothing short of death to intervene. Mrs. Meyer was just out of bed with grip, and the secretary, her husband, had been in the house all day nursing a feverish cold. Mrs. Lodge confessed to a headache, and Mrs. Goelet, quite contrary to her custom, had to touch up with a little rouge to look well. This, in spite of the fact that she is considered, I believe, the handsomest woman in New York. She is lovely like a tall Easter lily, only with color. Last night she had a little too much—but then, everybody had something wrong with them.

Mrs. Meyer entertains charmingly at all times, and the dinner last night anywhere else would have been a hopeless failure. She has a wonderful figure, dresses with taste, is highly educated, and has every element of social leadership. Her setting has been rather contracted heretofore, for her home on Connecticut Avenue was too small for her, and then, too, the street cars passed the house. One cannot be thoroughly at ease as a hostess if at any time one's dignity is to be broken in upon by clanging of bells and rattling of badly laid car tracks. It was a genuine pleasure to see her last night with spacious surroundings and tapestried walls. I predict she will have a great record as a hostess next season and, if she cares to be, a popular one as well.

The President is having another portrait painted, or rather has permitted another portrait to be painted. This time it is a young woman—and a very pretty one at that, he says. He invited me over this afternoon to meet her, which brought forth the remark from Mrs. Taft:

"If you enjoy a pretty face, Captain Butt, I would advise you to come."

I will give you my impression of the young woman and her work later in the day.

We ride this afternoon for a half hour. The physician will not permit him to do more, and he must go at a jog.

In the Evening.

Well, we did not have the ride and I met the artist. The President was to pose for her at three o'clock and then go riding later. At two-thirty the new minister from Venezuela, Señor Rojas, arrived with his two new secretaries, and was accompanied by Secretary Knox. The President went upstairs to put on his official robes, as he calls his frock coat, and remained so long that I finally went for him. I found him in his sitting room, calmly reading a book.

"You have hunted me out, have you?" he asked.

"Yes, sir," I said. "I am not worried about the minister, but the secretary looks so abused if he is kept waiting."

"Well, Knox thinks he is martyr at all times, and he is never so happy as when he has a legitimate complaint," he said.

And going down in the elevator, he said, smiling a good broad smile:

"So you have noticed, too, that Knox takes his office pretty seriously. I often think how Knox would enjoy playing the rôle of President. I know he thinks I am far too casual in my treatment of foreigners."

The new minister delivered his address in Spanish and the President had to laugh when in his address he read:

"It was with unfeigned delight that I heard you enunciate, etc., etc.," or some such nonsense, for he had not understood one word of what the minister was saying.

I went in the Green Room at three and found the little

artist there, really lovely and quite naïve in her enthusiasm. The President did not come over until five and by that time I was well acquainted and had been induced to put on a coat of the President's and pose for his clothes. But, unfortunately, the coat hung like a bag from my shoulders and helped on the portrait very little. The President tried to pose for a little while, but he was very tired and very weak. He fell asleep twice while standing up, and sat in a chair for a minute and was sound asleep.

While Mrs. Taft seems to be growing younger, he seems to be growing so much older. I looked at his face in repose and saw lines there, deep, deep lines, which I had never noticed before.

Of course we did not go riding. He soon went upstairs to rest and I remained with the artist, helping her clean the mess she made. Her hands were covered with oils and she had a smudge on her nose and she had dropped several large dabs on the velvet rug. I tried to wash it up with turpentine and made it worse.

To-night I dine at the Japanese Embassy.

ARCHIBALD.

Social Triumph for the Wickershams

Washington, D. C.
May 8, 1909.

DEAR CLARA:

The President certainly has bad luck these days of spring. No sooner did his fever and cold leave him sufficiently for him to resume his exercise and horseback riding than a bug flew in his eye and injured that feature so badly that he has now been laid up with it for several days and has had to wear a bandage over it. In consequence, the portrait is coming along very slowly, and poor Miss Swan is in despair over the results. She cannot possibly paint him while his eye is bandaged, though he says he is perfectly willing to have the bandage and all show on the canvas as long as he can put an end to the posing.

Delaney and I have entered into a conspiracy to try to keep the President well. Every time he makes a fool engagement which it is not necessary for him to keep, I am to try to break it, and if I fail Delaney will advise him as his medico to do so. I got him to break an engagement to attend the commencement exercises of the Blind Asylum, the first part of next week, and declared off the engagement to appear at the unveiling of the Longfellow statue yesterday. These things are too petty for him to bother with. Those who urge him to attend such exercises merely do so with a view of exploiting themselves. The engagement to attend the Board of Trade dinner has got to stand although he is not well enough to go.

In spite of the fact that it rained and thundered nearly all the afternoon, the garden party transferred to the house was very enjoyable. Mrs. Taft received in the East Room and the President stood with her a part of the time. She had every room on the lower floor open and also the doors leading onto the terraces from the State Dining Room and the East Room. The sun came out late and many of the guests wandered about the grounds and on the lawn, though the grass was soppy wet and the trees dripping rain water. The South Portico was a lovely picture and the view from the south windows was most picturesque.

Mrs. Taft was gracious and charming to everyone who came near her. She seemed to rise quite superior to rain and clouds and to the general upsetting of all her plans. In fact, I think she tried to compensate for the lawn feature of the entertainment. She really charmed her guests, and she had a little word of friendly gossip with every woman who passed her.

In the evening I went to dinner at the Wickershams'. It was one of the few delightful dinners I have attended this winter and was such a contrast to the long heavy dinner of the night before, given by the Brazilian ambassador. The evening was made memorable by a speech by Senator Root. I really think he is the most remarkable orator of this latter-day style of eloquence I have ever heard.

Mrs. Wickersham, I imagine, has been quite a belle in the past. In fact, she told me she had known General Beverley Robinson for years and she did not forget to find out his address when she came here and to look him up. Poor old man. He is bedridden, poor, and lives in what must have appeared to her great squalor. She went to his room and held his hand and heard him recall old days, and White Sulphur and Washington, when he was one of the greatest beaux of that period. He boasts that he never had a friend who was not a great social success and accounts for it on the ground that if they were not great successes to start with, he made them such.

I had never met her, but I had seen the pleasure which the general had got from her attentions and I was prepared to like her. She has a good deal of manner, but is a woman of the world, and, I imagine, a great help to her husband. I imagine she and the Attorney General are going in for a very exclusive society, and to have an invitation to their house will mean something before this régime is past. I can only judge of the dinner last night and the people about whom they talked. The conversation was pitched on a rather high scale and there was something about the house which gave one the impression of high birth and culture. She looks like a woman who would be socially ambitious to lead, yet when one talks to her one sees that she will not vie either with the MacVeaghs or Meyerses, but will gather about her home a very different set of people from those to be found at the average dinner at Washington.

He is thought by the President to be the most brilliant member of his Cabinet, and he said to me once:

"Archie, I will give Wickersham one year and then I will prophesy that he will be the most popular public man in Washington."

Mr. Wickersham's invitation to me last night was due solely to the fact that we have ridden several times together, and he took this way of evincing the fact that he liked me.

Their house is handsome, but small for Washington. They can never give dinners of more than sixteen, and a tea would crush the walls, yet I am certain that, modest as their home is, it will become a Mecca for the cultured and that the climber will clamber for invitations to it in vain.

Good-bye. It is Saturday and there is nothing to look forward to but the Board of Trade dinner.

ARCHIBALD.

CHAPTER VIII

WHEN MR. TAFT HITS HARD

Washington, D. C.
May 10, 1909.

DEAR CLARA:

The speech of the President at the Board of Trade dinner on Saturday night has caused much consternation, as it foreshadows what he is capable of doing when the opportunity offers. The dinner was arranged and planned with a view largely of committing him to suffrage in the District of Columbia. The most brilliant orator, Justice

Stafford, was put forward to convert him to this theory of District government. Whether his speech was reviewed by the *Evening Star* faction, I do not know, but there is a strong suspicion that it was and that it met with the approval of those advocating the franchise in the District.

On our way to the dinner, the President remarked to Colonel Crosby and myself that he intended to declare against the franchise, but at that time he had no idea of what was coming. He said he did not want to discuss the subject and that he hoped it would not be necessary to do so.

Justice Stafford was the only other speaker besides the President, and he was greeted with great applause by the three hundred diners when he arose. He spoke for an hour and, as the President said afterward, it was more demagogic than any speech he had heard in the last campaign. However, he created great enthusiasm, and such was his reception that I expected the President to change his line of argument and not oppose, openly at least, a sentiment which was being so enthusiastically received.

I turned to look at him and his face wore that half-cynical smile which is indicative of good-natured disgust. I knew, then, that he would stand to his guns, but I did not know that he would fire them with such vigor as he did. He not only declared against the franchise, but ridiculed Stafford and made him appear absolutely foolish. He belittled his judgment and denounced his entire theory of local government. I have never seen the President so aroused. He gesticulated and his voice rose to great heights. In fact, I felt that he was doing a little too much, but his whole judicial nature had been aroused by the speech of Stafford. As soon as it was over he left the hall and, seeing Senator Tillman near the elevator, he asked him to go down with him. The South Carolinian said:

"Mr. President, I did not believe it was in you. I sat there astonished that you had the hardihood to hit them as you did. I think that speech of yours settles the question of franchise for all times in this self-centered community."

ARCHIBALD.

Keeping the President on the Move

Washington, D. C.
May 15, 1909.

DEAR CLARA:

Little beyond routine work and pleasures have occurred worthy of note. I mean no reflection on my Chief when I put pleasures in the routine category. The fact that I denote this constant attendance on the President as a pleasure is complimentary to him and his good nature.

I do certain things with him each day. Whether I am feeling fit or not makes little difference, for nothing but downright sickness would cause me ever to fail him in anything he might want to do. Then, too, one gets interested in such a work as I do. To keep him up to the mark, to make him break engagements, and ride, even when I do not feel like it, to prevent him from yielding to lethargy, which is natural to one of his size, and to scheme to get him to the ball park and the golf links, and to buoy him up in many other ways becomes, in time, by constant performance, an interesting duty.

I never had to do anything of this kind with President Roosevelt. He did the thinking, the planning, the scheming for all his playmates. One never had to suggest to him to take exercise or prod him to keep his interest in sport alive. It was he who swept one off one's feet in a sort of whirlwind motion and, when it was over, left one exhausted, glad to yield to another playmate the place in the saddle, by his side, or to scale cliffs, or swim creeks. There is no use, however, to compare them at this late day. The records of the feats I performed with President Roosevelt were made at the time I was with him and under his wonderful, almost hypnotic, influence. But I am conscious that the routine work of the day now is harder. I do the thinking, the planning, the executing. The President is not easy to handle either. He moves on his own way, and it takes some device to sidetrack him and lure him to new playgrounds.

I was at dinner with Count de Chambrun, the military attaché of the French Embassy, the other night, and heard him describe his hunting elephants in Africa. Someone asked him which animal was the most dangerous to hunt and it was his opinion that it was the African elephant. For the reason, he said, that the skin was six inches thick and that he towered about twice as high as the average Asiatic elephant one sees in captivity. He has seen thirty men shoot into one elephant and yet seen that animal walk away without feeling a single shot and, in his measured and unconscious tread, kill two natives by walking directly over them. He says the grass is very high in this elephant country and it is most difficult to get out of the way of one moving rapidly.

I could but compare President Taft to this animal. He walks on so unconscious of surroundings and is so immovable in many ways. Yet I flatter myself that I do handle him and to his own good. The fact that he seems to want me with him wherever he goes causes me to think he approves of my methods. When I enter his office in the morning and he says he will ride, I will suggest that there is a big golf match on at Chevy Chase, or a new road open in the park—anything to change his routine and keep his mind active while taking exercise. Had he his way, he would ride in the same place every day and not vary it in the least. He gets accustomed to make a turn at a given point and it is like changing the course of Niagara to try to get him to make the turn elsewhere. I have tried making use of argument or suggestion, but he will say the same thing:

"Let us take the old road, Archie."

I have hit upon a plan which is better, when I think it time to change the course of riding or any of his routine life. If riding, for instance, and I want him to try a new road, I simply ride ahead of him and lead the way. I find that nine times out of ten he will follow. The tenth time he will do as he did the other day, go his own way—when I looked back to see where he was, we had separated and I had to follow. As I rode up at a gallop, I thought I saw a smile playing about his lips, but I am sure he felt that he had circumvented me and was enjoying it.

After dinner, just as I was going to bed, the "Night Riders" came by and howled me into my clothes again, and off we went on a ride.

، The Night Riders is an order which has come into being under the leadership of Alice Longworth. Any time, whether at ten or one o'clock, they might start off and decide to ride. That means that she and Nick, for he backs her up in everything she does, will start off and gather two or ten more, whatever the fancy may be, just as she gathered us up last night. It may be the Meyerses, or the Phillipses, or the Keepses, or any home where the inmates are known and beloved by the Night Riders. Out onto the lawn is the work of a second, and the howls and cat calls continue until the house is opened and the refreshments are served or something is done. At first there was some criticism of the Night Riders, but now the highest social honor one can have is a raid from the Night Riders led by the intrepid Alice.

ARCHIE.

Mr. Taft Takes a Nap at a Funeral

Washington, D. C.
May 12, 1909.

DEAR CLARA:

How was this for a busy day yesterday? Reported at the Executive Office at nine, got directions to see the Secretary of the Navy and arrange for a trip to Hampton on the *Dolphin*, which was accomplished in detail; at the White House on routine matters until eleven-thirty, at two-fifteen presented the Russian ambassador, at two-forty-five presented several hundred artists, architects, et al, to the President and Mrs. Taft in the East Room; at three-thirty was with the President in the Green Room at his request; at four attended the funeral of Mrs. Dalzell with the President, where we heard interminable reading of the scriptures; at five rode horseback until seven, and at seven-thirty went to the circus with Mrs. Taft and her sister. No wonder I woke up too late to see the President this morning, or that I am tired to-day.

Poor Miss Swan is very much discouraged about the portrait. I fear she has attempted what is too much for her and every now and then the President threatens to stop the sittings and then she rushes to me to help her keep him up to it. She is so pretty that it is hard to deny her any help even when I know it were better to stop them and give him the rest.

The death of Mrs. Dalzell is very sad and her husband seems nearly heartbroken. The funeral yesterday was pathetic. They had laid her out in the front parlor on a white divan, gowned in white silk. In one hand she held roses, and lilies were laid across her feet. I had seen something of his battle for her life, and his unselfish love for her, and his broken-hearted efforts to hold her a little

longer have given me some light into his deeper self,
which I can but respect and admire.

Chairs were provided for the President and myself in
the room, and other chairs were there for the Vice President and Mrs. Sherman, the Speaker, and other men of
note. I gave my chair next the President to Justice White.
In the midst of the services I saw the President fall asleep,
and I stood horrified when I heard an incipient snore. I
could not wake him up, I was not near enough to him, and
just as I had about made up my mind to walk over to him
to arouse him for fear he would fall into heavy snores,
Justice White fell asleep also, and I let them remain so,
for had either snored loudly I made up my mind to lay
it to the justice when comment was made of the incident.
It taught me a lesson; I shall not absent myself from his
side again at such a time, for it is my duty, as I construe
my duty, to protect him from such situations as to guard
his person from anarchists.

Day before yesterday we rode for two hours in a heavy
rain. He came back saturated. I was as wet as I was when
I went to swim Rock Creek with President Roosevelt. It
was raining when we started, and I asked him if he objected to a shower.

"No. The only things which do not bother me are the
elements. I can overcome them without a fight. All one has
to do to get the best of the elements is to stand pat and
one will win."

And so we rode for two hours in a rain which kept getting harder until it came in torrents. We talked about Mrs.
Taft, and he seemed to dwell with a good deal of pride on
the way she has managed her entertainments. He said, in
fact:

"Archie, I am very proud of the way Nellie has taken
hold of things at the White House. It was a difficult thing
for her to give any individuality to her entertainments

following so close on the Roosevelt administration, which was so particularly brilliant, but I really feel she has impressed her individuality on the few entertainments she has given so far."

After a while he asked:

"How did you like that gown she wore last Friday? I love to see her well dressed. I wonder what husband does not like to see his wife handsomely dressed."

(Had she been there she would have corrected him and said "gowned.")

"The only promise I extracted from her was one that she would not economize in dressing and, contrary to what I expected, she is keeping that promise. As you may have discovered, economy is her prevailing mood."

Good-bye,
ARCHIE.

CHAPTER IX

MRS. TAFT FALLS SERIOUSLY ILL

Washington, D. C.
May 17, 1909.

DEAR CLARA:

Mrs. Taft is seriously ill. What the result will be, even the attending surgeon does not seem to know. Mrs. Taft has done too much. The last of six dinners was given to-night. Every Senator and most of the important members of the House have been entertained during the past two months. In addition to this, she has planned and carried through two big garden parties and innumerable smaller affairs, besides inaugurating the driveway and realizing splendid success from the venture. To-day has been the one straw which has proved too heavy. I hope it has only injured the nerves and that the results will not be more far-reaching. I know what the day has been to me, and I shudder to think what the President is suffering.

When I went to the office this morning the President looked anxious, and when I asked him if there was anything I could do for him he said there was and asked me to make all arrangements for him to visit the Eye and Ear Hospital at two-fifteen, that Charlie was to be operated on for adenoids at one o'clock and he wished to be there as soon after the operation as possible. Both he and Mrs. Taft had an engagement to go to Mount Vernon on the *Sylph* at four o'clock to meet the Regents. They had invited the Wickersham household, including Sir Robert and Lady Radfield, and myself, to be of the party. This necessitated a change of appointments, and there was some lively phoning to the State Department to have some South American special commissioners presented at two instead of two-thirty. I then went to the White House and saw Mrs. Taft. She was looking pale, and evidently worried over the prospect of the operation at which she insisted upon being present. I suggested to her to let someone take her place, but she merely smiled at the suggestion.

At two o'clock I presented the commission, after which the President went to the Green Room to meet the Pierpont Morgans, Jr., with two English people—bankers, I think. It was nearly three o'clock before we reached the Episcopal Hospital, and we found Mrs. Taft just ready to telephone to the White House to see what caused the delay. The operation was successful, but there was a good deal of blood, and the poor boy was hysterical when he came from under the ether. This I learned from Mrs. Taft later. The President remained about a half hour, and together we returned to the White House with only time enough to change clothing and start for the Navy Yard. We had not reached Alexandria when Secretary Wickersham turned to me and said:

"Mrs. Taft has fainted. See if there is any brandy aboard."

Captain Williams dug up some rye whisky hurriedly, and I ordered some cracked ice to have applied to the pulse and temples. She was deathly pale, and in a few minutes seemed to revive but did not speak. I arranged a lounge for her, and we laid her on it. In a minute or two she staggered from this, and I led her, or rather half carried her, into the saloon. Still thinking it a faint, we left her with Mrs. More, her sister, and Mrs. Wickersham. I took the responsibility to order the captain to turn back to Washington. I called the President, and he went deathly pale, and as he entered the room where she lay he closed the door.

The trip back seemed interminable, and after reaching the dock we had to wait for the automobile. I practically carried her in my arms to the car. The ride home in the limousine was terrific. No one could do anything, and she made no motion and did not seem to be more than half conscious. I lifted her out of the car on reaching the White House and put my arm about her waist so as to give her all the assistance possible. The President had one arm linked through one of hers, and so we entered. I had also taken the precaution to order the doctor to meet us at the White House, and so Delaney was there. The President looked like a great stricken animal. I have never seen greater suffering or pain shown on a man's face.

There was this ghastly dinner on for the evening. I knew that this had to be gone through, and so I told him that Mrs. More would take Mrs. Taft's place and urged upon him the necessity not to reveal Mrs. Taft's condition, but to state to everyone that Mrs. Taft was exhausted after the day in the hospital. Mrs. More agreed with me. I had not been expected at the dinner, but the President asked me to remain, which I had already decided to do.

We kept her real condition a secret from those even in the house. I told the ushers that she was over the attack, and if anyone made inquiries to refer everyone to me.

I made light of the attack to the Wickershams, who called later, and when the dinner was announced, no one could have told of the tragedy in the hearts of those who knew, or feared, what the results might be. Mrs. More was brave and carried off the situation like a Spartan. Colonel Crosby did not suspect anything and did not think it worth while even to inquire after Mrs. Taft.

As the President entered the room with the blare of the music back of him, he smiled and passed among his guests in a most nonchalant way. But what a dinner! Every mouthful seemed to choke him, yet he never wavered in his duty, and I could not help thinking that he was fighting her battle, for it would humiliate her terribly to feel that people were commiserating with her. The guests seemed to enjoy themselves to a special degree, which made it all the more ghastly.

Senator Gore, the blind Senator from Oklahoma, was there. It fell to my lot to give him my arm and conduct him about. He and Mrs. Gore are seldom separated, and she went to dinner with him and prepared his food for him. He feels for what he wants with his fingers and most deftly uses his fingers to put meat and vegetables on his fork. It does not seem to be a bit unconventional the way he does it and his eyes are so bright in spite of their blindness that one wonders if after all he cannot see. His face is smooth and almost beautiful and his hearing is so acute that he seems to be able to listen to what one person is saying to him and also absorb a conversation several seats away at the same time. She is a nice-looking woman and devotes every second of her life to him.

While the men were smoking I slipped through the doors leading to the west end of the corridor to inquire after

Mrs. Taft. I had the doors everywhere leading to this part of the house closed, so as to prevent the music from reaching her. Delaney was there still. Just as I was going out the President entered, and I left him and the doctor together. From the smoking room we went out on the East Terrace, which Mrs. Taft had fitted up so beautifully for the warm nights. All the electric lights were shrouded in red paper, and the terrace was made like fairyland with palms and flowers. I know the beauty of the scene cut the President like a knife, for even I could but think of the pleasure she anticipated from this lovely tropical panorama she had taken such pains to prepare.

Delaney is there to-night. Just before leaving, the usher told me that the newspapers had heard something of her illness, and so the President prepared a statement for me to give out if I thought it well to do so later, announcing the fact that she had been exhausted by the nervous strain of the day and that a few days' rest would fit her again for her social duties.

As soon as I came to my room I read this statement to the Associated Press, and only just at this minute thought of my dear old friend Dick Oulahan, who is in charge of the New York *Sun* press service, and it is now twelve-fifteen. Dick says he fears it has missed his first edition, but I hope not. I almost dread to-morrow, but I hope for the best. If she gets through this attack with nothing more fatal than a temporary paralysis, she will be fortunate, and it will be a warning to her in the future. It makes me feel very reproachful. We have all been thinking for the President, and none of us ever seemed to have thought that she might be overtaxing herself. She always seemed so strong and self-reliant, however, that it was natural not to feel any anxiety about her.

This time to-morrow night we were to have been on the train for Petersburg and then to Charlotte, where there is to be a big celebration. Mrs. Taft has looked forward for weeks to this trip, and she has anticipated so much enjoyment in meeting Mrs. Stonewall Jackson, who was to be their hostess in Charlotte. Of course, she will not be able to go. He will go, however, if she is any better, for it would be a bitter disappointment to all interested if he should be forced to withdraw at this hour.

He knows what duty is in the face of sorrow. His mother died while he was on a trip around the world, and when he suggested backing down she insisted on his going and told him that even if it were certain that she would die, still he must put his family welfare above sentiment and sacrifice every emotion if his friends thought that this trip to the East and to Russia was essential for his campaign for the Presidential nomination. I have seen him suffer in the Philippines when a lesser man would have yielded to the advice of doctors and withdrawn from the tropics. He stands surrounded by sorrow now, but it will not swerve him from his duty as he sees it.

Good-night. May God grant a more hopeful outlook on the morrow.

ARCHIBALD.

Carrying on Despite His Troubles

Washington, D. C.
May 18, 1909.

DEAR CLARA:

I am leaving in a few minutes for the train with the President. We do not leave the city until sometime after midnight, but we go on the train at ten. But I cannot leave until I relieve your curiosity, if not your anxiety, about our First Lady of the Land. Without drugs of any kind she has slept almost uninterruptedly for sixteen hours, showing what an exhausted state she must have been in yesterday when the attack came on.

The President, and I, and Clarence Edwards, went riding at five this afternoon, and his account of his fears and feelings last night was most pathetic and makes me think that I in no way exaggerated the case. Delaney tells me to-night that she has undoubtedly improved, and he hopes that she will fully recover. Her old will and determination asserted itself to-day, when she arose from the bed without warning and attempted to walk.

One more chapter of accidents, and then I am through. The President was thrown from his horse this afternoon, but luckily not hurt. I am sure he is bruised and that he will be very sore to-morrow, but it was lucky that he was not killed. We were riding near the water's edge on the unimproved part of Alexandria Island when his horse took fright from the water, which suddenly became disturbed by a gust of wind, and wheeled. He simply wheeled from under the President and the latter fell on his back. The horse might easily have stepped on him, but instead of this he became frightened at the President on the ground and leapt to one side. I dismounted at once, and by the time I reached the President he was shaking with laughter, so much so that he could hardly get up. He mounted the animal a moment later and finished the ride. Later he asked me what I had thought when I saw him going.

"My only thought was, Mr. President, that the devil was certainly sitting up overtime to see what next he could do to the Taft family."

At which he laughed again and said:

"It certainly does look as if he were giving an extra amount of attention to us, doesn't it?"

He went to his wife's room and asked me to wait. When he came out he said that it was all right, that he would be ready to go at ten o'clock. He thought her condition even more improved than it was this morning. We have been able to keep the serious side of her illness entirely from the press, and the fact that he has not broken his engagements has completely disarmed the sensationalists. We were to go to Old Point and Hampton on Saturday on the *Dolphin.* If she recovers sufficiently to walk, she will accompany us, as the doctor says a light sea trip can do her no harm and may be most beneficial. If anything happens on this trip I shall begin to believe in a hoodoo and will start searching for it. It is not necessary to warn you not to breathe a word of any of this to anyone, but an extra precautionary warning may not be amiss.

Good-night. As ever,
ARCHIBALD.

Mr. Taft Meets Mrs. Stonewall Jackson

Washington, D. C.
May 21, 1909.

DEAR CLARA:

After two days and two nights of eating, greeting, and a little sleeping, and, I should add, a little speaking, the President returned to Washington this morning and I, of course, returned likewise. While very wearisome, still it was very delightful in many ways. The uncertainty of Mrs. Taft's condition dampened the President's enthusiasm somewhat, but as no one but the two of us knew of the actual state of health, no one else was affected by his anxiety, nor did he allow it to affect his reception of the hospitality of Petersburg and Charlotte. He was constantly asking for news and telegrams, and was somewhat relieved the first day, when at Petersburg, to hear that her condition was somewhat improved. Just before he made his address in the afternoon at Charlotte, he received a telegram announcing continued improvement. It really made a new man of him, and he spoke with a vigor and a

humor which would have been entirely lacking had he
been forced to address the crowd without this cheering
news. He has given up the Hampton trip for Saturday,
to-morrow, as he will not leave her again.

On our way to the hotel, the home of Stonewall Jackson's widow was pointed out to us, and when the President
saw Mrs. Jackson, he rose in his carriage and made her a
most profound bow. The crowd went wild, of course, for
she is the most beloved person in Charlotte, and from all
accounts she deserves to be. Simple, quiet, dignified, never
seeking notoriety or place, she moves among her people,
they told us, like an angel of charity, doing good and
living as thousands of other women on meager means are
living in the South. The President said to me of her later:

"I did not know just what kind of woman I had expected
to meet, but Mrs. Jackson is certainly different from anything that I had a right to expect when I remembered the
professional type of widows we are wont to know in and
about Washington. I find her so simple as to be charming,
so full of common sense as to be instructive, and so
womanly as to encourage gallantry toward her."

After the heavy rain, which came during the parade, I
dubbed him the modern Sir Walter Raleigh, and I see the
papers have taken it up. It was while the rain was descend-
ing in such torrents as to threaten to break down the canvas awning that the President noticed Mrs. Jackson,
sitting and holding up her feet to keep them out of the
water. He stooped as if to take hold of her feet, but evidently seized with another idea, he closed his umbrella,
which had a crooked handle, and putting this handle
around her ankle, he stood holding one foot from the water-
soaked carpet while she crossed the other foot over the
one he was holding and thus kept both feet reasonably
dry.

She is so very simple that it would never occur to her to

say anything for effect, and yet it seemed absolutely necessary for the press to have some word which passed between the President and Mrs. Jackson when they met.
I was besieged by the correspondents for some expression
which they might use. I had talked with Mrs. Jackson
some time, and she had referred to Mr. Taft as a wonderful harmonizer, so it came to me suddenly to put her ideas
in concrete and epigrammatic form to the Press Association. I said, without quoting her, that she was very proud
to welcome to Charlotte the great harmonizer of hearts,
which expression was immediately seized upon, and this
morning I see most of the dispatches, both from the Press
Associations and special correspondents, make use of this
phrase.

The President, in his guileless way, said:

"Archie, I did not hear Mrs. Jackson say that, did
you?"

I felt really conscience-stricken, but added:

"I think she said it while you were talking with Mr.
Hemphill, who interrupted you just at that moment."

Since I have been with Mr. Roosevelt and President
Taft, I do not like to deal lightly with facts. Both men are
very truthful. I know some do not think Mr. Roosevelt
to be, but rather than lie deliberately he would cut off his
hand. If anyone quotes him to the detriment of the state
he will denounce them as liars, but when it comes down to
perverting the words of a man or distorting history in any
way, he is truth itself. Of course it is a monomania with
Mr. Taft. So even to serve him I would not like him to
think I had misquoted anyone. I suppose most of "the
dying words of great men" are coined just in this way, but
I have not quite forgiven myself the partial untruth, and
I think that by confessing it here I may somehow wipe
it off the mind.

Nothing shows the lack of duplicity in President Taft

better than the speeches he made at this Charlotte celebration. It was held, as you may know, to commemorate
the Declaration of Independence at Charlotte, supposedly
on the twentieth of May, 1765. There is some doubt as to
the authenticity of this date, for there was a declaration
of a milder form voiced at a convention known to have
been held on the thirty-first of May. But for a North
Carolinian to express any doubt as to the first declaration
is to put his life in jeopardy. Every effort was made to
force the President to declare for the twentieth of May
convention. It was urged upon him that to do so would
be to carry the state of North Carolina without doubt
four years hence. Proofs in every form were produced,
but his opinion was unshaken, so that while he did not
declare against the twentieth of May convention he said
not one word which could be taken to indicate his belief
in it.

He made a splendid speech and made a wonderful
impression, but the real issue he left to the historians.
After the speech was concluded, Major Hemphill, the
irascible editor of the Charleston *News and Courier*, said:

"Mr. President, I admired the way you side-stepped
the Mecklenburg Declaration."

The President answered:

"I cannot bring myself to believe that there were two
conventions, one on the twentieth and another on the
thirty-first. While I am unwilling to endorse what appears
to be an untruth to me, I am equally unwilling to denounce
what appears to be sacred truth to others."

This is the end, for I am due to present the guests at the
indoor garden party this afternoon.

By the way, Frank Millet is painting a life-size three-
quarter portrait of me. It costs no money but only strength
as he wants over two hours a day. But as he is going to
make me a present of the work, I do not seem to have any

just complaint. He has me posed resting my left hand on my saber, the other hand holding my cap. When I remember that Fleming charges a thousand dollars extra for hands, I wonder at the generosity of Millet.

Good-bye for a day or two, no longer.

ARCHIBALD.

CHAPTER X

THE PRESIDENT AVOIDS ARREST

Washington, D. C.
May 24, 1909.

DEAR CLARA:

The hospital at the White House still holds its own. The President and I were to have gone riding Saturday, but when I got to the White House I found that he had gone upstairs and left word that he would not ride that afternoon. I waited around for a half hour and then got hold of Mrs. More and sent him word that if he would like to walk it was not too rainy. He laughed at what he said was a conspiracy, but came down in a few minutes. We went out of the front door and down by the office, where we picked up Price, one of the newspaper men who have to watch the White House. Price is from South Carolina and a splendid old fellow, true as steel and honest as the treasury. He is a Mason and has been talking Masonry to me until he has almost persuaded me to join the order.

We walked through the mist and rain, for it began to drizzle later, around the Monument, and the President expressed the desire to go up it. We found the keeper, but the fires were out and the elevator would not run. So we continued to amble on until we came to the flower beds in front of the Agricultural Department. Here a funny

incident happened which I see is still unmentioned among
the news of the day.

The President thought he would like to pick some
flowers himself for Mrs. Taft, and he went among the
roses, I among the peonies (I think they were peonies,
for they had no odor and were large), while Price began to
gather pansies. In a few minutes there was the greatest
yelling I ever heard, from the watchman, who put us all
under arrest. We came leisurely out of the garden beds
each bearing a handful of flowers. The old watchman, who
felt that here was at last a chance to justify his employ-
ment, began reaching for the flowers when he suddenly
recognized the President. The latter had already begun to
laugh and added now:

"I was just wondering how long we would be allowed
to steal Uncle Jimmy's flowers without being arrested."

The old watchman did not know exactly how to get out
of it, but said:

"I am put here for a purpose, and I have to obey my
orders whether it is the President or not."

"Right you are," said the President. "Do you want me
to go to the station house with you? But I must ask you to
let off these other gentlemen, as they were only acting
under my orders."

The old fellow was so embarrassed that he was speechless, so we simply walked off, and he lost his chance to
become famous for the minute by arresting the President
of the United States. Ever since the days of President
Grant, when a policeman was commended by him for
arresting him for fast driving, all policemen have dreamed
of a similar claim for notoriety. Once one attempted to
hold up President Roosevelt on some such trivial matter,
and he was promptly discharged the next day, so the story
goes. President Roosevelt wanted no nonsense around
him and knew very well if a policeman attempted to

arrest him it was merely for notoriety and to make a cheap display of authority.

Good-bye.

Hastily,
ARCHIBALD.

No Patience with Vulgar Plays or Tales

Washington, D. C.
May 27, 1909.

DEAR CLARA:

If you are going to let my letters distress you, I will cease to write them, but it is a great relief to tell you all I know and to unburden myself to you.

I understand perfectly how the illness of Mrs. Taft, and the tragedy it seems to lug into his administration, would affect any woman of high sensibilities. I am glad to say that she is better. As we went riding day before yesterday, she came to the window with Mrs. More and watched us start off. It almost brought tears to my eyes to see her thus. She tried to smile, but it was only a ghost of her old smile. On our return the President would not dismount until she had come to the window, and he threw her a kiss as he got off the saddle.

I would not have thought the President could be as attentive to anyone as he is to her. He seems to be thinking of her every second and looks for chances to do little things for her. It is rather unlike him in a way. The little things of life do not seem to fill up his mind. I know that he is very much unnerved over her illness, yet Mrs. More says that he never permits himself to appear serious for a minute when he is in her room. He laughs all the time and tries to amuse her. When by himself he sits for a long time, often simply looking into the distance.

We had left the nurse in charge of Mrs. Taft, and I had arranged for a box at the Belasco Theater to witness *The*

Revellers. I had not seen the play but presumed it was a musical extravaganza of some kind. I dined at the club in my evening uniform, and just before leaving, Will Denny asked why I was togged out and what was on. The moment you get in uniform everybody you know wants to know at once what is on the tapis. I said we were going to the theater, and he added:

"I hope it is not to the Belasco, for it is 'hot stuff.'"

So I was not entirely unprepared for what followed. The curtain no sooner went up than we were introduced to the loosest scene I have ever seen on the stage. Before it was half over I had sent the secret service man to order the motor car back, and as soon as the curtain fell on the first act and the lights went up the President turned and looked at me.

"Well, Archie, what do you think?" he asked.

"I think the sooner we leave the better it will be for the reputation of the Administration," I said.

"I do not care as much for the Administration as I do for my own feelings," he said. "I simply cannot stand such stuff. It makes me positively ill."

This morning I met Secretary Knox at the White House office and told him of the President's experience at the theater. He, it seems, had had a similar experience Monday. He and some friend went there knowing nothing about the play and left after the first act, just as we did. He told the President that if the matter got into the papers he hoped he would hit the play hard and denounce such filthy dramas.

"The audience last night," said the President, "was filled with young men and women, and I cannot imagine a young girl sitting through that first act unless she was simply afraid to go out. It has no humor, no wit, and the English is bad, and there is no excuse for the play except to appeal to the very lowest instincts."

Nothing has come out as yet, but I think it will have got out to-night, and then I hope to add a word here and there which will reveal the President in a new light to the people. He is one of the cleanest-minded men I have ever known, and anything smutty or vulgar is most revolting to him. He never forgives a man who tells him a nasty story, and I have seen more than one man go on the rocks as far as the President is concerned by repeating some dirty story or retailing some nasty gossip. I will not even repeat the things which are common gossip and well substantiated, simply because I know the seamy side of life is revolting to him.

> Good-bye.
> ARCHIBALD.

Captain Butt to His Aunt, Mrs. John D. Butt

> Washington, D. C.
> June 8, 1909.

DEAR AUNT KITTY:

The shadow over the White House has cast its gloom over me these past few weeks, for I think I have felt more sympathy for the troubles over there than I have admitted even to myself. I think I have been helpful to them also. I have worked unceasingly for the President, and it has been labor at times to keep him up to doing things.

Yesterday, while we were going over the links at Chevy Chase, he seemed to be so full of joy and interest in his game. I caught his eye and it seemed as if there was a world of misery in his mind. His great optimism has kept him up, but now I have seen signs that he realizes at last the tragedy which has entered his administration. He has got to keep up, and he has to think of everything but himself, but I am sure his great soul is wrapped in darkness over this continued illness of Mrs. Taft. After all, may not this very sorrow supply the one thing lacking in that soul? His optimism seems to be too great at times to surround him completely. Too great optimism may shut one off from the world just as too great selfishness or too much cynicism. Even this affliction, coming at this time, may be only the Great Hand molding him for greater good.

But to-night, good-night.

ARCHIE.

Taft Discusses Who Made Him President

Washington, D. C.
June 1, 1909.

DEAR CLARA:

I had quite a discussion last night with Mr. Charles P. Taft, who thinks he made his brother President. We were in the rear end of the special car of the President— Miss Helen Taft and Mr. Taft and I. I forget how the subject came up, but I said, relevant to something:

"Looking back, I do not see how a President ever becomes President; there are so few things he can do to strike a national note, and so many he can do which would seem to wreck his chances at the time for national office."

"Sometime when you are in Cincinnati come to the third floor of my house and I will show you how a President is made," said Mr. Taft.

I took the ground that no one could make a President, that the nearest thing to this which had ever been done was when Mark Hanna took up the cause of McKinley, but even McKinley had to have the record back of him, and had not accident made him chairman of the Ways and Means Committee, not even Mark Hanna could have done much with him. It is needless to go into the discussion which followed, but Mr. Taft, while admitting that character and records are necessary, adhered to the idea still, that all this would go for naught had there not been back of it all the master hand who knew how to handle men and organizations, how to pull the wires and how to control the candidate himself.

I took the ground that the people prepared themselves for a candidate of a certain type, that the candidate and ultimate President, unless he be the result of war or some distinctive concatenation of circumstances unlooked-for and unforeseen, represented the gradual development of an ideal of the people shaped by renewed conditions in the development of the country. Miss Helen agreed with me and thought that her father had been on the ladder for the Presidency ever since his appointment to the Philippines, and insisted that she had heard men of note prophesy at that time that some day he would become President.

The President listened to all this discussion about himself with an amused, playful smile on his face, and when we seemed to have come to the end of the discussion he laughed and said:

"What troubles Charlie is, he is afraid Roosevelt will get the credit of making me President, and not himself."

Seeing his brother start up for a fresh argument, he laughed heartily and said:

"Old fellow, I will not goad you into any discussion of this subject again, for we have had some heated talks on it before, haven't we? And I will agree not to minimize the part you played in making me President if you will agree not to minimize the part Roosevelt played. Possibly I had nothing to do with it at all and just you two did together, but my only hope is that you did not proceed in the same way which seems to have characterized Mark Hanna. While he had some good traits of character, no doubt, still I think he represents the worst influence which has ever appeared in American politics."

He said to me later about the matter:

"I am always amused at Charlie's determined position that Roosevelt had nothing to do with my nomination and election, and he grudgingly admits that he was for me at all, whereas to deny the determining factor he became in my nomination would be, not only the basest ingratitude, but to ignore the facts."

He went out of his way to say this to me, as if he wished to impress on my mind his own opinion in the matter. That is a side to Mr. Taft which makes him appear always to me to be big enough to have followed President Roosevelt. It is not so much his bigness but all absence of littleness which makes him wholesomely big. There is no doubt that Mr. Charles Taft was a factor in the machinery which made his brother President; but that brother, now President, will never admit any claims ahead of those of his predecessor.

Just as he punctured the claim of his brother, that the latter had made him President, so he laughed at a specious argument of mine while in Pittsburgh as to why he should watch the ball game from the seats in the grandstand rather than occupy some boxes in a most exclusive part of the stadium. He does not mind how much you play politics, but he never wants you to think that he does not see the truth just as it is. The first day in Pittsburgh had been carefully planned and thought out by the Committee of Yale men and the Citizens' Organization. It included a speech at the Arsenal and unveiling of a fountain in which certain women were to be starred as heroines, a luncheon at the Raes' regal home in the country, and then the rest of the afternoon to be spent among the fashionable people of Pittsburgh at the Country Club, the day to end at the Yale banquet at the Pitt Hotel at night.

The program seemed to be decidedly "classy." If Mr. Charlie Taft had been there at the time I would have talked the matter over with him, but he was not due until later. So, learning that a ball game was to be played there between the Pittsburgh and the Chicago Clubs, I went to the President's room and, without letting him know my reason for so doing, suggested that he go to the ball park in the afternoon. He readily agreed to go if the program could be so arranged, and I went to the Committee below and stated that the President wanted to go to the ball park. The Committee was unanimous in its protest against any change and simply said it could not be done.

"It will break the entire program," the Chairman said.

"That is what a President is for," I said, "to break programs."

"Where is the President?" they said. "Let us see him."

"You can't see him," I said. "He is writing his Gettysburg speech and will not allow anyone to come to him."

A pure fabrication, of course, for I knew if they ever got to him he would not insist on going to the game, as he makes it an invariable rule never to upset the plans of the committees.

"He not only wants to see the game," I said, "but he wants to see it from the seats, so you had better get together and get them to rope off twenty seats just to the left of the catcher and order the railroad to bring him in on a special from the Country Club not later than three-thirty."

Well, by simply ordering everybody about in the President's name I finally got the committeeman in charge of the police arrangements to change the police plans, the railroad committee to rearrange their schedule, and, over the bitter protest of everyone, the Committee on Arrangements to see the ball management and settle for twenty seats in the heart of the grandstand.

Of course, they were all mad. I would have been angry myself. The members of the committees, who anticipated riding with the President and growing important by contact, suddenly saw themselves spending the hours of the morning rearranging the program. I thought I had everything settled when the arrival of Mr. Taft changed the plan about the seats. Tom Laughlin, the brother-in-law who is in the rich set, and the others thought it undignified for the President to sit with the common herd, they said, and so told Mr. Taft. He agreed with them and thought the party should have four boxes, which are above the grandstand—and while one can see the game from them to a great advantage, still, it is impossible to be seen in them. However, I yielded, and another committeeman had to be sent to get the boxes instead of the seats. I had not entirely despaired, however, so I sent word by Wheeler, the secret service man, to get both the boxes and seats, and with this under way we began the day of speechmaking, feasting, and parading through crowded streets. It was while we were in the automobile that I said to the President:

"Mr. President, all arrangements have been made for the ball game this afternoon. We have both boxes and seats, but I do not believe you would enjoy the game from the boxes. They are very high up, and you are not able to see the individual plays as well as if you were below."

I purposely did not look at the President and tried to make my remark as casual as possible, but the President began to laugh, and I knew instantly that he saw my maneuvering.

"Archie," he said, "I am on to your little game. You don't care whether I see the game or not. What you want is for me to be seen, and I will tell you frankly I don't care whether I am seen or not, but what I really want is to see. Now, you can arrange it the best way you think, although I have no doubt that you will have your way."

And he laughed so that everybody in the motor became interested, and he had to repeat it over again, much to my discomfort and to his amusement. However, he was right. I had my way, for going out on the train to the Country Club I got hold of Mr. Taft by himself and hammered my arguments into him. And it would have been perfectly useless, Clara, for him to go to that game and sit perched in a box hidden from everyone. He might as well have remained with the Thaws and the Carnegies at the Country Club all the afternoon. So as soon as Mr. Charlie Taft agreed with me, we sent another committeeman to town with orders again to change the program and settle the line of police to the seats instead of the boxes. I think they all felt the logic of my position when the President entered the grandstand and saw those fifteen or twenty thousand people rise and shout themselves hoarse.

I let it leak out to the press how arrangements had been made for the President to occupy the boxes and how at the last moment he refused to do so, preferring to see the game where all the lovers of sport saw it and where he could see the crowd and hear the comment of the fans. The press throughout the country made more of this ball game than the rest of the celebration combined, including Gettysburg, and even the Secretary of State, who told me he thought it a great mistake for the President to go to the game, admitted to me later that it was the most popular thing he had done since his inauguration. The secretary actually forgot his dignity long enough to exchange his hot silk top hat for a Panama which some committeeman was wearing, so that he looked in keeping with the President, who wore a straw hat. The papers had such expressions as this:

"Taft has good, rich red blood in his veins. He refuses

to be exclusive and insists on being with the common people."

"Taft one of the people," and so on.

He enjoyed the game as I have seldom seen him enjoy anything, and I think he liked to be in the crowd, but I must confess that he would have enjoyed it just as much had he been perched in the loft as he did from the grandstand, but Secretary Knox would have been bored to death up there, and so would the others.

Mrs. Taft was not well enough to go to Pittsburgh; in fact, she only comes into the corridor of the White House when she can do so without running any danger of seeing anyone.

It is the hardest thing to keep the President from talking. He does not seem to realize that every word he utters is repeated and often exaggerated. At the garden party Friday, while Mrs. More and I were telling everyone who asked after Mrs. Taft that she was well again but that she was not downstairs, as the doctor thought the grass too damp for her to stand upon, the President was confiding to his intimate friends that Mrs. Taft was really very ill.

Coming back home, the President made this sage remark:

"I have come to the conclusion that the major part of the work of a President is to increase the gate receipts of expositions and fairs and bring tourists into the town."

Dr. Hadley started a conversation about Jefferson Davis and expressed the greatest admiration for his qualities as a leader and a man of action. Had it not been for Davis, he believes that the Confederacy would have ended much sooner. The President then related a conversation which he had once with Judge Lurton of Tennessee regarding Davis.

Mr. Davis had been in Nashville on one occasion, and

Judge Lurton had invited him to be his guest. He said that he had taken this occasion to ask Jefferson Davis who of the general officers, both North and South, had, in his opinion, developed the greatest skill and ability during the four years of the war. Judge Lurton said that Davis answered promptly that he had given that subject considerable thought and that it was his judgment that General Bragg showed greater development than any general officer in either army. Judge Lurton said that he disapproved this judgment to such an extent that he never asked the reasons for the opinion and was sorry now that he had not done so.

I think this has started all thirteen of us looking up the record of Bragg, for the opinion of Davis could not be lightly made on such a question.

Saturday morning.

Since beginning this letter I am more convinced than ever that letter writing as an art has departed from among us. I had thought to make an interesting account of all we did in Pittsburgh, but on looking over what I have written I find a lot of dry facts rather stupidly put together and with not enough side light on the President as Sorolla could put with one daub on his nose.

All this does bring to me one important thing regarding the President which might have escaped had I not so ponderously entered into a discussion of the regular troops. It is this:

President Taft will not hesitate to use these same troops when the occasion requires, and he came within an ace of using them in Georgia during the strike on the Georgia Road only this last week. He would have done so had the strike not been settled when it was. He got the news just after he reached Pittsburgh in a telegram from Carpenter and handed it to me with a statement:

"I am very glad of that. It saves me a very disagreeable duty."

That was all he said at the time, but since returning to Washington he has had a talk with the Commissioners of Labor whom he sent to Atlanta and they evidently told him some facts which he had not known before, for on the golf links last Wednesday, while he and I and Mr. Charlie Taft were doing the links, he said to me:

"Archie, I am perfectly astonished at Bacon's attitude in this last strike. Do you know he actually sent a telegram to the strikers sympathizing with their efforts to displace the colored firemen on the Georgia Road? Whatever had been his private sympathies, as a public servant he should not have done anything to infuse passion into the situation. I do not believe the solid men of Georgia will uphold him in such a small petty political play, for I cannot regard it as anything else. If the leaders of the people are going to pander to this prejudice, what can we hope from the lower classes?"

"Mr. President," I asked, "do you regard the situation there at any time as serious?"

"So serious that I had practically issued the order to patrol the line from Atlanta to Augusta with federal troops, and you know what that would mean in the South. But the law on the subject is so clear and my duty was so manifest that I should not have hesitated a minute had the strike not ended when it did."

There, that is Taft—Taft as he is going to appear right along, and you will see it develop in this way. I doubt if President Roosevelt would have used the troops except as a means to protect property in spite of the law. But President Taft will do anything if he has the law on which to base his act. The law to President Taft is the same support as some zealots get from great religious faith. And the fact that the law is unpopular would not cause him to hesitate a minute. My theory of him six months ago would have been, that in such a situation as he faced in Georgia last week he would have temporized and waited to see if things would settle themselves. I have had to shift my theory, for I have come to understand his faith in law, as law. If the South does not want to have the problem of federal interference to face, it had better not break the law of interstate commerce or permit its citizens to interfere with the mails.

I am not professing to admit my sympathy with him in this matter, for, like all Southern men, I have my prejudices regarding the use of federal troops, but he will not hesitate for a minute to use the troops from Oglethorpe and McPherson, should such an occasion arise. He loves the South and likes the Southern people, and he believes moreover in the Southern character. But he will not let his growing popularity there interfere with his duty as he sees that duty.

I do not know whether I quoted to you what he said to the newspaper men on his return from Charlotte. They had come in from the front car to pay their respects just before reaching Washington, and someone—Patchin of the New York *Herald*, I think—spoke of the effect he had made in the South and the apparent friendly feeling of the South for him.

"It is very necessary," he said, and I remember his words exactly, "for the South and the national government to get very close together, and I am going to do all in my power to bring about a closer union, not so much for the South as for the federal government itself. I am looking ahead fifteen, twenty, possibly fifty years, for in that time some very serious questions are coming up, problems which are as serious as the Civil War itself, and when they come up the federal government will demand the support of the South for the maintenance of Anglo-Saxon law as we have it in this country. The Southern people are our most homogeneous people and by nature the most conservative—not conservatism which comes from wealth and a desire to protect that which it has, but a conservatism which stands for precedents, for unwritten law, for association and for the preservation of the Constitution."

I had intended to quote this statement to you before, but it seems to me that I did not incorporate it in one of my letters. I deem it important to preserve it, for some day it may come up out of the past for use and guidance to others and an incentive to us in the South not to be betrayed into radical action by unsafe and unsound leaders.

Just as we were getting into the motor on Wednesday a telegram was handed Mr. Charles Taft which, after reading, he read aloud to the President. It was merely asking him to have a certain man appointed Collector of Customs somewhere.

"I wish people would not presume to think I can get any office I want, Will. It really worries me."

"Well, old fellow, they ought to know that you can get almost anything you want, for I do not know anyone else whose wishes are above yours."

"And for that very reason, Will, I do not like to ask you for things," said Mr. Taft, "and you may notice how few favors I have asked of this administration."

"Do you want that man named Collector?"

"I don't care anything about it," said Mr. Taft.

"Then we will let the other fellow hang on for a time," said the President, "in spite of the fact that he did all he could to defeat my nomination."

ARCHIBALD.

CHAPTER XI

THE PRESIDENT WANTS TO SMASH CHINAWARE

Washington, D. C.
June 9, 1909.

DEAR CLARA:

We are busy these days getting ready to move the White House to Beverly. Therefore I may be somewhat lax in the matter of letters for a few days.

The President said last night that it was a great deprivation to him to forego the Alaskan and Washington trip, but that he realized how right he was to do so when he saw the relief which Mrs. Taft showed when he told her.

"It has had a very beneficial effect upon her, and I think she worried over my leaving her more than any of us suspected, for she realized that she could not go with me."

The question of which china to take was discussed last night, and my suggestion was to take only the odd and broken sets, taking none, of course, with any historic value to it, such as the Lincoln, Jefferson, or Grant, and also leaving out of consideration the Roosevelt china, which is the only complete set in the White House. The President said:

"Wouldn't this be a good time to get some of the Hayes and McKinley china smashed and thus rid the White House of it 'by fair wear and tear,' as they say in the army?"

We had never thought he had even seen the Hayes and McKinley china to know it, but he evidently sees more than we imagine. The Hayes china is about as ugly as it is possible for china to be. Mrs. ——, who was Lucy Hayes,

called on Mrs. More at the White House the other day
and remarked that when her mother had chosen this same
china, they all thought it wonderful, but she would not be
willing to purchase it for herself now. You have seen the
same china about that time; I remember it. Every dish
and plate covered with cheaply and badly painted fish,
birds, flowers, all in colors which changed as a rule after
burning.

This afternoon we went to Chevy Chase, where Senator
Bourne and I played against the President and General
Edwards. The President likes to take advantage of the
Vice President's being away from the city and play golf.
The President is committed to the Vice President for golf
and fears to hurt his feelings by not asking him to join him
when he plays, for it gives Mr. Sherman such evident
delight, but his game is getting so bad that it gives the
President no pleasure to play with him at all.

Good-bye. With a lot of love,

ARCHIE.

Mr. Taft Sees the Wright Brothers

Washington, D. C.
June 11, 1909.

DEAR CLARA:

Edwards and I are pulling the President in different
directions all the time in the matter of the Catholic
Church. I do not hope to do more than minimize their
influence, and if I catch them slipping at any time, I shall
use it for all it is worth, being a narrow, bigoted Protestant,
in a way. But Edwards's influence is as strong as mine,
and, moreover, he is so plausible in his suggestions that it
makes it very difficult to overthrow his plans. I am sure
he expects their influence to get him something in the
future or else hold him to the position he has gained. As the

head of the bureau dealing with Porto Rico and the Philippines, he comes in contact with the Catholics at all times and, I think, yields largely to their demands, and he strengthens himself constantly by having the President pay them honor by calling at their convents and schools, and this, together with his own gratitude for what they did for him, makes it appear that he greatly favors their organization, if not their faith. If he sees a convent while we are out riding, he leads the President by it and incidentally suggests talking with the nuns or whomsoever he can locate.

I think it bad politics, and it will react disastrously on the President in the future if the Protestants get wind of the way he favors the Catholics. I told him that this society in Brookland, which he addressed last night, was supposed to be a special mission for the proselyting of Protestants and suggested that it would be well to keep clear of anything like endorsement of their plans and work. In consequence, he remodeled his speech and urged religious tolerance and spoke on general lines.

The Protestants in Washington never concern themselves with governmental affairs and are not constantly haggling for advantage in this department or in that, and leave it to the individual to secure offices and do not make it a church matter. President Roosevelt used the Catholic Church for his ends, but never permitted it to use him for theirs, and while he talked a good deal about religious tolerance, yet he was a Protestant to the backbone.

However, as the President goes on his own way largely, and is quite unconscious of the tiny strings which we tie here and there, he is not liable to be dragged out of his course one way or the other by the petty plans that either Edwards or I weave for him.

Enough of religion—and now to the Wrights, whom all

the world seems mad to honor. They were given a reception
and a lunch at the Cosmos Club and at three were presented the medals by the President. The Aëronautic
Society sent out the invitations to the White House, so
we did not know who was expected, and therefore some
complications arose which we could not see or prevent.
We did not know that the diplomatic corps had been invited, and it was only when I saw some of the ambassadors
being herded in the East Room with the seven or eight
hundred other people there that I realized the fact and
gave orders that if any more ambassadors should arrive
they were to be shown into the Green Room, where the
Wright brothers and their sister, a nice, interesting-looking
young woman with eyeglasses, were brought by arrangement with Representative Parsons, who seemed to be
managing them.

Just why Mr. Parsons assumed such a prominent rôle
I do not know. I made all the arrangements with him, and
he made the first speech and so preëmpted the subject
that he left little for the President to say. It may be a good
thing that he did, for I do not think the President fully
realized the opportunity he was letting slip by him. He
ought to have prepared a speech, and his remarks should
have been of such a nature that they would have added
another period, or at least semicolon, to our history. As
it was, he entered the East Room thoroughly unprepared
and did not seem to know what it was all about and hesitated, as if in doubt, as to the pronunciation of some of
the technical terms used by the speakers who went before
him. His speech was pleasant and jocular in a way, but
somehow I did not think it was the time for jocularity, for
the conquering of the air just at this time is the greatest
problem before the world. When Edith Wetmore suggested last night that his speech was a little undignified, I
resented her imputation with a good deal of vigor, though

I realized that she was voicing my own opinions and possibly the views of most of those who were present.

I had been prepared to meet modest, retiring types of men, but not as modest and retiring as the Wrights proved to be. Wilbur Wright is thin, clean shaven, and studious looking, while Orville Wright wears a mustache and looks habitually embarrassed. They are both so simple and direct in their manner that one wonders if they are really the two persons who are the center of the scientific watchers of this age and have been received and decorated by the great potentates of the world.

I met a man from Dayton last night who told me that in Ohio, for years, they were considered to be half cracked, and that it was not until of late, after Europe had crowned them as victors, that they were taken seriously. Indeed, the President referred to this himself, and wondered when the time would come when America would accept its own without waiting for the verdict of the rest of the world.

This is all I have got to say.

ARCHIBALD.

Golf, Dinner, and Mrs. Longworth's Wrath

Washington, D. C.
June 13, 1909.

DEAR CLARA:

Yesterday was quite a red letter day in local golf circles. The President and Allen Lard, a noted golfer, played in a foursome with the Vice President and Travis. The game had been arranged for several weeks, and consequently there was a large crowd at Chevy Chase to witness it. The President, as a rule, does not like a gallery to follow him, but as the members wanted to watch Travis and Lard, the President had to yield his wishes in the matter. However, the President played a very good game and made no very bad fizzles and added to his reputation rather than diminished it. He and Lard defeated their opponents by five holes up. The final hole was played before an immense gallery, who heartily applauded a very good drive of the President.

In the evening the President gave his first golf dinner. Strangely it did not get into the papers, or else it would have been headed something like this:

THE PRESIDENT DINES THE GOLF CABINET

Or—

THE GOLF CABINET IN SESSION AT THE WHITE HOUSE

The dinner was unique in one respect. It was the first time in eight years, I should say, that guests sat down to dinner there without evening clothes. The fault was due to the ultra-democracy of the genial Vice President and moreover was not endorsed by the President. The President said this afternoon that there was no excuse for Travis and Lard coming in morning suits, for he had invited these two over two weeks ago. He will remember it, and I doubt if either will ever receive another invitation to the White House. He recognizes the fact, however, that the Vice President is largely to blame, for he, it seems, told both of them that the dinner was informal and no one was expected to dress for the occasion. Just as we were leaving the clubhouse, the President invited Nick Longworth to dine with him also, and the Vice President volunteered the information that he was expected to come "just as he was."

"Is that the way the others are coming?" asked the President.

"I told Travis and Lard that you would expect them in that informal way," said the Vice President.

"I hardly think so," said the President, "for I invited both two weeks ago."

Senator Bourne and I and General Edwards exchanged looks and doubted our hearing, but, strange to say, not only did the golf champions appear in sack suits, but the Vice President as well. I donned the full dress uniform, and so did General Edwards. The others were all properly dressed with the exception of Longworth, who also wore a sack suit. And thereby hangs a tale.

This morning, before I was out of bed, the telephone rang, and Mrs. Longworth called me up to ask me how the President was dressed. I told her, and she then said that she was so angry with Nick for daring to go to the White House to dinner in a sack suit; that he gave her as an excuse that the President had expressed his wish in the matter and had worn one himself. She, evidently, had Nick treed, and she made him apologize to the President for such a breach of etiquette.

"He would not have dared to do such a thing under the last administration," she said with indignation, which was not feigned, for she is truly fond of Mr. Taft and will not allow any criticism of him in her presence.

The only rebuke the President offered was to attire himself more faultlessly than he would probably have done, had not the Vice President pretended to speak for him in the matter.

Charlie Taft returned to the White House again last week, as another case of diphtheria had broken out in his school. He is a young man of infinite resource, as shown by the way he crossed New York at night. The President asked him yesterday how he managed to get across New York by himself.

"Oh, I just wired the secret service police in New York that I was coming to New York and to have someone meet me and take me over."

I have not seen anything amuse the President more than this, and he wanted full details, and asked Charlie why he had thought to wire them at all.

"Well, one of the secret service men whom I knew at Hot Springs told me once that if I ever needed anything in New York I should let him know, and so I just let them know. That was all."

This precocity was quite up to that of Quentin Roosevelt. He played golf yesterday and posed with the ease of an old politician for the photographers, when they wanted to snap him in action. He is really better broken in to this side of the Presidential business than his father.

Mrs. More and Miss Helen are telling of a very funny visit they had from Mrs. MacVeagh yesterday. She is as kind and good as possible. She had called to ask that Mrs. Taft be sent to her home somewhere in New England for a month and brought photographs to illustrate how removed the house is from all other places in the neighborhood. After she had extended the invitation she asked Mrs. More if she might be permitted to look at the chairs in the State Dining Room. They accompanied her and were much surprised to see her draw from her little bag that she carried in her hands a tape measure and begin to measure the chairs. She explained, finally, that as she would be expected to entertain the President next winter she desired to have some chairs large enough for him and expressed the greatest surprise to find the chairs in the White House, which he is accustomed to use, about the same as she has in her home. She then measured the chairs in the Green and the Blue rooms and did not seem to think her request or action the least bit out of the conventional.

Of course, they told the President, much to his amusement. Miss Helen remarked that the tape measure would not have seemed so strangely odd had she not been simply loaded with diamonds and pearls as large as hen's eggs. The act, I take it, was more motherly than banal and was prompted by real affection for the President.

I will leave Monday night for New York and will motor down to Oyster Bay Tuesday morning. It will be my only opportunity to say good-bye to Mrs. Roosevelt and Miss Ethel. I shall probably spend the day with them and go on to Beverly Tuesday night. How long I will be in Beverly I do not know, but I shall not leave there until I have made all definite arrangements for the move.

Good-bye. Affectionately,
ARCHIBALD.

CHAPTER XII

CAPTAIN BUTT VISITS MRS. ROOSEVELT

Washington, D. C.
June 18, 1909.

DEAR CLARA:

I only returned this morning from a hurried four nights and three days trip to Beverly. I have only just made my report to the President, and as we have a golf game on this afternoon, I know there will be no time to write later, so I am snatching an hour at lunch time to jot down my wanderings.

I took the car and started for Oyster Bay to see Mrs. Roosevelt. I had telephoned her I was coming, and she told me to make my plans to stay to lunch. The road was so familiar to me that I kept on the lookout for this point or another and almost expected to see the President dash out of some road or swing by from one cut to another. As I passed the tennis court, I felt homesick for the Big Chief, and just then I saw Mrs. Roosevelt, walking across the lawn just as she had always done, with a light blue

gown on and a big white cloth hat. I stopped the motor
and went up the lawn to meet her.

It was all so nice, seeing her for the first time since she
left the White House, just in this way. She was looking
well, and her interest in everything was just as keen and
kindly. I told her all about Mrs. Taft, and she thought it
tragic. She said there had been so few happy women in
the White House; that she and Mrs. Cleveland were the
only two, as far as she could remember, who had been entirely happy there. Mrs. Grant may have been, but it is
hard to tell.

"I doubt if even I was entirely happy," she said, "for
there was always that anxiety about the President when
he was away from me. I never knew what would happen
before he got back. I never realized what a strain I was
under continuously until it was over."

"How did you spend the day," I asked her, "the day the
President left?"

"In the woods," she answered. "I and the children
spent it in the woods, simply walking about, talking, and
trying to think what the President was doing in New York.
But it was a dreadful day. I have never known but one
like it; that day when Archie's fate was in doubt and we
did not know if he would live or not. Each crawled into
bed about eight that night, and since then we have been
very happy and content."

She said she had heard often from Mr. Roosevelt, and
that he had up to this time killed ten lions and they had
shipped over twenty animals in all. Strange to say, she
said that nearly all the newspaper reports had been correct and that most of them had been corroborated by
letters from him later.

I left at three, and Miss Ethel, who was going to town
that day to spend the night with Virginia Osborne, motored with me. It was nearly seven when I got back to

the hotel, where I had dinner and spent an hour or two later on the roof, smoking and listening to the band concert.

Miss Boardman and I made an early start for the President's cottage at Beverly the next day and spent two hours going over it with the landlord, seeing what was there, what we would have to take with us and getting him to do as much as possible. It might interest you to know that there was plenty of china, but no table service or linen and no bed linen or blankets. But there were eight servant rooms over the stables, which made up for much. It is going to be dreadfully dull for Mrs. Taft and not overexciting for the President.

We lunched with Mrs. Leiter. She had on her lawn a charming swinging chair under an awning, and she offered one which I accepted for the back porch upstairs. It will be the very thing for Mrs. Taft to lie in during the day and watch the sea. Mrs. Leiter is a dear, kind soul, but rather funny at times, but not as funny as Dame Rumor would make her out to be. She did say to Miss Boardman that somebody was "not as lympathatic as we are, Mabel," meaning as loose-jointed as they were, as she illustrated later, but she is seldom ungrammatical, and most of her errors consist in using the wrong word at the wrong time or place.

Later. Eleven o'clock, night.

Mrs. Taft had quite a bad attack while I was absent, but the doctor says it was not part of this trouble at all, but was like an attack of biliousness.

The President cast a bombshell in Congress by advocating a tax on the incomes of corporations and also in favor of presenting a constitutional amendment permitting the federal authorities to levy an income tax. Senator Aldrich and Senator Lodge thought they had him weaned away from the income tax proposition, but when they thought themselves safe from this menace he slipped his message, when they were entirely unprepared for it.

Good-night.
Archie.

"Chloroforming" Aldrich and His Crowd

Washington, D. C.
Sunday, June 20th, 1909.

Dear Clara:

On our way to the White House, President Taft told me that he had invited the majority members of the Finance Committee of the Senate to dinner, and he wished I would come if I had no other engagement. As it happened there were several coming to us for dinner, but of course I said I had nothing else, and as I knew how Mrs. Taft was and I would have to seat the table, I changed from my riding togs in a jiffy and was soon back to the White House. The names were about the most portentous now before the country, for it happens that they have seemingly the power of life and death over our industries in the making of this tariff bill. This dinner was decided on this morning as a result of some news he had overnight.

The President has played some pretty shrewd politics of late, and instead of being duped by Aldrich and the other Senators, he has chloroformed them, as Senator Bourne explained to me yesterday while going around the links. I have known all along that he contemplated something unlooked for in this tariff business, for he has been doing something quite contrary to his habit, namely, inviting Senators here and there to breakfast with him at the White House at nine and talking with them long after office hours. Senator Aldrich has been among those he has juggled with, but I never suspected for a minute he would get a majority of the Finance Committee favorable to a tax on corporations and to an amendment to the Constitution providing for an income tax.

But one by one he lashed them together and committed them separately to his proposition and quietly sent in his messages which the Senate and the country at large is just comprehending. Several Senators have told me confidentially that his message took everyone by surprise, and none more so than the members of the Finance Committee. In one way it is funny. He has swallowed the entire Finance Committee. He has pocketed every ball.

It begins to look now as if there will be the corporation tax or else no tariff bill. If they defeat him, then he is the only one who can stand before the country. Every congressional fight in the next general election will be made on his recommendations. He said to me while riding this afternoon that "the insurgents," as he calls LaFollette and Cummins and Dolliver, as well as the Democrats, "should have seized upon his recommendations before the Finance Committee had done so before them. They cannot afford to fight my propositions and yet, if the Finance Committee puts them in the bill they will get none of the credit for them."

He feels that he has the upper hand now and has the entire situation in his own control. He has played some very deep politics, for just when they thought they had him sleeping he showed them he was never so alive in his life. His dinner to-night was to get the committee in line and together and settle upon some definite policy to put his recommendations into law.

Senator Root took in Miss Helen, and he and she and I sat at one end of the table, and I think we were the only people who talked at all. The others were all afraid to open their mouths, apparently for fear of committing themselves to some unforeseen proposition. Senator Hale tried to get the conversation to Mr. Roosevelt by making fun of some of his appointments, such as Daniels, whom Mr. Roosevelt appointed marshal of Arizona. Senator Lodge spoke derisively of the "two-gun men," the way President Roosevelt always spoke of Daniels, and there would have been a general firing all along the line had the President joined in the conversation; but he sat quietly smiling to himself, and that topic of conversation came to an untimely end.

The President did say that he was looking for some other place for Daniels, as Arizona thought it a reflection on the state to have as marshal one who had been in prison. Senator Hale asked why he did not send him to Africa, but, getting no reply, his flow of venom was stopped.

Senator Cullom said he heard that the new President of Cuba, Gomez, was sending Cuban funds to Paris, preparatory to going himself, and the President told the story of the tenderfoot who went to Oklahoma and got into a poker game. After losing for a while he watched the dealer and turning to his neighbor said:

"'Say, did you see that fellow deal himself four aces?'

"'Well, what the hell, isn't it his deal?' the other answered.

"I think Gomez thinks it is his deal," laughed the President.

I have never seen the President so talkative as he was at dinner. He can talk when he wants to, that is clear. He told anecdote after anecdote, and in fact carried the entire dinner. The only time the conversation became at all general was when someone mentioned the New York *Evening Post*. Then it was like an anvil chorus opening up. Each had a brick for the owner and editors as well, and each hurled it good and hard. Senator Lodge, with a rather superior air, said:

"I never read the paper. It is so mendacious that I don't have it near me."

Senator McCumber, who was sitting near me, said in his whisper:

"It is the first paper he reads."

This dinner, I am sure, was the culmination of the President's policy, and a good deal was settled to-night out on that portico. How securely he has bagged his game remains to be seen, but he is at least in a position now to fight openly, if the worst comes to the worst. This will give you some idea of the play behind the curtain and possibly make the open fight more interesting to watch.

Good-night.

ARCHIBALD.

CHAPTER XIII

ALL IS POLITICS AT THE WHITE HOUSE

Washington, D. C.

June 22, 1909.

DEAR CLARA:

Everything at the White House, for a time, was social. Now it seems to be all political. Nothing but conferences from breakfast until late suppers. The President is certainly testing that axiom proclaimed by me that the White House was the biggest political asset of an administration, to its fullest extent. One never sees anyone about the White House these days of heat and aggravation but who has something to do with the tariff bill.

This afternoon we went to the golf links, where Senator Bourne and I beat the President and General Edwards seven down, much to the disgust of the President. Several times I heard him swear under his breath, and once openly. He was off his game and has been for several days. I think it is due to the physical culture exercises he is taking from his New York doctor. I came back in forty-six, which was excellent for me, and won a word of praise from the President. He is always after me for playing carelessly. My theory of the game is that it should become a habit to play well and that it is unnecessary to do much thinking in the matter. I find that I do play better when I take time and make motions at the ball before driving or approaching.

Everything seemed to conspire to make it a pleasant day for the President, bar his golf. He told us, going out, that he felt now he had the proper number of votes necessary to pass the tax on incomes of corporations; that he had counted his last one the night before. Senator Root seems to think that the corporation influences have not had time as yet to get in their word on Senators, and he does not feel so sure that the requisite number is certain by any means. But the optimistic President feels reasonably sure that the bill will pass with the corporation amendment about the middle of July. He said yesterday that Root had been the greatest assistance to him during this whole fight, and his aid had been invaluable, for Mr. Root has had to work as an outsider, not being a member of the Finance Committee.

Speaking of the astonishment that some of the papers seem to express that Senator Root was in favor of this tax, the President said yesterday:

"The fact is that while neither Root nor I even got the credit for being the progressive members of the last Cabinet, we were the most progressive and the two who usually aided and abetted President Roosevelt in what were called his radical policies. I don't know if that would be a popular thing to admit just at this juncture, but it is true, and I felt that when the time came to push this program that I could rely on Root to stand by me."

We did not get back from the golf links until eight o'clock and learned for the first time that Mrs. Taft had

actually been for a motor ride. She seemed a little nervous,
Mrs. More said, but once out of the White House she
seemed to enjoy it.

Your affectionate brother,
ARCHIE.

Captain Butt to Mrs. Theodore Roosevelt

Washington, D. C.
June 22, 1909.

MY DEAR MRS. ROOSEVELT:

This is just to say good-bye to you and to Miss Ethel,
and to offer to do anything I can at any time for you in
Washington, in case dear Belle Hagner is not here.

I know you will be glad to hear that Mrs. Taft is better,
really better, though she is still unstrung in nerves and
seems to be in constant fear all the time that she may at
any moment become paralyzed, there is so much of it in the
family. It is largely morbidness now.

Good-bye, dear Mrs. Roosevelt. I wish there was something I could do to show you how deep my affection and
gratitude really are, for you and the President. Some day I
may be able to serve you, and then how happy it will make
me! Once more, good-bye to you, to Miss Ethel, and to
the boys, and bon voyage.

As ever,
Your sincere friend,
ARCHIBALD W. BUTT.

Congress Seeks the White House's Advice

Washington, D. C.
June 25, 1909.

DEAR CLARA:

The President's doctor thought he had sufficient exercise yesterday, so we went for a motor ride this afternoon.

The conversation was largely between the President and the Attorney General and related largely to the corporation tax amendment, which was offered in the Senate by Senator Aldrich to-day. The Attorney General laughed heartily when the President said:

"Well, George, for a man who has always eschewed politics of all kinds, you certainly have got knee deep in it. It remained for my non-political attorney general to draft a law for Congress. The strangest part is that the Congress was willing to have a member of the Cabinet draw up such an important amendment, for as a rule the Senate Committee on Finance is rather jealous of its prerogatives."

The Attorney General said that he was merely the instrument of the President himself, for while he had largely put the amendment into shape he only embodied the suggestions of the President. Secretary Wickersham then commented on the two dinners of which I have given an account in my last letters and remarked on the dramatic side of them.

"I scarcely think there were ever two more important dinners than those two given at the White House, certainly not two which are fraught with such importance or liable to have a more lasting influence on the laws of this country."

I was glad to hear him say this, for I deemed them not only of great dramatic interest but of great importance, yet I feared that I had possibly seen more in them than was really there, so accustomed have I become to note interesting incidents. I fear that I sometimes magnify the importance of events which happen there, or rather lend to them a dramatic interest which the results might not justify.

"It has been a long time since Congress has come to the White House for its advice," said the Attorney General, "and I do not know any incident such as the framing of this amendment ever happening there before."

"However," said the President, "I think that both Hale and Aldrich felt that unless they acceded to some of my views there would be no tariff bill. In fact, I said to them, when they first met with me on the subject, that it was either the corporation tax or the income tax or no bill at all, and Aldrich answered frankly, 'That is why we came to you.' Aldrich is frank if anything."

He then told of Representative Payne's objection to the proposition to frame any corporation tax, when he said:

"There will be a lot of amendments offered in the Senate, so why agree on anything now?"

"There will not be any amendments," answered Aldrich with a jerk of his head.

Senator Root then stepped forward and taking Speaker Cannon's hand said:

"Mr. Czar, let me introduce you to your fellow Czar."

At which there was a general laugh, and "the House and the Senate got that much closer together," added the President.

Good-night.

ARCHIE.

Jeff Davis, Senator Bailey—and Dress Suits

Washington, D. C.
June 29, 1909.

DEAR CLARA:

The President's bachelor dinner went off with great éclat last evening. Luckily the clouds cleared away about seven o'clock, and so the dinner table was laid on the West Terrace. There were forty places laid, but only thirty-nine were present, owing to the fact that Senator Jeff

Davis of Arkansas failed to show up. How can a state tolerate such a cad as he is? When he did not come, that is the epithet the President used of him. We waited until twenty minutes past eight, and then I reported he was still absent, and the President said:

"We will wait no longer on such a cad. I presume he thinks he is smart to play such a trick."

"Shall I remove his seat?" I asked.

"No, let it remain there as a reproach to the state that sends such a man to represent her in the Capitol."

When the invitation was sent him he called up Mr. Carpenter, the secretary, and said he had no dress suit and that he would not wear one if he had, and therefore he supposed the President would not want him to come. The message was taken to the President, and he sent him word, most kindly, to wear any clothes he had and that he would be just as welcome, but to come, that was all he wanted. Davis then said he would come and promised that he would be decently dressed. Carpenter asked him if he would send a written acceptance, and the Senator said, "No," that he had no time to write letters, but to tell the President he would be there.

You remember that Senator Bailey made the same protest against the dress suit to McKinley, and the latter told him unless he could come properly dressed he had better not come at all, and Bailey made a lot of alleged political capital out of it at the time. Now when Bailey is invited he wears not only a dress suit but one of the latest style, and his wife comes décolleté, with ropes of pearls around her neck.

The President told me not to give out the facts about Davis. If I thought it would do him any harm I would have the facts published, but I feel sure that this is just what would please Davis more than anything else and be what above all he desires. At any rate, he missed a beautiful entertainment, as charming as I have ever seen at the White House.

Good-bye.

ARCHIE.

Planning the Income Tax Amendment

Washington, D. C.
July 1, 1909.

DEAR CLARA:

We only returned from New Haven this morning. The change in weather from New England to Washington is very great, so much so that I smile when I remember some dear old ladies at Yale telling how insufferably hot it was there. Why, the President had to wear his overcoat when motoring.

Senator Aldrich's admission in the Senate that he accepted the corporation tax to kill the income tax is troubling the President, for he sees in this admission an effort on the part of the Rhode Islander to throw the odium of the tax on the President. Up to the present he seems determined to push the tax, and if others are weakening, he is not, at least.

Yesterday afternoon he and his two brothers, Mr. Charlie and Mr. Horace, and I went for a motor drive in the country about New Haven. By the way, the country around this old college town is very beautiful, reminding me somewhat of parts of Tennessee, that part which is hilly and cool.

The President laughed at Mr. Charlie over the fact that he would have to make the *Times-Star* of Cincinnati a partnership affair and not continue it as a corporation if he hoped to conceal the salaries they were all getting and the amount of money he was making.

"No," answered Mr. Charlie, "I will stand by you in this matter. It would not do for any of your family to run to cover."

"You are a trump, Charlie," said the President, hitting him on the back. "I did not consult you about this proposition, for I felt it would be contrary to your interest to endorse it, but I felt you would stand by me."

The President then recited the facts which led up to the corporation tax and why he advocated it instead of the income tax.

"I prefer an income tax, but the truth is I am afraid of the discussion which will follow and the criticism which will ensue if there is another serious division in the Supreme Court on the subject of the income tax. Nothing has ever injured the prestige of the Supreme Court more than that last decision, and I think that many of the most violent advocates of the income tax will be glad of the substitution in their hearts for the same reason. I am going to push the Constitutional Amendment, which will admit an income tax without question, but I am afraid of it without such an amendment."

He then told his brothers that the corporation tax was his own suggestion, first made to the Speaker of the House and later to Senator Aldrich.

Good-bye. Love to the old man.

Affectionately,

ARCHIBALD.

Camera Work at the Summer White House

Beverly, Mass.
July 4, 1909.

DEAR CLARA:

The papers all refer to the cottage, which is quite a tiny affair by way of a house, as the Summer White House. I have spent most of the day warding off newspaper men. I got the President's permission to present them in a body this afternoon, so I turned onto the lawn the entire lot, some forty in all, the majority of whom had cameras. He consented to pose, and so seated himself in a comfortable armchair and said with a laugh:

"Now, gentlemen, shoot me full of holes, for this is your last opportunity this season."

They walked around him in the most shameless way and "shot" him from every point of view. He made forty good friends out of them, however, but he always feels that it is at the sacrifice of dignity.

Later John Hays Hammond and Colonel Nelson of the Kansas City *Star* called on him, not together, however, as coupling them in this way would imply. Colonel Nelson is a great free trader and came to assure the President that the entire West is against the present tariff bill. Colonel Nelson came to Washington last fall, and he and President Roosevelt nearly came to blows over the third term idea. The colonel was a devoted friend of the President, but insisted that if he did not reiterate his position as to a third term he would be credited with hypocrisy, if not downright duplicity. The President was furious with him for intimating that his former declaration could be doubted, but nevertheless, when he returned from his ride that afternoon, he gave a statement to the Associated Press affirming his former declaration and settling forever any third term suggestion.

Good-night.

Your affectionate brother,
ARCHIE.

Enter Hughes, Who Outshines the Company

Lake Champlain
(On Board the *Ticonderoga*),
July 8, 1909.

DEAR CLARA:

I have got the President hidden in the pilot house and I think he is safe for an hour and a half, the time it takes to cross the lake to Burlington, Vermont. With him are the French ambassador and his charming, chatty little wife; the British ambassador, with his more stolid helpmate. Governor Hughes is walking the deck, and there are two secret service men at each door of the pilot house with instructions to admit no one.

This country is so beautiful and so many things have happened to impress me that I have taken advantage of this respite to write to you rather than follow the example of the Governor of New York and walk the deck. In fact, I never appear for a minute without someone tagging on to me to know what the President will do next, or if he can see some local light whose special claim is similar to that of ten thousand other persons in the community. I am forced to be pretty severe at times, and at all times I am forced to be firm, even sometimes to rudeness.

I forgot to mention also that Secretary Dickinson is with the President, but as the President dearly loves this hard-faced Southerner, he will enjoy his company rather than be bored with him. "Max," he calls him, and while the President admits that sometimes the Tennesseean's stories get a little long, he also says he would rather hear a poor story from Dickinson than a good one from anyone else. He admires the wit of his Attorney General, can listen officially to his Secretary of the Treasury, grows nervous under the placidity of the Secretary of the Navy, but he loves his Secretary of War. He looks at Dickinson while the latter is talking and keeps in a continual smile. He seems to be more amused in watching Secretary Dickinson than he is by what he says. By far, he is the most intimate friend in the Cabinet. The President can sit with the secretary for hours and discuss matters, and they hammer at each other like two boys in a debating society and then end each such debate with reminiscences of the days when they knew one another in Tennessee and Chicago.

At the end of this day the worst was to come—the banquet. It began at nine and did not end until after two o'clock. I sat between the cardinal and Seth Low. The cardinal remained only through the soup course and then withdrew, as he never remains out of bed after ten o'clock. He looks like an ascetic and no doubt his health, which is a matter of such concern to Archbishop Ireland and other aspirants, is due to the life he leads.

The speeches were all very good, but none compared with the address of the Governor of New York. The more I see of Governor Hughes, the more impressed I am with him. I have been with him constantly for the past two days and he is as witty and humorous a man as I have ever seen. He keeps the President constantly laughing with his witticisms, and instead of being the icicle I have always heard him described, he is genial, warm, and always gracious. He is stern in the matter of duty and simply refuses to do things when he disapproves of them, without giving any excuses or reasons. He declines to give interviews and rejects propositions in a perfectly ruthless way. In office he has but one mistress, and that is conscience, and those nearest to him say that he never flirts with it nor attempts to fool himself in the least.

I can see the President is hourly being attracted to him, and, strange to say, there is no suspicion of jealousy anywhere on the surface. He is greeted with as much warmth up here, where the true Hughes seems to be known and where he hails from, as the President, and sometimes is given a greater ovation. His speech at the banquet was a gem, each sentence rounded and balanced and every period a perfect one.

I am accustomed to see something of men of large caliber, but this man is about the biggest I have seen, it seems to me. I feel that he has only begun his career and he has far to go. The President alone shines out with him.

All the other public men that are here, other governors and state officials, and even those at the national capital, seem to be pigmies by the side of him. I may be judging hastily, but I don't think so.

His presence is magnetic, moreover. One finds oneself watching him and studying his face, not critically but in admiration and wonder. When he is thinking his eyes seem dead, and suddenly he comes to life, as if breath had been breathed into him, and his whole body seems to quicken and radiate life. I feel that it is a privilege to have seen him as I have, and my only regret is that when we reach the other side of the lake he will relinquish the seat of honor by the President to Governor Prouty.

Next to Governor Hughes and the President, the British ambassador carried off the laurels in the way of addresses and popular favor in the manner of their reception. Ambassador Bryce, strange to say, is very witty for a Britisher, and seems to possess what would be described as American humor. He knows, of course, the American people thoroughly, and is in great sympathy with them. He says he can tell, when he meets an American, from what state he hails, which I think may be somewhat exaggerated, but he maintains he can do this and has demonstrated his ability to do so on more than one occasion. He invariably begins his addresses in a humorous vein, then becomes serious, and invariably makes his audience sad before the conclusion. He is apt, while extolling the great men of the past, to wonder what the subsequent generation will think of this one, and as a rule his deductions are not very flattering to the present one.

The French ambassador, on the contrary, is always buoyant, always hopeful, and his wit is Celtic and not well adapted to an American audience, although he made a decided hit, when referring to the various and conflicting claims as to whether Champlain discovered the Vermont side of Lake Champlain or the New York side first, by saying that the best authorities in France were of the opinion that the discoverer came in a canoe and, looking up unexpectedly, saw both sides exactly at the same time. He talks so rapidly and so indistinctly that Secretary Dickinson, for instance, is never able to connect his sentences and professes not to be able to understand him even in a conversation around a dinner table. He speaks English with great ease and, while most of his speeches are extempore, he studies the subject matter for an address and is very familiar with the facts before he rises to his feet.

Love to Lewis, and tell him if my letters bore you to throw them in the fire unread. I feel that I am the manager of a large operatic troop, traveling everywhere with the same people and seeing each one do his part two and three times a day.

I am indebted to the President for the idea, as he likened us to a traveling show under contract to give at least three performances a day. To-day will not be very different from yesterday, just as yesterday was not greatly different from the day before.

Love to yourself

ARCHIBALD.

CHAPTER XIV

TAFT CALLS HUGHES THE "GREATEST ORATOR"

Washington, D. C.,
July 9, 1909.

Well, dear Clara, the traveling show is back, and as hot and disagreeable as Washington is, it is better than giving a continuous performance in a better climate.

Madame Jusserand said the Governor of New York [Hughes] had been the revelation of the celebration to her;

that she had found him to be everything which he was supposed not to be. The President then said this, and I quote him direct, for it bears out the general opinion of everyone who heard his marvelous speeches on this trip:

"I regard Hughes as the greatest orator we have in America at this time, and one of the greatest we have had in our history. He is the most wonderful extempore speaker I have ever heard, and when one thinks that each sentence is not only perfect in the ear, but carries in the nut some subtle truth, I would place him as one of the foremost orators of all times."

The opinion I expressed yesterday has been endorsed, and we can now look for the path he is to follow, or, more likely, to blaze.

Saturday Night,
July 10, 1909.

The President had the chairman of the Ways and Means Committee and the Attorney General to dinner to-night, and later I went by for them in the car and we spent an hour in Rock Creek Park. The President is in this fight good and hard and will not let up if he has to disorganize the House and cause the members to reject the report of the conferees.

We played golf this afternoon, General Edwards and the President against Senator Bourne and myself, and we beat them one down. Also we gave them the four best holes. I must say the President was handicapped, for he was thinking more about the tariff than he was about golf.

The idea of veto is abhorrent to him for the reason that the bill carries with it a number of Philippine tariff reductions, dear to his heart as well as the corporation tax. He does not like the conferees. It looks as if the Aldrich school and the stand-patters in the House were in absolute control. He has heard from the other side, and he thinks, if there is no other way to force terms, he can do so by encouraging the insurgents to rally and defeat the conference report. But one can't prophesy anything at all. The fight is going to be an interesting one, and all I can do is to watch and record the innings.

Good-bye.

Your affectionate brother,
ARCHIE.

An Iowa Senator Decries Prohibition

Washington, D. C.,
July 14, 1909.

DEAR CLARA:

Last night we went to dinner at Senator Newland's, where we met the entire committee for the Reclamation of Arid Lands from the Senate and some others besides. There was an expert with a magic lantern, who threw a lot of pictures on a canvas in the garden after dinner. These pictures showed the work which has been done since the appropriation was made seven years ago, and the amount of work accomplished is amazing. It is proposed to bring under cultivation over thirty million acres of land which up to seven years ago was arid and waste.

Senator Dolliver was the wit of the dinner. He picked up his glass of wine to Senator Bristow, whom he knows is a teetotaler, and said:

"Senator, I should like to drink to the health of your constituency."

The Senator responded most soberly:

"I am sorry that I cannot use wine even in such a good cause as that, but I shall pledge your health in water if you will permit me."

"Which I shall not do," said Dolliver, "as I desire to remain a little longer in public life."

Then, lifting his glass again, he said:

"You gentlemen where intemperance is an issue in your state have my sincere sympathy, for there is a lot of delicious damnation stored away in this small glass."

President Taft then told of the Methodist Conference refusing to accept Vice President Fairbanks as a delegate because he served cocktails at the luncheon he gave President Roosevelt, and accepting Senator Dolliver as one of the leading apostles in the Church.

"Such are the contradictions in our political system, that one state rejects poor old Fairbanks who never tasted a cocktail in all his life and another takes as a man to head its delegation to the National Conference a man who has given voice to such depraved sentiments as we have just heard him utter."

The Senator looked up and, with that smile which envelops almost as great an area as does the smile of the President himself, said:

"It only goes to show, Mr. President, that cocktails are not an issue in Iowa."

"As soon as it does become an issue there, you will find that Dolliver has never tasted a cocktail either," said Senator Bristow, who was still smarting under the Iowan's jocularity.

There was no tariff discussed at all, everybody keeping clear of the subject as if by mutual consent.

July 15th.

We dined last night at the French Embassy, the dinner being, of course, in commemoration of the fall of the Bastille. There were fourteen at the table, including Secretary Dickinson, Secretary Meyer, the Attorney General, the Newlands, the Longworths, and the Winthrops. After dinner we went to the roof garden, as the ambassador calls his upstairs back porch, where we remained until ten-forty-five. I made the motion to leave, for the President had told me that Senator Aldrich and Representative Payne were coming to see him at eleven.

The night was fairly cool, and the President enjoyed himself very much, especially the vivacious conversation of Alice Longworth. While he does not approve of her, he simply delights in her wit and her brilliant repartee. She was late, as usual, arriving after the President, an unpardonable offense in official Washington, but she made a star entrance and her apologies were so flagrantly absurd that she threw the assembled company into a delightful mood at once. He took both her hands between his and said, with a hearty laugh:

"Alice, if you will only stop trying to be respectful to me, I believe you would become so."

"And then I would bore you to death as the other women do," she said, sweeping her arm around the room.

Good-bye. With love,

ARCHIE.

July 16th.

Going out to Chevy Chase in the motor yesterday were the President, General Edwards, Senator Bourne, and myself. The President had lunched with Senator Aldrich, Cardinal Gibbons, and Representative Payne. The two politicians had asked to see him sometime yesterday and so he asked them to lunch. These two persons are seeking the President more now than he is seeking them. Going out in the car, the President heaved a sigh of relief as we passed out of the grounds and said:

"Well, I have made some advance, I hope."

The President then went on to say that he was being urged to make some headlines in the papers; some wanted him to throw down the gauntlet to Congress and assert that the bill had to be this or that, or else he would veto it.

"Now, boys,"—and these I think were his exact words; "Now, boys, I will tell you frankly what I am trying to do. I realize as well as anyone else does that I could make a lot of cheap capital by adopting just such a course, but what I am anxious to do is to get the best bill possible with the least amount of friction. I owe something to the party, and while I would popularize myself with the masses with a declaration of hostilities toward Congress, I would greatly injure the party and possibly divide it in just such a way as Cleveland brought dissension and ruin into the Democratic party. I wish to avoid this one thing. I shall do all in my power to retain the corporation tax as it is now and also to force a reduction of the schedules. It is only when all other efforts fail that I will resort to headlines and force the people into this fight."

Tariff Battle Under Way in Earnest

Washington, D. C.,
July 18, 1909.

DEAR CLARA:

When I left the President a few minutes ago, he said:

"Well, Archie, we have had a busy day of it. Now you can go home and go to bed, but I will talk tariff for another hour, and I am too tired to do anything but stand pat."

It was after eleven o'clock when we got back to the White House, having taken Representative Payne to his apartment on Vermont Avenue. It has been an average day's work for the President and it has been made memorable to him by, what do you think? No, not by victory over Aldrich, although that has been in the day's doings too, nor by counteracting some Machiavellian scheme of the Speaker's, but because he beat all his former records in golf at Chevy Chase, doing the course in ninety-four.

You have possibly seen it published that he has done the course in ninety-four, but he never did it before, and we who gave the hints by which the reporters arrived at these figures gave them to boost the Presidential game a little. He did not return from the links until half-past seven. He has gone through the day in fine shape and I am inclined to think he has enjoyed every minute of it.

I found all plans for golf upset. The President was at lunch with Senator Warren and I felt the lunch would last a long time, as he had been waiting to get hold of Senator Warren on the wool and hides schedules. Senator Warren did not leave until a quarter to three, and then Senator Aldrich and the Speaker arrived. While they were on the South Portico a message came from the State Department that the Chinese Embassy had received a cable from the Emperor and wanted to know when the chargé could come to deliver it. I asked the President and he said, "At once." This meant a uniform, and so, telephoning the message, I took the motor and hurried home, bringing back with me my dress uniform, which I hastily donned in the breakfast room. I was in full state by the time the Chinese arrived, and they did not notice that I had on no collar and was without my side arms.

Shortly after they arrived the Speaker and the Senator left, and the President entered with much dignity into the Blue Room to receive the message from the Chinese Emperor. He seemed to be very much pleased, for after they left he handed me the message and said:

"I think that quite a diplomatic victory."

Then he told me that there had been reasons to believe that the foreign diplomatic agents at Pekin had, by the use of money with the Chinese officials, frozen out American capital in the improvements to be made in the Eastern Empire. The President had, on receipt of this news, sent a personal cable to the Emperor, stating his great interest in the improvement of China and his personal interest in the welfare of the empire and expressing the hope that American interest be considered in the contracts and loans to be negotiated. The answer he received to-day was a personal assurance from the Emperor that orders had already been given in compliance with the President's wishes in the matter.

It was then four o'clock, but we got hold of Senator Bourne and started for Chevy Chase, where he and the Senator played a twosome with the result above mentioned. It was late when we got back, and he asked me to stay to dinner, which I did, eating out on the West Terrace. The dinner was an interesting one. He talked to me freely about the tariff. He had served notice on Senator Warren, he said, that if he did not withdraw his fight on free hides he would force an inspection of the wool schedules which would be worse than anything the Senator could anticipate.

"I have told them all," he said, "that free hides is the keynote for this bill. I will have nothing less than free hides. I also want free iron ore, free coal with reciprocity, free oil, and less duty on lumber. I am also opposed to the duty which they have put on gloves and stockings. This is not the time to talk of building up new industries by protection, and it is foolhardiness to run counter to shibboleth and that is what the opposition to this duty on stockings and gloves amounts to."

Then he made this remark, which smacked so much of President Roosevelt that it made my blood tingle:

"I have tried persuasion with Warren, and if that does not do he can go to hell with his wool schedule and I will defeat him without compromise."

I then told him what President Roosevelt had said in my presence when some of those who had visited him in Augusta intimated that with the Taft inauguration would come a complete reversal of all the policies of the Roosevelt administration, how some had said that the government would be turned over to the enemy again. He seemed to be very much pleased when I told him that Mr. Roosevelt's only answer had been:

"Do you not know Taft? He will fool all of them yet."

It seems, looking back now, that President Roosevelt was the only one who knew the man, and it only shows his knowledge of men—that even when those nearest to Taft were predicting failure, Roosevelt never seemed to doubt him.

He then told me that he feared Nick Longworth would be defeated for Congress at the next election, and said that he wanted to take care of Nick and Alice before they were humiliated by defeat.

"I do not care so much about Nick, but she is Roosevelt's daughter, and I always want to look out for Nick on her account. I would give him a mission abroad if they would like it, or I would make him Governor of Porto Rico, and what a queen she would make there!" And then he laughed and added, "Until she got tired of it! Or I would send him to Cuba."

He then asked me what Clarence Edwards expected and what were his ambitions. He is only a detailed brigadier general, and the President thought he would like to be made a brigadier general in the Line. I told him I thought the army was expecting such a promotion and was fully prepared for it.

"If," I said, "all the insular possessions could be placed under one bureau and another Cabinet post created, I think the general would be willing to resign from the army to enter the Cabinet in this way."

He said Congress would not consent to a new Cabinet place and it would be out of the question, and so the meal came to an end with nothing definite either for Clarence or Nick, though I shall sound Alice at the first opportunity as to what she would like in case of an emergency.

At ten o'clock we went out in the motor for Representative Payne and drove for an hour. He talked tariff all the time and reiterated his former expression that unless there were free hides there would be no tariff bill, and when Mr. Payne said he was in favor of the duty on gloves and stockings, the President said frankly to him:

"Then, old man, I will have to fight you. We won't quarrel, but I shall use all the influence I have to defeat this schedule."

It is this perfect frankness which disarms all the old crowd and even upsets Aldrich's estimate of human nature.

It is now half-past twelve. I think I have earned a rest, don't you? Do you realize, dear Clara, what an insight you are getting into governmental affairs and how results are obtained? I know you follow the intricate ways, which, I grant, are dark, and tricks, which are, however, not altogether vain, with intelligence, but do you follow them with any degree of enjoyment, or do they seem trivial by the side of the health of Julia and the digestion of Lewis, or sink into insignificance in comparison with the wit of Ann and the gentle humor of Frank?

Good-night,
ARCHIBALD.

CHAPTER XV

A BREAK IN THE GOLF CABINET

Washington, D. C.,
July 22, 1909.

DEAR CLARA:

The first break in the so-called golf cabinet came today. It was due evidently to jealousy of the real Cabinet. We started from the White House for Chevy Chase about three o'clock, and in the car were the President, General Edwards, Senator Bourne and myself. On our way we stopped at the Maryland Theater, a five-cent show on North Street, to see some moving pictures in which the President was seen in review at Petersburg and Charlotte. I appeared in them only once, which showed me that my effort to keep out of the line of the camera is not without some good results. I noticed the President was in a very bad, rather a silent humor. He was not jocular, to say the least, and all the efforts of Senator Bourne to draw him out met with failure. He was silent all the way to the club.

We left Senator Bourne at the club proper, and the President, General Edwards, and I then went on to the bungalow where we keep our clothes. Just before reaching there, the President said:

"A funny thing happened to-day at the Cabinet meeting. Old Knox most solemnly protested against my continued intimacy with Bourne on the ground that it alienated other Western Senators from me and was bad politics in general. I asked them to provide me with a golf companion, but none offered to fill his place."

That was all he said, but when I went to his office this morning he did not mention golf, and I finally said that young Hoerstmann, one of the champions of Chevy Chase, had been anxious to take him on sometimes. He thought for a few minutes, and then said he would like to try him, as he thought he might learn something from him.

"From now on poor old Bourne is a dead card, so to speak, and the worst of it is, he will never know why he has been dropped from the playmates list."

It seemed to me that a shiver ran down the spinal cord of General Edwards, for he doubtless thought he would be the next one to go. Ties mean very little to the President when friendships are formed in a political or official way. I do not think it is so in his earlier friendships. His devotion to such men as Judge Lurton of Tennessee, to Secretary Dickinson, and to others whom he has met through his law practice and on the bench may be different in a way, but if he gets it into his head that it is wise to drop someone from his list, he does so without the slightest compunction. I feel certain that when he feels that I have outlived my usefulness to him he will send for me and say that, as much as he shall miss me, he still feels that he is doing me an injury by keeping me longer from my legitimate duties in the army. If he thought I was making enemies for him or causing him to be criticized for too much favoritism toward an individual army officer, I am certain that he would not let any gratitude for past services stand in the way of my leaving him for a minute. I am inclined to think that this element is indicative of largeness rather than smallness.

Coming back from Champlain the other day, he said to me:

"Archie, I do not know what I would do without you," and I was so embarrassed that I left the car to keep from answering.

It was the first time he ever intimated that I was of any service to him. He shows me many favors now. Too many, I think, for I think it would be wiser to scatter these trips among the various attachés at the White House, but it seems my hour and I accept it as such.

Good-night,
ARCHIE.

Mr. Taft's Way with Friendships and Duty

Washington, D. C.,
July 23, 1909.

DEAR CLARA:

I have just been rereading my last letter to you, which letter I did not mail last night for the reason that after I had written it I feared I might have given you some erroneous impression of the President or done him some injustice. In fact, last night after I had got in bed my mind kept dwelling on what I had written you, and I came to the conclusion that the judgment of anyone based on that letter would most certainly be erroneous and so went to sleep resolved to destroy it the first thing this morning. When I reread it again this morning I decided to mail it to you; that if taken by itself it might give one a wrong impression of President Taft, but taken with other letters it could not be misleading, and, moreover, it seems to have so much that was pertinent in it that I thought it wise to let you draw your own conclusions, even possibly thinking that my deductions were based only on my own fear of being some day removed and in a way preparing you for such a contingency.

Whether his indifference to people in general comes from his experience on the bench or whether it comes from a high sense of what he owes to the state, or is in line with his sense of duty, I do not know, but I do know that he can remove people from office, that he can refuse to grant favors, with an indifference which is impossible to most men of his apparent type.

Senator Root appears cold, yet Senator Root binds his associates to himself with hooks of steel, and will hold on to friends and hold friends in office long after they have ceased to be useful, merely on account of the humanity that is in him. He looks like a piece of refined steel, and the President, who looks all warmth, all fervor, all humanity, can deal out the cards which make one shiver at the touch. Yet he is filled with the humanities, so to speak. His sympathy, his love for human nature, is, in a way, in the abstract, and he never permits his heart to govern his mind.

Both McIlhenny, the Civil Service commissioner, and

I appealed to him to issue an executive order putting Clarkson Galleher in the classified service, but without avail. Galleher failed on his examination, and he was considered such a valuable clerk that his chief, the quartermaster general, and everyone who had anything to do with his work, recommended that he be classified by an order merely for the good of the service. His father, Bishop Galleher, was an intimate friend of the President. Yet he turned down John McIlhenny and myself with hardly a thought in the matter. He walks very straight and is not swerved from the path he has marked out himself as the path of duty.

Now about Bourne. He never wanted to play golf with Bourne and every time General Edwards would suggest it to him, he would say:

"Sometime, sometime."

He told me that he wanted to avoid just those intimacies which brought so much criticism on President Roosevelt, and for that reason he did not ask this or that person to ride with him, and was content to be just with me or with General Edwards. I told the general yesterday that he was to blame for this Bourne incident, and he acknowledged it. The trouble is that Bourne is a very engaging man, and once he had played with the President, he continued to link game to game until the President did not see how he could put an end to the intimacy without hurting Bourne's feelings.

The President is very complacent. He is so complacent that sometimes people fall into the erroneous opinion that he is soft. He is only complacent so far as it is convenient to be so. He puts up with a lot of dictation from me apparently, but it is convenient for him to do so. I make things easy for him, but I do not fool myself that I am necessary to him or that he continues this connection with me for any deep affection he has for me. He told his sister-in-law that I never annoyed him as other people do; that I never talk to him when he is worried; and I think that is really my chief advantage over others about him. I may be over-modest, but it is better to err on this side than take myself too seriously.

Last night we dined at the Longworths', and Alice made a charming hostess. The only other guests were Mrs. Townsend, the Newlands, and myself.

These last two letters almost cause me to forego letter writing and resort to a diary. They seem to be such failures as letters. I am helped to this conclusion by a remark that Alice Longworth made last night. After taking the President home, I returned to the Longworths', where we chatted until after twelve. We got on the subject of records and she said that she had kept a diary of the first two years in the White House. I remarked that I would have thought she would have kept a diary of comment rather than one of facts and incidents alone.

"It takes very brainy people to make comments worth reading," she said, "and I doubt if my judgment would have been equal to analysis of events as they transpired about me."

This remark lingered with me longer than I would have had it do, and I still do not find an answer to it in my own case. I am prone, I fear, to be prolific in comment, but facts alone are dry materials to record, and then I find that I enjoy airing my opinions even if they do not pass beyond the horizon of my immediate family.

This afternoon I am going to play golf with the President. When I asked him what he wished to do this afternoon, he said golf, and when I asked him with whom he would like to play, he looked up quizzically as if he expected me to read his thoughts and said:

"With you, old man."

But I have asked General Edwards to join us for fear he may think that influences are at work against him.

Goodbye. Your affectionate brother,

ARCHIE.

Indignation Over the Glove Tariff Plan

Washington, D. C.,
July 23, 1909.
Midnight.

DEAR CLARA:

I have just returned from a motor trip through the park. The President dined with Mr. Hoyt, and I went by for him at ten. He and I and General Edwards played golf this afternoon, and he played against our best ball, yet defeated us three down. This will show how he is improving.

Senator Payne and Senator Aldrich had a hurried conference with him this afternoon after he came in. They came over to ask him how he felt on the subject of the glove schedule. He told them that he did not believe this was the time to build up a new enterprise by protection and was opposed to the duty which the House bill carried on this article. Then Senator Aldrich told him that he was greatly embarrassed, as Speaker Cannon had come to him and insisted on the glove schedule for the reason that Representative Littauer was anxious for it and that he felt committed to him. He further said that he owed his victory to Littauer and therefore it was a personal matter with him and that he would insist on the duty which the House had put in the bill on gloves.

The President was most indignant. He said it was the most bare-faced piece of personal legislation he had ever heard of and that the reason which Cannon gave made it all the more impossible for him to agree with it.

"It is nothing but the pound of flesh that Littauer is demanding," said the President to Payne and Aldrich, "and I should think that Littauer would be ashamed to use such an argument, and I should think that Littauer would be more ashamed to hold the Speaker to such a bargain. I let both Aldrich and Payne know that I was horrified at such a proposition. I felt it was a betrayal of the party, and of the country, for nothing but a personal venture."

The Senator still insisted that he was greatly embarrassed, and the President then said that he would send for other members of the committee, which he did, and urged them to stand firm against the glove schedule— with what result we shall see.

He is a mystery to these men with whom he is dealing, for he refuses to make any bargains with any of them, and while he is not averse to an honest compromise, it must be an honest one, open and above board. He is very anxious to have the Congress pass a law authorizing the tariff commission. The Speaker is opposed to it for the reason that he says there will be no guarantee that a protectionist will be put on it, and that he fears the President will name college political economists. One word to the contrary would get the bill through the House, but he refuses to give guarantees to anyone. He said yesterday when someone told him what the Speaker had said about college professors:

"I am not a damn fool and I am a protectionist, but I don't propose to say this much to the Speaker, and if the bill is passed I will appoint the commission without his assistance."

Good-night. This is my second letter to-day, but I thought this of sufficient interest to record. It does not put either the Speaker, Littauer, or Senator Aldrich in a very enviable light, but it illustrates something in the character of the man in whom I am interested and whose fight makes it worth while to note. In the school in which the Speaker and Aldrich were trained such methods were considered perfectly legitimate and neither can see anything wrong in it. But to the school which Roosevelt made fashionable and which is exemplified in President Taft, such methods are scarcely short of dishonesty.

How his answer to them would have delighted President Roosevelt! The latter would have probably impaled them in a message or a speech had they made this proposition to him, but the President will make nothing known, and will fight them in another way. It illustrates the difference between the two men. The result will be the same, though the method of reaching it is quite different. Roosevelt would have felt ferocious with the Speaker. President Taft feels sorry for him.

Good-night,
ARCHIE.

CHAPTER XVI

A REPROOF FOR THE MARINE CORPS

Washington, D. C.,
Sunday, July 25, 1909.

DEAR CLARA:

The President gave me a rather disagreeable duty to perform yesterday. Coming back from Chevy Chase, he said:

"Archie, seeing Colonel Denny and Colonel McCauley at the club reminds me of the fact that I am getting tired of having the orders of the Navy Department curtailed by Marine Corps officers lobbying at the Capitol, and the next time I hear of any such influence being used to check the government in its plans for this corps, one gentleman will find himself in the Philippines and another at Guantanamo. If you are interested in these gentlemen, you might give them a hint to this effect."

I know of course what he meant, and that his suggestion to me was an order to convey this remark to them. He referred to the influence which the Marine Corps has built up in Washington by admitting sons of every Congressman who happens to have a boy who has failed at everything else. The corps is very unpopular in the navy, and at the request of this department President Roosevelt ordered the marines off the ships. Such was the influence of the corps that Congress set aside the order and directed that they be used at first aboard of the naval vessels. They are now attempting to secure additional advantages through legislative action, and this is what the President intended to hit when he sent to Colonel Denny and Colonel McCauley the above message.

I found out that McCauley has done little, only doing what he has been forced to do to keep his standing with Colonel Denny, who holds over him always the threat of the Philippines. They have been to see me separately and together, and Colonel Denny has not been able to so convince me of his sincerity, for I am inclined to think that he intends to urge his friends in Congress to do nothing more on the ground that the President will take just such action as he indicated he would. This, of course, will cause Congressmen to become all the more determined to look out for the interests of the marines. I warned them both against just such action, and I am sure that McCauley will stand by the compact, but I know that Denny has already seen one member of the House and conveyed to him just what action the President proposed. I told the President last night just what they had asked me to tell him, namely, that both sent him their assurance that in the future neither they nor any of their corps, as far as they could help it, would in any way attempt to direct legislation.

I did not discuss the merits of the Marine Corps with the President at all, but confined myself solely to the message which he gave me to deliver and brought to him the profuse apologies of the two officers.

The President said that sooner or later the marines would have to leave the ships; that as a distinct body the corps had become almost useless, and as far as the navy was concerned it was an actual detriment. These details are only tiresome to you, though you may be interested in seeing just how this big President goes about to reach results.

Good-bye,
ARCHIE.

Summer Days at the White House

Washington, D. C.
July 28, 1909.

DEAR CLARA:

Monday I played golf with the President at Chevy Chase and later went to Fort Meyer to see Orville Wright make his official flight in the aëroplane which he and his brother are testing for the government. The wind was very high, and it looked as if there would be no flight, so we went to the shed, where Mr. Wilbur Wright showed his machine to the President and explained its mechanism. He was greatly interested.

The wind died down later. While unable to make the endurance flight, Orville Wright went up and remained soaring in the air for nearly fifteen minutes. The machine sailed up against a heavy wind, and the novelty of the flight was due to the fact that he did not use the weight and pulley to get it started. It was the first time the President had ever seen the machine fly, and he was as enthusiastic as a boy over the feat. I had never seen it either, and somehow I could not arouse any interest in it at first. But this indifference disappears as soon as you hear the buzz of the propeller and see the huge machine mount with the lightness of a bird into the air.

Thousands go out every afternoon, but up to Monday the President had continued to play golf until dark, preferring this exercise to watching the Wrights. Monday there was to be the official test, and he felt he ought to be present; so we went to the club at half-past one and finished in time to reach Fort Meyer by six o'clock. The Wrights held a sort of reception in the shed, and most of the Cabinet and the leaders of the House and Senate, and of course Mrs. Longworth, with several other women, were present.

Mrs. Longworth has never missed a day, and she has done much to make it a fashion for society to go to the Fort and witness the flights. She takes a tea basket with her. She invites those who visit her in her motor car to have tea and lemonade, and if they accept the latter they are agreeably surprised to find a delicious gin fizz instead of the less harmful citron drink.

Those few who have remained here this year feel repaid. There are only the Longworths, the Newlands, the Winthrops, Mrs. Townsend, and the Jusserands who are to be had for a dinner, and in consequence these are at every dinner given at the Country Club or at the Newlands', or in fact anywhere at this season.

The President has had another portrait painted. It gives him a very florid face and reddish hair, and, as Mrs. Longworth told him, it looks pudgy.

"But I am pudgy, Alice."

"Not as pudgy as that, Mr. President, and I would not have it."

I think he likes it. As far as I am able to find out, he is the only one who does.

Mr. Charlie Taft is going to send on the Sorolla to hang

in the White House for a time. This portrait is a perfect delight to the President. I think it makes him feel younger. Sorolla met Millet, who asked him how he would paint the President.

"I am going to send that smile down to posterity," the Spaniard said, and he has done it.

I think I told you that the firmness of the man is shown in the hand. He is holding something in his right hand, and while the face is breaking into a smile, his hand shows strength and firmness. I said it was a pity he had not held some document of importance when posing, since so much of his character was to be shown in the hand. This I remarked while showing him a copy of the *Metropolitan Magazine* which contained an engraving of the portrait. He then told me that the paper was an important document of vital importance to one person. He said that as he was leaving the office a petition was brought to him to delay the execution of a murderer in Panama—a Spaniard by the name of Reyes, I think he said. He had refused a pardon once before, and the petition had now been sent to him, signed by the majority of men of influence on the Isthmus. He was thinking of this all the way over and was still thinking of it when he entered the room.

"As I sat down I had about made up my mind that I would not interfere with the law and, I presume, was gripping the petition rather ferociously when the jolly little Spaniard spoke to me and I looked up at him, my face breaking into a smile as it always did when I looked into his quizzical little face. It was at this sitting that he put in the hand and sent me grinning into the future."

I think this is rather an interesting incident, don't you?

Midnight.

I told him that the head waiter had told me that the cigars at the White House were too good, that if we had poorer cigars the guests would not smoke so many. This seemed to amuse him very much, and he told me to continue to buy the best tobacco to be had, and then said:

"Never in my life have I been able to be as generous as I would wish, and always I have had to retrench in entertaining others from necessity. This is the first time in my life I have ever been in a position where I could let the innate feelings of hospitality have full scope, and I propose to indulge this weakness to the utmost for the next four years. I would rather entertain people I don't like than not to entertain at all, and it gives me the keenest pleasure to see a lot of fellows sit on the South Portico and to know that they are really enjoying what is mine to give them. So while I am here they will have the best."

What he says is true. I have never seen a man who more thoroughly enjoys entertaining.

We played golf and then later went to Fort Meyer to see the Wrights make the speed test, flying to Alexandria and back. But the wind was too high, and the crowd had to trudge it back to Washington.

We were late in returning and so did not get to the dinner at the Country Club until nearly nine. Mrs. Townsend had got together twenty agreeable persons, and in every other way the dinner was a charming midsummer diversion. After dinner the President and Senator Aldrich sat apart from the other guests, and no one went near them. Once he called to me and directed me to send a telegram to Loeb in New York to have a glove expert report in Washington at once. Later he told me to telephone to him, and I was an hour trying to locate the collector, but finally reached him at the Yacht Club at Oyster Bay and gave the President's order.

Love to Lewis and yourself.

ARCHIE,

Captain Butt to a Friend

Washington, D. C.
July 30 [1909].

MY DEAR MEGGS:

Long ago I have ceased to do any other work. President Roosevelt began to use me very much as a general uses an aide, and it is the same thing under Mr. Taft. I appear with him everywhere in uniform and travel with him always. I see nothing of local society save an occasional lurid night at the Longworths', or dinner with some old-time friend.

Write me when you get lonely again, but don't fire a Pythian dart at me again in the suggestion that I like this life. It is only given to me to strut across the stage at this time, and very soon I will disappear in the scenery of the Philippines or Cuba, and then it will all be as if this hour had never been. It doesn't count for much except to those people who are impressed by snapshots in the press and daily mention of one's name in print. I know the game, and I don't overestimate it.

With love to any friends who may be hanging about drinking mescal, and with the same old clasp of friendship for you, I am, as ever,

Your sincere friend,
ARCHIBALD.

Victory for Mr. Taft in the Tariff Fight

Washington, D. C.
July 30, 1909.

DEAR CLARA:

The end is in sight, and we may get away from Washington by the middle of next week, certainly not later than the end of the week. The conferees have agreed, and the report will be made to-morrow to the House and Senate. It is a complete victory for the President and rather a humiliating defeat for the Speaker and, I fear, the Vice President.

The President sent me word this morning to come to lunch early, as he wanted to spend the entire afternoon on the golf links. There was a deathlike silence about the White House which indicated that something of an unusual nature had happened. There were no telephone messages from anyone at the Capitol asking for appointments, and there was every appearance of negotiations between the White House and the Capitol having been severed. The President came over at half-past one o'clock and seemed rather silent and worried, I thought. Then he told me what he had done.

The conferees had again appealed to him to recede from his position on lumber and gloves, and he sent them word he would answer by note. He prepared it very carefully, and while he did not threaten Congress, he gave them to understand that he would not sign any bill which carried with it more than one dollar and a quarter on rough lumber and which carried a greater duty on gloves than was contained in the Senate bill. It was at his instigation that the House duty of something like four dollars on gloves had been cut to something near a dollar, and he refused to capitulate.

"They have my last word," he said, "and now I want to show my scorn for further negotiations by spending the afternoon on the golf links. I do not want to return, so I will dress there for dinner and go direct to the Winthrops' without coming back to the White House."

This plan was carried out. I motored to the club with him, where I left him playing golf with Buck McCammon, and I returned to Washington for some papers which he wanted to see and also to bring back with me the two glove experts who were to arrive at five o'clock. It was after six when I got back to the club, and while I changed into my uniform he held a short interview with the custom officials. We motored from seven until eight, when we entered the grounds of the Winthrops'. We were a half hour early but fortunately found Mrs. Winthrop dressed and ready to receive the President.

We had been there for ten minutes, possibly, when the message came by phone from the White House that the conferees had agreed and had accepted the rates as laid down by the President. For a minute he remained perfectly silent, staring incredulously at the paper before him. Then his face wreathed itself into a smile, and he said:

"Well, good friends, this makes me very happy."

I was the first to speak, and I said:

"Mr. President, I have watched the struggle, and I congratulate you."

"Did you expect me to weaken, Archie?"

"Hardly that, sir, but I was afraid they might convince you."

Beekman seized his hand and congratulated him, and then Mrs. Winthrop did a most characteristic thing. She went over and kissed him.

We sat possibly for fifteen minutes longer before the Eustises, who were house guests, came down and others came in. Most of that time he said little and sat apart thinking. The other guests had all heard the news before leaving town, and as each arrived he or she would offer congratulations. The Secretary of the Treasury was quite happy, and Alice Longworth fairly danced before the President in her delight. The Postmaster General had been arrested for speeding, coming from Fort Meyer, and did not arrive until dinner had been announced, and he never heard the news until dinner was half over. He seemed surprised, for I think he had serious doubts if the President could win the fight, and, in fact, he had gone with a delegation of Congressmen, urging harmony for peace's sake.

We did not leave the Winthrops' until nearly eleven o'clock, and as we motored through the park he said:

"I should not like my hostesses to hear me say so, but the pleasantest thing about these dinners is the ride to and fro."

At the White House there was no one waiting for him, and when he asked if there were any messages, he was told there was none of any kind. He entered the White House lonelier in his victory than he had been in his fight.

I came home at once to write this letter to you as a closing chapter to a book. It is the end as far as he is concerned. There may be trouble to get the votes now to pass the bill in the Senate, as we heard later that several Senators were threatening to bolt, but that is not his fight. The party must provide the votes for the final passage. He may help to win over some recalcitrants, but the personal equation is eliminated as far as he is concerned—and the fight is over.

Good-night.
ARCHIE.

CHAPTER XVII

THE PRESIDENT IN REMINISCENT MOOD

Washington, D. C.
August 1, 1909.

DEAR CLARA:

President Taft played golf yesterday with Buck McCammon, and I dined with him last night. As we were coming home, he said that Colonel Harvey, the editor of

Harper's Weekly, was coming to dinner. He had asked no one to meet him, and he had a horrible feeling that he would go to sleep if left alone with the editor. He asked me to come and see if I could get one or two members of the Cabinet. It was then seven o'clock, so I sent word to Alice, the cook, who since the Longworth dinner is never caught napping and is prepared for any number the President may spring on her at the last moment.

I finally got the Attorney General and Secretary Mac-Veagh, and we dined on the West Terrace, and later smoked on the South Portico. They remained until eleven o'clock, and then the President and I took a motor ride, which always rests him and puts him in good condition for a healthful sleep.

Colonel Harvey would be an interesting talker if he were not such a dogmatist. He eliminates all conversation by the first remark or comment he makes. He closes all avenue for discussion by his announcement of his opinion on any subject which may be mentioned. Even Secretary Wickersham, who is a marvel in matters conversational, simply retires before one of these Harvey pronunciamentos, and there is silence until someone else becomes sufficiently intrepid to start another subject. Once he came in the Blue Room with me to look over some records, and the conversation between the President, Secretary Mac-Veagh, and the Attorney General opened with the volume of a roaring Niagara compared to the timid remarks which had been ventured during dinner and while Colonel Harvey was present. After they had left the President said:

"I cannot think of a pleasanter recollection for anyone to carry with them from Washington than an evening spent on the South Portico of the White House. I remember once spending an hour here in the time of General Grant, and that evening still stands out more distinctly than any one evening in my life.

"There is something about the atmosphere of this South Portico which challenges your thoughts for the past and brings to your mind the fact that every President, since Monroe at least, has come here when worried and from this spot has renewed his courage for the fight—and most likely their best dreams were dreamed right here. I love to feel that Jackson must have been looking down this vista when he made up his mind to veto the bank bill, or that it was here that he decided to stand by Peggy O'Neil, just because she was a woman; and that Lincoln's great soul was refreshed from this point; and that even Cleveland became stronger as he looked on that glorious white shaft of Washington.

"I know that Theodore loved this spot as he did no other in the White House, and his most brilliant sallies of wit were made here, and that when the world seemed to be all awry it was here that he and Mrs. Roosevelt would sit, and his tempestuous nature would receive just that influence which made him one of the greatest figures the country has ever seen."

I had never seen him in just this mood, and I felt that his soul was moved to great secret thoughts, and that his words were but an echo of them. I could but think that it was the only time I had ever heard him speak of President Roosevelt as Theodore, and I knew he felt in very close communion with him just then.

We got into the motor and never spoke, and we rode for nearly an hour without a word, and, stranger than all, he never slept, and when I glanced at him to see if he were asleep, he was looking hard into the fleeting darkness ahead.

"Good-night, old man," was all he said as he got out of the motor and went indoors.

Affectionately,
ARCHIE.

More Echoes of Colonel Roosevelt

Washington, D. C.
August 3, 1909.

DEAR CLARA:

Yesterday we played golf; the President and Senator Bourne in a twosome, and Mr. Lawrence Abbott, of the *Outlook*, and I. I got to know the Abbotts in the last administration and to have great respect for both the father and son. He told me yesterday that Mr. Roosevelt had written to his father that he had already written four of his articles for *Scribner's* and kept up with his writings as he progressed with his hunt. Just as soon as he finishes his articles on the hunt for *Scribner's*, he will begin to uncork his editorials for the *Outlook*.

Mr. Abbott told me that the magazine had taken a prodigious bound in circulation and public sale since the fact became known that Roosevelt would be connected with it. Heretofore, the management has never put the magazine on the newsstands, but they have been forced to do so now to meet the demand, before Mr. Roosevelt has even begun to launch his real self into the periodical.

I received such a nice letter from Mrs. Roosevelt yesterday. She is with her sister, Miss Carow, in Italy, but leaves for Paris next week to educate the children, she says, through an endless sightseeing tour. She says she is very content and very happy and has not regretted for a moment that they are no longer in the White House, but feels a deep sense of relief when she reflects that her life now can be natural and that she has to see only those persons whom she really likes and who really like her.

I wrote to her to-day and reminded her of the wonderful record she made as mistress of the White House and how she has linked herself to the great women of this age, and that not even would Dolly Madison be held in more affectionate regard by the people of this country than would she. There must be hours of loneliness when she misses all that came to her in Washington, and moments when she is apt to feel cynical, seeing those people who were prone to pay homage to her and her husband doing the same to other people, and so I never write to her that I don't, just in a sentence or two, try to bring to her mind what she was to the White House and to the people of this country, and what she will be to them as the years recede and history is written. When I get on the subject of Mrs. Roosevelt I am apt to continue at great length, so, fortunately for you, Anna has announced lunch, and I am hungry.

Good-bye. With a lot of love for both of you, I am again,

Affectionately,

ARCHIE.

A Special Dinner at the White House

Washington, D. C.
August 6, 1909.

DEAR CLARA:

The tariff bill is off the President's hands, and we are off to Beverly to-morrow. It passed the Senate at two o'clock, and a few minutes later the supplementary resolution correcting what was said to be a "joker in the bill" was introduced in the Senate and passed that body an hour later and then went to the House, where it was passed a little after four. The President was waiting anxiously for news, and while he said he would go to his room and sleep he was unable to lose consciousness even for a cat nap, and it is the first time I have ever seen him show any excitement save the hour before his first state dinner at the House, on which occasion he confessed to nervousness. The resolution had to be enrolled—for without it there would have been no reduction on shoes—making it ten minutes to five before the bill was ready for the President's signature.

He decided to go to the Capitol to affix his signature to this measure as well as to a number of other bills, so we left the White House at a quarter to five, the President and his private secretary and I, and were at once escorted to the President's chamber on the Senate side. There were all the members of the Cabinet who are in the city and a goodly number of Senators and some few Representatives.

The President signed the general bill first and then the Philippines bill. The pen with which he signed the tariff bill he gave to Representative Payne, but the one he used in signing the Philippines bill he told Carpenter to keep for himself. I think he intends to send it to the Philippines, but he may retain it as an heirloom himself. I think he feels it to be a greater triumph to secure the passage of the Philippines bill, giving free trade to the islands, than he does in the passage of the Payne-Aldrich bill. He signed a number of other bills and distributed the pens of the usual number of relic seekers to be found in every assembly of this character.

The Senators came in to say good-bye, and the President had an individual greeting for each one. He noticed that Senator Bourne did not come at any time he was at the Capitol and remarked upon this later. A number of Representatives came in also, but it was impossible to say good-bye to them all, so he only spoke to those few who came up to speak to him, waving at the others as he saw them look in the room and pass the door. A terrific thunderstorm broke out while he was preparing to sign the bill, and at once the newspaper correspondents seized upon this as a note of warning from the country, indicating that the bill would be received by a storm of protest when the features of the bill were understood.

The President wanted the dinner served on the terrace, but the storm prevented, and the dining room never looked lovelier than to-night. We served sherry, hock and water, and champagne. There came near being a contretemps on the subject of champagne. We had in the wine closet fifteen bottles of a very good champagne, but the President thought it was not good enough to serve at his Harmony Dinner and told me to get some extra fine wine. I thought it perfect nonsense to serve vintage wine to most of those people, so I bought four bottles of the very finest vintage wine I could get at the Metropolitan and gave directions to serve this wine to Senator Root, Senator Hale, the Speaker, the Attorney General, and several others, who are *bon vivants* in their way and great connoisseurs of champagne.

I was sitting next to Nick Longworth, and to my horror I noticed that the waiter, in serving the wine, passed me by and filled up Longworth's glass and later came back to serve me from the vintage wine, which I had not told him to do. I was drinking Scotch and soda. I loathe the taste of champagne. Nick promptly fired an arrow in the sky in the shape of a remark that I was serving two kinds of wines and possibly palmed off inferior brands on the un-suspecting. I laughed at his suspicions and said we were serving a vintage wine and ordered the waiter to keep Nick's glass filled. The next time he passed I took the bottle as if to look at the year and allowed Nick to get a glimpse of the label, which satisfied him; but he has what is known as a searching eye, and had he discovered what I don't think he really suspected, I would never have heard the last of it.

Senator Root complimented the President on the dinner and the delicious wines, and also told him that it was the first time he ever dared to take a cigar at the White House. By the way, I have just ordered from Cuba five thousand cigars in two sizes to be made especially for the

White House, the larger size to be known as "The Administration," and the smaller to be called "The Cabinet." By the time they land here they will cost about thirty-five cents apiece, but one cannot better spend money at the White House than by serving good wines and good cigars.

The President never takes anything to drink at all, but is most profligate in making others imbibe. I do not see how he sits through these long dinners and banquets without taking enough merely to exhilarate him, but he takes no alcoholic liquors of any kind and seems to be much the better for it.

ARCHIE.

On Vacation at Beverly, Mass.

Beverly, Mass.
August 10, [1909].

MY DEAR CLARA:

I have dated this letter the tenth, though it may be any date between the sixth and the eleventh or twelfth, for time has been passing in a sort of dream for the past week. I only know that we left Washington last Friday, and that this is Wednesday, and that I have done nothing but play golf all the morning and motor all the afternoon, seeing these strange little New England towns which are scattered along this coast.

We reached Beverly at nine. There were very few persons to meet us. These people thought, because President Taft wanted to enter quietly on the last trip, that he desired to be left alone at this time, so there were comparatively very few to welcome him, which he did not notice and which distressed Jimmy Sloan, the secret service man, considerably, as he thinks it a mark of disfavor if Presidents do not have to bite their way through crowds.

The President's face lighted up with the keenest enjoyment when I told him that Mrs. Taft was in the motor outside. He hurried out and gave her a kiss—several of them, the papers say—which could be heard by everyone present. Mrs. Taft was looking better than I had expected to see her; in fact, she looks almost normal except for a certain pallor, which I do not like. The President gives at least the half of each day to her and never permits anything to distract him from this duty. He plays golf every morning, either at Essex or at Myopia, and returns to lunch at two o'clock. The rest of the day is hers. He sits with her and talks and tries to make her forget her illness, and in the afternoon they motor. He always seems to want me to go with them, and I make no engagements which will conflict with what he desires. I feel that at this time I am some help to him, for I carry my share of the conversation and try to interest her in the many little details which he would not think to give to her. Very often Mrs. More and Bob accompany us, but most frequently there are only the four of us—the President, Mrs. Taft, Mrs. More, and myself.

We have all the motors with us, and still they are hardly sufficient to meet the demands of the family. Miss Helen has her engagements and Bob his, and Charlie is never quiet for an hour. When he is not on the water he wants to go to see Dick Hammond or play golf at Essex or tennis at Monserrat. When I spoke of hiring another chauffeur to-day for the landaulet, Mrs. Taft objected, but the President thought it wise to get one.

"Let them have a good time while they can," he said. "In four years we may all have to become pedestrians again, and I want them each to look back upon this portion of their life with the keenest relish. They are not children to be spoiled by a little luxury now."

That is very true. I have never seen people more natural

and wholesome. Not one of them shows the least signs of what might be called the "swelled head." They have inherited the kindly genial nature of the President and the hard common sense of the mother. The President says Charlie is the only grafter in the family who feels that what is the government's is his and is ready to accept any gift which comes his way.

The President does not permit much business to come to him now. He feels that he has earned a good rest and will take it in his own way. It is a very simple way, but it is his way, and he enjoys it. He likes to do the same thing in the same way every day and resents any effort to estrange him from this course.

Good-bye,
ARCHIE.

Gay Days in the Taft Family

Beverly, Mass.
August 15, 1909.

DEAR CLARA:

I have never seen anyone so keen about motoring as the President. He simply revels in it. As we were flying along the main road the other afternoon, he said to Bob and Helen:

"Well, children, enjoy this all you can, for in four years more you may have to begin to walk over again."

He loves to joke his wife about the time when they will go back to what he calls the lower middle class. It is a term which Miss Marisa Herron has made use of a good deal in the family. She is a great wit and once made the Laughlins furious by saying that Mr. Taft and Mr. More were the only members of the family who did not belong to the lower middle class, "as they were the only members of the family who lived by their wits." Mr. More is a scientist of no mean ability, and the President speaks for

himself. Mr. More is here now and has put his foot down
on his wife's remaining longer. He says this notoriety he
is getting is hurting his reputation as a scholar. I told
him of the remark that Douglas Robinson made to Nick
Longworth when he married Alice.

"Nick," he said, "when I married a Roosevelt I did so
in ignorance. It never occurred to me that I was marrying
into a Presidential family, but with you it is different, and
when you find yourself bullied and ignored or hung on the
family like a tail to a kite, you will not be able to plead
ignorance, for you are doing this thing with your eyes
open."

More said he was ignorant also, that when he married
his wife Mr. Taft was not regarded as even a possibility.
She is going back with him, and I am sorry to see her
leave, for she has such splendid poise and is so sane and
normal that she has a most healthful effect on Mrs. Taft.

I am glad to have met Mrs. Charlie Taft. She is witty
and at all times full of fun and good humor. She was one
of the great heiresses of Ohio, but is so natural and kindly
that one would never suspect her of either great wealth or
high position.

A great many invitations are being pressed on the President, but I am declining them all. He only goes to those
houses where he is intimate, much to the disgust, I think,
of the Bostonians who live on Commonwealth Avenue in
the winter and on the North Shore in the summer. I am
refusing my invitations likewise, for the reason that I
never know when I will be able to keep an engagement,
and moreover I am so dead tuckered out when night comes
that it is a pleasure to hear even the droll whine of my
own landlord, and finally to fall into bed, exhausted.

The President called on Mrs. Evans (I am now writing
at night, having finished sixty miles in the motor) this
afternoon, and we found the widow quite cheery. She

asked the President if Mrs. Taft had tried the New Thought treatment. He said she had not, and began at once to back-pedal from a Christian Science discussion, I thought. She said it was only teaching people to rely on themselves, and the President, with a laugh, said that Mrs. Taft must have tried the New Thought years ago, for she was about the most self-reliant person he had ever chanced to meet.

With love, I am as ever, your affectionate brother,

ARCHIBALD.

CHAPTER XVIII

A LETTER FROM AFRICA

Beverly, Mass.
August 17, 1909.

DEAR CLARA:

I am sitting crouched over a fire to keep warm, or rather to thaw out, for the President would play golf to-day, in spite of the fact that it was blowing a gale and raining hard. He and I and Mr. Charlie Taft went around together, and when we came into the Myopia clubhouse we might as well have been in swimming with our clothes on. But every nerve was on edge with battling with the wind and rain. The day was made memorable to me by what the President said going out to the links.

"I cannot tell you, Archie," he said, "what you have meant to me during these past months, and I want you to feel that I appreciate everything you have done for me. I want to tell you, moreover, that you have used such tact at all times and shown yourself such a gentleman in every way that words fail me when I try to express just what I do feel for you."

I received a letter from President Roosevelt yesterday,

which I read to the President. . . . He evidently has no stenographer, for it is written in longhand by himself, and he hates so to write.

Love to Lewis, and with much for yourself, I am as ever,
                    Your affectionate brother,
                                        ARCHIBALD.

Captain Butt to Theodore Roosevelt

                                Beverly, Mass.
                                August 17, 1909.
MY DEAR MR. PRESIDENT:

I have wanted to write to you for some time, but hesitated to do so on account of your expressed desire to be alone while hunting, and I felt that you would receive all the news of any value from your own immediate family. But since receiving your letter dated June 27th, but only received within the past week, the impulse to write you is too strong to be resisted longer.

I had heard from Mrs. Roosevelt that you continued well, and I knew you to be happy. I have thought of you each day, for there is nothing about the White House that is not connected in some way with dear Mrs. Roosevelt and yourself. Of course, everyone there has had to readjust themselves to the new conditions, and with the exception of the minor changes in the servants, everything remains pretty much as it was.

Mrs. Longworth would tell you that there was a Victor Talking Machine in the Blue Room and a bearskin on the floor, and while the old *intimes* would find fault with this, I am so glad to see old customs followed and the dear old place kept just as you and your family planned and carried into execution. Mrs. Taft will not even order any new china, but says the Roosevelt china must be continued as the White House china and much that is there now in broken sets she thinks ought to be destroyed, but of course fears public opinion too much to wield the hammer.

The President has continued me as his personal aide and keeps me near him at all times. Even now I am here at Beverly, acting as a buffer largely between the persistent curio seeker and himself. I find that he is not able to extricate himself from situations as you were wont to do, and he really needs someone like myself to keep a weather eye open at all times for him. The confidence which he seems to impose in me comes, I feel sure, from the warm words you spoke to him of me, and I try to serve him loyally and faithfully, though it is hard to give anyone the same unselfish devotion that those around you felt at all times. He is kindness itself, and I am not unmindful of the remarkable advantages I have been afforded in serving two Presidents and at a period when everything which is done becomes of precedence and national import. Just how it is going to be to go back to looking after mules and studying the problems in the quartermaster's department I am not sure, though I try not to take my post too seriously, so that when the call comes for more active service elsewhere I will be all the better fitted to answer it.

The tariff fight is the only important matter which has come up for consideration since you left, and I know you will be pleased to learn that the President whipped the old-timers out and that the allies were as badly defeated in Washington as they were in Chicago. Senator Aldrich, Senator Warren, and the Speaker, and the old-time standpatters, misinterpreted altogether that smile, and I could but remember what you said of him once, that he would fool them all when the fight opened. I sat up with him during that fight, and the record of it will be interesting some day. He used the White House as a great political adjunct in the battle and tried to coax when it was possible. But when that failed he used methods which reminded me of some of the methods which made the Executive feared in the past. He is not pleased with the bill, but got certain fundamentals incorporated in it which he feels made the measure one which he could sign.

Possibly long before this the papers have told you of the fight and the humiliation of the allies. At one time he was in a very sluggish state of health, but recently he has got stronger, and I think will be able to preserve the country from the sage of Utica, New York, for at least four years. I flatter myself that I have done something in the way of keeping him from lapsing into a semi-comatose state by riding with him and playing golf, a game which I have had to take up much against my inclinations, as I have never cared for it, and I am only beginning to become sufficiently proficient to enjoy it. I have always thought the game itself secondary to the walk around the links and the blueness of the sky and the greenness of the grass. But of late I am beginning to suspect it may have charms of which I have been ignorant. Whereas in the old days I had corns on my right hand from tennis, now my right hand is as delicate as that of a girl, and there are corns on the left hand, the change of hands showing the change of administrations.

We leave here on September the fifteenth for a two months' swing around the country, and I am to go and largely manage the trip.

Mrs. Taft is not at all well, and I fear it will be many months before she recovers. This state of health in his wife has been a source of constant anxiety to the President, but his optimistic nature shines out healthfully through all his troubles. I do not believe it possible for her to resume her duties at the White House next winter, though the President tries not to see her condition as it appears to the rest of us. His optimism in this tragic matter, as in everything, shines out like the sun, and I dread the awakening for him.

I write to you fully about matters, for I am sure he would find no objection to my doing so. I read him your letter to me and told him I was going to write to you and would give you all the news, if he had no objection.

"I wish you would," he said, "and I will write to him also, although he owes me a letter."

The papers are still filled to overflowing with any scraps of news they can gather, and there seems to be the same fanatical interest in everything you do. Pardon me for the use of the word "fanatical," but that word alone describes the interest which the people of this country seem to take in you. I feel it myself, and it seems to me that everyone I meet, save a few of the enemy, is pulsating with it. When it was known that I had a letter from you the clerks in the office here, Forster, Smithers, and good old Jimmy Sloan and Murphy, each one who had served you in any way, hung about me until I would tell them something of what you said, and each seems as delighted as if he had received it himself. Nothing but loyalty and devotion everywhere, and each of us finds it perfectly compatible with the service we can give your successor, for he seems to have no desire to change men and get new faces about him, but rather seems to cling closest to those who served you the most devotedly.

I want to make you feel, away off there, when you finally get this letter, how you are loved and missed. If what I have written sounds at all like flattery, Mr. President, then I will have to stand for the charge, but I don't think I ever felt even flattery toward you and certainly tried always to be truthful. I have one address, but I am fearful you have progressed far away from it, and so I will send this letter to Mrs. Roosevelt and ask her to forward it to you. I am writing this letter on the typewriter myself, and not dictating it, so you will pardon the seeming casual appearance of it, but my handwriting becomes more illegible as I move onward in life and I know you have not the time to dawdle over a badly written letter.

Give dear old Kermit a lot of love, and if he is not careful, use the stick; for his trip makes his life too valuable to jeopardize now by foolhardiness.

Mrs. Roosevelt was looking well when I saw her; and if her eyes were not to see this letter, I would tell you how altogether lovely she was looking the last time I saw her at Oyster Bay. The seven years at the White House without ever having made a mistake will shine like a diamond tiara on her head some day.

Belle seems reasonably happy, although she had another brother down with typhoid fever, and she misses you and Mrs. Roosevelt more than she can admit, for to admit it always brings the tears to her eyes.

Hoover has charge of the White House this summer, and the office is being enlarged to take in the old tennis court. I would rather see this sacred soil built over than to see a second story on the old office, a thing which came near to happening.

I see a good deal of the Longworths, but I tell Nick that his wife is all that I have left to love from the last administration, so he puts up with a great deal of pattering around from me. It may interest you to know that Mrs. Longworth has lost none of her popularity since the fourth of March. It seems to me that she is even more entrenched in her position and that she is as strong without the White House as a background as she was with it for a setting. She is most discreet at all times, and her conduct has greatly endeared her to the President, who has more than once spoken in the most affectionate way of her manner to him and his family. He said to me the other night:

"I wonder if Alice and Nick would like to go abroad. I would give them any post they would want, or I would send them to Cuba or to Porto Rico if they preferred to

remain nearer home. I do not know how the next elections
at Cincinnati will turn out, but I want them to feel that
they can have any post in my power to give and whenever
they want it."

I thought he said this for me to repeat to Nick, which I
did. The latter smiled and said only that he hoped to remain at home for a while.

Good-bye, dear Mr. President.

> With a great deal of love,
> ARCHIE.

An Anecdote of Dr. C. W. Eliot

> Beverly, Mass.
> August 22, 1909.

DEAR CLARA:

By the way, I heard a good story of Bishop Lawrence
the other night at dinner. Dr. Eliot has a reputation of
saying often the very thing he should not say. One evening,
while discussing the death of Phillips Brooks, Dr. Eliot
said, after dinner while the men were smoking:

"We should have a quiet, commonplace man to succeed
Brooks. A man with culture, education, but with no claims
to oratory or brilliancy, just such a man as—why, Lawrence, you are just the man. You are just the man! You
should be Brooks's successor."

And so he was.

> Good-bye. With a lot of love,
> ARCHIE.

The President and Pardon Cases

> Beverly, Mass.
> August 23, 1909.

DEAR CLARA:

The President needs diversion when he gets hold of
pardon cases. He is busy with a number of them now, and

he is invariably worried with them. He goes very carefully over each (this is the judge in him), and unless there is some excellent legal reason he is not moved by them. He told me yesterday, going to the Boardmans', that he was greatly worried over one especially, a case of peonage in Alabama. The offender is an Iowa man who became a lumber manufacturer in Alabama and is now in the penitentiary.

"I have never seen a case for pardon so adroitly worked up," he said. "The Governor of Alabama, the Senators, the Representatives, and the various leading politicians of the adjoining states have all petitioned for his pardon. Senator Cummins of Iowa and the Iowa legislature and a host of others made a special plea to me. I have been over the case most carefully, and I have decided not to be moved by the petition, for I am convinced that the man was guilty."

I said to him:

"I should think, Mr. President, the most nerve-racking cases would be those from death sentences and life imprisonment."

"I do not allow myself to be moved by anything except the law. If there has been a mistake in the law, or if I think there has been perjury or injustice, I will weigh the petition most carefully, but I do not permit myself to be moved by mere harrowing details, and I try to treat each case as if I were reviewing it or hearing it for the first time from the bench."

I am busy now arranging for the military reception to President Diaz of Mexico. The Mexican ambassador called on the President and intimated that the President should be received, when he makes his first call on the President of the United States at El Paso, with military honors. A Latin's idea of military honors and those of the President of the United States are somewhat different. The President has directed me to direct the Chief of Staff to send one or two squadrons of cavalry to El Paso, but no more. I have written to the Chief of Staff to call on the Secretary of State for advice and then to write to me as to what our foreign office thinks is proper.

The Ambassador also asked what aides the President would have with him, as the Mexican President desired to have aides only of equal rank. The President replied that he would have only one, a captain. But I think he should have more, and I will suggest at the proper time that the officer in command of the cavalry be ordered on special duty with the President when he returns the call on the President of Mexico, and accompany him to the dinner which Diaz will give him on the evening of the sixteenth of October in Laredo, just on the other side of the river from El Paso.

When I left Mexico I never expected to see this great old man again. I was with General Ransom for a while in Mexico, when he was there as ambassador. I was not officially accredited to the Mexican government, but went in the capacity of private secretary to the general. While he was absent the President accepted an invitation to open the mines of Santa Anna, which had been destroyed years before by an explosion, and he went accompanied by a great military escort and the entire diplomatic corps. My experiences were most interesting, and I have always carried with me a picture of Diaz as I saw him on that trip.

ARCHIBALD.

CHAPTER XIX

BREAKING A HUNDRED ON THE GOLF LINKS

Beverly, Mass.
August 24, [1909].

DEAR CLARA:

Our summer holidays are drawing to a close, and I shall not be sorry to see the last of them. The President, however, hates to see them pass, for he knows at the end of them he will begin speechmaking.

"If it were not for the speeches, I should look forward with the greatest pleasure to this trip," he said. "But without the speeches there would be no trip, and so there you are."

The President says he will outline about four speeches and insert certain portions of them in each speech he makes and by throwing in some local color each one will have a new dress.

"If not a new dress," he says, "it will have new bows and ribbons, which will pass for the same thing. I would give anything in the world if I had the ability to clear away work as Roosevelt did. I have never known any one to keep ahead of his work as he did. It was a passion with him. I am putting off these speeches from day to day, and the result will be that I shall have to slave the last week I am here and get no enjoyment out of life at all."

I might predict that he will not have a speech written by the time he leaves Beverly. He will possibly have the outlines of the one he is to deliver in Boston on the fourteenth prepared, but that will be all, and he will spend the first two or three days on the train preparing speeches; but as to preparing them cut-and-dried fashion, as President Roosevelt did, he will not. If I am wrong, I will tell you, but I believe it will be a good bet, with odds too, that he will not get to work on them until after he leaves, when the pressure is really on him to do something.

I won five dollars on his golf game Saturday. I think I told you that a good deal of money had been put up on his game, and the club had been very much divided in its opinion as to whether he could make the course in less than a hundred. Herbert Leeds, who is the great golf expert at Myopia, gave it as his official opinion that he would never make the course under a hundred. Pap Golf, as Leeds is called, has great pride in his judgment and a number of club members put faith in it and backed his judgment with bets. I had my doubts whether he could do it or not, but when I heard Richie Simpkins and Leeds talking about his game I took Richie on for five dollars last Saturday, the very day he made ninety-eight. In fact, Richie held me to the wording of my bet that he would make it under a hundred, and when I disputed the terms of the bet he was backed up by Leeds, and I refused to withdraw and, out of loyalty, let the bet stand.

Imagine our surprise when we came in to find that he had made it under a hundred. I understand that over a thousand dollars changed hands, though the exact amount cannot be ascertained, as the betting at Myopia is a very silent affair. The secretary got him to sign his name, and George Sheldon, who was playing with him, certified to the score, and the leaflet on which he keeps his scores was torn out of his book and will be framed and hung on the walls as a souvenir. You see, Myopia is the hardest course in the world, and ninety-eight is about equal to eighty-five on other links. While it is nothing for the professional, yet it is a rattling good score for the middle-class player. I have never seen him so happy over anything. I think he showed more pleasure over it than he did over the passage of the tariff bill. Mrs. Taft takes the greatest interest in his game always, and the news that he had made it under a hundred made her most happy. She went up to him and kissed him when she heard it, a mark of great favor from Mrs. Taft, for she is not demonstrative as a rule in public.

Good-night.

ARCHIBALD.

The President's Sense of Dignity

Beverly, Mass.
August 25, 1909.

DEAR CLARA:

This morning I played golf with the President, and he beat me two down. We play the rubber match to-morrow, I having beaten him the last time we played together. We are considerably troubled by persons wanting to get into the golf cabinet. Col. Fred Crosby was the latest applicant and has played with the President before at Murray Bay. The President granted his request to take him on for a game, but was so displeased with the letter asking for the engagement that he is not likely to accord him another game. He began his letter "Dear Taft," and the intimacy, in view of the President's position, did not warrant such familiarity, and the President said so plainly to Mrs. Taft. It came out in a discussion with Miss Helen and Mrs. More, when the former said that it was correct to speak of the President as Mr. Taft. She thinks the custom of always addressing him as Mr. President undemocratic and ought not to be encouraged. In the height of the argument Mrs. Taft arrived and agreed with Mrs. More and myself, and gave as an instance the President's anger at Crosby's familiarity. He did not show it to Colonel Crosby, but I think it will be the last opportunity the handsome Colonel will get to be advertised as a golf companion of the President.

There is nothing snobbish about any of the Tafts, least of all about the President. His sense of dignity is genuine, and he has no false pride to contend with. They always enjoy Mrs. Leiter's attempt to make them into royalty by addressing the President as "Excellency" and speaking of Mrs. Taft as "Her Excellency." The President likes to be democratic, but he knows what convention requires and resents very quickly the slightest infringement of the dignity of his position or the respect due his great office. I have noticed that his old friends never call him "Bill" but once. I have heard his old classmates say they would always address him as "Bill" or "Taft," but they invariably drop into "Mr. President" a second time.

Even the Frank Ellises soon ceased to call him "Will." He says nothing to put a stop to it, and seems to smile just as blandly as if they addressed him in the most respectful manner, but there is something about him that seems to forbid a repetition of the familiarity. He says that most people, unless they be fools, come to a proper understanding of the fitness of things after they have made the first venture toward familiarity; the experiment brings about a readjustment in the proportions of things without any hint or snub from him.

But he will not permit any undue reverence for his person either. For instance, he always accords to a lady motoring with him the seat on the right of the vehicle, although custom has established the precedent that the President always takes the seat to the right, no matter who is with him. President Roosevelt always took the right seat, or rather, Mrs. Roosevelt would never occupy it herself or permit anyone else to do so, but President Taft accorded this courtesy to his wife and now to every woman who happens to ride or drive with him. He does not like to be called "His Excellency" any more than did President Roosevelt, and while he laughs at Mrs.

Leiter, he will not permit it in others. Whenever he sees the dear people waiting to see him he invariably repeats a remark Mrs. Leiter made to Mrs. More on one occasion, and gets a lot of fun seemingly out of it. The Washington Dame of Fashion came once to take Mrs. More driving on the speedway, just after Mrs. Taft had opened it up for concerts. After she had made one or two turns she said to Mrs. More:

' "Now, my dear, we will go over and speak to Her Excellency, and then we will walk among the people. They like to see us, and I think it very kind to show ourselves."

Mrs. More said she had on a very simply made lawn gown, and by the side of the wonderful velvet creation worn by Mrs. Leiter she looked like a badly dressed companion. The Tafts have a lot of fun among themselves. A note of Mrs. Hammond to Mrs. More and Miss Helen, when she invited them to come to the Gloucester celebration, "to leave off their hats and put on their jewels," caused no end of amusement in the family.

Good-night. With a lot of love to all,

ARCHIE.

At Dinner with Mr. Frick

Beverly, Mass.
September 3, 1909.

DEAR CLARA:

It has been rather a dreary week of golf and motoring, and, added to this routine, the President has been suffering with lumbago, which makes him play very slowly and of course detracts from the pleasure of the day's sport. However, the chief thing to do is to keep him well, and he is so unselfish towards others that it is not hard to make a few sacrifices for him.

The most notable thing we have done since I last wrote

to you was to dine at the Fricks'. Yes, what he failed to accomplish by himself he brought about through Secretary Knox. The President wanted to see the Secretary of State and wired him to come to Beverly, and there was nothing more natural than that he should visit the Fricks, for he and Mr. Frick are both from Pittsburgh and fellow millionaires.

It was Secretary Knox who suggested a golf game, but I saw that the press carried only the fact that the President played with this cabinet officer. It was Mr. Knox, again, who asked the President to dine at the Fricks', and the President, good-natured and complacent, yielded of course to his premier. I felt that I had done all I could do to keep him away from the Fricks' so, I was rather glad of an opportunity to get a whiff of the outside world for one night. Had I written you the evening of the dinner or the day afterwards, I would doubtless have told you only of the people, the house, and the cataclysm of melody which poured from a hundred-thousand-dollar organ, and of the Romneys, the Turners, the Gainsboroughs, and the Van Dycks which meet the eye wherever the vision falls in this marvelous home. While there, it all seems so natural. The house, a perfect palace hidden away among the trees, seems the proper place for the old masters. The owner is so modest, apparently, and unobtrusive, that when enjoying the fruits of his millions it never seems to occur to one to ask how the pictures got there any more than how he has managed to gather around his banquet board the people who were there.

The marble rooms, the wonderful organ, which he keeps a musician to play upon constantly, the splendid collection of modern paintings I could possibly have condoned, but when you are seeing famous men and women of England painted by still more famous artists, hanging on his walls, you feel ashamed of the people who let these pictures go, and blush for the man who bought them. I suppose the price of one's ancestors can be reached in time, if only the bidder is sufficiently rich.

As I entered this home, I felt as Aladdin must have felt after he had rubbed the lamp. The table is indicative of the house. It is of mahogany and round, and it is enlarged by circle after circle of mahogany being added, extending wave after wave to take in all that can be purchased to sit around it. I did not feel it at the time, but I do now. The President and every old North Shore denizen there had been haggled for just as the Romneys and the Van Dycks had been bought. I heard one woman say, looking at a lovely portrait of a young mother:

"How could they let her go?"

She went, doubtless, just as the woman who had asked the question had come to dinner. I know the Bryce Allens, and doubtless they were among the coterie who at first scoffed at the efforts of the Fricks to reach society. But there we all were: the President of the United States, and around him grouped the best the North Shore had to offer. There are possibly a few who still hold out, but they will be there in time, just as that last Van Dyck, which they had such a hard time to get, found itself there finally. No, my dear Clara, I have not got the indigestion, nor am I prone to be cynical, but the effects of that marvelous dinner have worn off and I see things clearly.

Possibly it shaped itself in my mind more distinctly when the President said to me that Frick wanted to give him a reception merely to afford him an opportunity to meet the men of the North Shore. The bid was so cleverly put. It came through Secretary Knox, who said that Frick hated to be persistent in his attentions since the President had declined to come to luncheon. We were together in the motor on our way to Magnolia to call on Colonel Nelson when he told me this and asked what I thought.

I saw it all as I see it now. The President was to be bought just as the portraits of men's ancestors had been bought, except that Knox was doing the buying instead of the art collector in New York. I did not say it quite this way, but I said what was in my mind and I was glad to find an echo of this thought in his, for he said he had put Knox off and would decline it now altogether.

There is to be a fair at the Myopia on Monday, given for the farmers of this region, and I shall try to turn that fair into a reception for the President. If he must have a reception, it will be to meet the proper people and in a proper way and not be hung out as an advertisement sign to Frick.

I am glad I saw Romney's first portrait of Lady Hamilton, but can anything be more vulgar than the presence of these paintings in this house, or even in America? No wonder that we are looked upon as purchasers and not collectors, and that we are hated for the wealth which the world cannot resist! The one redeeming feature of the whole thing is the fact that Frick really enjoys his gallery, and I must give him credit for having an appreciation of the paintings apart from their value.

We spent the forenoon and a part of the afternoon on board the *Sylph*, watching the races of the boats of the sonderclass off Marblehead. The wind was soft, and the racing slow, but the myriad little sails dotting the horizon made the day worth while. There are several days more of racing yet, but the President will not see them again. He will give the cup to the winner on the ninth. He has ordered the *Mayflower* to Beverly and intends to give a buffet lunch on that occasion.

We had intended to start for Haverhill at three o'clock, as the President wanted to call on Justice Moody of the Supreme Bench, who has been brought to his home there very ill, but just as we were starting a Dr. Fisher, a reformer, called to protest against the President taking sides, as he said, against Gifford Pinchot, who is at the head of the Forestry Bureau. The President says Pinchot is a fanatic and has no knowledge of discipline or interdepartmental etiquette, and he will not stand for such insubordination as he has been guilty of. He got very angry and raised his voice several times, so that we could easily hear all he was saying in the House. Mrs. Taft said:

"Yes, he is very angry. When he raises his voice like that he is always mad."

There was no doubt in anybody's mind but that he was very angry. Mrs. Taft is improving very rapidly now, and the President is very optimistic that she will be able to resume her duties in the winter, but I fear she will not be able to do so.

Good-night. With love,
ARCHIBALD.

CHAPTER XX

MR. TAFT AND THE YALE SPIRIT

Beverly, Mass.
September 6, 1909.

DEAR CLARA:

Secretary Ballinger arrived while the President was on the golf links and he made the sixth at lunch. He came laden with portfolios—all bearing the case of Pinchot, I imagine—and to-night he and the President are thrashing out the matter. I don't see how it is possible for both Ballinger and Pinchot to remain in the Interior Department, and it would be a pity to cut off Pinchot in the work he is doing, but the President thinks him in the wrong. If his chloroform system fails to produce the result for which he hopes, then I fear he will stand by his secretary and let the reformer go. The President is not over-indulgent toward reformers, especially that class who see evil motives in everyone else's acts save those few who agree with them and who are suspicious of everyone who does not agree with their pet schemes. It would hurt Mr. Roosevelt very much to have Pinchot let out, and I fear it would array against the President all that set of men who look upon themselves as purists in politics.

To-morrow we motor to Boston, and the President will spend the day frolicking with old Yale boys in Brookline. I hear a great deal of the Spirit of Yale. I should say the Spirit of Yale is youth. The Yale men never seem to get old as other people do. The Pres dent himself is boyish and much prefers play to work, and when they get together they are like schoolboys out on a holiday. They don't only act young, they *are* young, and I look with surprise at the caperings of their minds. I have heard so much of the Spirit of Yale that I am really beginning to see what it means. It stands for youth, mental and moral, for loyalty and sincerity. The President is not unlike fifty others of his age whom I have met, and, what seems strange to me, he is never bothered by Yale men either seeking office for themselves or for other people. They seem to be singularly free from that ambition which was aroused in so many Harvard men during the last administration, namely to use every means to hoist themselves in office. There seems to be an unwritten resolution among all Yale men not to trouble the President with applications for office, feeling that when he has offices to distribute to Yale men, he will know to whom to give them without any solicitation from them.

I will take advantage of the outing to-morrow to run into Boston and take out an accident policy in the Travelers for any old thing might happen on a thirteen-thousand-mile trip.

What do you think of Cook in the South? The best opinion up here puts him down as a monumental faker, and the President has his doubts as to the validity of his claim, but when Cook cabled to him the President was forced to congratulate him; but as you may have seen, in a very careful way, basing his congratulations on the report of Cook himself, and not on any belief he might entertain on the subject. The President says if Cook has not found the North Pole, then he is the greatest faker of the age—and that is something accomplished!

Good-night.

ARCHIBALD.

Roosevelt Appointees in Most Offices

Beverly, Mass.

September 10, 1909.

DEAR CLARA:

The death of General Corbin was really a shock to me. I cannot forget that he could have prevented my appointment in the army and on the contrary did much to encourage me in seeking my commission. What I think of him is of little importance, but the President said this of him yesterday coming back from the Myopia Club:

"There was never so cordially hated a man in the army, I suppose, and never one so unjustly hated. Everyone who failed to get promotion in the Spanish War blamed Corbin for it, and those who did get the promotions gave him no credit, when in fact he looked only for the good of the army first and to the welfare of the McKinley administration secondly. I know General MacArthur blamed Corbin for Chaffee's promotion ahead of his own, and yet I know that President McKinley chose to make Chaffee a major general before MacArthur simply because MacArthur would not carry out the policies of McKinley. MacArthur is now writing a history of the Philippines, I am told, and you will find that he will flay Corbin, and without a scintilla of justice in his attack.

"He was a tremendous worker and with the capacity for great things. He was strictly honest, and even that has been the subject of attack by some people. When he declined a favor he did so without that graciousness which takes away the sting, and when he bestowed one he did so in a brutal sort of way that left the recipient under no obligations. His great weakness, to my mind, was his desire to associate in purely a social way with wealthy people and those possessing great social place. That weakness came, I presume, from a consciousness in the past of his own ability and a natural desire for social position, which was never gratified until too late to be of any great enjoyment to him.

"The press, even now, while giving many of his fine qualities, are still harping on these old stories told in their day to his detriment and rehashing the scandals, none of which was true. At the same time they are lauding to the skies Harriman, as corrupting an influence as ever appeared in American life. After my nomination Harriman sent me word that he would do all in his power to aid my administration, a promise on which I put no reliance at all. I sent him word the only way he could aid me was to obey the laws of his country, which I might add he never did in his life."

The President has inherited a great burden from the old administration. I heard him say this to Mrs. Perrin of Cincinnati a few days ago when she was calling on him:

"My chief trouble comes from the fact that I have no offices to distribute. If it were not for Roosevelt, I would in all likelihood not be President. I know some differ, but that is my opinion nevertheless. Not only did I have his support, but the support of all his friends. The whole administrative part of the government was for my nomination and election. I can no more turn out these men than Roosevelt could have done without some just cause. I suppose I have fewer offices to fill than any man who ever found himself in the White House."

It is not his nature, however, to turn people out of office either. He shows not the slightest desire to fill his own offices with other men. He has only made three changes in the personnel of the executive offices, and he would not have made these had not Carpenter done so before he arrived in Washington. He is troubled just now as to the successor to Whitelaw Reid, Ambassador to England. He says he sees no one on the horizon but Seth Low. He does not think him especially equipped for the post, but he asked me:

"Can you name anyone else?"

I thought it over for a time and finally said: "If you were a democrat, you might find material in Thomas Nelson Page."

"But, Archie, I am not a democrat, though some of you people down South seem to think I am, and that first post in the diplomatic service should go to the party in power."

He offered it to Dr. Eliot, and I think he was relieved when Dr. Eliot declined it.

With love,
ARCHIE.

Chicago Children Parade for Mr. Taft

On the train at Milwaukee
September 17, 1909.

DEAR CLARA:

We are now thoroughly launched on our one-night stands, as the President calls this tour. This morning at breakfast he asked me how I was pleased with him as a popular show, and I had to confess that he was so far a success. I never expect to see again such a reception as he received in Chicago. We arrived there at half-past eleven and motored through nine miles of streets, each side being lined with children three and four and sometimes ten and fifteen files deep, making in all about eighteen miles of school children. They each wore red or yellow paper flowers and looked like lovely, bright-eyed little soldiers. The President was very much moved by the demonstration and said more than once:

"We can sometime doubt the motives of adults, but the cheers of children are sincere."

In one respect the reception he got in Chicago was unfortunate, for in no other place can there be given such an ovation. Chicago does everything on a mammoth scale. As we passed through the crowds going to the ball park, the President said:

"One can't touch the hem of Chicago without feeling an electric thrill."

Secretary Dickinson remarked: "And few can touch her hem without feeling virtue go out of him also."

ARCHIBALD.

CHAPTER XXI

RIFT WITH ROOSEVELT ON THE HORIZON

[Washington, D. C.]
November 14, 1909.

DEAR CLARA:

If I remember rightly, my last letter was dated somewhere near Milwaukee about the middle of September. I had hoped to find time on the trip to keep up my letters to you, but after two or three futile attempts I had to forego them and resort to a diary, which I dictated to a poor overworked stenographer each night, a copy of which I mailed to you and which I now want you to send back in order that I may strike out the few personal comments which it contains and file it in the records of the White House. This record is of great value officially, but I must confess that it is even more dreary than the newspaper accounts of the trip which have flooded the country for the past two months. I hardly dare to hope that you have even read it, for it was largely a rehash of what you must have read in the papers, although it contains much that is of historic interest to future biographers of Mr. Taft. It at least has the value of being true, which cannot be said of any of the accounts which have been sent out from day to day as the trip proceeded. I was constantly surprised to see how little of what the press would regard as news of the day was worth recording in a permanent way.

However, the correspondents may have been in the same position as I found myself, somewhat afraid to write all the truth. In fact, that is the main reason why I did not write to you after leaving Milwaukee. While there may be no harm in writing of one's impressions, as I write to you, still to have those impressions made public either by chance or theft, or to have them reach the hands of those commented upon, would lead to disastrous results. The President knows that I keep very full notes, but in what way I keep them, or how fully, he does not know, and it might be a shock to him to come across suddenly some criticism of him where he felt he had the right to have only commendation and praise. He thinks that my records are all of an official character and he thinks this of great importance. They are important as far as official acts are concerned, but what leads to those acts and what motives prompt them are of greater interest still.

I know that many think that nothing should appear in a man's biography save those things which he himself has approved or made official; but this theory, if carried out, would permit the weakling often to go into history equal with the strong, the immoral with the virtuous, and the crafty politician with the statesman. It is only by getting sidelights on the public man that you really see the man at all and are able to judge of his public acts, and how much are the results of his advisers.

For instance, it is interesting to know that when the President started out on this trip he spoke with the greatest difficulty; every speech he made was a labored effort, yet before he had half concluded it he was as felicitous as it is possible for a man to be, and instead of dreading to make a speech he delighted to make one and felt so certain of himself that he would often speak when no speech was expected from him—and even at times when it was not desired. Before the close it got so that if anyone even raised his glass to him, he would take the occasion to rise and speak for five or ten minutes. He repeated himself very little, and before he reached the Pacific coast he had accustomed himself to adapt his remarks to the locality and give to each address some local color that would largely make up for any brilliancy which might be lacking in his oratory.

I do not think his speeches will read as well when put in book form as they will be pleasing to those communities in which they were delivered, and there will be none of them for which he might be ashamed. He was unfortunate in starting off his trip with a speech praising Senator Aldrich. This, with a Winona speech in praise of Representative Tawney, had a very bad effect throughout the West. They were both honest, and he believed that both men had been greatly slandered by the press and the public's opinion in which they were held. He soon learned that it was not a popular thing to praise a man even in his own district, for in most cases these men had reached Congress through some political chicanery of which the decent element in the state is ashamed, or else done something while in Congress which the best-minded people will not endorse. He began by picking out the worst types to endorse. Whether Senator Aldrich is a horse thief or not, the entire West and South so regard him, and to the former section, especially, he is regarded as the one man who is at enmity with their interests.

President Roosevelt had educated the public to hear the truth about public men, and so, when the President began to praise Aldrich and Tawney and Senator Tom Carter of Montana, it hardly knew what to expect. But he soon dropped this crusade and I think I was able to assist him to reach this conclusion. He has been largely won over by Aldrich, and I think he feels grateful to Tawney for doing what he did in the matter of increasing his salary and assisting in passing the bill allowing him traveling expenses. But he has little respect for Tom Carter.

The same thing is true about Speaker Cannon. The President simply hates him and expresses his contempt for him whenever he can do so, yet he openly flattered him on the trip down the Mississippi, was photographed with his arms about his neck, and appeared to endorse him whenever they spoke together. At the same time he wrote to Secretary of State Knox that he should be driven out of public life, that he was a constant reproach to the decent self-respecting element of the country. He is doing all he can to encompass his defeat to Congress and the Speakership, yet he constantly gives him strength by appearing to approve both him and his actions.

I have never known a man to dislike discord as much as the President. He wants every man's approval, and a row of any kind is repugnant to him. If by saying the word publicly that would defeat Cannon, I believe he would say it, so sincere is his dislike of the Speaker, but he does not feel that he is strong enough to say it and so he takes the opposite tack, hoping to aid in his defeat by private innuendo. But the Speaker is too wily for him. I saw how he maneuvered to get the President in constant juxtaposition to himself and how he made use of that position to further his own ends. He gave several openings which would have afforded President Roosevelt, for instance, many opportunities to kill him politically, and which Mr. Roosevelt would have taken advantage of, too, by the way. But the President let them go by, leaving the impression that he actually endorsed the old vulgarian.

So much in the President's character can be explained by his complacency. He believes that many things left to themselves will bring about the same result as if he took a hand himself in their settlement. He acts with promptness and vigor when he has got to act, but he would rather delay trouble than seek it. Of course that is just the opposite view to the one which would be taken by President Roosevelt. The President everywhere endorsed the Roosevelt policies, yet in each state he entered he affiliated with the men whom Roosevelt disliked the most and whom he was wont to call the "Enemy."

Jimmy Sloan was with President Roosevelt for seven years and was more of a friend than a detective to him. He said that the President would not be able to placate Mr. Roosevelt with speeches unless he followed them up with acts. He then related to me a conversation he had with President Roosevelt the last time they went to church together. He said that Senator Lodge had just left him and undoubtedly had been filling his mind with suspicion, but he made the pertinent remark:

"Jimmy, I hope I am not mistaken; that my policies will be made into law; but I may have to come back in four years and enter the fight."

It is just this which I dread and which I hope will not come about. But there is a great deal of feeling between the friends of the two men now, and while each has been able to keep out of it, there is no telling when one or the other may be brought into it.

I found that in the West President Roosevelt is as popular as ever, even more so, and while the West gave a most enthusiastic welcome to the President, one could discern a fanatical devotion to his predecessor which would mean following him any length in upholding the doctrines which he preached.

The Ballinger-Pinchot controversy will not down, and the friends of the two men are lining up on either side. I look forward to Mr. Roosevelt's taking some action which will be in support of President Taft and which will put a quietus on all this talk and gossip now being spread, and the only person who can complicate the situation at all is the President himself. If he is led into dismissing Mr. Roosevelt's closest friends and upholding the men whom President Roosevelt denounced as the corrupting influences in the government, then he may bring about a breach which it will be hard to bridge.

If Pinchot resigns, nothing will convince Mr. Roosevelt that he was not forced out. I know that the President does not want to force Pinchot to resign, yet he will not tolerate insubordination, much less criticism of himself. It is getting pretty foggy, but my faith rests on the loyalty of President Roosevelt and his wonderful political sagacity.

As yet the President has not said one word which could be construed into the slightest criticism of Mr. Roosevelt. On all this long trip, when opportunity after opportunity has been given him to say or do something inimical to Mr. Roosevelt, he has either kept his own counsel or else spoken in terms of only loyalty and affection of the African hunter. I have waited and watched for some sign of disloyalty, and the nearest approach to it has been in his affiliation with men whom Roosevelt despised and condemned, but this may have been only to make friends of the righteous and not to rebuke the prejudices of Mr. Roosevelt.

While it is useless to guess what will or will not take place in the next four years, it is of interest to set down the fact that the President, while endorsing the Roosevelt policies in nearly every speech, did consort with the men most obnoxious to Mr. Roosevelt; but this may all work its way out in such a complete and logical form that the President will have shown wisdom which neither Jimmy nor I could comprehend at the time and which will even meet the endorsement of Mr. Roosevelt himself.

Both Jimmy Sloan and Joe Murphy tell me that the crowds were much larger when Mr. Roosevelt went through the West, but I do not see how it was possible for any man to have a more cordial reception than was tendered Mr. Taft everywhere he has been. There was some coldness discernible in the Middle West, but there only; and that was due to the unpopularity of the tariff bill in that section. The farther west he went, the greater the enthusiasm in his reception, and when he reached the South his receptions were unprecedented. But this was due to his position in the Negro question. The Negroes have greeted him coldly everywhere, and he in turn has done nothing to placate them. In no place has he pandered to them, and he has seemed to avoid them everywhere. He dislikes the Negro, and his highest ambition is to eliminate them in politics. His determination to recognize only white men in the South has given him a popularity there which is marvelous.

I heard him tell Cecil Lyon in Texas that he would not name a single Negro on the census boards and that he must not recommend one. He also told Mosely in Mississippi that he wanted the culture and the education of the South to have a voice in the government and not the carpet-bag type. The most impassioned speeches he made were those in the South, and I cannot but think he will be able to do much in bringing some of the Southern states to him should he be renominated.

He stood the trip remarkably well, for two reasons chiefly: he has no nerves, and he really and sincerely likes people. He likes different types and he enjoys studying them. Whereas most people in his position try to avoid handshaking, he prefers it to sitting down and resting between times. He is a very hard man to handle on account of his complacency. He will stop a dozen times on his way in and out of a room to shake hands with anybody who calls to him. He shows a good deal of political sagacity at times, too. Even when he does not want to shake hands, he will stop and make it appear that those around him won't let him. Jimmy and I got so tired of this on two occasions that we let him alone and followed the line of least resistance ourselves. As they crowded in on him, we would simply stand idly by and let him shake hands until he finally called a halt himself and looked appealingly to us for help. One was at Los Angeles and the other at Augusta. He said to me afterward:

"Why, in the name of heaven, didn't you come and take me out of the Cummings's parlor? I was almost dead and I felt I could not stand it a minute longer."

I told him I thought he wanted to see all their friends, and he said: "Well, don't think the next time. Just come and get me."

But he does not realize what an effort it is to be dragging him away all the time, especially when he seems to resist. While I got out of patience with him often and as often got to a point where I would have liked to tell him a few truths, yet on the whole I came back from this trip feeling more real affection for him than I had ever felt for him before, and this in spite of the fact that I think he is a more selfish man than I had suspected. I have come in from a hard day's work worn out and then been sent for to play bridge until one and two o'clock in the morning. The fact that I would go to sleep at the table would not cause him to quit until he would get sleepy. I saw him angry only once or twice, and then it was with Carpenter and Mrs. Taft, who kept sending him the New York *Times* with adverse editorials in them on him. He finally telegraphed to both not to send him another paper with adverse criticisms of him; that they did no good and only angered him.

Another time was with me, when we reached the Grand Canyon. Some people interested in the trail down the canyon, especially Governor Sloan and the Representative from that district, persuaded him to make the descent. I knew that he ought not to do it and entered my protest, but he waved me aside and refused to listen to argument. The night before we reached the canyon I went to him and for about the fifth time started on my argument why he should not go. He turned to me, and I think he was really angry, and said:

"See here! You go to hell! I will do as I damn please sometime."

I saw there was no use to argue further, and in fact I was so full of laughter that I could not have gone on without showing my amusement, and that night before retiring he announced with the braggadocio of a big boy that he would ride down the trail the next morning. He was not to leave the train before eight, and I was out bright and early to see what else he could do. I arranged for a drive twelve miles away and lunch there, and then for a drive to Sunset View in the afternoon. Going to his room while he was dressing, I said:

"Mr. President, may I come in for a few minutes' talk?"

"I suppose you are going to talk about the trail again," he said, and I admitted as much.

I then told him that I had learned that he would have
to dismount from his horse several times and that the trail
was very narrow and this was a difficult thing for a man
of his size to do. Moreover, I reminded him that his meeting with Diaz was only two days off and that he would be
so stiff and sore that this meeting, instead of being one of
pleasure, would be most uncomfortable. I did not mince
words with him at all, for I had no idea of letting him run
the risk of breaking his neck and imposing the Vice President on the country as the Chief Executive.

He heard me through and finally turned to me with his
face very red.

"Well, damn it, you can have your way; but I'll tell
you one thing. I will get even with you some day—and
with John Hammond, too," he yelled, as I went out of the
door, for he knew that I had Mr. Hammond as an abettor
in my plans.

He really was put out, for his pride had been excited
and he hated to back down, especially as he had sworn
with an oath that he would go. Postmaster General Hitchcock was with us and just then he was trying to placate
the territories, and so when the matter was brought up,
he agreed with Sloan and the rest, and this brought about
some coldness between him and John Hays Hammond.
Mr. Hammond said he was a fish with no blood in his veins
and would throw down anybody to curry a little favor
with the President or with some political henchman. Altogether it was not a happy day, except once when the
President got a glimpse of the trail down in the valley.
I felt that he admitted to himself that I was right, though
he has never made such an admission to me and the nearest he has come to it is that he said that doubtless his wife
and Cabinet would think I was in the right.

But on the whole he has a wonderfully equable temper
and a very sweet disposition. He believes the best of every-

body and will not tolerate anyone retailing gossip to him about this or that public man, and even when he thinks it might be true he prefers to think to the contrary. He calls himself an optimist and he exceeds any I have ever met. Even when he knows a man to be bad, he prefers to think he is so by accident and not by design. I was struck with this yesterday when I went out with him to play golf at Chevy Chase. Senator Bourne was along, and the President said on the way out:

"Well, I find on my return everybody full of despair and predicting all sorts of evil. One member of the Cabinet tells me that there is a cabal of the Roosevelts' friends to force an issue between us and another that Pinchot has got to be dismissed. Still another tells me that the reformers don't believe that I intend to push any of the reform measures instituted by Roosevelt and that hell is to pay everywhere. The trouble is that they don't believe me when I say a thing once. The corporate influences did me the honor to say that as between Roosevelt and me they preferred me, but they were also equivocal in their compliments by admitting that I was not sincere. I think the next Congress will show my sincerity. I can't reiterate and reiterate, for when I have said a thing once I see no reason to repeat it; and what's more, I will not repeat my position. I have told the Cabinet that if I had done anything to be ashamed of or had said anything which might have brought on them all this gloom, then I would feel some regrets possibly. But I have done nothing that I would not do over again, and therefore I must feel that their troubles are either imaginary or else someone else is to blame."

This is Sunday, and I am spending the day in the house getting my things straight and writing to you. I went last night to dine at the Townsends', and this afternoon I had to put on my uniform and attend a celebration at some

Catholic church with the President. He asked me to come
to dinner to-night, and as I had declined and got him to
excuse me last night, I could not beg off again. I had
promised to dine with Ovey, but sent Charles, the White
House footman, to explain my predicament to them and
make my excuses.

With love, as ever,
ARCHIE.

CHAPTER XXII

REFORMING THE WHITE HOUSE'S DINNER CUSTOMS

Washington, D. C.
November 17, 1909.

DEAR CLARA:

Mrs. More has gone and Mrs. Tom Laughlin has come
in her place. I dined with them last evening and went to
the theater later. We had a rather jolly evening until the
last moment, when in getting out of the limousine I
mashed the President's fingers in the door and he yelled
out in pain. I know how it hurts, and I felt terribly sorry,
but it was really his fault, for while I got out of the wrong
side of the machine in order to help out the women, he
reached over and took hold of the encasement in order to
pull himself up, and so when I slammed the door it caught
his fingers. He said nothing, but hurried upstairs to put
his hand in hot water, and when I saw him this morning
he did not feel much the worse, though the ends of his
fingers on his right hand were swollen and blue and the
nails had already begun to discolor.

We had ridden in the afternoon and I took that opportunity to talk over matters for the coming social season.
It is going to be a short season and everything will have
to be crowded into a month and four days, as Lent comes

on the fourth of February. I made a number of recommendations which the President has accepted, and he offered as many more, so between us I think the matter of receptions and state functions will take on a very different character from any they have had in the past.

In the first place, I have got his consent to cut down the receptions more than half. Congressmen, for instance, who have always been invited to every reception, will only be invited to the congressional. The 388 correspondents, instead of being pandered to and invited to all receptions, will be scattered through the four, and no person save the head of the army and the navy and the Cabinet will be invited to all.

This suggestion gave to the President an opportunity to carry out a design which has been in his mind for some time. He has never liked the idea of giving a reception to the diplomats and then having the diplomats leave while a few choice people remained to have supper in the upper corridor of the White House. The Judiciary has always resented this system, while the receptions to Congress have sunk to such a low ebb that only a handful of Congressmen ever come to the reception given in their honor. The President, therefore, has decided that at the reception to the diplomats, the diplomats will be invited to remain to supper in the State Dining Room, and the Judiciary will be invited to remain for supper after their reception, the Army and Navy likewise at their reception, and Congressmen and Senators will be given special invitations to supper at the close of their receptions. When the President spoke to Mrs. Taft last evening at dinner, she was most pronounced in her objection to it. She did not object to cutting down the lists, but she protested against serving supper, both on the ground of economy and trouble.

Mrs. Taft is not going to take part in any of the social affairs this season. The doctors have told the President

that if she attempts to do so they will not be responsible
for her condition at the end of it. What they fear is a re-
lapse, and every effort is being made to keep her in com-
parative seclusion. She has improved greatly. I was never
so struck with her improvement as last night.

"Now, my dear, you have agreed to retire for this
season," he began, but she interrupted him to say:

"I don't care, I am going to have a voice in this household."

"You shall, my dear, but it just happens that when you
think the matter over you will agree with me."

"I will never agree with you if it is to feed all those
people."

"Well, I am the boss this season and I am going to have
those in whose honor we are entertaining remain for supper, and I know you well enough to predict that you will
see that the supper is a good one."

Mrs. Laughlin and I kept out of it, and later Mrs. Taft
said she still objected to the scheme, but that she would
have to yield. So to-day I began to cut the list, to rearrange the classes, and to order the cards for the season.
Poor Netherlands, who had charge of this work last year,
left all records in a most deplorably mixed state. There
is no one to take up the work, and so I have agreed to
manage it with Mr. Young, who has always had charge
of the dinners, as my assistant.

Most affectionately,
ARCHIBALD W. BUTT.

Mr. Taft in Moods Grave and Gay

[Washington, D. C.]
November 17, 1909.

I had a ride for an hour and a half with the President
this afternoon. We did not start out until after five o'clock,

and it was dark at a quarter to six. The President, seeing the crescent, with Venus very bright and very near to it, asked me if I remembered when we had last seen it. I could not tell him, and he then said:

"Why, at Corpus Christi. We were on the porch at Charlie's, and the star was hanging just as it is now."

We rode on for a few minutes in silence and then he said:

"When one looks at Nature, it is not hard to accept the faith of our fathers, is it? There is so much that is infinite around us that a personal creator is not difficult to accept. But the greatest argument for a God is law—law that works more accurately than any which can be devised by man; in fact, we only mar law and the logic of law. It is too unerring to be chance; it works up or it works downward; there is no stagnation, no cessation.

"Theodore and I used to discuss these matters a great deal, and he and I differed very little, if indeed we differed at all. He was as good a Unitarian as I, and had I been born in another church I would have abided by its tenets just as he has by those of the Dutch Reform. He believes in churches and church organization, and so do I. I think I shall always remember him with the greatest pleasure in those conversations in which we discussed the infinities. We often differed in our premises, but usually we got together in our results."

We rode most of the way in silence, but just before we came in he began laughing and explained by asking me what I thought was the funniest incident of the trip. I told him the time when he was making a speech in the open air in Birmingham and someone called out: "We love you, Bill," and when he asked what was said, several voices called out: "We love you, Bill." And the quick response he made when he called back:

"It might have been right to dissemble your love, but why did you kick me downstairs?"

"It is strange that the two funniest incidents should have happened at Birmingham, then, for I think the funniest incident was that when Governor Comer suggested that I send him as minister to China and the uproarious applause with which the suggestion was received by the people of Alabama. I never saw a more comical situation than the moment when he realized that the crowd were laughing at him instead of with him," and the President went into peals of laughter again over the memory.

November 18, 1909.

We leave this afternoon for Norfolk, where we are to attend an oyster bake and do other things of a tiresome and wearisome nature. I spent most of the morning dictating plans for the receptions for the winter in accord with the wishes expressed by the President the other night. I have drawn up a sort of protocol—covering all changes, and they are very sweeping—which he is to take up with Mrs. Taft on the boat to-night. If he agrees to all I have set down, there will be a revision of the social list which will cause as much consternation in Washington as the revision of the tariff did throughout the country.

The President has a very clear idea of how things ought to be done and is willing to lend his help to popularize entertainments at the White House. The changes proposed will not be popular with the mob which has been accustomed to assault the White House at the affairs, but it will be popular with people in whose honor the entertainments are given and those who will be included in them.

I will not return until some time Sunday; in the meantime I leave Aunt Kitty here in the care of Palmer and Synington. Mrs. Taft is going with us, but she will not participate in any of the festivities, but will remain on board with the doctor.

Sunday, November 21, 1909.

Before leaving, Chandler Hale came over to the White House to present the new Belgian minister, who read his address to the President in English. I was standing immediately behind the President when I saw him suddenly begin to feel in his pockets and finally to look hopelessly at me.

I knew at once that he had forgotten his reply, prepared so carefully by poor old Adee. I asked the usher, but he said the reply had not been sent to him; that they were always given the President as he left the office for lunch. I saw it was a hopeless quest I was on, so I went to the Blue Room again and found the President making an extempore reply, filling in time by talking about trade relations with Belgium. At the conclusion he laughed and told the new minister that he had left his formal address somewhere, but that he would send it to him later. The minister replied that he was fortunate then, as he would have had two addresses instead of one.

After the Belgian had left, Dr. Wu, the Chinese minister, called to present the Baron Liang, an uncle of the present Emperor and a brother-in-law to the Regent. We were to leave at four, but I feared we would never get away, for when the President and Dr. Wu get together and begin to discuss the East there is no telling when they will stop. The captain telephoned up that we ought to leave on time as the tide was very low, but one can't hurry the President. The baron talked no English and simply grinned at the President. He cannot be of much importance, for the minister did not even take the trouble to interpret for him half the time and never pretended to tell him the complimentary things the President said of him or his people.

The conversation was carried on entirely between the President and the minister, and both laughed uproariously over their jokes. I felt sorry for the little baron, who was left out of the conversation entirely. The President said to the minister, at the close of the conversation:

"Doctor, I want you to make it known to your government that it can trust us implicitly, for we do not want any of your territory. We only want your trade"—and as he said this he gave the minister a poke in the side, and they both laughed as if they were in perfect accord. "You can't grow too independent or too strong for us. I only wanted to get a share of that loan in order that we might be able to have our say in the councils of other nations when matters concerning China were being discussed. It was of greater value to your country than it was to us for the United States to have an interest in the loan."

As the old minister left, the President said:

"I think Wu a great old villain, but I like to talk to him. He is the wittiest Chinaman I have ever met and he thinks he is being advanced in Western civilization when he cultivates the art of lying."

We took a special train at noon for Cape Henry, where some eight hundred people had gathered at the Casino to give an oyster roast in honor of the President. On the train with us was Andrew Carnegie and a friend of his, Sir Horace Plunkett. Mr. Carnegie is more shriveled up than ever, but he is very humorous and at times witty. The President says like all wily Scotchmen he is funniest when he does not mean to be. He loves to talk about giving his money away, and amused and interested the President throughout the ride by giving him some of the plans he had for making himself poor. One thing which he said especially caught the attention of the President. He told the President that he really had no sense of ownership and always thought of all this money as belonging to someone else. The President repeated this to young Rockefeller, the one who married the daughter of Senator Aldrich, and he said:

"I should hate to test the truth of that statement by trying to make a run on his bonded securities."

The oyster roast was fine, the oysters the largest I have ever seen. The President ate a dozen of the raw and I do not know how many of the roasted. He said it was the first time he really enjoyed the flavor of an oyster. But the luncheon was a mob. One could not hear one's self speak. Everyone advised the President not to attempt to speak, but when Representative Moore offered a toast in a voice which could not be heard two feet away, the President mounted on a chair, a very rickety one at that, and made a very happy after-luncheon address.

I could but wonder what thoughts were going through the British head of Sir Horace and if he was able to detect the deep love and reverence for the President over the noisy demonstration. The President had Carnegie and a party of friends in his car on the way back to Norfolk, but he fell asleep just after the train pulled out from the station and said he never heard one of the jokes which were told for his benefit on the way back.

We dined at the home of Fergus Reid, a rich cotton factor, but a scion of an old Virginia house, at eight, where we met Dr. and Mrs. Eliot of Cambridge, a very beautiful woman by the name of Mrs. Englis, of Baltimore, and a number of other local society people. It was a good dinner, though one could see it had been prepared by a caterer, for the terrapin was served in these modern bird-nest effects, and each course smacked of the high-class restaurant. What a mistake for people not to have their dinners served by their own cooks and in their own kitchens! Old diners like the President and I can detect a caterer's dinner by the way the caviar is placed on the toast.

November 23, 1909.

We had rather an interesting afternoon at the White House. The President did not leave his office until after two o'clock and he had an engagement with the Austro-Hungarian ambassador at two-fifteen and another with the French ambassador at two-thirty. Baron Hengelmüller appeared promptly on time, and I ushered him into the Green Room. The President had not left the lunch table when the French ambassador arrived, and I showed him into the Red Room. Senator Borah and a Mr. Cobb of Idaho came to lunch with the President, and so Mrs. Taft decided to have her lunch alone in the breakfast room. At two-thirty I told the President that the Austrian ambassador was waiting and had been waiting and seemed to be fretting.

"Let him wait," said the President. "A man with the name of Hengelmüller should not want me to leave my lunch."

So I pranced up and down the hall hoping to keep the old Austrian entertained by my martial tread. Ten minutes more, and I saw the old man peer out of the Green Room and beckon to me. I went in and found him in a rage. Diplomatic to the last, he said in his most foreign manner:

"I must apologize for mistaking the hour, but I understood that two-fifteen was the time set for me to pay my respects to the President. I am so sorry I have mistaken the hour."

I replied most calmly that he had not mistaken the hour, but the President was late himself and was detained at the Cabinet meeting. He looked his rage at me, for he knew I was lying and I knew he knew it, for the President's laughter in the State Dining Room could be heard even then in the Green Room. But I bowed profoundly and called him "Your Excellency," and then sought Jusserand in the Red Room. I told him he would have to wait and then whispered to him that the Austrian was waiting and had been waiting for over a half hour, which seemed to amuse the Frenchman very much.

"I do not mind waiting. I like to wait when I can recline on the red lounge."

I told him to lie on it; that I would wake him if he was asleep. Taking me at my word, he half lay down and put his head among the pillows.

In ten minutes Hoover, the usher, came rushing to me, saying that the President had left the dining room and had entered the Red Room by the side door, and was even then with the French ambassador. As I entered, the President was laughing at the contretemps and was preparing to sit down with the French ambassador, who, wily little cuss that he was, was for beguiling him into doing it too, to get ahead of the Austrian. I insisted upon the President's seeing Hengelmüller first and he yielded. The President dismissed his other guests and, as he entered the corridor with me, said he had found Jusserand fast asleep when he entered. As I entered the Green Room the Austrian was fairly foaming at the mouth, but he swallowed his spleen to enter the room with both hands extended, smiling as if he were the most content diplomat in existence.

Of course, Hengelmüller was right to be angry. It is wrong to keep an ambassador waiting. The whole theory of his rank is opposed to it, but as I have remarked before, you cannot hurry this President of ours. President Roosevelt was accustomed to leave the lunch table on such occasions, rush through the audience, and finish his lunch. But President Taft keeps them waiting, and, moreover, does not mind it in the least.

We rode later in the afternoon and did not get in until late. He told me, apropos to being late always, that it was his nature and he could not help it. He said that the press was urging him to finish his message so that it could be sent all over the country by mail, but he was not going to do it, and the press would have to send it by wire.

"Roosevelt," he said, "could always keep ahead of his work, but I cannot do it and I know it is a grievous fault, but it is too late to remedy it. The country must take me as it found me. Wasn't it your mother who had a servant girl who said it was no use for her to try to hurry that she was a 'Sunday chile' and no 'Sunday chile' could hurry? I don't think I am a Sunday child, but I ought to have been; then I would have had an excuse for always being late."

Mrs. Roosevelt will arrive from Europe to-day. Remembering this and seeing one lonely little bud on the trailing rambler on the south steps of the White House, I picked it and slipped it into my pocket. I enclosed it in a short note of welcome home to her, thinking she would appreciate it, for I think she was fonder of this part of the White House than any other, and she always looked forward to the first flowers on this vine and was sorry when the last had gone.

⟩ Alice Longworth came in town yesterday for a day and left at night for New York to meet her mother. No one knew she was here until a fire broke out on H Street almost opposite the Metropolitan Club, and at its height Alice was seen approaching. A cheer went up at the sight of her and she held a regular reception.

"What is more natural than that I should make my first appearance at a fire?" she laughed.

Dinner invitations are pouring in, and it keeps one busy declining them. I have accepted one at the Italian Embassy and the Walshes', the Clovers', and the Boardmans'. One has to pick and choose these latter days in Washington, for if you attempt to accept every one that comes you will be swamped in a week.

CHAPTER XXIII

THE SUPREME COURT AND STANDARD OIL

Thursday, November 25 [1909]
Thanksgiving Day.

We went to St. Patrick's Church to-day, walked for two hours in the afternoon, and, while the President had a quiet family dinner at home, I went to the Italian Embassy to dine to meet a lot of young officers from the ship *Etruria*, which has anchored off the War College.

The President has added walking to his various forms of exercise. From now on I presume it will be a semi-weekly occurrence. Reminds me somewhat of the old days when I would go into President Roosevelt's office and ask if he had any orders for the day. If the day was wet and drizzly, I could invariably expect the reply:

"Archie, you might get into the hobnails."

Yesterday the President had a very trying day; one engagement after another kept him confined to the office almost without a break until six o'clock. I was on hand with the horses at four o'clock. At half-past five he sent me word to send the horses away, but for me to remain, as he might be able to walk. At six he came out of his office and said:

"I'll be damned if I am not getting tired of this. It seems to be the profession of a President simply to hear other people talk. Come, let's take a walk."

We started around the circle back of the White House, intending to walk around it five times, but the first proved so monotonous that when he saw the lights down Pennsylvania Avenue, he said:

"I have not been on F Street or Pennsylvania Avenue since I was President. Let's take a try at it."

We crossed by the Treasury and walked seven blocks without the President's being recognized. This, too, when I was in uniform with riding boots! Lots of people glanced at me, but their eyes got no further, thinking I was one of the soldiers from the barracks. He seemed to enjoy it hugely. In fact he said he felt like a schoolboy playing hookey. We walked down as far as Seventh Street and then turned to come home. On our way back he was recognized several times, but no one spoke to him. Whitehead, one of the correspondents, walking rapidly, was about to pass him when the President reached out, took him by the arm and said:

"See here, not being recognized for a time was some fun, but Archie and I are getting lonely."

I believe he is the first President since Harrison to walk on Pennsylvania Avenue, or so the papers stated the next day. When Wilkie, the chief of the Secret Service Bureau, heard he was on the streets alone, he telephoned to his two representatives telling them never to let it happen again.

While in Norfolk I read the telegram to the President announcing the decision of the Supreme Court in the Standard Oil case. His only remark was:

"Bully for that!"

But since he has heard something of the effects of that decision he is not so sure that it will not be a boomerang. In fact he told the Attorney General yesterday that unless there was some remediable legislation the whole commercial structure of the country as now existing would go to pieces.

"I want to read the business interests of this country a lecture, but it should have some warning before the law becomes too drastic. It should not be taken by surprise."

Of course Mr. Roosevelt's answer to this would be that when the Anti-Sherman Law was passed the warning was given and nothing would have delighted him more than taking evil-doers, as he terms all trusts, by surprise. I hope for his own good the President is not going to take a backward step in this matter, for it would do more than anything else could to bring about a separation from Mr. Roosevelt. If he believes that any injustice is being done any interests, the fear of a split here or of disapproval anywhere will not cause him to halt, I will say this for him: he is the fairest-minded man I have ever met, I believe.

When we got back to the office he insisted on all of us going to the White House to have a Thanksgiving drink. When we got in the Red Parlor, he ordered Scotch and soda for us and an orangeade for himself. The Attorney General said he would rather have a cup of tea if he could get one, and his suggestion was followed by all of us. We sat for nearly two hours, and I don't think I ever heard the President more candid or more interesting. He told the Attorney General that his defense of Aldrich had met with little approval anywhere.

"I may have made a political mistake in doing it, but I have the satisfaction of knowing that I said what I believed. The muckrakers think Aldrich has captured me, and I think I have captured Aldrich. The results will show which is right."

The Attorney General said: "Mr. President, I suppose you know the heaviest burden the administration has to carry?"

"You mean Cannon?" asked the President

"Yes, Cannon," said the Attorney General.

"I recognize this," said the President, "but I don't see how we can defeat him. Parsons is out against him, and some very hard things are going to be said when the next fight for the Speakership comes up, but I feel that Cannon will win out, and then I hope that his friends will get together and give him a dinner and a loving cup to commemorate his victory and that he will take that opportunity to say 'Nunc dimittis' and retire. I found in the West that he is getting to be too heavy a burden even for his friends to carry much longer."

As much as the Administration dislikes Cannon, it does not feel strong enough to defeat him; even this the Attorney General had to acknowledge.

The President made this pertinent statement:

"If I am defeated for the next nomination, I think it will be by Hughes. And I don't think he will allow his name to be used unless he really feels that I have no chance to win. I do not think Theodore Roosevelt will allow his name to come before the convention. I may be mistaken and many around me tell me I am, but nevertheless that is my firm conviction. He will have his own way of doing it, but I think you will find I am right in my judgment of the man. But I always think of Hughes as a President. I will have a chance to offer him a seat on the Supreme Bench. He will be inclined to accept, and he will waver and he will then consult his wife, and she, I think, will be the final influence which will cause him to decline it. But if he does not accept the Judiciary, I expect to see him President some day."

"He is the coldest man I have ever known," said Mr. Wickersham. "The politicians around him will know that he means nothing to them for the future and they will see that the other politicians of the country know this also."

[*Major Butt has omitted quotation marks at the beginning of the next paragraph, but the context indicates that he is quoting the President.*]

That may be true and I know it to be so, but one of the marvelous things about him is that he is strong enough to force the men who dislike him the most to stand by him. By far he is the strongest man before the people to-day except Roosevelt. I think his greatest fault is his failure to accord credit to anyone for what he may have done. This is a great weakness in any man. I think it was one of the strongest things about Roosevelt. He never tried to minimize what other people did and often exaggerated it. He did this for two reasons: first because his impulses were all generous; and secondly because he knew it was a fine political thing to do.

Good-night.
ARCHIBALD.

Alice Longworth's Varied Humors

[Washington, D.C.,]
December 5, 1909.

DEAR CLARA:

I have had an entire day to myself, the President being laid up with a severe cold, and when he has a cold it takes him days to recover from it. Mrs. Taft is inclined to laugh at him when he suffers from grippe or a cold, but I think it is a serious matter. His whole great frame seems to collapse. However, I took the day off and went to church with Aunt Kitty, much to her astonishment, and later called on some people with her who have entertained her since she has been visiting me. It is rather a difficult thing, entertaining anyone just now, for I never know when I am to have an evening or afternoon that I can call my own.

It is even more unsatisfactory for those who happen to have the misfortune to be visiting me than it is for me. I do not like to put my own engagements before those of the President, and yet not to do so occasionally means getting myself at times into some very embarrassing positions. Last Saturday night, for instance, I had no previous engagement and when I thought the coast clear I sent to the theater and got two tickets for my aunt and myself. At five minutes before eight the call came by phone from the White House to see if I could come there and play bridge. There was no one whom I could get to take my aunt, and when I looked up she wore such a woebegone expression of disappointment that I told the usher to say that he could not find me, that I had already left for the theater, and, the usher being a fellow Mason, I knew he was to be trusted not to betray me. But I felt remorseful the entire evening and I did not enjoy the play at all, and I fear that I communicated my feeling to Aunt Kitty. It was the second time only that I had put myself before the President's wishes; the other time being when I went to dinner at the Townsends' when he needed me at the White House.

I have been called to the telephone three times since I began this letter and each time have been invited to dinner, the last time to the Pattens'. I have declined six dinner invitations to-day, which is indicative only of the scarcity of men in Washington just at present. I make it a rule to decline all invitations and then later, if I feel like going, to telephone to the hostess that I can come if she still desires my presence. That sounds fearfully snobbish, doesn't it? But in reality these people take advantage of one by the way they rush invitations out a month ahead. And those who invite one over the phone never deserve anything better.

The season is so short this year that there is a perfect scramble to get certain of us who are considered in the select oyster class, and woe betide the innocent who accepts the first invitations which come in. Many may not be as frank as I am to you, but it is the man in Washington who thinks he confers the favor when he accepts an invitation. Of course, when one is climbing, one's mental attitude is somewhat different; but after having reached the top a contempt for all invitations makes one doubly valuable to a hostess. In my case, it is not scorn, contempt, or even indifference to the attentions of friends which causes me to assume this attitude, but merely a proper sense of proportions.

A man who takes himself seriously in this social business here at Washington is lost from the start. I do not flatter myself that it is any wonderful charm I possess which causes me to be inundated with invitations, but the fact that I am a man, presentable, well dressed, fairly entertaining in conversation, save when I am in a bad humor, and can always be pointed out to the assembly as the aide to the President. Yet when Alice Roosevelt and I had a row the other evening and she was blaming me for being late at a dinner and accused me of getting spoiled, telling me that after all I was only invited around because I was at the White House, I became furious and said that I had had the same attentions in Washington before even the Roosevelts came to Washington. Having made me perfectly furious, she then proceeded to laugh in my face and accused me of being not only spoiled, but childish as well.

Alice is really wonderful. When she is out of humor she will insult her best friend, and the next day be so penitent and charming as to make one feel the culprit. It is an art, I find, to insult people and then force the one insulted to apologize. She possesses it to perfection.

I told Bertie de Chambrun, the military attaché of the French Legation, and brother-in-law of Nick Longworth, that I had decided to have nothing more to do with Alice. We were playing golf, and he laid aside his club and went into hysterics, saying that he had made up his mind to do the same thing many times and that he as frequently changed his mind when she was ready for him to change it. I said no; that I intended to be polite, but that I would never go to her home again, nor would I ever invite her to any of my poker parties, at which she always wants to be present. He bet me six balls that I would be in her home before January the first. I wanted to make it a dozen, so certain was I that nothing could induce me to enter her house, but he feared that a dozen balls would be too great an inducement to cherish my resentment.

That next afternoon I met her in the Elkins' hall, as she was going in to see Katherine.

"Butt," she said in that hurried little manner of hers, "you are just the man I want to see. You must come to dinner Tuesday night. There will be no one but the Newlands, the Kemps, Katherine, Stumm, the Oveys, and you and I, and Nick."

I hurriedly told her I feared I had an engagement.

"Then break it," she said. "You must come; only our little crowd and, if you come the Howards will come and we'll have an old-time hectic night."

I still pleaded a partial engagement and said good-bye quickly, for I felt myself weakening. Later in the evening she called me up, and the next morning at the White House. The result is I am going, and she will be lovely for another two months, and then will come my turn to be angry with her again.

De Chambrun says it is all this which makes her so irresistible. The fact of the matter is she doesn't care a hang whom she insults for the reason that she knows her power to make friends again. The only person she cannot entirely placate is Mrs. Taft. The President is as much under her influence as any of the rest of us. He gets dreadfully put out with her at times and then comes around completely when she is nice to him. He was fearfully angry with her at one of the garden parties, when Mrs. More was receiving in the place of Mrs. Taft. Alice resented the fact that the President permitted Mrs. More to stand ahead of him and would not speak to her first, but waited until the crowd had passed and then came from the other direction. But the President got over it and quite forgave her.

She makes a mistake in not placating Mrs. Taft, as she

underrates her influence with the President. It was Mrs. Taft, evidently, who kept Nick from being sent to China as minister. I had not known that Nick was ambitious in this line; in fact, he told me once that he did not know of a single foreign appointment he would be willing to accept. But he evidently changed his mind, and on account of his wife, I imagine, for she loves the East and especially China. I did not learn of this from the President but from Mrs. Taft. She told me that Nick had asked to be sent to China and was willing to resign his seat to accept the mission, but that she simply would not have it, as she thought neither Nick nor Alice fitted for this post under the present conditions. I suppose the President put it on different grounds, but the real reason for his refusal was the opposition made to it by Mrs. Taft.

The President did not go out of the house to-day. He spent it in his study and most of the time with Senator Root, discussing the Anti-trust Law. With the exception possibly of Attorney General Wickersham, Senator Root is the closest adviser of the President. The President takes very few men into his confidence at all, or rather he has the appearance of taking all men into his confidence; but in reality he takes them in only so far as he will be able to use them for his own legislative ends. He is different with Root and Wickersham. He depends on them for advice and on their brains to formulate measures which will come within the law. Both are constructive types of statesmen, and the President never submits any proposition to Congress involving any constitutional or legal point without first submitting it to these two men. If it is approved by them, he feels pretty certain that it will hold water.

December 8, [1909].

I went with the President last night to the Red Cross reception at the Boardmans'. It is a bad precedent the

President is setting. He will find it a hard matter to accept one invitation and not another. Besides, he cannot stand it. He has promised to go to a reception at the Highlands Apartment House to-night, given by Representative Boutell. I have urged him not to go, for if he does he will have to go to others of a similar nature. However, he has his own system and it may be the very thing which will accrue to his advantage in the long run.

He is determined to do all he can to tie Congressmen to himself. He does not do this from a purely selfish motive, for he feels that the President should do what he can to uphold the position and dignity of Congressmen and their wives, and not to accept the attitude usually held by Chief Executives, namely, that of ignoring members of the House and Senate in social matters. He not only wants to have them at the White House on every occasion, but he evidently intends to show his attitude to others by going to their little entertainments. It is certainly a gracious thing to do, but it will be a great hardship. It has got to be the fashion to ignore the entertainments of members of the House and the Senators, save a few millionaire members, and it is to counteract this attitude of Washingtonians that he intends to attend their entertainments.

The list of those to be invited to the diplomatic reception was shown to the President this morning. By careful pruning we got the list down to eleven hundred. The President said it was so small he would add a few Congressmen, but only those whom he knew personally. He went over the list of Representatives himself and checked them after this fashion:

"Adams; that's old Adams of Georgia? He's a countryman, but I like him so we'll include him," and so on down the entire list.

When he got through, he had added one hundred and thirty-one members of the House with their families, and when he began with the Senate he checked all of them through the K's, and then said:

"Oh, invite all the Senators with the exception of Senator Davis of Arkansas. A man who accepts an invitation from me to dinner, and then refuses to come without sending an excuse, will not get another."

So the list has jumped to over seventeen hundred. We sent it to Mrs. Taft, and when she gets through it may be down to eleven hundred again. I have saved the list he marked, as the names represent those whom he regards as his personal friends in the House. It is going to cause some jealousy among those who are not invited, but it will bear the stamp of individuality, a thing which no state reception has borne for many many years past.

December 9, 1909.

The papers this morning announce that Judge Warrington may be appointed to the Supreme Bench in place of Justice Peckham, who died—which only indicates how near they get to the truth sometimes, for Judge Warrington is here in behalf of Judge Lurton of Tennessee, who is on the bench with him. The President told Judge Warrington he was going to appoint him, Judge Lurton, but not until he had heard some of the other interests which were to be presented in behalf of other candidates.

To-day I lunched with Campario, the naval attaché of the Italian Embassy. We had spaghetti cooked in the real Italian style. He is a fine fellow and is madly in love with Eleanor Terry, daughter of Admiral Terry.

My last letter was terrible. I read it over and I am still holding it, doubtful whether it were wise to send to you. It seemed to be full of such utter nonsense and it does not seem to reflect much credit on me personally. One would have to know me very well not to think it the letter of an arrant snob. But if these letters are of any value, they are so by reason of the truth which is apparent in them, whether it be hurtful or otherwise. I must not spare myself, and if I feel like a donkey, then let me write myself down one. I know I am not a snob, but if my actions are such as to make me appear to be one, then let the evidence show on the surface.

When my melancholy moods are on, they last long enough to counteract the few moments of purely personal and frivolous ones. I never make an ass of myself without knowing it, and I am conscious of resembling one in my last three letters to you. The mood reflected in them comes from cynicism, I think, rather than from sheer frivolity.

Another horseback ride by myself this afternoon, and later I am dining with dear Belle Hagner alone and will sit late into the night talking to her. She always brings me back to earth with a thud, and when I feel the world getting too much to my liking, a good wholesome hour spent with her has the same steadying power as an hour with Wordsworth. She is just as wholesome and not quite as prosy.

December 12, 1909.

The President attended the Gridiron dinner last night, Carpenter and I going with him. I was invited by a committee from the club and therefore felt certain that I would be what the name implies, roasted. The President expected me to be also, and going down in the motor he said as much and added:

"I am getting very tired myself of these dinners, and if they are at all rough with me this evening it shall be the last one I will attend. It is an undignified thing to do at the best, and yet it is very difficult not to accept, as all other Presidents of late years seem to have made it a custom to do so. I presume that both you and Carpenter will come in for a fair amount of roasting."

The dinner proved to be rather a tame one, on the whole. There were the usual stunts, such as finding the lost mince pie, in which Roosevelt was discovered when it was cut; a rather good skit on the suffragettes, and another in which a medium delivered messages from the spiritual world to guests at the table. The club sang two verses, one to the Speaker and one to me. The one to me was most complimentary and was written by Commissioner West. The refrain was: "Archie's in the White House now." Of course, it is something, as one of the members said, to be mentioned by the Gridiron at all, but to be mentioned in a complimentary fashion was almost unprecedented. I sat next to the Speaker, and we had rather a jolly time together. We were so placed as to occupy conspicuous positions when the songs dedicated to us were sung.

The Speaker and I had quite a discussion as to Mr. Roosevelt. He expressed great admiration for the ex-President, but said:

"Roosevelt was a man of transcendent genius, but if he had been followed by another President, a counterpart of himself, one as forceful and as daring, the system of free government would have ceased to exist in the country. I remember when the anthracite coal strike was on and he brought about a compromise. It was a great achievement, and I told him so, and then I asked him what would have happened if the miners and railroad operatives had refused to compromise. He looked at me for a few minutes and answered, 'I would have seized the mines and the roads and would have given the freezing people coal, and Congress could have impeached and be damned.' And he meant it, too. He was one of the few men I have ever met of whom I was afraid. He never guessed how afraid I was of him, and I took particular pains not to let him know."

ARCHIBALD.

CHAPTER XXIV

Mr. Taft Visits the Bowery

[New York]
Wednesday,

We did not get back from New Haven until after eleven
o'clock. After dinner we went to Carnegie Hall, where the
Methodists were holding their jubilee. The President made
a speech.

After this meeting the President went to the Bowery
where he made a speech to about five hundred of the un-
employed who had gathered there for a midnight meal.
I enjoyed this expedition, for it was flavored with dramatic
coloring. In the first place, the night was frightful, high
winds and sheets of water, so that it even came through
the roofing of the landaulet. We had let no one know we
were coming, but at nine I sent word to the mission, which
is run and managed by a converted Hebrew, that the
President would visit the place. Those who were inside
were told that if they remained they would see the President, so the audience was not a picked one as I feared it
would be, but was made up of the tramps and the unem-
ployed who had gone there to get a supper. Services are
held there every night, but it is not necessary to attend
them to get a warm place to sit out of the cold and to get
something warm in the stomach.

The President entered the platform from the rear
through an alley, and his entrance was the occasion for a
great ovation. The superintendent seemed to have perfect
control of the men, and he catechized them as to who the
President was, for what he stood, and made them respond
to each question. Then he introduced the President, who
made as fine a speech to the hoboes as he had made a poor

one to their more prosperous brothers at Carnegie Hall.

I have often been struck by the humanity of the President, but it seemed more exemplified here than I had ever seen it before. The superintendent had said that it was a long step from the White House to the Bowery, and that it was a great thing for the President to step from such an exalted place to one of the lowest and most despised on earth. This superintendent did not mince words when talking to these people, and it seemed to me that he had put the President at a disadvantage in dwelling on the difference in positions and pointing to the contrasts existing between the social strata each represented. But the President has a wonderful way of probing into hearts, and he went right at the operation. He told them there was not quite the chasm between them that the superintendent might make them believe; that they must not think of their fellow citizens as greedy oppressors, for their hearts were open to help the suffering.

"If there is one thought I would convey to you," he said to them, "it would be to hope on, forget the difficulties, the disasters of the past, and go ahead with the thought of the future and the big things it may have in store for you."

It was simply a message of hope, but their faces brightened and there was many a wet eye before he finished. I was glad he went there, and I have thought better of John Wesley Hill for taking him. I am afraid that John Wesley was thinking more of the political effect than he was of the good results to be obtained for the cause of charity, but then God uses queer means to bring about his results at times. I don't think the President saw or cared for the political side of it, and the dramatic feature of his visit to the Bowery made no appeal to him. He was simply moved by the message begging him to come and bring some cheer at the Christmas time to the outcasts of the Bowery.

Another nice thing the President did was to have the former secretary of the President, Mr. Loeb, at the dinner. Mrs. Loeb was there also, and it was so nice to see them. Mr. Loeb and I sat next to each other and talked as if it might be our last chance this side of the grave. I told him what Speaker Cannon had said to me the other night at the Gridiron dinner, regarding President Roosevelt and the coal strike. He denied it and said that President Roosevelt never said any such thing; that he believed Cannon was making up the conversation out of the whole cloth.

ARCHIBALD.

Taft Says He Is Not "Anti-Roosevelt"

[Washington]
December 19, 1909.

DEAR CLARA:

The President was very despondent coming back from New York. He went to bed immediately on arriving at the car and did not rise until we reached Baltimore. I never saw three brothers more devoted than these three Taft men.

This afternoon General Edwards and I walked with the President from three until six o'clock. The conversation was rather rambling and uninteresting. He is still worried over the District commissioners. He says there is some doubt about Hemphill's being a citizen of Washington, and there is quite a protest against Merriam. Still Merriam has some strong backers and may overcome the President's present disinclination. He says he hopes Congress will investigate the charges against Secretary Ballinger. He thinks it will then be shown just how lenient he has been toward Pinchot.

"Of course, Roosevelt would have come back at those preferring the charges and would by now have them on the run, but I cannot do things that way. I will let them go on, and by and by the people will see who is right and who is wrong. There is no use trying to be William Howard Taft with Roosevelt's ways."

He then said: "I am not criticizing Roosevelt, but simply saying our ways are different. I would not have had him attempt to be calm and dispassionate, for he would have failed, whereas he was a brilliant success in his own way. But I get rather tired hearing from his friends that I am not carrying out his policies, and when I ask for one instance they cannot name one.

"I have decided to make Wood chief of staff simply because I know that Roosevelt was anxious to have it done. With Loeb at the head of the customs in New York and Meyer at the head of the navy, and with Wood at the head of the army, I do not see that I am open to the charge that I am anti-Roosevelt. I have got to have a clear understanding with Wood, however, for I am inclined to think that, coming after Bell especially, he will have plans of such magnitude as to be unable to accomplish anything. Already he is talking of shaping the American army after the German. Such a scheme is not practical and is un-American. I want him to work with what he finds, improve that, and not attempt too radical a change.

With love,
ARCHIE.

"I Will Never Catch up with My Work"

[Washington]
December 22, 1909.

DEAR CLARA:

There is a good deal of fault finding on the part of Congressmen that they are kept waiting for hours and then fail to see the President, but he cannot be hurried, and if he permitted himself to be, they would still be clamoring for more of his time. He will sit and discuss some subject with a man for fifteen minutes when the visitor does not deserve five seconds. The President takes all men seriously until it is too late, and so they wear him out and each other too.

When President Roosevelt said he would walk at three he would not have allowed the recording angel to stop him, but the men are different and their ways are different, and of the two methods pursued one hardly knows which to admire most. President Roosevelt seized his visitor by the hand, wrung it hard, and sent him flying out of the nearest door; and strange to say, the visitor, as a rule, thought he had left of his own accord. President Taft presumes that each man is as serious as himself. When he makes an engagement with a Representative, for instance, he listens to all he has to say. Those waiting on the outside rage, but when they are admitted they do the same thing, and so it goes on. He said this afternoon:

"Archie, it seems to me I will never catch up with my work. Just when I think I will catch up, something like this requiem mass for Leopold to-morrow comes up, and everything is thrown behind again."

I thought to encourage him by saying: "Mr. President, President Roosevelt was here for seven years, and he figured out that when he left he was still two years behind with his work."

But it did not seem to relieve his mind, for he said:

"But there is so much to be done, and so little time to do it in, I sometimes feel very discouraged."

The reception of the new Chinese minister yesterday was quite impressive. He and the old minister, Dr. Wu, called at the same time and each had his own suite with him. It was the first time since the death of the Emperor and the Dowager Empress that the Chinese had appeared in full court raiment. They were as gorgeous as flamingoes. The reception was very interesting to me, for it was the first time we had had an opportunity to put into practice the new system adopted by the State Department for a full-fledged legation.

The two ministers were shown into the Green Room and the President entered the Blue Room. I went to the Green Room for the old minister, passing two junior aides standing at attention at the door leading into the corridor. After he read his letters of recall and the President responded, I made a sign to the juniors and they conducted the incoming minister with the Secretary of State into the Blue Room. The new minister had asked for the old to remain while he presented his credentials, as he spoke no English. It was a most solemn performance. He mumbled along in Chinese for five minutes, and the President could hardly refrain from smiling as he caught the eye of the outgoing minister. Dr. Wu did not exactly wink, but he looked a deprecating sort of look and practically said:

"What do you think of my successor?"

After he had finished, the secretaries were escorted in, and the introduction was made in Chinese. Dr. Wu did not help his successor out at all, and it was evident that he enjoyed the awkwardness of the situation.

On Friday the new Japanese ambassador is to be received, and it will require both the senior aides and the army and navy and six junior aides. The State Department gets the credit for formulating these protocols, as they might be called, but they were worked out in my own Machiavellian brain and so arranged that Crosby is almost entirely eliminated, and he does not even enter the room with the ambassador. His duties were purely perfunctory and he had enough to do to annoy me.

I fear I am one of those people with a disposition which would not brook a rival. I must either be in full charge or else let someone else take charge. President Roosevelt largely centered everything about the White House in

my hands. Well, it either had to continue or else I would
not have remained. The rank of captain was pretty far
down the line to assume as much as I wanted, but I feel
that I have succeeded and I also feel sure that the entire
service at the White House is for the first time on a dignified and decent plane. I have had the State Department
designate me by name everywhere in the orders for the
reception of ministers and ambassadors as "Chief Aide,"
and I have had the President to approve the documents,
so that when Crosby protested against the program, which
seemed to eliminate him as a factor, the Secretary of State
merely pointed to the President's approval, and that ended
it. But after I leave there will never be any question again
as to authority or precedence, for the Chief Aide at the
White House will be what I have made the post to be.
It was always the most conspicuous place near the President, but it never carried with it any written authority
until I wrote it in myself.

The next step is to abolish the other place entirely and
have the President's aide given extra rank and pay. That
will hardly come in my time; but whenever I leave I shall
have it so arranged that the step will be easily taken. I
am sure I could have Congress do it now, but I do not
want to use the influence I have got to benefit myself
pecuniarily.

With love,
ARCHIE.

CHAPTER XXV

THE PRESIDENT GOES CHRISTMAS SHOPPING

[Washington, D. C.]
Christmas morning, 1909.

It is a white Christmas in Washington. The skies were
clear last night when we went to bed, and this morning the

ground was covered with snow and the flakes are still tumbling one over the other in their haste to reach the earth. I am remaining in the house all day and will go out this evening to dine at the White House. So the day at least promises to be peaceful. As long as the absence of my mother continues to be the most notable event of the day to me, it can never be a happy festival to me. But I love to remain in the house with her things around me and spend the hours thinking of her and of our lives spent so much together.

My friends have remembered me generously to-day, but nothing has given me as much pleasure as the books sent to me by the President. They were just what I wanted, but that is not surprising when I tell you that I picked them out myself. We went on a shopping tour together yesterday afternoon, and it was a regular lark.

As Count Moltke left, the President said: "Now, how long will it take you to get out of that uniform?"

I said ten minutes, as I had anticipated his wish and had sent my civilian clothes to the White House. We did not even avoid the crowd by going back of the Treasury, but went full sails down Fifteenth Street to Pennsylvania Avenue. The streets were crowded. Very few people noticed the President, and those who did merely raised their hats and said "Merry Christmas" in passing. At the Willard we ran head on into four convivial spirits emerging from the cellar bar of that hotel. It was a nice, merry-looking party, but they were very much abashed when they saw the President. They were effusive in their apologies, and as he raised his hat to them and hurled his "Merry, Merry Christmas" to them, they righted, and with a "Merry Christmas, Missure President," passed on for the next saloon, laughing uproariously.

It was quite the thing in my time, not so very far away, to make a tour of the Avenue and take a drink in each bar, going down one side and repeating the program coming up the other. I recognized the spirit of those we had met and rather longed to be one of them. I knew they were having a good time of it.

We went in at Galt's and the President called for some traveling bags. There was only one and the price was a hundred dollars. I insisted that it was too heavy and too costly, and suggested, much to the chagrin of the salesman, going to Becker's on F Street, where they kept a larger supply. We went out Eleventh Street and then up F. It was the first time he had been on F Street since his inauguration and he enjoyed every minute of it. He said he felt like running.

At Becker's we found the bags to be costly, but finally the President saw one for seventy-five dollars which he liked very much. He said he wanted two and he would get this one and the other one at Galt's. I still persisted that it was too much to pay and finally he said:

"You go to the devil, Archie. This or the other one is for you; now do you like it or not?"

I was really abashed, for it never entered into my head that he was going to give me a present, so I said:

"Mr. President, I don't want you to give me anything but what you have already given me, your confidence and good will."

"Do you like this bag or not, that is what I want to know?" he said.

"Of course I like it, sir."

"Do you like it better than anything else you see?"

"Yes, sir," I answered again.

"Do you like it better than anything you don't see?"

I hesitated and finally said: "Mr. President, you are not to be dissuaded from giving me something?"

"I am not," he said. "Now out with it."

"Well, then if you are determined to give me something,

I would rather have some memoirs down at Brentano's than anything else."

"Good," he said, laughing. "Down to Brentano's we go." And we left the store, the salesman looking broken-hearted.

Brentano's was crowded, but we edged our way in and I found at last Mr. Norman, the manager, waiting on someone else. I whispered to him to come and wait on the President. He asked what he could do with the other customer.

"Drop him and let him stand," I said, and we left the customer, a well-dressed, nice-looking man, evidently a gentleman, perfectly bewildered. We made our way to the shelves where the memoirs were to be found, and as we passed through the crowd one man spoke to the President and reached out his hand. I simply gave him a punch in the stomach and hissed "Fool!" to him under my breath. The President asked me after we left what I had done to him.

"Oh, I only whispered to him not to begin to shake hands, that it would start the whole store doing it."

I had been longing for the *Memoirs* of Cellini and had told Mr. Norman laughingly a few days before that if anyone came in and seemed doubtful what Captain Butt would like, to suggest Cellini and the *Life* of Whistler. So I promptly called for Cellini and when the President got them he wrote in the first volume, "To Captain Butt with the affection of William H. Taft," and then asked me what else I wanted. I said nothing and he looked at Mr. Norman, who said:

"Yes, he does, Mr. President," and then repeated my conversation of the day or two before. So he called for Whistler and in the first volume wrote: "With the affectionate regards of William H. Taft," and then, taking out one of his cards, which I had provided for him when we started out, he wrote on it: "To Captain Archibald W. Butt, with a merry Christmas from a companion of his many hours," and told the manager to put the card with the package and send it to my house.

I suggested to him to get a book for Clarence Edwards, and at Norman's suggestion he chose *A Beau Sabreur*, and I took it to Mrs. Edwards last evening when I went there to dinner. The general has gone to Porto Rico, but I hung it on the tree and later when it was opened it greatly pleased Bessie, who took much pride in showing it to the others who were invited in.

We went back to Galt's, where the President bought a silver-mounted pin-cushion for Mr. Winthrop and some silver knives for the secret service men. By this time it seemed that everybody was cognizant that the President was out shopping, for he was recognized on all sides. No one attempted to interfere with his personal liberty, and yet everyone who saw him wished him a Merry Christmas. It was really quite exhilarating and joyous. He had his fun, too. Whenever he would make a purchase he would say, "Please charge that to me," and would ask: "Do you know who I am?" or "Is my credit good?" and when he wanted something sent to the White House he would say, "Send that to me," and add: "Do you know my address?" or "Do you know where I live?"

The papers this morning make a lot out of the fact that the President went shopping, and while the accounts fill much space they have none of the facts, but much conversation which they make up and which I must say I have read with interest, even knowing that none of it is correctly quoted. I think it speaks very well for the storekeepers that they did not give the list of purchases, which they might have done with impunity.

Good-bye. God bless you all.

ARCHIBALD.

Anxious to Avoid Rupture with T. R.

[Washington, D. C.]
December 31, 1909.

This will be the last letter to you dated 1909. On the whole, the year has been a fairly successful one for me. Judging from the standpoint of the world, I suppose I have been successful, if success consists in being constantly in the public eye and envied by many men and sought after by as many women. From the standpoint of my mother it has not been successful, for after all I have not done much which is lasting unless it be in these letters to you, and I have begun to doubt seriously whether they would be of much interest to anyone save you and me, and possibly to some old historian a hundred years hence who wants to learn how the people at the White House ate, slept, and in what manner they conducted themselves.

We left Washington on the morning of the twenty-ninth, in the coldest weather we have had here for many years, to attend the wedding of the President's niece in New York. The roads had just been opened, but the trains were still running far behind schedule time.

The President put in all his time on the train working on his special messages which he is going to send to Congress as soon as it reassembles after the holidays. His first one deals with the Anti-trust Law and Interstate Commerce Commission, and the second will have to do with the conservation of natural resources. I think the President begins to feel that all this talk about his failure to carry out the Roosevelt policies in the matter of conservation is the result of a well-organized conspiracy to injure him throughout the West. He does not believe that President Roosevelt will endorse such a thing, but the fact that Pinchot seems to be behind most of it gives the

President great concern, for there is no doubt of the devotion of President Roosevelt to Pinchot and his belief in him. However, the President is going to try to circumvent them by putting on the statute books laws which will show better than anything else his desire to conserve the resources of the country.

I find that the President draws a long bow and shoots far. He does little to counteract such moves at the time they are being made, but he hopes to be able to show the malice of their motives at the crucial time. Mr. Charlie Taft said to him after the wedding:

"Will, I am getting tired of this Forestry Bureau business, and I don't know but it would be a good thing to let Pinchot out!"

"I am beginning to think that is just what he wants to force me to do, and I will not do it," said the President. "If the whole contention is the result of some sort of conspiracy, Pinchot's dismissal would only bring about what they are trying to do, an open rupture between Roosevelt and myself, and I am determined if such a rupture is ever to be brought about that it shall not be through any action of mine. Theodore may not approve of all I have done and I don't expect him to do so, but I shall try not to do anything which he might regard as a challenge to him. No, Charlie, I am going to give Pinchot as much rope as he wants, and I think you will find that he will hang himself."

His brothers are the same conservative type as he, and they approve of his course. Politically they are not as sagacious as he. For instance, just after we reached the house in the morning, Henry Taft said to his brother that Senator Aldrich was in the city and was most anxious to see the President.

"Tell him to come here," said the President.

"That is not what he wants," said Mr. Taft. "He is at the home of J. Pierpont Morgan, and they are having a conference there, and they want you to come to it if it be possible."

The President sat thinking for a few minutes, and before he spoke his brother said again:

"You have got plenty of time to go before the wedding, or I can send you down in the motor after the wedding if you prefer."

The President said: "Telephone Aldrich that if Morgan wants to see me he can come to Washington. Aldrich ought to know that what he suggests is impossible. There is only one place where men like Morgan can see me, Harry, and that is in Washington."

As a sequel to this conversation, when we returned to Washington this morning at eight o'clock Morgan was waiting for the President in the Red Room. He evidently did not want the interview to become known, for he came at seven in the morning, the hour the President was supposed to arrive, and nothing of it got into the papers. I do not know the purport of the interview, but I imagine it was of some importance to Morgan and the money world, else he would never have got out of his bed at that hour. The President is not afraid to discuss matters with a man like Morgan just because he is rich, and he has a good deal of respect for the banker also, and great faith in his judgment.

The fact which strikes me as inauspicious is that Senator Aldrich was back of the interview. I feel that the Rhode Islander is the most sinister influence around the President. The President thinks he has captured Aldrich and can make him do anything he wants of him, but I fear it is the case of the wolf in sheep's clothing.

To-night I am going to a dinner at the Larz Andersons' and later dance the cotillion with Miss Ovey. The Clomans are here, and I am having some friends to meet them at an eggnog at my house at five on the first of January. I made out my list before going to New York and had the invitations written at the White House and sent out yesterday. I wanted to have not more than fifty persons, but to my horror I learned this morning that there were over two hundred on my list. Fortunately my house is large, but unfortunately my pocketbook is small. However, I will wager that it is a great go. My friends embrace both the Bowery and the Four Hundred, so it will be a mixture.

Good-bye.

ARCHIE.

Captain Butt Gives an Eggnog Party

[Washington, D. C.]
January 2, 1910.

DEAR CLARA:

Fortunately it is Sunday. There ought to be a law making the New Year begin on Saturday, which would always provide a Sunday for rest. The reception at the White House was a success, and the reception at my house was even a greater one. That at the White House was an average size, though I had expected it to be much larger. About five thousand five hundred passed in line, but to have been equal to that held by President Roosevelt after his inauguration it should have been three thousand more. We started it promptly, and it was over by half-past two. Mrs. Taft received with the President for three quarters of an hour and then retired.

I know you are more interested in my afternoon than in the White House reception. Well, everybody who was invited came, and more also. Upwards of three hundred people came altogether. I was really flattered, because I know how people, especially the crowd I run with, hate teas or anything given in the afternoon.

The scene was quite brilliant. Mrs. John Hays Hammond served the eggnog, and the café parfait was served from the buffet. Major Cheatham came in to help me with the eggnog, and the people went wild about it when they ate it. It was too thick to be drunk. Here is what was in it: Ten quarts of double cream whipped very stiff, twelve dozen eggs, six quarts of Bourbon whisky, one pint of rum. I rented a huge punch bowl and kept the rest in tubs in the pantry. That at the bottom was as thick as that at the top. It was made by my mother's old recipe and for fear you don't know it I will send it to you, for I have never tasted any eggnog to equal it.

For one dozen eggs, use one quart double thick cream, nearly one quart of whisky and two tablespoons of Jamaica rum. Beat the yolks to a cream, add a dessert spoon of sugar to each egg, and whip again. Then add whisky and rum slowly. The cream should be whipped very stiff, and so should the whites of the eggs. When mixed it will remain indefinitely without separating.

My eggnog lasted until the last guest had gone, but there was hardly a spoonful left over.

I invited a few of the attachés and included in my list, never thinking they would come, the Austrian ambassador and Baroness Hengelmüller, the French ambassador and Madame Jusserand, and the Netherlands minister and Madame Loudon, and the Moltkes. All came but the French ambassador. People like Mrs. Townsend and the Pattens, who seldom go out to afternoon affairs, were all present and helped to give cachet to my party. I invited only those whom I liked personally, and I did feel pleased that all came. I fear I am not as thoughtful in similar matters.

Good-bye. A Happy New Year to you and Lewis.

ARCHIE.

CHAPTER XXVI

AMONG THE LADIES OF THE CABINET

[Washington, D. C.]
January 3 [1910].

DEAR CLARA:

The President took away the breath of some of the old-timers yesterday by paying a personal call on Judge Lurton before the new justice had called on him. While those persons who are always looking to the dignity of the Chief Executive were somewhat shocked, yet the people as a whole, I am sure, like this little human touch in their President. It was purely an accident. We were out walking in the afternoon, and the President found the mud and snow so disagreeable down on the mall that he had started to return when the lights of the Willard gleamed through the trees and reminded him that his old fellow jurist had arrived only that morning in Washington. I fell back and got one of the secret service men to hasten ahead in order that there would be no delay when we reached the hotel. We entered by the F Street entrance, but already the news that the President was coming had spread in the corridors, and there was a visible stir everywhere on the ground floor. We found the new justice was out and the President looked at me quizzically, as much as to say again:

"I find you have none of my cards."

But I surprised him by taking some out of my pockets.

"You got ahead of me this time," and he laughed, remembering the time in New York when he was making some purchases and asked me for some of his cards, and I had to confess that I did not have any with me. His reply then was:

"You are the hell of an aide, not to have some of your chief's cards with you."

Since then I always go armed with them, for there is no telling when he will call for them.

The administration circles are becoming somewhat amused over the apparent rivalry between Mrs. Wickersham and Mrs. Meyer. As the wife of the Attorney General, Mrs. Wickersham ranks the wife of the Secretary of the Navy. These two women are the most imposing women in the Cabinet, and their little contentions make them a mark for much good-natured gossip among the others.

Mrs. Wickersham really went a little too far on New Year's Day by holding up everyone who passed and having a chat. She was so affable that at times the President was kept waiting for the line to begin to move again. We had to get word to Mrs. Wickersham to permit the line to move more rapidly. This was, of course, greatly enjoyed by Mrs. Meyer, who took the opposite tack and stood frozen in apparent scornful disdain of those persons passing down the line who seemed to give Mrs. Wickersham so much pleasure.

Mrs. Taft sees so very little of the women in her Cabinet that she will not be able to bring harmony among them, and, moreover, she would not take the trouble to do so even if she were well.

Mrs. Roosevelt always set aside one morning a week for a meeting of the Cabinet ladies. It took a good deal of time, and there was considerable rumbling among them, but they always came; their husbands would see to that. But remembering how distasteful these meetings were to her personally, Mrs. Taft announced at the very outset, even before the inauguration, that she would do away with the custom of bringing the Cabinet ladies together like school children every week for (as she called it) a lecture. But it was just through such meetings and enforced exchange of views that contentions and jealousies were kept out of the Cabinet circles, and doubtless they helped in many ways to keep the *entente cordiale* among the women of the Cabinet.

We will watch the little quarrel between these two good ladies with some interest and report from time to time, for I am sure it will be of far more interest to you than politics.
Good-night.

ARCHIBALD.

A New Sort of Presidential Reception

[Washington, D. C.]
January 5, 1910.

DEAR CLARA:

The reception to the diplomats last night was a great surprise to everyone who attended it and was pronounced by everyone, save Alice Longworth, the most beautiful reception ever held in the White House. It was like a reception in a private home. There was none of that formality and stiffness which have made the receptions at the White House in the past a thing of horror not only to those who came but to those receiving. The old order was done away with entirely, and everything which had been done in the past was reversed. For instance, it had been the custom for years for everyone to file in two by two from the street and passing through the State Dining Room to enter the Blue Room from the Red Room and then walk through the Green Room into the great White East Room. It was the epitome of stiffness and angularity. This time the diplomats entered through the south grounds and came up the private stairway into the main corridor and then entered the south end of the East Room which was reserved for them.

The public, for there was no special list to be admitted through back doors and side doors, entered through the east entrance by the Treasury and were allowed to fill the East Room at once. It was like holding a great reception here before the reception began. People saw their friends and chatted with them, and all had an opportunity to see the diplomats forming into their line. When the Presidential party came downstairs and entered the Blue Room, they faced in just the opposite direction from the way they had always faced in the past. Captains Johnson and Van Voorhis admitted the guests into the Green Room in single file, and I presented them to the President.

The doors of the dining room were not to be thrown open until ten, and Mrs. Taft's orders were that the supper was to be ready at that hour. Knowing that the dining room should be open at the very beginning, I gave the surreptitious hint to have everything in readiness and then told Osterhaus, who was in the Red Room, to have the dining room opened five minutes after the reception began. I do not know what would have become of the crowd had the State Dining Room remained closed longer, for the congestion was already great in the Red Room and the west end of the corridor, when the doors were suddenly opened and the diplomats promptly hastened to the supper table. Everything worked out just as I had planned. It was the first time in the history of a diplomatic reception that the diplomats remained until the close. The President has been receiving congratulations all day on the success of the reception, which pleases him mightily.

Mrs. Taft remained down much longer than she did on New Year's Day and has had no bad results from the exertion.

Good-bye.

ARCHIE.

"What Will Roosevelt Think?"

[Washington, D. C.]
January 7, 1910.

DEAR CLARA:

Everything is in a perfect whirl here—breakfasts, luncheons, dinners, and dances every day and night. I am only going to those houses where duty prompts me to go, but it seems to me their number is far in excess of what it is either for my good or pleasure to enter. Luckily the President has been so busy of late as not to require me every afternoon, so that I have been able to snatch a little rest between five and seven. He has settled the commissioners for the district, and his appointment of General Johnston and Mr. Rudolph appears to meet with general satisfaction. When I went to him this morning he heaved a sigh of relief that the commissioners were off his hands and asked me what comment I had heard on their appointments. I told him that they seemed to please everyone.

"But one trouble is no sooner over in this office than another arises," he said, and pointed to a column in the paper regarding Pinchot. "This is something I will have to decide for myself."

And when I asked him if he wanted to ride or walk and suggested that he take some exercise he said:

"No, I have got to wrestle with Pinchot. The trouble has come to a head sooner than I expected."

I left him really feeling sorry for him. He has been very lenient with the forester, but this last letter of Pinchot to Senator Dolliver, practically attacking the Administration itself, demands some action on the part of the President. He hesitates to dismiss only on account of Mr. Roosevelt. He knows Pinchot is courting dismissal, and the President has said more than once in my presence that he would not

make a martyr of him. He regards this last attack of
Pinchot as a piece of insubordination almost unparalleled
in the history of the government, and yet he hesitates to
let him out. I am inclined to think he will suspend him
pending the congressional investigation, and if he is able
to substantiate his charges he may be reinstated. But what
I know of Pinchot leads me to the belief that he will not
remain in the service. Each move he makes now is to force
the President to dismiss him.

I have felt this coming, and I knew it would prove the
issue of the Administration. My only hope is that Mr.
Roosevelt will not be led into taking any side until he
himself has looked into the matter. I do not believe he will
uphold Pinchot's insubordination, as much as he may
regret that the services of Pinchot will be lost to the government.

But my chief is wrestling with the spirit to-day. He
looks haggard and careworn. I saw him several times during the afternoon and he looked like a man almost ill.
He is weighing Pinchot in the balance, but he is weighing
also the consequences of his own act with Roosevelt. All
else is as nothing to him. I know it. I believe he loves
Theodore Roosevelt, and a possible break with him or the
possible charge of ingratitude on his part is what is writh-
ing within him now. He can't say to his advisers, "What
will Roosevelt think?" His very question would be misunderstood even by the members of his cabinet. He expected
all sorts of troubles to come up in his administration, but
I think he had hoped to be spared this one.

I blame Pinchot, however, for not trying to coöperate
with the President to enact into laws the policies of Mr.
Roosevelt in regard to conservation. The President has
been working to this end, and yet during all this time never
once has Pinchot offered to be of the least practical assistance, instead of which he has been traveling over the

country making charges against everyone in the Administration with the exception of the President, and now in this last letter he practically attacks him. This letter comes out at the very time, too, when the President is writing a message to Congress urging legislation on the conservation of our resources.

Midnight.

While I was writing the above late this afternoon, the President had settled the Pinchot controversy once and for all by ordering the dismissal of Pinchot. He gave out his letter to-night, and it is a calm, dispassionate document which I think will appeal to everyone but the old line muckrakers. I have not seen the President since, but I know how sick at soul he is. He did not falter after he made up his mind. But no need to discuss the matter further. It has gone into history. What effect it will have upon the fate of the man who wrote it is hard to predict now. I am fearful of the result, but I do not see how he could have done less than he did.

With love,
ARCHIE.

CHAPTER XXVII

PINCHOT DISMISSED AFTER ADVICE FROM ROOT

[Washington, D. C.]
January 9, 1910.

I spent some time with the President this morning and went walking with him this afternoon. He is like David after the death of the child borne him by the wife of Uriah the Hittite. He looked refreshed and even fairly happy. As I entered he looked up, smiled, and said rather cheerily:

"Well, Archie, I will take up my routine again. I have done all the harm I could. Come for me at three, and let's get some pure air in our lungs and the cobwebs off my brain."

He and I left the office at four-thirty in the car and motored out five miles toward Tennellytown, where we got out, dismissed the car, and started on foot. He talked most freely about the matter uppermost in his mind. He said that nothing had distressed him as much. He had not dismissed Pinchot without deep thought and consultation. He said he sent for Senator Root, and at first Root advised against his dismissal, but asked to be given time to look over the correspondence and read the letter to Dolliver. Later he came back to the White House and said to the President:

"There is only one thing for you to do now, and that you must do at once."

The President said the entire Cabinet was in accord with this view, and that he believed that when Mr. Roosevelt saw the correspondence he himself would wonder why he had delayed action as long as he had.

I do not anticipate any rupture between the two men over this matter, but I do fear one between them in connection with the President's friendly attitude toward Aldrich, his defense of Tawney, and his association with the men whom Mr. Roosevelt was wont to call the "Enemy." I think I know Mr. Roosevelt well enough to judge what his opinion will be in the Ballinger-Pinchot matter, but he will be inclined to judge the President harshly for taking counsel of Aldrich and Tawney and for his complacency of Cannon. The President sees it all and understands the situation. Of course there is nothing else discussed here to-day, and everyone looks for a counter move on the part of Pinchot.

Taft's View of New York "Society"

[Washington, D. C.]
January 12, 1910.

DEAR CLARA:

For the first time in the history of the White House, I suppose, women were seen smoking in the East Room. Alice possibly has smoked thousands of cigarettes in her own apartments, but never before at a public function have women smoked in the East Room. I hope the press will not hear of it. Baroness Rosen, the wife of the Russian ambassador, started it; but the President, after all, was to blame.

As I approached him after dinner to tell him that coffee and cigars would be served on the floor above and to suggest his making the move, he asked me to get some cigarettes and a match. I got them from the band leader, the others having all been taken upstairs, and when I gave them to the President he handed one to the Baroness and, lighting a match, applied it to the debased weed himself. No sooner had she lighted one than Baroness Hengelmüller drew out from her pocket a gold case and lighted one herself; and so it started, and nearly every European woman in the room was smoking in five minutes. I am glad to say that the American women did not indulge, not even the American wives of the European diplomats. Alice Longworth stole into the Green Room where she had her few puffs, showing that even she dreaded the comments of the wives of the Americans present.

After the last guests had departed the President asked us to go to his study and eat apples, which we did, munching them for a half hour. I never saw anyone so devoted to apples. He thinks everyone else likes them as much as himself, and Mrs. Taft says he would feed his family on them if he could.

And now for the opera. We heard *Lucia* Monday night, and with Madame Tetrazzini in the leading rôle and the Irish tenor as Edgardo. The President pronounced the House the most brilliant one he had ever seen, the whole tier of boxes being filled with men and women whose names are household words in the world, and Tetrazzini was at her best. She was fairly quivering with excitement. She made her entrance with a deep European courtesy to the President and sang at his box the entire evening. Alice Longworth accused him of having a flirtation with her. Certainly she gave him most of her attention. He led the applause and made them give several encores. Once after a number of sweeping deferential courtesies to his box, the President turned to the rest of us and said, laughing:

"She does not realize that the only difference between us is that she is on one stage and I on another. I feel that I am acting just as much as she is."

He was very much pleased with the Irish tenor, and I told him McCormack had brought a letter of introduction to me and was very anxious to have the honor of meeting him. The President asked me to bring him to lunch the following day, which was, of course, yesterday. He is very boyish; in fact, he is only twenty-five years old, and I suppose the youngest tenor on the grand opera stage. He has all the wit and humor of his people. Miss Parsons and Miss Louise Taft were enthusiastic over the fact that he was to come to lunch, but there was a general slump in his direction during the meal when he incidentally referred to his wife. He went down about ten points on the curb.

He greatly amused the President by retailing to him the factional rows in the company between the Italian and the French factions and how rejoiced the Italian faction had been when it was learned that the diplomatic dinner would prevent him from attending the French performance of *Thaïs*. He said that Tetrazzini had voiced the sentiment of the Italians when she exclaimed on the stage before the entire chorus: "Oh, Blessed be God who has given us this advantage over our enemies."

His brogue is very pronounced, but one does not notice it in his singing. His voice is not as heavy as some of the others one hears, but its quality is wonderful, and he thinks in three years more he will be able to sing *Aïda* with ease.

I wish you could hear Tetrazzini, Clara. She has greater power of execution than Melba, but her voice is not as sweet or as rounded. She is a marvelous actress, and one almost forgets the flesh in the play of her features and the graceful movement of her arms and hands. Hers are the daintiest hands in the world. When I went back of the stage to give McCormack the President's invitation to lunch, he insisted on taking me to her dressing room. We found her manicuring her hands. I kissed her hand, and McCormack said it would take fifteen minutes to get the spot cleared away again, and she added, laughing, that all the company joked her about the time she spent on her hands, and confessed that had she spent as much time with her face as she did with her hands she might be more pleasing to the President.

"But after all," she said, "I can do nothing with my face, and I shall try to keep my hands young as long as possible. I seldom see my face, and my hands are always in sight."

I was to have gone Friday to a dinner and a cotillion at the Cornelius Vanderbilts' in New York City, but she wired me this morning that an uncle-in-law had died and that the dinner and dance were postponed until February fourth. I do not much mind, especially as I was to have danced it with Mathilde Townsend, but she had chucked me over to dance it with Peter Gerry, and we had such a

confounded row as to take away all the pleasure connected
with the dance. It was to have been my first official plunge
into the New York "Four Hundred." I have been to dinners there and met most of them from time to time, but I
have never seen them en masse. When I told the President
where I had expected to go he said:

"Well, since politics keeps me out of the Four Hundred,
it is well to have a representative there. It is strange," he
said, speaking seriously, "of how much importance that
set thinks itself and of how little importance it is in fact.
A labor union of as many people would have more influence in the world than they."

We took a long walk yesterday afternoon and got back
so late I barely had time to shift into my uniform for the
diplomatic dinner. Mr. Kellogg, the "trust buster," as he
is called, went with us. We motored to the McLean place
on the Tennellytown Road and walked back. Nothing but
politics was discussed. Kellogg is going to run for the
Senate from his state, either Minnesota or Wisconsin, I
do not know which, and the President promised to help
him for all he had done for his administration and that of
President Roosevelt. They talked very frankly about the
chances of the President for another term. Kellogg was in
favor of declining all patronage to any man in the House
and the Senate unless it was to be used to aid the President's nomination for a second term. The President did not
take this view. He said that he would not appoint a man
to office knowing him to be opposed to him, but he would
rather not have the question raised.

"For, after all, Kellogg, a number of our best Presidents have had only one term, and there is nothing dis-
graceful in not having two. I am trying to act as if there
were not another term. I believe, too, that it is good politics. If I stand for anything, it is for being straightforward
and natural, and it is unnatural to try any other rôle."

Kellogg gave him a full account of what the Pinchot-
Garfield-Dolliver people hoped to do and said that the
whole trouble was a part, as he described it, of "The Back
from Elba plot." The President said he knew all this, but
it did not trouble him. He was still of the opinion that
Roosevelt would not lend himself to their plans and that
he would have his own way of disposing of the matter on
his return.

Jimmy Sloan, who was walking back of us just near
enough to hear the conversation, took me to one side after
we came back and said that he thought the President was
fooling himself about President Roosevelt, that he had
reason to believe that he would take the nomination (in
1912) right out of the hands of Mr. Taft, if there was the
slightest reason to think Mr. Taft was not carrying on his
policies. I have always taken the other ground, but Jimmy
was for seven years with Mr. Roosevelt and was very
close to him. He is rather an astute little politician also.
We were just by Lafayette Square, and Jimmy said:

"Captain, you did not know it and no one did, but Mr.
Roosevelt got sore on the President before he left Washington. We were coming back from a walk one night, and
it was just about in this place, when he said, turning to me:

"'Jimmy, I may have to come back in four years to
carry out my policies.'

"That was all he said, and I made no answer. But I
have thought of it a lot since. And there is more in the cry
'Back from Elba' than either you or the President think. I
hear a lot that you do not hear, and so does Latta, and I'll
tell you that a lot of people are fooling the President."

I give you this little bit of political gossip for what it is
worth. It only shows what the other side of the matter
really is. Jimmy Sloan seldom talks to anyone, and the
fact that he struck this note of warning to me is significant.
I wish Sloan were not in the secret service. He is capable

of so much bigger things, and some day he will have them, I feel sure. We are very close. I look upon him more as a friend than as a subordinate, and he is the very embodiment of loyalty. In speaking of these two men whom he has served he said to me once (I think I may have told you at the time):

"In many ways, Captain, I like this man better than the other. He's finer in some points, but he does not see as the other saw things."

Subsequent events may prove all this to be utter rot, but then again Jimmy may prove to be a much better prophet than I. My faith is founded on what I think is an intimate knowledge of President Roosevelt, and my ideas as to what he will do under certain circumstances coincide with the President's estimate of him.

Good-bye, for I must be boring you. With love,

ARCHIE.

An Argument with Secretary MacVeagh

[Washington, D. C.]
January 20, 1910.

DEAR CLARA:

The President is not very well to-day, and what is more important to you is that I am not either. I am all stuffed up with grippe, but there is not as much of me to feel badly as there is of the President. He has had a cold ever since he went to the Requiem Mass of King Leopold.

We motored to the Treasury Department, where Secretary MacVeagh met us on the sidewalk and got in the car. Secretary MacVeagh started in at once to tell the President that he was opposed to the publicity features of the Corporation Tax Law as far as the small corporations were concerned, and the President rather discouraged him by saying that it was the publicity feature which appealed to him more than any other part of the law. The secretary saidit was meeting with the greatest objection everywhere; he thought the collection of the tax would result in good, whereas the publication of the facts regarding the small corporations would only bring about great discontent and no special good. The President said he thought many small corporations had a good deal that should be made known and that it could meet with only healthy results.

"Even you," said the secretary, "would not like all your business matters to become public property: what income you had and from what source it was derived."

"I would not mind in the least," said the President, "would you?"

"I certainly would," said the secretary, "and I should do all I could to evade the law."

"Then you would be one of those we are hunting for," added the President. "No, MacVeagh, I am in favor of letting the law work out as it was framed to do. To me the publicity feature of the law is the only thing which makes the law of any special value, for it is not going to be a great revenue-producing measure."

And now good-night. With love,

ARCHIE.

CHAPTER XXVIII

MR. TAFT PICKS A WALTZ PARTNER

[Washington, D. C.]
January 24, 1910.

DEAR CLARA:

It was at the Southern Charity Ball the other evening that the President took us all by surprise by dancing in the crowded ballroom. He loves to dance, and, strange as it may seem, he waltzes most beautifully. He was in his box holding a sort of levee, surrounded by all the climbers in the room, when he pointed to a young woman, dressed simply in pink with a pink rose in her hair, and asked me who she was. I did not know, and he said it did not matter, only he had been watching her dance, and she was most graceful and light on her feet. I slipped to the back of the box, called Horace Westcott, who was chairman of the floor committee, and, pointing out the young woman who had caught the Presidential eye, suggested that he bring her to the box and present her to the President. He did so and she proved to be a Mrs. Pierce Horn, a daughter of the Confederate general, A. P. Hill. The President immediately asked her to dance, and they mingled with the other waltzers, much to the astonishment of everyone present and to the delight of the floor committee.

This simple act of the President has made her famous, now, the country over. The next afternoon the papers had her entire history and that of her husband and father, and also her photograph, and one cannot pick up a paper from any part of the country now without seeing references to the beautiful Mrs. Horn. The President rather enjoys the notoriety of his simple act, for many of the papers have written editorials on his democratic simplicity. His only desire to dance was to keep his legs quiet, he says, but as soon as he did so I passed the word to the papers, for I saw in it what the advance man of an opera troupe would call "a good ad."

Good-bye. With love,
ARCHIE.

Not Worried by a Wall Street Slump

[Washington, D. C.]
January 27, 1910.

DEAR CLARA:

There is a panic in Wall Street. All the morning the President has been besought to issue a statement tending to quiet conditions. For two days past stocks have been tumbling, and everyone who has lost five cents, or who thinks he may lose, blames the President. In the meantime he is more amused than anything else and refuses to take the matter seriousiy. When out walking yesterday afternoon, he opened up his mind to me on the subject.

"They don't frighten me at all with the cry of panic in the stock market. There is no reason for a panic, and these fellows bring about the trouble themselves, and when it goes farther than they anticipated they rush to the Chief Executive for a statement to quiet things again. It has just percolated into the heads of some of those people that I mean what I say, and I don't have to reiterate my sentiments every five minutes to convince them that my messages are my decrees and that they are not written for political effect but to secure legislation."

He laughed heartily over my description of the members in the Metropolitan Club weeping in their soup while they told each other that everything was going to the damnation bow-wows.

"It is just as well for it to come at this time and for the money people to know that I intend to prosecute all forms of illegal transactions. No corporation doing a legitimate business need have any fear. It strikes me as rather funny that I am being blamed for the high prices on the one hand and the falling prices of stocks on the other, but I shall not be forced into making either explanations or excuses."

Several public men, one being Jim Hill of St. Paul and the Northwest in general and another being Fred Upham of Chicago, besought him to issue a statement and hinted that the Board of Trade banquet last night would be a good place to make it, but the President merely smiled at all the suggestions and, instead of talking on financial issues last night, spoke merely of the necessity for this country to own its own embassies and legation buildings and to pay its representatives abroad higher salaries.

As soon as he sat down a flashlight picture was taken, and we then went to the Vice President's on Sixteenth Street to a reception the like of which has not been seen in Washington since the days of the Fairbanks'. As we approached, the President said:

"It looks like a regular Vice Presidential evening."

We had difficulty to get in, and it was like the Capitol on Inauguration Day except there was no order. I got in front of the President and simply backed through the crowd, making way for him inch by inch. We passed down an unending line of Shermans.

All the Diplomatic Corps must have been invited, but not one was to be seen. The President remarked on this while returning home and then said:

"By the way, I don't want any special attentions shown to the Bernstorffs of the German Embassy. Was not he one of those who asked to be excused from attending the Judicial Reception on account of the death of Nabuco?"

I told him he was.

"Did I not see that he and his wife attended the Bachelors' Cotillion the next night, while Nabuco was still unburied?"

I again said "Yes," and then the President said:

"It is not worth noting officially, but bear this in mind, for I want both Bernstorff and the Countess to learn sooner or later that I have noticed this breach of etiquette and that such discourtesy does not go unnoticed even in our democratic government."

I was somewhat surprised to see them receiving at the cotillion, and I showed my surprise by shaking hands with Mrs. Meyer first and only bowing stiffly to the Bernstorffs. I think they caught my meaning. They will feel sure that I reported the matter to the President, whereas he learned it himself, and what surprised me was that he remembered that they had not appeared at the White House reception.

The President is not over-partial to the Germans, and he has no liking at all for Bernstorff, whom he thinks very much of a prig. He has never thought the same of him since he saw him playing golf with a lady in his shirt sleeves. He did not object so much [to the lack of a coat] as he did to the fact that he wore a pink shirt and red suspenders.

I take my Third Degree in Masonry to-night. I wish you would tell Lewis. Has he taken all three or just the first two degrees?

Good-bye,
ARCHIBALD.

Under the Fire of the Publishers

January 29, 1910.

DEAR CLARA:

The President practically got rid of his cold that he contracted at the Nabuco funeral, but last night when we were going to the Publishers' dinner he said that it had returned with renewed force, and he felt worse than he had at any time since he had it, which in reality dates back to the requiem mass of Leopold. He is so tired that he cannot resist any microbe, however small. He makes engagement after engagement, and when it comes time to meet them he tries to get out of them, and by doing so I think he makes more enemies than if he declined in the first place.

He allowed himself to be wheedled into a dinner of the National Board of Trade, and at the last moment, just as we started for a walk, he said: "Is there no way I can get out of this dinner to-night?" and I answered promptly:

"Certainly, sir. We can notify them that you cannot come before ten o'clock, at which time you will make your speech."

This was the program carried out, and I hear he has given great offense and is being criticized severely for cutting their dinner to go to the theater. I asked him at the same time if he would do the same thing at the Publishers' dinner last night, and he thought not; yet while I was dressing to accompany him I got the message that he would not go until ten, preferring to have his dinner at the White House. I was sorry he did this, as glad as I was to have chicken and rice at home, for the dinner last night was given by the Publishers' Association of the United States and represents all the big publishers in the country, including the leading magazine men and writers.

This was the association whose dinner he promised to attend in New York and which he did not attend on account of the blizzard then raging. They were very much distressed at the time and felt keenly his absence. Since then the situation has been complicated by his message to Congress recommending that the postage of books and magazines be increased in order to make up the deficit of sixty-three millions of dollars occurring annually in the Post Office Department. So while they ostensibly are meeting in Washington for other purposes, they are here to lobby against this increased postage, and I fear they think the President is too hasty in the matter and blame him for accepting the statement of Hitchcock without a proper investigation. The position he took in his message was, of course, a most impolitic thing to do, for it arrays against him practically the entire magazine world of the country, but this is just like him. He found that the deficit was largely due to the low rate of postage on magazines, and, without thinking of his own interests in relation to them, set the entire association against him by advocating an increase in the postage.

But all these things made it more necessary that he attend their banquet after he had accepted the invitation. Yet when the hour arrived he simply sent word by phone that he would come in after dinner, and in consequence, when he got there, there were a lot of sour visages around the tables. It was a very large dinner, possibly six hundred people being present. Hopkinson Smith, whom I introduced informally to you before he was the presiding officer, at once presented the President as "a President whom the people love." He said that the country admired many Presidents, but he thought that Taft would be mentioned as the one the whole country loved irrespective of party or section. It was a happy introduction and put him in touch with his audience at once and relieved the unpleasant situation.

The President made a very delightful after-dinner speech. He was most happy in his phrases and so jovial and genial (no one in the room except myself knew how he was working to be so) that when he sat down he was given quite an ovation. He left everyone in a happy frame of mind and passed over the matter of increased postage in a jocular way that left no scar and dispelled any impression which the association might have had that he was in some way hostile to the publishers of magazines. I was sitting next to Mr. Abbott of the *Outlook* and near Pinchot, and they were both open in their expressions of praise of the speech. It was the first time I had seen Pinchot since his dismissal, and we took up the line of friendship where we had left it in the West, and, without referring to the estrangement between himself and the President, we talked of him and his speech as if there had been no estrangement at all. Mr. Abbott told me he was going to Khartoum to meet Mr. Roosevelt and asked me what message he could take for me.

"Simply that I am devoted to him as ever and have tried to serve those of his family who are left here with the same interest as if he were still in the White House."

It was while Joe Cannon was still making a speech that Mr. Abbott told me he had a letter from Mr. Roosevelt which he thought very significant. In it, he said, the ex-President wrote that of late he had received letters from friends advising him to delay his return until after the next congressional elections, but that he had decided not to do so, and he used this rather enigmatical expression:

"As much as I should hate for the White House to see Cannon, Tawney, et al., defeated, I fear I will be unable to delay my return on that account."

I did not see exactly what he meant and looked to Abbott for an explanation. He said that it meant only one thing to him: to wit, that Mr. Roosevelt would take part in the next election to bring about their defeat.

A great number of the publishers whom I was wont to see in the last administration came up from time to time to speak to me, and it was like a reunion of the Roosevelt luncheon parties. Every man there last night had Roosevelt uppermost in his mind. I think the President realized that also.

On our way home, the President said:

"That speech of Dolliver's was the most demagogic attempt I have ever heard him make. It was cheap and unworthy even of him. I wonder if the thinking men present saw what an insincere effort it really was. I had to admire old Cannon for the way he presented the facts, for if any man in the world has the need of the magazine writers of the country, unless it be myself, it is Uncle Joe."

He then asked me how I liked his speech. It was the first time he had ever asked the question. I told him frankly that it was the very best which could have been made under the circumstances, that he got over the thin ice with remarkable felicity and never put his foot in the water once.

"Most of the magazine writers will never see anything but Roosevelt and will never approve of any methods except those of Roosevelt, so there is no need for me to be hypocritical with them."

I said nothing, for there was nothing to say. I always know how people who have once been under the influence of Roosevelt feel. We seem to know each other by instinct. Having once come under the charm of that personality, there is no escape from it. If I, who love the present man and know the great beauty of his character, feel as I feel toward the other, what must be the depth of feeling of those who have not the same opportunity to know President Taft as I have nor to be under the same obligations to him? One felt Roosevelt in the air last night, and I could but reflect what would have happened had it been the other instead of the President who entered the hall.

Enough of speculation. Ethel Roosevelt arrived yesterday to visit the McLeans. Every moment of her time will be taken up in entertainments in her honor. Alice Longworth has allotted to me luncheon on the third of February, when I will have ten of her old friends to meet her. Mrs. Townsend called me up on the telephone this morning to say she wanted me to try to get her to remain longer and come to her. Among those whom I have invited to meet her is young Baron von Stumm of the German Embassy, whose engagement to Constance Hoyt is announced this morning for the first time. It is a love match. He was a great pet socially and is one of the most eligible parties in Germany, his family being very wealthy and powerful. Hers is a good family in point of lineage, but they are not wealthy and the father has some subordinate post in the State Department. One hears a great deal of international marriages which are made for wealth, but very little is written of those founded on love, such as this one, and that of the Grennards and the Oveys, and a dozen others which I could name.

Good-bye. With love,
ARCHIE.

Mr. Taft's Optimism Lags

January 30, 1910.
Midnight.

DEAR CLARA:

The President was a little pessimistic to-night. He told Senator Bourne that he thought it would be impossible to elect a conservative man to the Presidency next time, that the whole drift of the country was toward radicalism. He said they had managed to handle it within the party up to the present time, but he saw signs of a complete break within the Republican party and feared the La Follette, Dolliver, Cummins element would dominate the situation in the next election even if it did not join with the more radical element of the Democratic party in the West.

"Sooner or later I fear we have got to turn the government over to this element and let it demonstrate its incapacity to govern the country. One thing I have decided to do, that is to play no politics. I am going ahead as if there were no second term and pay no heed to the demands of this element. If the party comes to my point of view, well and good; if it doesn't, I am content to step down after four years. It is a very good thing for the country to have this outlet to its feelings. Sooner or later the country will demand its dose of Bryanism or its equivalent, and I am in favor of never again using such efforts as we did in the past to stay it. Educate the people if we can, but whatever the country thinks is right, whether it is right or wrong, it is right for it to have. Something has been radically wrong in our legislation in the past that such combinations have been formed under our laws and that we have to resort to all sorts of special legislation to counteract it. It may be that after all the opposition may have some remedy which we are unable or unwilling to try."

Both the Senator and General Edwards tried to see things brighter, but the President did not see it as they did.

"We are prosperous, and the signs of the times point to greater prosperity, yet there is a great deal of unrest and discontent among the people."

Good-night.
ARCHIE.

CHAPTER XXIX

CAPTAIN BUTT AT THE VANDERBILTS' DANCE

[Washington, D. C.]
February 5, 1910.

DEAR CLARA:

Let me tell you in the first place how thankful I am that you came through your sickness, and then proceed to my gossip. This being the first time a member of the Butt family has actually penetrated into the heart of the Four Hundred, I am sure you will want to know the particulars and what impression this much-talked-about set made upon me. In the first place I was distinctly disappointed, and so were Miss Townsend, Alice Meyer, and Count Moltke. Thinking this over, I am not sure but that it is a compliment to the Four Hundred, for after all we were only disappointed in that the people were not more beautiful, the house grander, the favors more costly, the dressing more ornate, and the general scene more brilliant.

I do not know just what we did expect, but it was like any other dance, not as beautiful nor as brilliant as we are accustomed to see at the Townsends', the McLeans', the Hitts', the Wadsworths', or a dozen other homes here, but then it was not a great event in the lives of the New York people who were there. It was merely a dinner dance, but somehow we were keyed up for something quite extra in grandeur and brilliant in appearance. The Countess Moltke belongs more or less in that set, and going over on the train she kept wondering what they would think of her husband, for it was his first introduction to New York's elect. I knew Mrs. Cornelius Vanderbilt and her home, but I had never seen her friends massed for battle, and I felt interested but with no feeling of awe.

Miss Townsend had gone over the day before and had wired me not to fail her, as she expected to dance the cotillion with me. Alice Longworth was going as a house guest, and Secretary Meyer and his daughter were coming on a later train. The Marquis de Villalobar was on the ground, and unless Ann Ide, Mrs. Bourke Cockran, can be placed to the credit of Washington, we constituted the Washington contingent.

There were a hundred and seventy dinner guests and we were placed at small tables of eight and ten persons. Much to our mutual disgust, I was placed at the head table and Miss Townsend at one lower down. All the rank that was there came from Washington. Moltke sat on the right of the hostess, Villalobar on the left, and I, evidently taking rank as the President's aide de camp, sat one below Moltke. Hoerstmann, whom I forgot to mention above, a second or third secretary of the German Embassy, came next below me, much to his surprise, I think; and others at the table were the host, Cornelius Vanderbilt, Captain Paget, son of Lord Paget; Lord Innes-Kerr, a brother of the Duke of Roxborough, and one or two millionaires, one being John Jacob Astor.

My neighbor, who was a Mrs. Warren, evidently a great

local wit, told me that their set resented Astor's betrayal
of the set by permitting the secrets of the Four Hundred
to be dragged through the Appraiser's Court when his
mother's pearls were shown to be part imitation and her
ballroom chairs to be only gilt.

Poor Cornelius Vanderbilt looked bored to death. It
seems that he hates this sort of thing, and all during dinner
he looked like one treading water and calling for help.
He is thin, wears a pointed beard, and his eyes are very
sad. He talks little and has none of the social chit chat
that goes to make up social reputations. He is deeply
interested in mechanics and engineering. His wife tells
me that while she is doing the art galleries and modiste
shops, he spends his time, when they are abroad, inspect-
ing bridges and studying ship building.

This is interesting only because he is a Vanderbilt and
his father practically cut him off with a few millions because of his marriage to Grace Wilson. She is a splendid
woman to whom all New York looks up and on whose
shoulders the leadership of Mrs. Astor will fall. She makes
a charming hostess, gracious and sweet, and possesses the
art of speaking to each guest as if he or she were the one
person necessary to the success of the ball. Her jewels
were wonderful. She wore a filigree work of diamonds
which literally covered her neck, and the back of her head
was likewise covered with a plaque of diamonds, while in
her corsage she wore the famous Princess Mathilde diamond rose. It is a full-blown rose on a stem with some
leaves and buds, and the whole is made of delicate filigree
work of diamonds. I could not believe at first that it was
a diamond creation. When I admired it at the late supper
she told me it was formerly the property of Princess Mathilde Napoleon,. and that when her jewels were sold
"Neely" had purchased it for her, knowing how fond she
was of such ornaments. She says she does not care for large

diamonds, but her taste is for small white spotless diamonds in unique settings. The rose and cluster is possibly six inches in diameter.

My right-hand neighbor was somewhat of a good-natured gossip and pointed out the celebrities to me. She confided to me that Lady Paget was undecided whether to wed her son to Mrs. Leeds or to Mathilde Townsend. Of course I saw to it that Mathilde heard of this gossip, and when Paget came later to speak to her, he was given a freezing smile of welcome.

The room was filled with Dyers, Gerrys, Drexels, Jays, Cuttings, Goelets, Harrimans, and others whose names one sees in the papers every day but seldom meets. Harry Lehr was there, petted by women, but shunned by the men. Countess Szechenyi with her Austrian husband, a rather decent-looking fellow, was there, and so was Mrs. Willie K. Vanderbilt, recently divorced from her husband. The fact that she was there was a proclamation of Mrs. Cornelius as to which side she espoused. Mrs. Craig Biddle and Mrs. Robert Goelet were the handsomest New York women there, but none of them compared to Miss Townsend or Countess Moltke.

The dinner was most indifferent. It was evidently a Sherry dinner. The supper at one in the morning was much better. The food was good and hot and had the appearance of being cooked at home. After dinner I did not join the men, but Miss Townsend and I sat alone in the ballroom while the others peered at us through the door and nodded their heads. A cinematograph amused the guests after dinner, and the cotillion did not begin until after twelve. As the ballroom filled up, Miss Townsend and I went to other rooms. Secretary Meyer, coming by, said that we could have talked just as well in Washington and wanted to know why we came.

The favors were handsome, but not too much so. I got

three sets of opera glasses, one of which I will send to you, another pair to Arrington, and keep the third.

When I first began this letter I thought the Vanderbilt ball deadly dull, but looking back at it and seeing it from a receding distance, I think I must have enjoyed it, for I am giving a lot of time to it this morning, am I not?

Good-bye. With lots of love to you and Lewis and Bessie,

I am, as ever,
Your affectionate brother,
ARCHIE.

Colonel Roosevelt Homeward Bound from Africa

[Washington, D. C.]
February 9, 1910.

DEAR CLARA:

The President said yesterday, while walking (he and I being out together), that if there was any cohesion among the Democrats at all they would most certainly secure the next House of Representatives; but as badly disorganized as the Republicans are, the Democrats are entirely without organization. An effort is going to be made to rally all the forces with the return of Mr. Roosevelt. In fact, a committee has asked the President if he will go to New York to greet him. While he has given no answer yet, he is inclined to do so. The only question in his mind is that of the dignity of his office. He is not so sure that he, as President, ought to go to New York to welcome a private citizen, even if that citizen is an ex-President, a great personal friend, and the man to whom he acknowledges he owes the fact that he is now President. This view he is not giving out publicly, but it is that which may deter him from going.

He fears, too, that by going to New York he may appear in the attitude of trying to placate Mr. Roosevelt if the

latter has become disgruntled with him for any cause. I
believe that he will be caught up in the Roosevelt enthusiasm when the time comes and that nothing could
prevent him from going. In which case I will go also, I
presume. If he does decide not to go, then he will send me
with a letter of welcome, which, personally, I will like
all the better. Somehow I think his going might be misconstrued by many people, but not by the ex-President.
I think before Mr. Roosevelt returns he will manage to
make it known to the President in some way whether it
will be agreeable for him to be met by him or not.

Since writing to you last, we attended the Gridiron
dinner, where most of the evening was taken up in skits
relating to Mr. Roosevelt. Coming home the President
said:

"Archie, nothing shows what a hold Theodore has
on the public mind more than the dinner this evening.
Even when he is away and in no way interfering in politics, such is the personality of the man that almost the
entire evening was wit and humor devoted to him, while
the President with most of the Cabinet present and all the
big men of the country were hardly mentioned. He oc-
cupies our minds as much now that he is away as when
he was in our midst. It is a strange hold he keeps on the
minds of the people."

This was not said begrudgingly, but as a fact merely,
and one which did not seem to trouble the President at
all. I think he feels that if he is renominated it will be
because of Mr. Roosevelt, not in spite of him. A man
of tremendous personality himself, he still lives in the
shadow of that other personality, and, as unfortunate and
unfair as it is, his acts challenge attention largely by
comparison with the acts of the other. He is so broad as
to show no resentment even if he feels it, and I am inclined to think he feels none whatever.

Night before last I went with the President to the
"Salon of Miss Boardman." There were very few people
of prominence there. This is the first effort possibly ever
seriously made by anyone to establish a salon in Washington. I think the President makes a mistake to go to them
as often as he does, but he is very fond of Mabel Boardman and will do a great deal to aid her in any direction.
She has found her life's interest in the Red Cross work of
this country, and for the work which she did at the time
of the earthquakes in Sicily she was decorated by the
King of Italy and presented with a coronet of golden oak
leaves. She went on the memorable trip to the Philippines
and China with the President, then Secretary of War, and
chaperoned Alice Longworth. Her friendship with the
President was cemented by their famous journey, and since
then she has ever been regarded as his closest woman
friend.

Yesterday he complained to me that he had made too
many engagements for the evenings; that he was very tired
and began to feel greatly fatigued mentally.

"I am afraid, Archie, that I do too much to sustain
properly the dignity of the office of Presidency. I know
Alice thinks I make myself cheap by doing and going so
much, and doubtless that is the general comment, but it
is not my nature to remain shut up in the White House
when my desire is to mingle freely with my fellow kind.
What do you think?"

I could not tell him that I thought he did go too much,
but I said what I thought to be perfectly true: that he
carried his dignity with him wherever he went and that it
was unnecessary to house it and himself in his library. He
is always dignified, and no one in the world has a better
idea of his own dignity, and no one would ever presume to
infringe upon that dignity a second time.

Yesterday we had such a nice luncheon party at the

Jusserands'. There were there only the ambassador and his wife, Admiral and Mrs. Cowles, John McIlhenny and his lovely young wife, the Beekman Winthrops, and myself. We were in some way connected during the last administration, and the luncheon was to bring us together again.

The presence of Mrs. Cowles rather prevented the same freedom that once existed between us, as no one seemed to know just how she felt regarding the new administration since the Back from Elba cry had been raised and the Pinchot episode had entered as a wedge between the two administrations. Mrs. Cowles is very deaf, so I had to speak rather loud to be heard, but it was evidently a relief to everyone when I said in a bantering way:

"We are certainly glad to have you here, for those of us of two administrations have had a hard time of it lately and we need a recruit."

Mrs. Cowles enjoyed the reference and said in return:

"I cannot be a recruit, for I too am under suspicion by those who would draw a line and make us take sides."

From now on, dear Clara, I am not going to be able to write as often as I have in the past, a fact that may be more a blessing to you than otherwise; but the fact is I have got to begin to study for my majority. It has come on me so suddenly that at any time now I may be called up before the examining board. It would never do for me to fail, and I must run no chances. I may not be ordered up for six months, but I want to be prepared when it comes.

I hope you are better and will soon be out again. With a lot of love I am, as ever,

Affectionately,
Your brother,
ARCHIE.

Taft Advised Not to Meet the Boat

[Washington, D. C.]
February 13, 1910.

DEAR CLARA:

Loeb came to see me for a few minutes at the banquet, and we discussed the advisability of the President's going to New York to meet Mr. Roosevelt. We agreed that he ought not to go; that it would be misunderstood; and, moreover, Mr. Roosevelt would not like it. In the first place, it would be forcing the President of the United States to play a secondary rôle, for on the day of his return, as Loeb put it, "it will be a T. R. day and there will be no other note sounded." He had come up to me after the name of Roosevelt had been mentioned by the toast-master and there had been such an ovation as had not been accorded to the President himself when his name was mentioned. At my instigation Loeb met the President and told him frankly that he ought not to come to New York, and that any advice to the contrary was not well considered. The President agreed with him and said he would not be influenced to come, but instead he would send me with a letter and a word of welcome.

The speeches on the whole were quite ordinary, the best being Governor Hughes's.

Good-night,
ARCHIE.

CHAPTER XXX

PLANNING TO OUST DEPEW AND WOODRUFF

[Washington, D. C.]
February 14, 1910.

I fear this will prove a record day for Senator Depew and Lieutenant Governor Woodruff of New York. The

President sent me word to come by his office with the open car at a quarter to five, as he wanted to be at the Capitol at five o'clock. Promptly at that time we were there, and he asked me to let Senator Root know that he was waiting for him. He wanted to get it done as soon as possible and not be seen, I think, but luck had it that the Pinchot-Ballinger investigation had just been concluded and everyone who came out of the big Senate office building saw the President and hung around until Senator Root joined him.

The President launched into the object of the drive at once. He began by telling the Senator that he was sorry he had not come to the New York conference, that Depew was there and his absence had been construed to be a disapproval of the selection of Griscom. The Senator said that he had wanted someone else, but that he had been most pleased to see the way Griscom had taken hold of the committee, and he had not written to him merely for the reason that he was very busy and had delayed doing so. The President then suggested to him that he write, as he felt it would strengthen Griscom in the work he had to do.

"And now, Root, to business. It was an important conference and much may come out of it, but you must meet Hughes. He is anxious to see you and I think you ought to see him. He thinks there is a good chance to elect a Republican governor on the state ticket, but he says we had just as well go out of business as to offer Depew to the people again, and Timothy Woodruff must be eliminated."

"That's easier said than done, especially the latter," said Senator Root.

"I have thought that over too, and discussed it with Hughes, and we see our way out, I think. If you agree, we can simply wipe Depew off the slate; that is all there is to be done in that matter. He is seventy-six years old, and that will be the excuse for doing so, but we all know that he is out of touch with the modern thought, and while the people have apparently forgiven the old charges, they have in reality not done so, and they will not stand for his reëlection. As to Timothy, I think I can bait a hook which will catch him. He has long had a diplomatic bee buzzing in his head. I am not willing to give him a mission, but I can give him second place on this South American mission with Henry White at the head. I think we can bell him with this offer."

"I suppose the State Department can act for you in the Woodruff matter, but who will tell Depew?" asked Senator Root.

"Well, we thought your relations with him were such that you might best do it," said the President.

"Not on your life," laughed the Senator. "Won't it precipitate a fight in New York which will be more disastrous than were he to remain in the race?"

"I think not," said the President. "You mean between the friends of Hughes and Roosevelt. Hughes does not mention himself as a candidate and seems to take it for granted that if Roosevelt will accept the nomination he can be elected. I do not think Hughes will be a candidate with Roosevelt as a possibility. He himself suggested that, if Roosevelt would agree, we could have the convention pass resolutions endorsing Theodore for the Senate which would commit the candidates for the legislature. I doubt whether he would consent to such a resolution, but if he is willing to accept the Senatorship at all, he might prefer to make the fight for it without committing the Republicans in advance to his candidacy."

Senator Root made no comment on this statement at all. Possibly the President knows or was able to judge of what was passing in his mind, but I was not able to say whether the suggestion of Roosevelt for the Senate met with his approval or not. It would mean, of course, yielding the leadership from New York to another in the state. The President continued:

"As to Depew, I don't know who will break the news to him if you do not. Hughes may find a way. I find him more resourceful than appears on the surface."

We had a good dinner, very simple, the only meat being a large well-cooked beefsteak, the President's favorite food, and when Mrs. Taft has it, it is a concession to him, for the rest of the family do not care much for beef.

ARCHIE.

Mr. Taft's Forgiving Disposition

February 16, 1910.

Arthur I. Vorys, of the National Committee which managed the Taft campaign in the election, took a motor drive with us in the afternoon before the dinner. The President spoke most freely with him about the campaign three years hence. He told Mr. Vorys that he rather expected to see Roosevelt elected to the Senate, and he was in favor of running Loeb for governor in New York. He did not feel at all sure as to the election of Loeb and regretted that he was not a better speaker. They might find someone else, but at present he was rather inclined toward Loeb, though he thought Governor Hughes was not. If Roosevelt wanted the Presidential nomination, he thought he could have it for the asking, but he did not think he would accept it, but would support him. In which case, he said, he was very doubtful as to the outcome, for he would have the tariff to defend, and the high cost of living would be charged up against him, and should there be a panic he would get the credit for that too. He scoffed at the suggestion of adopting different methods from those he was now pursuing and told Mr. Vorys frankly that he would continue to carry out the policy he had adopted, and if the people wanted to try a different party next time he would acquiesce without bitterness or complaint.

Coming home, the President said he was going to offer a place on the South American mission to Judge Lamar of Augusta. There is no salary connected with it, but the President said it would last from June to November and all expenses were to be paid. He thought Mrs. Lamar would like it, whether the judge did or not. He is offering the first place on the commission to Henry White, the former Ambassador to France, whom he removed for some slight to himself and his wife when they were traveling in Europe several years ago. Nothing shows the bigness of the man's character better than the fact that he is now willing again to appoint Mr. White on a diplomatic mission, and while it is not a permanent appointment, it is a post of great honor and may lead to a permanent appointment later.

The President himself told me the facts in the case of White. It seems that when a very young man White was an attaché to St. Petersburg when the President's father was minister there. It was natural to suppose that he bore some loyalty to the Taft family and would serve it when occasion presented itself. But when he was first secretary —acting chargé, I think, in London—Secretary of War and Mrs. Taft were in that city and asked for certain courtesies at the hands of the embassies. They were shown through a minor secretary and in a way so begrudging that naturally the Secretary of War and Mrs. Taft felt the keenest resentment.

Since his return Mr. White has made Washington his home, and whenever the President and he have met they have spoken most amicably, and the President, I think,

has had cause to revise his opinions of Mr. White and the
nature of the discourtesy, although the subject has never
been mentioned between them. Mrs. Taft has apparently
forgiven the offender and is now one of his advocates
before the President.

A. W. B.

The President's Opinion of W. J. Bryan

February 21, 1910.

DEAR CLARA:

In the afternoon we went walking, the President, Senator Bourne, John Hays Hammond, and I. We motored
first through the park and walked back from Tennellytown. Most of the conversation was regarding the political
situation. The President said to Hammond that he would
feel very hopeless about leading the Republicans to
victory next time if it were not for the disorganization of
the Democrats.

"Do you know," he said, "I believe that Bryan will
force his nomination on the Democrats again. I believe
he will either do this by advocating Prohibition, or else
he will run on a Prohibition platform independent of the
Democrats. But you will see that the year before the election he will organize a mammoth lecture tour and will
make Prohibition the leading note in every address."

Senator Bourne said: "In many ways I think the career
of Bryan and the leadership he retains more remarkable
than the career of Theodore Roosevelt. His powers in this
direction are wonderful."

"They are," said the President. "When the history of
this period is written, Bryan will stand out as one of the
most remarkable men of our generation and one of the
biggest political men of our country."

ARCHIE.

An Encounter with the Storers

[Washington, D. C.]
February 22, 1910.

The dinner and musical this evening at the White House were very pleasant affairs, both of them. The dinner was especially delightful. It was small and made up of friends of other days, in a way. There were Justice and Mrs. Lurton, the Secretary of War and Mrs. Dickinson, Bellamy Storer and "Maria" his wife, the Nortons, Professor Emory, and those of the household, including myself. I drew Mrs. Storer. It was the first time she had been in the White House since her celebrated controversy with President Roosevelt, and it was, therefore, the first time I had met her.

I could think of only one thing and that was the "Dear Maria" letter, which in reality made her famous. Since meeting her I am sure President Roosevelt was right. But withal, she is extremely interesting and amusing, but a most incorrigible gossip—yes, much worse than I am even to you. I gossip for a purpose; I make myself gossip, when in reality I don't care a hang what people are doing as a rule, but I think their doings worth preserving in a way, and then they may lighten the burden of these letters to you somewhat. Mrs. Storer kept me laughing throughout the dinner. She evidently thought I was much more receptive than Secretary Dickinson, on the other side of her, and therefore gave me all the benefit of her wit.

After dinner we went into the Green Room, where we had coffee, and later the men went to the President's study to smoke. We had no sooner got there than a messenger came telling me that Mrs. Taft wanted to see me at once.

"For heaven's sake," she said, "either take that cartoon out of the study or keep Mr. Storer from seeing it."

I knew at once what she meant. It is the original drawing of a cartoon which appeared in some of the magazines and was sent to the President. It shows Roosevelt at the wheel in a big touring car with Mr. Taft sitting by him. They are racing for dear life, and back on either side of the road which they have traveled can be seen the fragments of the Philippines, Cuba, trusts, railroads, undesirable citizens, and what not, and underneath is written "Roosevelt to Bill: 'Is there anything ahead of us, William?'" The last object passed by the motor is an old hen shown in midair, just having escaped from the wheels, and flying for life with several feathers dropping from her tail, and the hen is marked in rather large letters "Maria." The cartoonist, whoever he is, really got some points of similarity between Mrs. Storer and the figure of the hen. I could not look in the direction of it without laughing, and the President, seeing me eye the cartoon, began to laugh and yet talk against time to keep the husband from seeing the joke.

Mrs. Laughlin told me a rather good conundrum which is going the rounds, and while it is at my expense, still it is sufficiently good to repeat. The question is: "Why is the White House nearly?" and the answer is: "Because it is all Butt." I am writing all this twaddle to-night because I know I will be too tired to-morrow morning to write a word, and we leave at eleven o'clock for New York.

Good-night,
ARCHIE.

Two Public Dinners in New York

[Washington, D. C.]
February 24, 1910.

DEAR CLARA:

I returned from New York with the President this morning after one of the most trying trips I have had since

I began this continent-trotting existence. Up until after two o'clock both nights, and up again at seven each morning. The New York papers all spoke of the President's tired look, and commented on the fact that he looks much older than he did six months ago and has lost much of his joyous and happy manner.

He does look older. I can see him aging every day, but as to being in a bad way or on the verge of a breakdown, I cannot see it at all. He does too much and is wearing himself out with all sorts of gymnastics before breakfast and walking in the afternoons, then going out nearly every evening. I know it is telling on me, and I am much younger and—well, I started to say stronger than he is, but when I see what he undergoes and still continues to keep afloat, I doubt whether I am stronger than he after all.

The whole trip was somewhat a revelation to the President. There have been so many adverse criticisms of his administration lately that he had with philosophic humor begun to accept [the belief] that he was extremely unpopular and had failed somehow in his duty as others might see that duty. When Governor Murphy told him that New Jersey was prepared to give him a rousing welcome, he said:

"Ah, Governor, don't try to deceive me as to the sentiments of the dear people. I have been hearing from the West and the East, and the South seems to be the only section which approves of me at all, and that comes from merely a generous impulse, for even that section would deny me its votes."

This he said laughing, and then added seriously: "But what makes me really tired is the hysteria and hypocrisy of the present day; the hysteria which followed the crusade of Roosevelt and the hypocrisy of those who want to keep on the crest of the hysteria."

The dinner at the Plaza given by the New Jersey Society of the Order of the Cincinnati was like a thousand such dinners, only it was more coldly formal and less exhilarating than such dinners usually are. There were only eighty at the dinner, and the speeches were of a most conventional character. I would have enjoyed it more had I been there in capacity of a gentleman, and not as an aide thinking of politics and the best play to make for my chief. I soon saw there was nothing in this gathering for him, and as he had promised that he would attend a dinner of the lieutenants of the New York Police Force at the Waldorf later, if he could leave the first dinner in time, I began to plot to get him away from the Plaza early in the evening. He is so decent himself that he does not like to appear rude to people, and as he had come to New York for the Cincinnati dinner he said that he would remain as long as they desired him to do so.

I knew the other dinner was a big thing politically, and the influence of nine hundred lieutenants of police scattered throughout Greater New York was not to be minimized. The Cincinnatis did not want him to leave their dinner at all, for obvious reasons, and they began to delay the game. However, he spoke first, and then I began my maneuverings. I moved nearer to him and at the right moment told him that the Committee of Police were waiting to escort him. The committee consisted in a telephone message from me to the Waldorf to say that he might be late and to have the Committee at the Waldorf entrance to meet him when he arrived.

After the next speech I asked the President of the Society to announce that the President must leave and to ask the members to remain standing as he passed out. This was an old dodge I have practised often. It never meets with success at once, but after one or two speeches more the toastmaster, feeling that he has delayed the departure far beyond what was expected, consents to make the announcement. It happened as I anticipated, and the President remained for two more speeches. Then we got away exactly on schedule time and entered the great ballroom of the Waldorf at ten minutes after eleven.

It was a great sight. On the floor were some nine hundred police lieutenants, all in uniform, and the boxes were filled with their wives and daughters and sweethearts in bizarre colors which made the effect very striking and picturesque. As the President entered, every man and woman waved a small silk flag. The enthusiasm, like all enthusiasm of this character, grew on what it fed upon, and they yelled for five minutes. In public life one accustomed to be in it feels at once that thrill which comes from contact with people who either know things or do things. One felt at once that the dinner was made up of people who were in touch with the affairs of the political world, and no point in any speech was lost on them. The President made a splendid speech under the influence of the popular demonstration given him. The next day, the dinner of the Cincinnati was hardly given a notice, and the dinner and his speech to the policemen covered columns.

Good-bye.
ARCHIE

CHAPTER XXXI
THE STORY OF A BOMB AT THE WHITE HOUSE

[Washington, D. C.]
Sunday, February 27, 1910.

DEAR CLARA:

I came back to the office and waited for the President, who wanted to walk, but he was too tired to make the start and at six o'clock backed out altogether. He had decided in the morning not to go to the theater, so I was free to go to the Meyers' to dinner and later to the musical at Mrs. Patterson's home in Dupont Circle.

She does not entertain often, but when she does it is always in a way that tells. Everybody wanted to sit back, but Geraldine Farrar, the soprano soloist, insisted upon having the front row of chairs filled to keep her warm, as she expressed it. I was glad that we were forced to move afterwards, for it gave me a good view of the wonderful back of Miss Farrar, which has added to her reputation as much as her wonderful voice has done.

By the way, do you remember my writing to you last February, telling you of a bomb which had been found in the White House grounds just before President Roosevelt went out of office? I may not have thought much of it, not even enough to make mention of it, for it soon passed out of my mind. Well, I heard more of it to-day, while in conversation with Lieutenant Moore, then stationed at Washington Barracks. The bomb had been sent with great secrecy to the engineers for examination, and they found it to be a time bomb. It was wound up and set when found, but evidently had not begun to run, he said. They started the clockworks going and, as a mere matter of precaution, at the appointed time they got some distance from it, though they did not expect it to explode. However, it did go off with terrific force, and had they been near it they would have been blown to pieces. Another piece of news he gave me concerning it was the inscription on it:

FROM YOUR FRIENDS OF THE TWENTY-FIFTH INFANTRY

Affectionately,
ARCHIE.

Mr. Taft's Judgment of John Marshall

[Washington, D. C.]
Sunday evening, February 27, 1910.

DEAR CLARA:

I had such a delightful walk with the President this afternoon that I cannot refrain from putting it in a letter to you. We started from the White House in the open car. There were John Hays Hammond, Senator Bourne, and I, and the President. We chatted on politics; in fact, the President did most of the chatting. He rather raked up hill and down dale those people who charge him with Aldrichism and Cannonism and who then refuse to give him aid to pass the very bills to which the platform and the party stand pledged.

We continued down North Capitol Street until we reached Rhode Island Avenue, when Mr. Hammond suggested that we turn down that thoroughfare, but the President insisted on going to the Capitol and then walking through the Mall. We went by the west entrance of the Capitol and passed under the statue of Chief Justice Marshall. The President stopped, looked up in the bronzed face, and started to turn away when Mr. Hammond asked:

"Would you rather have been him than President?"

"Of course," said the President. "I would rather have been Marshall than any other American unless it had been Washington, and I am inclined to think that I would rather have been Marshall than Washington. He made this country."

We walked on and then, as if reaching some conclusion, he said, stopping in his walk:

"Taking it all in all, I think Washington was the greatest American, the greatest man, I almost believe, of his generation. Marshall is certainly the greatest jurist America has ever produced, and Hamilton our greatest constructive statesman. There you have my opinion of our greatest men."

"Does Marshall size up with the great English jurists?" asked Mr. Hammond.

"I think with the greatest of them," said the President.

Good-night.

ARCHIE.

Taft's Reasons for Giving a Dinner to Cannon

[Washington, D. C.]
March 4, 1910.

DEAR CLARA:

There has been so little of importance happen within the past few days that I have not thought it necessary even to attempt a letter, but to-day comes as a reminder that the new Administration has now been in power just one year. When asked by Mr. Hemphill, called the "deacon" by the President, whether he liked being President, the latter replied:

"On the whole, yes. I would rather be Chief Justice of the United States, and a quieter life than that which comes at the White House is more in keeping with my temperament, but when taken into consideration that I go into history as a President, and my children and children's children are the 'better placed on account of that fact, I am inclined to think that to be President well compensates one for all the trials and criticisms he has to bear and undergo."

The dinner last night was very heavy and stupid. The President decided several weeks ago to inaugurate as a regular State function this dinner to the Speaker of the House. Heretofore President Roosevelt had always given the Speaker a dinner, but it had never taken on the character of a State function. President Taft has formally inaugurated it as one, and last night he had fifty-four guests to meet the old fellow. It is true the guests were made up largely of members of the House and Senate and consisted largely of those whom he had not had at dinners before, so it answered a double purpose.

While walking yesterday, Mr. Hemphill asked in his peculiarly insinuating way:

"How does it happen that you are giving a dinner to that old reprobate, Joe Cannon?"

"That is what all the insurgent newspapers out West are asking," said the President, "and if I could answer them as freely as I can you, they might see the wisdom of my doing so without misunderstanding my motives.

"In the first place, the Executive should give a dinner once each year to the Speaker, no matter of what political faith, personal character, or reputation. Roosevelt always gave him one in a half-surreptitious way, and since I felt duty bound to entertain him officially I decided that I would inaugurate a Speaker's dinner as one of the State dinners of the year and would so include it on all the official programs. Next, I feel really under obligation to Cannon for the way he is coöperating with me in getting my bills presented to Congress and passed there. Those who are denouncing me the most for apparently favoring Cannon are standing idly by as far as the administration measures are concerned, or else they are actually opposing them merely because they want to see them fail. I recognize those who help me, and whatever may have been my prejudices about Uncle Joe, and whatever may be my private opinions now, I am grateful to him for the part he is playing toward my administration, and I am going to evince that gratitude, as I am doing to-night.

"Those who think that Roosevelt would have come into

the open against the Speaker at this juncture do not know that when I entered office it was with the avowed intention to defeat Cannon if it were possible, and that it was Roosevelt who persuaded me to hold up until I could count the votes whereby I could defeat him. Before my election I had decided to declare war against Cannon, and after my election I pledged myself to fight him tooth and nail. The first message I got from Roosevelt was to make peace with Uncle Joe, and when I came to Washington I called to see Roosevelt and told him that Cannon ought to be defeated, and while he agreed with me, he said:

"'That is all right, but you can't do it, and if you try and fail you defeat your own administration. Better make peace and get along with him as best you can until you get what legislation you want through, and then,' he said, laughing, 'let nature take its course.'

"I half reluctantly let up in my fight, and I have been suspicious of him all through, but he has been so square with me about my bills that I am forced to feel grateful, for where I had a right to look for assistance I have met with treachery and deceit. And now," he said, turning round laughingly and striking Hemphill on the back, "do you think me such a *particeps criminis* to entertain Uncle Joe?"

"You can always argue me out of my position as to yourself, but I reserve the right to stand pat on Uncle Joe."

Villalobar has gone, and his successor has been named. The latter is Señor Riano, formerly here as secretary, who married Alice Ward of this city. Nearly all the diplomats in Washington now have American wives, and it is doubtful whether the government feels complimented or otherwise. It makes a conspicuous list, if not a long one. There are Madame Jusserand, Countess von Bernstorff, Madame Louden, wife of the Netherlands Minister; Countess Moltke, wife of the Danish Minister; Countess de Buisseret, wife of the Belgian Minister, and a number of attachés and secretaries. It must be said of them that they are all high-class women and stand head and shoulders over the wives of the other diplomats, but the wisdom of this policy of the governments can be doubted.

One thing which happened yesterday which may be worthy of note and which I forgot to mention: Just before dinner Senator Crane came in to the White House to say to the President that the insurgents were trying to defeat the amendment to his Postal Savings bill—that amendment which permits the President to use the surplus in time of war or any great emergency. The insurgents claim that Wall Street is behind the amendment and that it is placed in the bill to aid Wall Street in times of panic. Be that as it may, the President, when he heard that Senator Burroughs was considering the wisdom of voting with Cummins and the others, called him on the phone and said to him what he had heard. I do not know what Burroughs said, but the President said afterwards that it was a mere excuse. The President said:

"I thought you were an Administration Senator."

He said Burroughs answered: "I am an Administration Senator, but——"

"There is no 'but' in it," said the President. "The way to be an Administration Senator is to vote with the Administration"; and while Burroughs was trying to explain, the President angrily hung up the phone. He will watch what effect his disciplinary measure will have to-day. That is the way he wields the whip lash when he knows he holds the whip handle. Burroughs wants his help in Michigan, and he will have to jump when the President cracks the whip, and the President does not mind cracking it when he has the power.

Good-night.

March 5, 1910.

We had a most delightful evening at the Boardmans'. There were no Cabinet officers present, but a number of the assistant secretaries. It was the best selected dinner of semi-official character which I have seen given in Washington. There were the Nortons, the Winthrops, the Bowers, Senator and Mrs. Crane, Mrs. Keep, the Longworths, Andrews, the young director of the mint; General Davis, the Griscoms of New York, and a Mr. and Mrs. Davidson. Mr. Davidson is the new power in the financial world, a man of wonderful energy and nerve, who has practically made himself, and who is now a member of the firm of Pierpont Morgan & Co. There were a number of others present.

Davidson is a young-looking man, but one sees the marvelous force in him that attracted Mr. Morgan to him. The President spent most of the evening talking with Mrs. Norton, but later he was joined on the sofa by Alice, who kept him laughing over her witticisms.

The President is in good humor over the passage of the Postal Savings bill through the Senate. He said that Burroughs came in to see him this morning and took both his hands in his and said most sententiously:

"Mr. President, you know I never had any other idea but to vote for that bill."

We went out by ourselves this afternoon and talked from the minute we left the White House until we got back.

"I have made up my mind, Archie, to one thing: that I will not play a part for popularity. If the people do not approve of me or of my administration after they have had time to know me, then I shall not let it worry me, and I most certainly shall not change my methods. I am going to be honest with myself, whatever else I do. I cannot be spectacular, and I will not be insincere with those I deal with. If I did as many of my friends want me to do, and play the rôle as Roosevelt played it, I would be accused in the first place of imitation and then denounced as a hypocrite, and both would be true."

This followed upon a remark of mine that I had felt at first that he ought to use methods which I had seen used to such advantage by Mr. Roosevelt, and that I did not see at first how he could possibly win the country to himself by other means, but that I had been forced to change my mental attitude and to feel that any other rôle than that which he had essayed would have been unnatural and false.

ARCHIE.

CHAPTER XXXII

SEEKING AID FROM ALDRICH AND CANNON

March 7, 1910.

In the afternoon, pretty well covered with mud too, I started out with the President. He directed the car to go by the home of Senator Aldrich, as he wanted to see him. We found the Senator indoors, and the President asked him to go for a ride. Something interesting I knew to be on the tapis. We usually go to the park and follow the Connecticut Avenue line, but with Aldrich in the machine I directed the chauffeur in a low voice to go out the unfrequented thoroughfare of Nineteenth Street, and as we would reach byways and side streets I gave directions until we finally reached Fourteenth Street. It had turned very cold, and the wind was very high, and the chairman of the Finance Committee of the Senate was almost frozen and asked if the top could not be put up as he was not accustomed, as we were, to these open-air rides. I fished him out a sweater from under the seat, one belonging to the President, and the President made him put it on. It would have encircled his body twice. With this compromise we went on with the top down, but owing to the wind it was disagreeable to all except myself, who took off my hat and let the cold wind do as it might with my hair.

The President had a number of important things to say to Aldrich, who had been away. The President frankly told him that since he had gone nothing had gone right and begged him to remain in Washington as much as possible until his bills had passed. He told him that Jonathan Bourne, who had been expected to the Speaker's dinner, had declined at the last moment in order that he might not be able to talk with him about the Postal Savings bill, and that when he had sent for him to come to see him, he had remained away with some trivial excuse, which accounts for the President's anger toward him and his determination to have nothing more to do with him. Aldrich said Bourne was all right when he himself left; that evidently Dolliver and Cummins had frightened him from the administration measures.

The President then told Aldrich what he was anxious to see him about especially. It was a plan he had on hand to defeat the Cummins and Dolliver faction in the next election in Iowa. He said that he had had Hepburn and some of the stalwarts, as he called the old Allison Republicans of that state, to dinner, and that they felt that if they had some outside help in the way of money they could make trouble for Dolliver and Cummins in the state. The President said he was unwilling for Hitchcock to enter the fight, as he thought it should be done apparently from within the state. To this Aldrich agreed, and said that he would see what money could be raised among certain friends of his to aid Hepburn on the grounds that it would be a campaign of education. He said that it might be done by private subscription and that he would aid the cause himself, and the President said he would also contribute his share.

He said that Dolliver and Cummins and Beveridge should not, under the guise of republicanism, stir up trouble within the party and try to defeat the administration measures without some retaliatory measures being undertaken against them. Senator Aldrich agreed with the President that Senator Beveridge, while apparently acting with the Administration, was organizing the insurgent element for its most effective operations. Senator Aldrich told the President that he should withhold all the patronage from Dolliver, Cummins, and Beveridge as far as possible, for the sooner they were made to quit the party councils, the better it would be for the party.

As we got back to the House the President said:

"Well, Archie, I had to descend to politics this afternoon. I believe in fighting the devil with fire. I don't propose to have my administration a failure simply because of the hostility of Dolliver and Cummins. After I write my bills on the Statute Books, they can then do their worst, for the record will have been written and the law will be there."

I think he said this to me as a sort of an apology, for he felt, I think, a little bit ashamed himself of entering into political plots with the Rhode Islander as a matter of retaliation. I wish I could trust Aldrich more than I do. He is so far out of sympathy with the West and the South that I fear he may get the President too far out of touch with the people too.

March 9, 1910.

The President is leaving nothing to chance as far as his bills are concerned. Yesterday, as we started from the White House, he told his secretary to telephone the

Speaker that he was on his way to the Capitol, and if the latter had nothing to do he would like him to take a motor ride with him. As we left the White House and proceeded up Pennsylvania Avenue, he said with a smile:

"I am following to the letter the injunction to make friends of the mammon of unrighteousness, so that, when those who ought to be my friends fail me, I will have others to fall back upon. I am not very accurate as to Biblical quotations, I am told; but that is the purport of the text, and it seems to find adaptation and fulfillment in me at the present time."

We got the Speaker, but when he saw the car was an open one and how high the wind was blowing, he balked and asked the President to go with him in his closed one. The President laughed at him for being what Mr. Roosevelt would call a mollycoddle, and taking off his sweater, the one which Aldrich had worn the day before, gave it to the Speaker and made him get in and button his coat high in the neck. Then we started on the same old route to the park, passing down Pennsylvania Avenue and keeping well in the open, as I felt no shame for the company we were in. Moreover, the Speaker is one of the most dramatic characters we have in public life, and after all is said and done, one of the most popular, and it rather strikes a popular chord than otherwise for people to see the President and the Speaker riding together. They are such different types that I always enjoy seeing them together and, even more, hearing them talk, for the President, with all his persuasive powers, cannot get the Speaker to say he believes a thing to be good if the old man thinks to the contrary. For instance, yesterday, when the President began talking about the chances of the Postal Savings bill in the House, the Speaker said:

"Mr. President, I don't want you to think that I blame those fellows who are opposing this bill, as much as I dislike those who are actually engaged in the work, for I wish this cup could pass from our lips or, better still, had never been handed us to taste. But it was put in the platform, and therefore I am willing to aid you to carry out the party's pledges in the matter, but I think it a decided step toward populism; and what I want to see done is so to frame the bill that it will be as little objectionable in this direction as possible. I am getting so damned tired, Mr. President, of this everlasting yielding to popular outcry against wealth that unless we put a check on it somewhere there is no telling where it will lead."

"Exactly," said the President, "but those fellows in the Senate who are opposing this bill are not doing it for any reasons which you have given, but merely to make trouble or else to freight it down with heavier populistic burdens."

"I believe that," said the Speaker, "and that is why I have such a contempt for those who are fighting you and am willing to give you my support."

"And now——" said the President.

"And now," said the Speaker, in imitation of the President's caressing tones, "we are coming to what you really wanted to see me for. I am beginning, Mr. President, to know that what is really in your mind to do is about the last thing you mention."

And as the President began to laugh, the Speaker added:

"So fire away, Mr. President, when you are ready; but temper your wind to the shorn lamb."

"All right. Then it is this: About the only promise which Roosevelt extracted from me, and about the only one I gave, was not to divide the fleet between the Atlantic and the Pacific until after the completion of the Panama Canal at least; and to try to add two battleships a year until the completion of the Canal, and by that time the fleet would be of sufficient strength to divide if necessary.

Now, what I want of you is to pull off your coat and work for those two battleships."

"Nothing illustrates better than this the difference between our last two Presidents," said the Speaker. "Roosevelt never wanted but two at a time, and yet he always asked, even demanded, four a year, hoping thereby to get two. You, on the contrary, want two and ask for two. While I am opposed to more than the two-battleship idea, I will help you all I can, and I will begin at once to count noses and then let you know of the prospects of getting the bill through. You may have to interfere in legislation and see a few obstinate members, but I am inclined to think we can put it through in spite of Tawney."

"Yes, I know Tawney is opposed to the idea, and I cannot ask him to change his ideas on the subject, for he has always opposed the building of these ships. I think his opposition to the policy was the real cause for disaffection between Roosevelt and him, but I think I can counteract his influence."

"What I should like to see done," said the Speaker, "is to build one ship a year and enlarge the personnel of our sailors and officers so that we could keep in commission at all times the quota of ships and have an army of seamen at all times trained to their work."

The President had no idea he would be able to win Uncle Joe over so readily to his two battleships, as he had heard that he stood with Tawney against them. As soon as the conversation began to run out, I turned the car homeward and soon landed the Speaker, half frozen, at his home on Vermont Avenue.

ARCHIBALD.

The President Saves Part of His Salary

[On the train.]
March 15, 1910.

DEAR CLARA:

We have used up all of the twenty-five thousand dollars appropriated by Congress for the President's traveling expenses, and a part of this trip he must defray out of his private means. There are seven more trips planned between this time and the first of July, and unless Congress gives him the same appropriation for next year and makes it retroactive, he will use up a large part of the salary he and Mrs. Taft have laid aside. He hopes Tawney will see that it does become retroactive, but it is possible for Congress to refuse to give it to him at all.

I heard him tell Mrs. Anderson, while we were motoring after the funeral in Pittsburgh the other day, that he and Mrs. Taft had saved just thirty-four thousand dollars this past year. He gives her a check each month for two thousand dollars, which she has invested, and he said that on the fourth of March he had in the Riggs National Bank just ten thousand dollars and gave Charlie Glover a check for it to put into some mortgage. He hopes to save thirty thousand dollars each year of his administration. If he does not have to defray his own traveling expenses, I think he will be able to save more than this amount next year, although he thinks this year will be more expensive than the last one. He has been lavish in his entertainments and never seems to have thought of money. I don't think either he or Mrs. Taft expected to save more than what he gave to her each month, and I think it was quite a surprise to her to find out that he had a balance at all.

I will write on my return.

ARCHIE.

The President and the Politicians

Erie, Penn.
March 18, 1910.

DEAR CLARA:

. . . The President heard this morning for the first time of the all-night session in the House and the evident attempt to dethrone Speaker Cannon. The insurgents and Democrats took advantage of the absence of many of the regular Republicans to offer a resolution which, if passed, practically eliminated the Speaker from the control of the House. The President did not get excited over the accounts and was unmoved even when cipher dispatches began to pour in from Washington urging him to return to Washington to save the regular organization from defeat. His Secretary sent several, one with a message from the Attorney General asking that, if the President should come back, he let him know in time, so that he, Wickersham, could meet him in Baltimore or some other place and give him his views as to the situation. The President sent an answer at once to Carpenter, saying:

"Have never for a moment thought of going back to Washington. I could do nothing under the circumstances if I went, and while I am sorry not to be in Washington at so critical a period, I think that my giving up my trip would be misconstrued and would be of no practical use."

But the day promises to be a busy one for us, for at each station now there arrive cipher dispatches which Wagner and I have to get out at once, and as we near Buffalo I will have to give up any further attempt to finish this letter. I have been writing it piecemeal, but it will give you some idea of the day and its importance.

Good-bye. Hastily and with love,
ARCHIBALD.

"Uncle Joe" Puts up a Fight

Off Rochester.
March 19, 1910.

DEAR CLARA:

We are just leaving Rochester, where we had a most delightful reception. Everybody was nice, and the President could not have had a more enthusiastic reception than was given to him by the people on the streets and at the banquet last night. We had a most sensible reception committee, for after conducting him to the hotel they left him to the free enjoyment of the luxuries they had provided, untrammeled by solicitous courtesies. We all enjoyed ourselves except the poor stenographer and myself, who spent all the time between our arrival and the banquet deciphering telegrams from Washington and putting others in code.

The President received every bit of news which came from Washington regarding the fight on Speaker Cannon, but made no comment and declined, as he had done in the morning, to take any part in the fight at all. He seemed to think that the insurgents had deliberately planned this coup during his absence, so as not to involve him in the battle, and also with a view to preventing him from making any appeals to them which it might be embarrassing for him to make or for them to ignore. However, it does not seem to bother him very much, not as much as I thought it would. In fact, after reading the papers at the breakfast table this morning he looked up, laughed rather roguishly, I thought, and said:

"Well, Archie, I think they have got the old fox this time. It would be funny, if he got the best of them after all, but Crane's last dispatch would indicate that the regulars had given up hope."

This referred to a dispatch which came just before we went to the banquet, telling the President that the Democrats and the insurgents clearly had a majority. Continuing, the President said:

"However, even if they don't beat him this time, it indicates one thing: that the old man has got to go and that he can never be elected to the Speakership again, if indeed he can retain his seat in Congress. He told me that if he was ever beaten by a test vote in the House he would resign. It will be interesting to see if he will, but I don't see how he could do otherwise. But it is fine to see how he is fighting. That is the quality I admire most in Uncle Joe: he does put up a good fight."

With love,
ARCHIE.

CHAPTER XXXIII

A VISIT TO GOVERNOR HUGHES IN ALBANY

New Haven, Conn.
March 21, 1910.

DEAR CLARA:

I find the President and I are constantly pulling in opposite directions. When he is alone he is thinking how soon he can be mingling with his fellow men again. When I am with my fellow men I begin to plan at once to be alone again and to get him by himself. It is only when I can get him by himself, safely locked in or asleep, that I can be alone. He is essentially a gregarious animal. He says so himself and loves to have people about. He likes to have someone in the car with him when he is reading or studying, and if he is at work, he works better if he has someone in the room with him.

Saturday night [in Albany] when he and Governor

Hughes sat down in the Library after coming in from a late banquet, I tried to slip upstairs and get to bed, for I was worn out; but he saw my maneuver, I think, for he said:

"Governor, I am sure Captain Butt would like a Scotch and soda with you," and he made a motion for me to remain, so down I sat and never got up again for two hours and did not get to bed until after half-past two.

I must confess that after a while I got interested in the conversation of these two men, and the time passed more rapidly than I had thought possible.

The conversation was largely on politics, and the Governor gave to the President a succinct account of the reforms he was trying to bring about, and the picture he drew of New York legislative work seemed pretty dark to me. The President then touched on the Governor's future and told him frankly that he thought it his duty to run again for the governorship, and then told him what Senator Root thought also, and said that the entire hope of the party seemed to rest on him. The Governor told the President that he could not do it possibly, and nothing the President said was able to change this determination. The Governor said he could not afford it; that he had four children, and that every year in the executive mansion had cost him over and above his salary eight to twelve thousand dollars.

"I do not dare to run the chance of breaking down mentally. I must get out and make my family safe while I am able. I think we can find someone to run who might win, provided we throw overboard Tim Woodruff and Depew and do not stand for such men as Barnes in this city and Aldrich in Rochester. The Democrats, I believe, will nominate a very strong man—Judge Keogh."

Saturday night we went to a University Club banquet at the Ten Eyck Hotel [Albany], where we heard some very good oratory from Earl Grey, the President, ex-Governor Francis of Missouri, and finally from the Governor. I never heard Governor Hughes in better form. He spoke as one almost inspired, and Earl Grey said afterward to the President that he had never heard a more eloquent man. He seemed to be carried away with the Governor. He is a most wonderful man, not yet fifty, and has a power for good seldom possessed by any man. If he is ever President he will startle the world, I believe. I don't see how he will ever make it, with the President and Roosevelt ahead of him. I said this much to the President at breakfast this morning, and he said:

"I don't know the man I admire more than Hughes. If ever I have the chance I shall offer to him the Chief Justiceship."

Another thing the President has decided to do is to appoint General Barry superintendent at West Point. He had decided upon General Bliss, but General Barry brought all the big guns of the Catholic Church to bear on the President. . . . As he says, being a Unitarian, he does not feel as hostile toward them as do others, but I feel that it is a very dangerous precedent he is establishing. . . .

Good-bye.
With love,
ARCHIE.

Taft Hears Pinchot Will Meet Roosevelt

[New York,]
March 22, 1910.

DEAR CLARA:

We lunched with Mr. Henry Clews, in a round dining room with a stained-glass vault, about a round table, and with well-rounded and mellow wines. It was beautifully done, and every detail would bear the closest scrutiny. He invited the leading educators and editors of the city to meet the President. We drank to his health in some port said to be a hundred years old, and I think it must have been, for it had that old tar rope odor which comes with very old port.

I sat between Mr. Seth Low and Cornelius Vanderbilt. The latter has just been named chairman of the reception committee to welcome back Mr. Roosevelt, and he is all up in the air as to what to allow and what to keep out of sight. My suggestion to him was to make the ex-President the whole show, to give him a long route to travel over, and to permit only a few Rough Riders to escort him and these to be supplemented by the police. I did not think Mr. Roosevelt would want a great military parade for himself now that he was a private citizen, nor did I think it was the proper thing to do. I told him the simpler the reception the better it would please Mr. Roosevelt. He told me that he had talked with Loeb on the subject, and this was his advice also, but it seemed to find endorsement with no one else.

I was much interested in seeing the editors of the big dailies. As a rule they are men about forty, and simple, earnest-looking men, rather ungainly and awkward. Brisbane introduced me to most of them, and I gathered from what they said that they had been most agreeably impressed with the President. Brisbane said to me:

"The fact of the matter is, none of us has ever given the President a fair show as yet. We have all been judging him by the standards of his predecessor, and we have yielded to the public clamor for him to use the attacking methods of Roosevelt. We are beginning to see him rightly, and I think he will win out if this Roosevelt homecoming does not upset all plans and purposes of thoughtful men."

The talk now is all Roosevelt, and there is the wildest enthusiasm over his return. I suppose the fate of everyone politically is largely in his keeping, and if he should want to be renominated again, nothing could prevent it, for it could come from the West alone in its present state of mind. No one recognizes this more than the President, and he said yesterday that he believed Roosevelt was stronger to-day with the people than he had ever been at any time in his career. He was rather thoughtful all the afternoon after he learned that Mr. Roosevelt had sent for Pinchot to join him in Europe. The papers so announced it, but I don't believe it to be true; rather I think Mr. Pinchot has gone to meet him on his own account, and I so told the President.

"Yet it looks like a straight tip which has been given out on the subject," said the President. "It would seem strange to me for Roosevelt to do that, but he may want to hear from him, first hand, Pinchot's side of the case. Of course, I can say nothing until he asks me, and he may not give me that opportunity. If they put it before him squarely, I am not afraid of the result."

But I could see that it worried him, not on account of the effect on his own political fortunes, as you might think, but he hates to think that his friend has misjudged him to this extent.

Good-bye. With love,
ARCHIE.

Mr. Taft Displays Great Patience

[Washington, D. C.]
Easter, 1910.

DEAR CLARA:

The President looks very badly, I am beginning to think myself. He is white-looking, and his pallor does not seem healthy. I may be getting nervous over him, but I wish he would not tie himself to his desk as he does. He is under a great nervous strain, and he has a very hard summer before him.

It is hard on any man to see the eyes of everyone turn to another person as the eyes of the entire country are turning to Roosevelt. I wonder if you feel it down South as we do here. Everything is on the *qui vive* for the return of the Hunter. He is certainly the first citizen of the world to-day, and how wonderfully he is handling himself amid it all!

The President never swerves from his silence for a minute except in praise of the ex-President. I never once heard him murmur against the fate which keeps him almost in a secondary place in the public eye. He accepts it as he does everything else, with profound patience and generous philosophy. President Roosevelt, of course, is playing his part too. I believe he is doing just what he says he is doing, expressing no opinion on politics and keeping his own counsel within himself. They both have hard parts to carry through, but I believe the President's is the hardest. He feels that somehow he is misunderstood and that his very honesty of purpose is doubted, and while he is resigned, nevertheless, his heart weighs him down at times. If he only had not the double burden to bear: that of the public and that which comes from his own fireside. No one knows how he suffers over his wife's illness. He bears up beautifully under it, but as the weeks go by and there does not seem to be any permanent improvement, his hope sinks pretty low at times.

I know how it affects me—and think what his own feelings must be. What really makes me almost ill with indignation, at times, is the fact that we have all our lives heard the American people say: "Oh, if we only had a President who did not think about a second term"; or, "If we only had a President who could act with independence and not be hampered by the second-term fetish."

And here they have one and they don't even appreciate

the fact; if they do, it gives only cause for criticism. I don't
believe he ever thinks about a second term, or, if he does,
merely as something not even to be desired.

Good-bye. Love and lots of it to both of you.

ARCHIE.

Social Chatter of the Capital

[Washington, D. C.,]
March 31, 1910.

DEAR CLARA:

Just why any officer wants to be an aide at the White
House, when he has no duties except of a most perfunctory
nature, it is hard to see. We use them to dance with the
unattractive guests at the White House and to accompany
official parties to Mount Vernon and at the large receptions, to stand as lay figures about the rooms and corridors. We also make use of them to present representatives of unimportant countries and states and to attend
Mrs. Taft at her teas.

I made up my mind when I first came that I would be
an aide as an aide should be or else eliminate myself. I
have succeeded to that point where I am the only aide, so
to speak, and have eliminated everyone else. It brings its
troubles with it, but you have the satisfaction of knowing,
when it is over and done with, that you were not a cipher
and that in your little time you played a conspicuous part
and possibly were of some service both to the man and to
the State. Just why I should enter upon a dissertation of
the uselessness of aides in general and illustrate my own
dogmatic disposition in particular, I scarcely know, save
that I agreed to write to you of what was in my mind, and
this subject has forced itself upon me to-day in reviewing
the events of last evening.

However, I won Mrs. Meyer's renewed respect last
evening, for when the President went on the platform at

the big drill hall at the Navy Yard, where the ball was being held, Mrs. Meyer was completely out of sight, and the President stood surrounded by people of minor importance and mostly family. Mrs. Wickersham had edged herself next to the President, and Mrs. Meyer, the wife of the Secretary of the Navy, seemed to be obliterated. Here is where I come in—and where I usually come in. I went to her and said the President desired her to sit at his right and, offering her my arm, led her to the President and, putting a chair next to his, told her the President desired her to be with him. The small fish fell back, and the President, realizing that I had done the only right thing, accepted the situation and looked his approval. The drill of the jackies then went on, and the Presidential box was in a dignified attitude to receive it and pay it proper attention. My act was not lost on the Secretary or Mrs. Meyer, nor any of the navy people present, and the fact that I did it all by the orders of the President eliminated the personal side of it, as far as I was concerned, yet emphasized the fact that I was looking only to the best interest of my chief.

I hurl this bit of etiquette at you to illustrate merely the hundreds of ways an aide may be useful, and the importance of being both eyes and ears to his chief.

The Postmaster General, Hitchcock, is giving a dance and cotillion to-night as a return for all the favors he has received. He is the bachelor member of the Cabinet and is being angled for a good deal by the would-be married. He is as cold blooded as a fish, and yet he has pink skin and red hair. His eyebrows are light red and his eyes steel blue. His rise has been rapid. Only a few years ago he was a stenographer, and through a fortuitous circumstance he became an assistant in the Post Office Department and there saw his opportunity to build up a Republican machine, intending to use it for Cortelyou, but was forced by the Roosevelt Administration to throw it to Taft. As a reward he was made Postmaster General, and here he is entertaining the best the Capitol City has to offer, a power politically and an eligible partee matrimonially.

This is a good ending.

Good-night.
ARCHIE.

CHAPTER XXXIV

THE PRESIDENT'S MANIA FOR TRAVEL

[Washington, D. C.,]
April 2, 1910.

DEAR CLARA:

We are leaving at five for Worcester, Mass., for just what purpose I am not certain. We are going to see "Aunt Delia," I know, but for what else I have not the foggiest idea. The President takes these trips just as a dipsomaniac goes on periodical sprees. Most people commiserate with him, thinking that they tire him out, when in fact they are the greatest recreation to him, and he enjoys every minute he is out on one of them. I come back bedraggled and worn out, and he returns from them refreshed and reinvigorated. It is almost freakish, the ghoulish delight he gets from traveling.

Good-bye.
ARCHIE.

Roosevelt, Taft, and the Vatican

[Washington, D. C.,]
April 4, 1910.

DEAR CLARA:

We got back from Millbury and Worcester this morning, having had a very delightful day with the President's Aunt Delia. She lives in a nice old-fashioned Colonial home, just the sort of home one would imagine she would live in, after seeing her.

We were late getting into Washington, and none of us on the car was called until nine o'clock. Mr. Clark, one of the Interstate Commerce Commissioners, returned with us, and he and I were the first to come out. The first thing which caught our eyes, of course, was the refusal of Mr. Roosevelt to meet the Pope, or rather his refusal to meet him if any conditions were to be attached to his visit. It was especially interesting to me, for the reason that everyone here had been prophesying that Mr. Roosevelt would not get himself involved in the same mesh which entangled poor Mr. Fairbanks in his recent visit to Rome. I never dreamed that the Vatican would, for one moment, repeat the mistake it made in the case of Mr. Fairbanks.

I was much interested to see how the President would take it, for he is sailing on pretty narrow seas as far as the Roman Catholic Church is concerned. As he came out I handed him the New York *Herald*, which contained the fullest account of the incident. He made no comment, and although breakfast was on the table he sat down and read the account through and then proceeded to other news. He came to the table without making any comment and Mr. Clark, evidently anxious for some comment from him, opened the subject, but the President said nothing at all. As soon as he had left the car the President turned to me and said:

"Archie, I am very sorry this thing has happened, but I do not see how Roosevelt could have done other than he did. I cannot imagine what the Vatican is thinking about or what sort of advisers the Pope has about him. If this sort of thing keeps up, the life work of Leo will be completely offset by Pius the Tenth, if he continues his present policy."

Of course this incident makes it most important that

the fact that the President sent his photograph to the Pope be not made known. In the present temper of the people it would have a most disastrous effect upon the President's popularity and would unite the whole Protestant world against him. I hope you will not make mention of the fact to anyone. This only goes to show how secretive you must be of anything I write to you. I fear some overzealous Catholic may give publication of the fact to offset the cry which this incident is going to raise against Rome, but I should hate it to get out through any fault of my own.

I don't for a moment think that you are not the soul of discretion, and this warning is merely to impress on you the necessity of keeping my letters very carefully concealed from other people. It is a burden to impose these letters on you, I sometimes think, though you are flattering enough to say that you really enjoy them.

The very fact that the President was waiting until we were alone to make any comment on the incident only shows what confidence he places in me and emphasizes the obligation on my part not to betray his confidence. This incident will unite the Catholics on him more than ever, and they will to a man stand back of him later on. My great fear is that the Protestant world will, sooner or later, realize to what an extent the Catholics endorse him and will become hostile to him on that account.

Good-bye.

ARCHIE.

Captain Butt to Captain J. R. M. Taylor

[Washington, D. C.,]
April 5, 1910.

DEAR JOHN:

When do you come back? It must be time for your regiment to return.

Every day of my life is such a busy one these days that time means practically nothing to me. The whole of American life is agog now over the return of the Great Hunter from Africa and his refusal to see Pius Tenth if his visit was to have any strings attached to it. The anti-Catholic feeling is more intense in the United States to-day than it has been for years, since the old Know-Nothing Days.

Every effort is being made to bring about a split between the President and Mr. Roosevelt, but up to the present time these machinations have been unsuccessful. I hope to bear the royal dispatches to New York when Mr. Roosevelt arrives. I am strongly advising against the President going over for the "Return from Elba" celebration.

Yesterday afternoon, when I went to his office to get him out to ride, I met a number of correspondents, among whom was Oscar Davis. You remember Davis in the Phillipines. He really is among the best of them. They were each one of them complaining bitterly of the fact that they could get no news these days from the White House.

"Only this afternoon," said Davis, "he killed four good stories: one that there was going to be a shake-up in the Cabinet; another, that he had not received one word from Mr. Roosevelt; another, that the Cardinal had called to talk about the incident in Rome; and the other, that he would lead off with a campaign speech at the Ohio dinner Saturday night."

"What are you going to write, then?" I asked.

"Nothing," he said.

"Then I will give you a subject to tackle. Why don't you dwell on the fact that nothing will divert his avowed determination to give this country four years of peace, whether the people want it or no? Only yesterday, on our way from Worcester, Mass., he told me that he would see that this country had peace for four years if he had to cram it down its throat."

And this is his idea. He really cannot be swerved from it—and another thing, he does not care whether he gets credit for anything which is done or not. He was so afraid that he would get the credit for settling the tariff war, which properly belonged to him, that he made haste to give it all to Knox.

But I did not intend to run on in this fashion when I started, except that I know you are interested in what kind of a President he is making. His sense of humor carries him over a good many pitfalls, and sometimes there is a touch of Lincoln in the way he makes use of anecdotes to illustrate a point. Here is one worth preserving and which I have not told to anyone before. I had intended to write it to my sister, to whom I write very fully, now that my dear mother is gone, but I am sure you will appreciate it quite as keenly as she would.

The other day I had an engagement to accompany him to the Brewer funeral, and he was detained so long in the Cabinet room in a conference with Western Senators and Representatives that I had to break in on it to get him started. In fact, Secretary Knox was waiting to go with him also, and as the minutes were slipping by the secretary said:

"Butt, I think you can go in and make him come. I cannot, or I would take the initiative."

So I went, and there I found Senator Smoot, Senator Chamberlain, Senator Dixon, Senator Hughes, and Senator Nelson, and Representative Mondell, and Senator Borah. They were there to protest against the passage of a bill the President wants passed, which legalizes the withdrawal of land from the public settlement done by both him and Mr. Roosevelt. He doubts whether these withdrawals are legal as they stand now. He, however, was evidently determined to push the measure, and the faces of the men with him all seemed to be flushed from excitement when I entered. Senator Borah said:

"Then, Mr. President, as we are to understand it, you are going to do as you damn please without consulting the interests of those states mostly affected."

The President was smiling at the time, and he continued to smile. I only saw that little glint come into his eyes which I know indicates when he is angry. But he laughed, rather chuckled to himself, and then said this:

"I might answer you more directly, but I will merely tell you of an incident which occurred a good many years ago in Watertown, Conn., where my brother Horace has a school. There was an old school teacher there, who determined to have order in his school or else have no school at all, and so one day he picked out the son of the most cantankerous farmer in the neighborhood to dismiss. The father came to the school house to tell the teacher that he must receive back his son, which the teacher refused to do. Whereupon the farmer got exceedingly angry and finally said:

"'It appears to me that you expect to run this school as you damn please.'

"The old pedagogue fixed his eyeglasses and looking calmly into the face of the irate father, said:

"'Your language is coarse, your manner offensive, but you have grasped my idea.'

"Now gentlemen, I leave you this little incident to chew upon, for I cannot stand longer between Brewer and his grave. Good-day."

And he went out still smiling, even patting Borah on the back as he passed him, to take away the personal sting he might otherwise have inflicted.

Good-bye. With love,
ARCHIE.

Taft Contradicts Cardinal Gibbons

[Washington, D. C.,]
April 6, 1910.

DEAR CLARA:

The President, the Secretary of the Navy, and I went riding this afternoon, which fact is hardly worth recording save that it relates to an incident of some importance which took place immediately before we started.

We had intended to leave the White House at half-past four, but Cardinal Gibbons telephoned, asking for an engagement at five, and the President decided to wait for His Eminence. He was with the President less than a half hour. I had been waiting at the House, and thinking I might hurry him up, went to the office. The cardinal had gone, and it seems that on his way out he had been held up by the usual corps of newspaper men who hang about the executive offices. They asked him, of course, if the incident at the Vatican had been discussed by the President and himself. . . .

Knowing of the determination of the President not to be drawn into any comment on the subject, I hastened to his private office, where I found him reading the *Star*. I told him what the reporters had said to me, and he became very angry. . . . The President saw at once what construction might be placed on his interview with the cardinal and thought that Mr. Roosevelt would have every reason to feel aggrieved that he should make any public comment on the matter. He told me then to go outside and tell the correspondents and reporters to come in to his office. I rounded them all up, and when they came in they repeated to the President what they had said to me. They said the cardinal had given it to them officially and that they would be forced to use it. Then he told them they must send his denial at the same time, and he dictated a flat contradiction of what it was stated the cardinal had said, and with this off his mind he hurried over to dress, and by six we were on our way to Alexandria Island.

Good-night.

ARCHIE.

CHAPTER XXXV

CAPTAIN BUTT'S HEART INTEREST

[Washington, D. C.,]
April 9, 1910.

I went to a dinner last evening given by Sowerly, the naval attaché of the British Embassy, to Admiral Sir Percy Scott. He is a quaint, dumpy little man, quite of the naval order, no frills and furbelows. It was altogether the best appointed and best arranged dinner I have seen given outside a private house in Washington. I was much amused at his reply to Mrs. Townsend, who was a Miss Scott, as to what branch of the family of Scotts he belonged. She, of course, is the Grande Dame in Washington society, and her father was a man of power and discernment in Erie, Penn., but I doubt if he was possessed of any great polish or culture, and I don't suppose, from what I know of him, that he ever cared a rap about his family. But the Townsends and the Thornes have coats of arms and crests on everything which belongs to them. So when Mrs. Townsend asked him about his family, he naïvely remarked:

"Oh, we are nobodies at all. I have wanted to find out something about our family, but I never could."

Such modesty in Sir Percy was quite unexpected by Mrs. Townsend, and she was so taken back that she could make no reply at all.

I sat between Mathilde Townsend and Katherine Elkins. I have seen very little of Mathilde of late, for the reason that there has swum into her sea one Peter Gerry, son of Elbridge Gerry, the New York millionaire, and from the first I have suspected that it would end at least to the contentment of Gerry. Mathilde confided to me last night that she thought she would marry him but was anticipating an awful row with her mother in consequence.

Up to the present time Mrs. Townsend has been able to break up all the affairs of Mathilde of which she disapproved, but she has never been able to bring about one which would have been pleasing to her. She is ambitious for Mathilde to marry a coronet at least, and her heart was set on the Duke d'Alba, who was very much in love with her and asked her to marry him. It would have been the most brilliant marriage any American girl has yet made abroad, as marriages are counted in the world there, but she would not marry him and refuses even to return to Europe while he is unmarried. Count Jerome Bonaparte; Dearing, an Englishman; Ordin Robbins—all have at times appeared to be the favored ones, and she has been supposed to be engaged to each of them at various times in her career, but she has been engaged to none of them, though I think she always liked Jerome Bonaparte better than the others.

I, who have grown accustomed to analyze my deepest feelings before you, fail completely here. I had always thought that the announcement of an engagement to anyone else would have been a terrific blow to me, for there is no use to attempt to conceal the fact from you, after all I have said of Mathilde, that she is the only woman who has ever dominated my mind and heart. I think deep down in my soul I felt that she would never marry me. She has the greatest capacity for friendship I have almost ever known in woman and the least capacity for love. Even now, when she tells me she will marry Peter

Gerry, I cannot bring myself to believe that she loves him. It may be I think this because he is so thin and anæmic looking. But she said to me:

"Archie, I have got to marry some day, and Peter seems to be the most suitable man I have ever met. He has everything I have, and he never bores me. He will have his things, and I will have mine, and we will travel and motor and ride. Mother would not have me marry any American, and I so hate foreigners that I cannot think of one as a husband save with repulsion. She will oppose my marrying Peter, but it would be the same if it were you or Jerre or anyone else. She has her heart set on D'Alba. I like old Jimmy, but she would find him an expensive luxury."

And so on. We talked all the evening, and I marveled at myself that I was able to discuss the matter with her at all, for, Clara, my heart was cold and my throat dry and choked. I went through the night like one in a dream and woke this morning as if someone had died in the night. I shall move on in the same way. It will not make any difference in my daily routine, and I fall back on my belief that I was not intended to be one of the happy people of the world, that if I succeed in leaving a record fairly decent, I shall have done what I had set out to do, and I shall not ask for more from the world and not pine away for what I might have had. I have written all this merely because I had set my hand to the task of being frank in everything, even where my own wounds are exposed. I shall not mention her again, save only as one who has passed out of my life into that world of New York and Newport, into which I have peeped but will never enter.

Sweet sister-in-law, when I think of the quiet even tenor of your life and the sweetness of your disposition and the delightful humor you shed about you, I envy Lewis the happy lot he has made his own.

ARCHIE.

Charlie Taft's Way with the Reporters

[Washington, D. C.,]
Sunday Morning, April 10, 1910.

DEAR CLARA:

The President, laughing, told the table of the game the day before, how he had been defeated by the Vice President and myself and yet how the papers had printed the fact that he had defeated the V. P. and I was not even mentioned.

"You don't have to play good golf if you have someone to do the official lying," he said, and I thought he looked rather roguishly at me.

"You don't mean to say that the Vice President beat you?" said Mrs. Taft.

"He did yesterday, my dear, but if I live four years I will give him such a beating that he will not recover from it."

"I don't understand," said one of the Anderson girls.

We all laughed, but the President said quite seriously:

"My dear, all I have to do to beat the Vice President is to live."

Helen told a rather good story on little Charlie, who is wiser than most of the family in many ways. She said she had been sitting in the upper hall when she heard him answer the telephone, and after several "What's thats" she heard him say:

"There is not a word of truth in it, and you can so state it."

"No truth in what, Charles?" asked Helen.

"Nothing. Only a reporter called me up to say that the paper had a report that I was going in long breeches, and I told him there was nothing in the rumor."

ARCHIE.

Alice Longworth's Stinging Wit

April 12, 1910.

DEAR CLARA:

Sunday evening I dined at the White House. After dinner Senator Bourne, Mrs. Exstein, Mrs. Taft, and General Edwards played bridge in the Red Room; the Anderson girls were in the Green Room with two young beaus from Cincinnati, while the President and an old classmate of his, Mr. Clark, and Mrs. More and I sat in the Blue Room, talking at random and occasionally hearing Caruso on the Victor. These old classmates talk very freely with the President and ask some rather embarrassing questions. For instance, Mr. Clark asked the President if he thought Mr. Roosevelt would run for the Presidency at the next election.

"I don't know," said the President. "I don't think he will want to, but the country may demand it of him; and if he does, he will most certainly be elected. I have not heard from him and I have not written to him. Root has written to him and given him a résumé of the events of the Administration and also his own version of the Ballinger-Pinchot dispute. I suppose Pinchot will fill his ears with prejudicial tales, but that I cannot help and I cannot checkmate. If he comes to Washington I shall discuss with him most frankly every act of the Administration, and even should he have committed himself to Pinchot, I have no doubt but that he will change his mind after he learns the facts from me or Root in conversation.

"It is a strange contradiction in Roosevelt's nature, but he has no pride of opinion at all. He does not mind how often he changes his mind if he thinks there is some reason for doing so. I have known him to commit himself to some proposition in the morning and reverse himself five times before evening. But each change was the result of some new information rather than the result of indecision. I have no fear that he will form his opinion in this matter hastily. Should he do so, he will reverse it just as readily when he sees the correspondence and learns of my attitude toward Pinchot. Pinchot is a socialist and a spiritualist, a strange combination and one that is capable of any extreme act. I think Roosevelt knows him thoroughly and will possibly reach the truth of the matter out of his own mouth."

I was to have dined with Alice, but of course went to the White House when the President asked me to dine. While I was spending a rather sober evening, Alice, with Katherine Elkins and Billy Hitt to back her, was paying calls on her friends in unique fashion. When I returned home I found an envelope addressed to me. It contained the ace of spades and the deuce of spades torn in half. This was supposed to indicate that I was not deuce high since the arrival of Peter Gerry.

She called me up to tell me what fun they had had and to give me some account of it. They motored all over town leaving cards in this manner, and at some of the houses the joke took a poignancy that must have found the quick. For instance, Senator Kean of New Jersey lives with his three old sisters, and Alice left therefore three old maids and a knave. At Preston Gibson's she left two queens of diamonds and the nine of diamonds, the "curse of Scotland." Preston first married Miss Field, who possessed a fortune, and when they were divorced he married another fortune in Miss Grace Jarvis, the niece of Senator McMillin. She hit Eleanor Terry and Campario, whose engagement everyone anticipates, though not yet announced, by leaving at the Terrys' a jack of hearts and the joker. At the home of Mrs. Patterson she left for the Countess Gyzycka a torn and disheveled queen of diamonds; the Countess is now seeking a divorce, having paid a thousand dollars for the possession of her child. On Richie Simpkins she left a Yarborough, a whist hand without a face card in it.

When I told the President of this last caper of Alice's, he said:

"There is always a sting in Alice's wit."

But how novel and how cleverly executed!

ARCHIBALD.

Captain Butt to Captain S. A. Cloman

White House Office,
Washington, D. C.,
April 17, 1910.

MY DEAR KID:

Socially, Washington is as mad as ever. Mathilde Townsend, I understand, is to marry Peter Gerry, and last night Mrs. Townsend wept on my shoulder, feeling hopeless as to this marriage, because she wants Mathilde at least to have a coronet, even if she has to pay for it. My suggestion that she invoke the Anti-Trust Law to prevent the marriage and secure the services of Attorney General Wickersham to bring action against the combination of so much capital did not even strike her as funny.

Eleanor Terry is going to marry Campario if either can get the price of the license, while Katherine Elkins is undetermined whether she will marry Billy Hitt or go into a convent.

Alice Longworth is still the dauntless leader of the Night Riders, and the other night upset the whole of Washington by leaving a series of playing cards among her friends, which had a sting in each hand. As far as I can find out, I am the only person that is not mad.

Good-bye. With love to both, I remain, as ever,

Your friend,
ARCHIBALD W. BUTT.

Taft on Roosevelt's Greatness

[Washington, D. C.,]
April 19, 1910.

DEAR CLARA:

Last evening's cotillion was just what I needed to clear up the season's obligations. I danced it with Eleanor Terry, and by staying late and having no White House guests on my mind I was able to dance with every woman to whom I have failed to show some attention during the months gone by. When I have not had White House guests to look after, I have been handicapped by Mathilde Townsend, who never wants to dance and usually has kept me sitting the entire evening in hallways and obscure corners, making a sort of Roman holiday for her. She wanted to dance last night's cotillion with me, and I promised to hold myself in reserve for her to make a final appearance, but at the last she backed out, which left me free for Eleanor and general maneuvers.

Later.

When I got to the office this afternoon I found the President closeted with William Jennings Bryan. They were together for at least an hour, while correspondents and photographers waiting on the outside hoped to get a glimpse of the two men together and learn what they discussed. In consequence we were late in starting to ride. He told me that they had discussed South American affairs, especially matters pertaining to Porto Rico.

"I was more favorably impressed with Bryan to-day than I had ever been before. We talked freely, and he seemed to desire only to impart to me the real conditions. In consequence, I have decided upon several changes in the administration of affairs in Porto Rico."

He sent a cable to Governor Colton to wire at once the purport of the discussion he had had with Mr. Bryan. We met Secretary Meyer on the Potomac driveway, and he rode with us for an hour. On joining us, he said:

"Do you really think Senator Hale is going to retire?"

The President said: "It does sound too good to be true, but I think he is. I am sorry to see Aldrich leave the Senate, but I think Hale's retirement will be a distinct gain.

"You know, Meyer," he said a few minutes later, as if coming to a conclusion, "I think this is an age of small men. I do not think either our House or Senate begin to have the big men in them of former years, even of more recent years than those of Clay, Webster, and Calhoun. We are not as strong in either House as we were in the time of Carlisle, Reed, Turner of Georgia, Crisp; even McKinley on the Ways and Means and Henderson on the Judiciary committees seem larger and more forceful men compared to the present heads of those committees in the House now. In the Senate there has been a decided retrogression in our leaders. It seems to be true of legislative bodies throughout the world to-day. There are no great figures on the English political stage, or in Germany, or Austria, or any of the European countries. There is a pettiness about this immediate period which gives me some concern. I believe we are undergoing some change of which we are unmindful. It may be one of the periods which come frequently before some great epoch, the apparent stagnation which comes immediately before the crystallization of some great world thought or movement."

He stopped talking as quietly as he had begun. He was over Meyer's head, and the latter made no response, or else he showed his wisdom by remaining silent, or possibly he disagreed and did not like to say so. At any rate, when the President spoke again it was merely to say:

"I don't suppose there was ever such a reception as that being given Theodore in Europe now. It does not surprise me that rulers, potentates, and public men should pay him this honor, but what does surprise me is that small villages which one would hardly think had ever heard of the United States should seem to know all about the man. The receptions which are accorded him in small obscure towns and hamlets are most significant. It illustrates how his personality has swept over the world, for after all no great event transpired during either of his administrations and no startling legislation was enacted into law. It is the force of his personality that has passed beyond his own country and the capitals of the world and seeped into the small crevices of the universe."

The secretary asked the President what would be Roosevelt's chief claim to greatness, and the President answered promptly:

"His rousing of public conscience. What else he will do it is hard to tell, for he is still a very young man, but up to the present time his power over the imagination and his inspiration to the public conscience is his predominant claim to greatness; that is, as I see it."

Good-night.
ARCHIE.

CHAPTER XXXVI

TAFT TALKS OF THIRD TERMS

[Washington, D. C.,]
April 22, 1910.

DEAR CLARA:

I went riding this afternoon with the President and Frank Kellogg. The latter is known as the "Trust Buster" of the last two administrations. He is a lawyer of considerable reputation and entered politics from Minnesota as a recreation. He does not seek office, although I think he would like to be a United States Senator. He is at present head of the State Central Committee in Minnesota and has become a power on account of the confidence which has been imposed in him by both Mr. Roosevelt and the President. This much by way of introduction to him, if I have not already introduced him to you before in other letters. However, all this is merely to give weight to what he told me while we were sitting in front, or rather I should say in the rear, of the White House yesterday afternoon, waiting for the President.

He told me that President Roosevelt really had no objection to a third term *per se* and that his determination to quit at the end of his last term was due solely to other reasons. He said he was summoned to Oyster Bay in July, 1907, and when he got there the first thing President Roosevelt said to him was that he feared the party was getting ready to renominate him.

"I don't want it, and yet the party has no right to put it to me in this way. It should not be up to me to accept or to decline it."

"How are you going to prevent it, then?" Mr. Kellogg asked; and he said the President answered:

"There is one man who can prevent it, and that man is Taft, and he can only do it through such men as yourself coming out boldly for him. You must go to Washington, see my other friends such as yourself, and each one of you announce yourselves for Taft, and then the public will accept my determination, expressed in my statement the night of my election, as sincere, and will begin to choose their delegates for someone else."

"I then asked Mr. Roosevelt," said Mr. Kellogg, "why he had ever written that statement, and his answer to me then seems of the greatest importance. He said: 'I did

it because I had determined to make a fight on the corporations, on the railroads especially for their rebate
systems and their pass systems, and all the other evils
which I felt it time to throttle or check. I would have been
greatly hampered in my work had there been the possibility of another term ahead of me, and so I decided to become a free lance as far as politics was concerned.' I have
no reason to doubt what he told me; in fact, I became certain that he had given me his real reasons for his declaration later, as the campaign proceeded."

"Up to that time were you for a third term for Mr.
Roosevelt?" I asked Mr. Kellogg.

"I was, and was one of his friends who had not seriously
accepted his declaration not to run again, and was doing
all I could at that time to bring about his renomination.
But after that talk with him, I came back to Washington,
then went West, and have never swerved once in my
loyalty to President Taft since that day. I tell you this
merely to make the point that should he desire to become
President again, there will be no moral reason within himself to fight out as to a third term."

Then they (the President and Mr. Kellogg) talked over
the prospects of the next fall elections, and both seemed
reasonably certain that the next House would be Democratic.

"It is only to be expected," said Mr. Kellogg. "I shall
never forget going to Mr. Roosevelt before your nomination and telling him that there was a great demand for
tariff reform in the West and I thought he should send a
message to Congress demanding tariff revision. 'No,' he
said, 'God Almighty could not pass a tariff bill and win
at the next election following its passage. The only time
to pass a tariff bill is the first year of a new administration,
and trust to have the effects counteracted before another
Presidential election.'"

Mr. Kellogg spoke openly of the effort to have Mr. Roosevelt run again for the Presidency and the belief that he would not do anything to encourage it.

The President said:

"Roosevelt is going to have a hard time when he returns. I really feel sorry for him. His rôle is even more difficult than the one I have to play. Every man with an ambition, every new movement, will try to drag to him and to it the ex-President, and whether he will be able to keep out of all I don't know. One thing I feel certain of, Frank, and that is that he will never be President again. I base this belief entirely on the anti-third term sentiment in this country. It is much deeper than is supposed. People are afraid of it, more afraid of it in a man like Roosevelt than in a weaker man like Grant. I don't mean to say that Grant was a weak man in the common acceptation of that term, but when it comes to politics and moral determination he was infinitely weaker than Theodore Roosevelt. Should the party believe that it could only win with Roosevelt and should it force the nomination on him, I do not think he could be elected. The strongest man the Republicans can put up, in my opinion, is Hughes. He would be stronger than Roosevelt and infinitely stronger than I would be, and if party success should demand someone stronger than I am, I would gladly see it turn to Hughes."

"If you cannot be reëlected," said Mr. Kellogg, "then Hughes could not be elected. Of that I am certain. I count on your gaining strength right along now."

"Well, if the worst comes to the worst, I can play the rôle of Harrison and allow myself to be put up merely to be knocked down. If the party foresees defeat to this extent, I think I owe that much to the party."

Good-bye.
ARCHIE.

Hughes Appointed to the Supreme Court

April 25, [1910].

DEAR CLARA:

I am as happy over the acceptance of Governor Hughes as if I were responsible for the Supreme Court itself. I do not know of anything which has given me as much real pleasure, and the President—well, he is fairly beaming with delight. Coming back from the exercises at the Howard University, he said he felt that Hughes would never have accepted had he not come in contact with him as he had done at Champlain and at Albany later on.

He sent at once for the Attorney General and gave directions to have the appointment made out and ordered Latta to take it to the Senate at once, if the Senate was in session. I left the room as the Attorney General entered, and it was four o'clock when Latta came through the secretary's office with the appointment. The President signed it, and then we started for the automobile. As we passed the press room the President stopped and looked in, as if to tell old Bill Price of the *Star* and the other newspaper men who are usually there, but everyone, thinking that the day's work was over, had gone. The President said as he settled back in the big Steamer:

"Well, I think I have scooped the boys this time."

The President did not speak again until we reached the entrance of the University and then it was to say:

"Yes, Archie, that is a great appointment. How do you think it will be taken?"

"It will be a monument to your administration," I said. "There was every political reason why you should not have made it and apparently every reason why he should not have accepted it."

"Yes," he said, more to himself than to me, "such an appointment makes politics look petty."

When we got back to the office it was too late to ride, so the President went in and sent for a copy of his letter to Hughes, which he let me read. It was written in longhand and he frankly told the governor that he wanted him to accept the vacancy caused by the death of Brewer, realizing at the same time what he would have to give up should he do so. He then said that he had always believed that some day he would be President of this country and also he realized that he was a poor man and that within ten years at the practice of law he would build up for himself a fortune. He then told him, if he desired to decline it for any reason, that he would offer him the next vacancy, even if it were the chief justiceship, for that was the place he had always hoped to see him fill if he ever went on the Supreme Bench at all. After he had signed the letter, he added quite a long postscript in which he asked the governor not to construe this remark as a promise of the chief justiceship, should it become vacant in his term, for there was no telling what exigency might arise, but he felt that such a mind and force should be at the head of this bench, though he felt that he should not commit himself at the present time. He added that he did not believe in the theory, seemingly prevalent, that promotions should not come from the bench.

April 26, 1910.

We are busy this morning arranging for the reception of the Imperial Highness Prince Tsai Tao. He arrives Thursday morning, and we will meet him with a troop of cavalry and pay him every honor. He is the brother of the Regent and Chief of Staff of the Chinese army. I received a letter from Fletcher, our chargé, last month, telling me of the intended visit and asking me to see that he was given a fine reception, as he was not only a great personage in the Empire, but a "good sport," to use his exact language, and deserving of recognition on this account alone. He is to be accompanied by Lord Li Ching Mi, who is a son of old Li Hung Chang, who was given such an ovation wherever he went a number of years ago, when touring the world.

There are some ten or fifteen in the suite, and it ought to be a very interesting ceremonial. The President will receive them in the afternoon, and in the evening he will give a stag dinner of fifty persons. He keeps adding names, so there is no telling how large the dinner will be. He told me he wanted the Prince on his right and the Speaker of the House on his left. The Vice President will be there, so we will pivot from him opposite the President. There are two ambassadors to be present, the German and the Mexican, and according to all customs the German ought to sit at the left of the President. Just why the President has decided so to honor the Speaker I do not know, but I presume the reason will show up along the line somewhere before the dinner is over. I fear diplomacy is being sacrificed for politics. But as long as it is not the British ambassador, I don't mind pushing the diplomats down a peg.

I hate this sort of business. I don't mind it so much for the White House, but I have calls on me from all over the country, and every request suggests some difficulty that has to be acted on separately. Some new problem arises all the time. For instance, the Americus Club in Pittsburgh, which is entertaining the President at a banquet next week—or is it this week? I don't know—sent me the list of guests to seat. I found among them the Governor of the State and the Secretary of State and several ambassadors and cabinet officers. I arranged it more by instinct than anything else and placed the Governor of Pennsylvania over the Secretary of State. Fearing this might offend the little bantam Secretary of State, I thought it wise to submit it to the State Department. At once a storm broke over my head, and the department yielded every point except that the Secretary of State must take precedence over the governor. I took the ground that the head of a sovereign state ranked in fact every person present within his own state except the President, and we finally decided to leave it to the Secretary of State himself. I explained my theory and Assistant Secretary Wilson combated it. Secretary Knox at once decided with me and ordered that hereafter this order be made a precedent in the department itself.

I find it very easy to bluff the State Department, for after all the men at the head of it are governed by some precedent established in the past by some people who had no idea of etiquette or social comities. I hope, before I give up my present detail, that I will have established certain rules which will be permanent in the government here and afford precedences for future guidance in the matter of official etiquette.

Do you remember my telling you some months ago to keep an eye on Fletcher, that he was certain to rise in his profession? He has been given a mission as a reward for his excellent work in China as chargé, and is now on his way to report as Minister to Chile. They could have done worse than appoint him Minister to China, but the department was afraid he was too young and that the Orientals would not have regarded his appointment as a compliment. He is one of the most popular diplomats there, however.

Good-bye.

ARCHIE.

A Quiet Evening in the White House

[Washington, D. C.,]
April 28, 1910.

DEAR CLARA:

The President and John McIlhenny and I went riding and covered about eight miles. While we were on the Speedway, General Miles was thrown from his horse and had two ribs broken. When we heard about it a shiver went through my spinal cord, for I am always expecting something like that to happen to the President. When I express any fear for him he always says with a laugh:

"Well, those who take up the horse must perish with the horse."

And that is all I get from him.

He and Mrs. Taft dined alone last night, and when I dropped in later to see about the reception to the prince from China, I found as lonely a picture as I have ever seen, or so it seemed to me. They were sitting together on the long sofa in the Blue Room, he asleep and she very wan and pale in appearance.

Are the reports of snow and a freeze in the South exaggerated, and is the cotton crop greatly damaged?

ARCHIE.

Mr. Cannon as a Social Success

[Washington, D. C.,]
April 29, 1910.

The dinner last night was a great success. The art of the other cook was missing, but what we lacked in actual foodstuffs we made up in music, picturesque costumes, and good humor. When I went to see Mrs. Taft later, she asked me what I thought of the new cook. I could not conscientiously praise her, so I spoke of the flowers and the music, and she, very quick to see the point, added:

"I must say I thought the boned turkey not so good and the salad bad."

Whenever the President has a stag dinner, Mrs. Taft has her dinner served at the same time, but in the Breakfast Room, adjoining the State Dining Room. She keeps her housekeeper's eye on the meal in this way, at the same time getting the benefit of the music and the general hum at the dinner table. It makes her feel less lonely, and she never has anyone dine with her on these occasions.

The next time the President entertains foreigners, I hope he will leave out the Speaker. He was the last to arrive last evening. The Prince and Lord Li came in late, after most of the company had assembled, and taking his Imperial Highness by the arm I led him among the forty-odd guests and presented him and Lord Li to each. When the Speaker came in with Senator Bailey, I asked them if I might present them to the guest of the evening, and Bailey said he would be most pleased to meet him, but Uncle Joe said loud enough for Lord Li, I feared, to hear him:

"You mean for me to go over there to meet that Chink?"

"Not unless you desire to," I said, "but he is the guest of honor."

"Oh, all right, I will do as you say, but it goes against my pride for an American free-born citizen to cross a room to meet a heathen Chinee."

The scene was in strong contrast to the one later in the library while the men were smoking, when Uncle Joe, a little the worse for the dinner, amused the entire room by keeping one arm around the shoulders of the Prince and the other around the neck of Lord Li, with a cigar stuck at seventy degrees out of the corner of his mouth, telling them all about the Constitution and government in general and airing his ignorance of Eastern affairs.

Lord Li was earnestly trying to interpret to the Prince

what the Speaker was saying, but he was unable to translate the slang of the old fellow, even if he understood it himself, which I am sure he did not. When he was hugging them he was punching them in the ribs, and finally they began to poke each other in the ribs as a sign that they understood at least the humor of the situation. The President called me and, whispering that he feared the Prince did not comprehend the wonders of Uncle Joe, suggested to me to separate them. Later the President did rather a graceful thing, I thought. He escorted the Prince and Lord Li to the living end of the corridors where Mrs. Taft was and presented them to her. As I joined her for a moment later, she said:

"The Prince is really the prettiest man I have seen in a long time."

I told you yesterday, he *was* handsome; and last night her words described him even better. He was dressed, or rather gowned, in all his robes of royalty—a dark blue shirt over which he wore his brilliant yellow jacket, the sign of his station. On his head, and never removed, was the brilliant headpiece which men of his rank wear at all times.

Good-bye. With love to Lewis,
ARCHIE.

CHAPTER XXXVII

TRAVELS AND POLITICS

Cincinnati,
Wednesday night, May 3, 1910.

Everything seems to be going wrong for the President just now, and he shows considerable bitterness over the situation. He was so confident that his railroad measure would pass the Congress and so wanted it that he keenly feels the possible defeat of it.

While we were in the Music Hall to-night, listening to the splendid performance of Judas Maccabeus, a telegram was brought to me which I opened and found to be from the Attorney General. The latter told the President that the insurgents were in control of the bill and had practically disemboweled it, or would do so on the morrow. He advised the President to make a public statement and place the blame on the men on whom it belonged and call attention to the fact that there was not a Republican majority in the Senate; for those who called themselves Republicans were voting with the Democrats.

The President seemed so happy in his old town, surrounded by old friends and family, that I hated to break in on his thoughts and his enjoyment, but he does not like to be kept in ignorance, so I handed him the telegram. He sat for a while looking into space and not hearing a note of the beautiful solo "Sound the Alarm," which was then being sung. He made up his mind during these few minutes what he would do, for he leaned over and whispered to me that he wanted to see the stenographer as soon as he left the hall. When he did so, and as soon as he got to the club, where Mrs. Maxwell was giving a supper in his honor, he sent a telegram to the Attorney General that he would not make a statement, as he was not sufficiently advised to do so intelligently; that for him to become abusive now would only further complicate matters and impair other measures which he hoped to get through.

This was very indicative of his mode of action. He was feeling most resentful, and he would have loved to pick up the club, but he exercised that restraint which is most characteristic of him and which gives him such poise in the midst of agitation and turmoil.

We reached Cincinnati this morning, and I was surprised

to see the little enthusiasm shown on his arrival at his old city the first time since his inauguration. I expressed my surprise, and the secret service man who had been with him even before he was inaugurated said it was always this way in Cincinnati. They know him so well here that there is no curiosity to see him, and they take it for granted they are pleased to see him. It may be that Ohio is becoming like Virginia in the past—the presence of a President does not excite it as it does other states, which are not so accustomed to them. However, I think the reception was very poorly managed, and with a proper parade and blare of trumpets the home town could have called the attention of the country to the fact that Cincinnati at least had not joined in the howl against her favorite son. But if his reception on the streets was lacking in enthusiasm, it was compensated for by the warmth of reception he received from people of his own social class, for all day he was surrounded by old friends and members of his family whose pride and devotion to him were manifested in every way.

St. Louis,
May 4, 1910.

It is always delightful to visit St. Louis. It warms the President's heart to get the reception which always comes to him here. These people have the art of entertainment down to a science. They never do too much, and they always seem to be considering the pleasure of their distinguished guest rather than edging and pushing for individual advantage.

A. W. B.

On train between St. Louis and Cincinnati,
May 5, 1910.

At breakfast this morning the President, Norton, the Assistant Secretary of the Treasury, and I sat for a long time talking. The President as a rule likes to dawdle over the newspapers at breakfast, but this morning he got interested in discussing the future development of Washington and American cities in general, and from McKim's plans for Washington he got to discussing Root and the part the latter played in this work, and then Roosevelt, and the old days when he and Mr. Root were in the Cabinet together. He said:

"The fact of the matter is, I get a good deal more credit for what was done than I deserve, for after all, when I came into the War Department I merely followed the way opened up by Root, and to him more than to anyone else is due the credit of revival in interest in art and architecture in Washington. It was not until he came there and saw the possibilities of developing the capital in artistic design that he began to make a study of the old plans of L'Enfant with a view of adopting them for the newer Washington. He is really a lover of architecture and painting and sculpture, and to gain his ends he brought to bear on men who might oppose his ideas all the diplomacy and forethought of which he was capable."

Turning to the old cabinet days, he said laughing:

"What a time we used to have there! Root and I were what were called conservative members of the Administration, Root being a good deal more conservative than I at times, I fear, but we were the two whom Roosevelt sometimes did not advise as to what he was doing until after it was done for fear of meeting opposition—as, for instance, when he wrote that Judge Humphrey letter. That letter would never have been written had he consulted us or brought it before the Cabinet."

"That was one of the things which caused us in Chicago to speak of debauching the judiciary," said Mr. Norton.

"Well, the fact of the matter is," said the President, "Roosevelt had a good deal of contempt for the judiciary.

He did not like the delay of the law when he felt the public weal was to be served. You know, you hear now that he is not unlike Napoleon, and it is becoming popular to speak of him in comparison to Napoleon. There is something in the comparison, to this extent at least: Roosevelt saw no reason why he should not reach results direct, and he never bothered about the means as long as the ends to be obtained were for the public good. But when he would get into hot water, he would send for the conservative members of the Cabinet and depend upon us to get him out of it.

"How well I remember—Archie, I think it was before you came to him—the time he was pressing his rate bill. He left his old friends and got tangled up with Clapp and Chandler and Tillman and Bailey, and when everything seemed to be in a hopeless snarl he sent for Lodge, Tillman, and myself. I shall never forget that meeting. We saw at once what was wanted, and after he diplomatically called for help Lodge told him this incident. Lodge could always speak very freely to him. Neither Root nor I would have dared to say it.

"'Theodore,' said Lodge, 'you remind me of what Mrs. Blaine said once when some of her friends went to her to commiserate with her about the way her husband occasionally became attracted by a new pair of eyes and followed them to the exclusion of all else. "How you must suffer, dear Mrs. Blaine," they said, "when Mr. Blaine leaves you so much for other women!" "Well," answered Mrs. Blaine, "I don't mind as much as you think, for I have lived a long time with Mr. Blaine, and I have gone through with this sort of thing a good deal, but I always know that after he has followed someone else for three or four weeks he will get sick, and then he is certain to come back to me. You can always depend upon sickness overtaking them if you only have the patience to wait."'

"Roosevelt took it good-naturedly, but I don't think he liked the story very much. Roosevelt's methods were essentially those of the old sailor in *Huckleberry Finn*, I think it was, who decided to hang a sailor for killing a nigger. When the crowd of citizens came on board to protest against the action, his reply was, 'Well, didn't he kill the nigger?—yes. Oughtn't he to hang for it?—yes. Then why not hang him?' But they persisted, 'He ought to have a trial, he didn't kill the nigger,' and so on. He always came back to the direct way. Roosevelt believed in administrative justice, and as a rule he was seldom wrong; only he ought more often to have admitted the legal way of reaching the same ends."

When we reached Cincinnati we made a stop for fifteen minutes. Mr. Charlie Taft came to the depot, and he and the President had a few minutes together. After the train pulled out the President said:

"Charlie is swept off his feet by Ballinger. He sees no way but to let Ballinger out of the Cabinet, and I am just as strong in my determination to take no action in the matter as long as nothing is proven against him. If Ballinger himself offers to leave and should present his resignation, I suppose I would feel justified in accepting it, for after all he is not a personal attaché of myself, but a public servant, and the people have the right to have servants whom they have confidence in; but I shall not ask for his resignation, and I am not so certain that I would accept it if offered. It would depend on the way it was done."

The President has taken the greatest fancy to Norton and talks most freely to him, far more than he would to some of his cabinet. The President went to his room for a few minutes, and after he left Norton turned to me and said:

"I don't want to see him call for Ballinger's resignation, but I think it the most selfish policy on the part of Ballinger to remain. He is the heaviest burden on the President, and the people in the West will never get close to the President until he rids himself of Ballinger. I don't see how two such men as Pinchot and Ballinger, calling themselves gentlemen, can have acted toward this man as they have done and still regard themselves as gentlemen. Each are equally culpable in my mind."

Good-bye.

ARCHIE.

[Washington, D. C.,]
Friday, May 13, 1910.

DEAR CLARA:

The President has named Mr. Roosevelt to represent us at the King's funeral. With him and the Kaiser present, it will be a wonder if the poor corpse gets a passing thought.

Good-bye.

ARCHIE.

The President Is Troubled

[Washington, D. C.,]
Sunday, May 15, 1910.

DEAR CLARA:

The only shadow on the day is the mood of the President, which was black and pathetic. He is feeling very keenly the way the party is splitting up, but what he feels more than anything else in a political way is the efforts which the Pinchot people are making to drag him into the investigation. Yesterday they brought out as a witness a stenographer of Mr. Ballinger's, who took an affidavit that the President had not written the opinion himself, which he claimed to have written, but had simply O. K.'d what Mr. Ballinger submitted to him. The President showed the utter falsity of the statement by producing his own letter and the sworn statement of the secretary who had taken it down, but for a President to be forced to offer proofs to substantiate his own statement is reaching the limit. He said to me this morning:

"For a long time I did not believe the reports that the whole trouble is the outcome of a well-organized conspiracy on the part of Garfield and Pinchot to discredit my administration, but I am beginning to believe it to be true. I have tried to have this investigation impartial and conducted on legal lines, but I am to be forced to enter the fight, and if I do, I shall make public such facts as will utterly annihilate Garfield and those who are behind this matter."

The President had to leave before the close to meet a lot of Senators, whom he had called together with a view of bringing a little peace into the distressed Republican ranks. He pocketed his pride and asked men for whom he has no respect at all to join the conference. The list of those there is interesting to me, for I want to see what effect the meeting will have on some of them, especially on Borah, Brown, Crawford, Burkett, and Piles. The full list is: Senators Root, Borah, Brown, Crawford, Dixon, Carter, Nelson, Flint, Jones, Brandegee, Smoot, Burkett, Sutherland, Piles, Nixon, Guggenheim, Heyburn, Crane, Aldrich, and Gamble.

I wish we were going riding this afternoon, but Mrs. Taft has corralled the President for a motor trip to Goldsborough's farm out beyond the University. Goldsborough claims to be able to produce the best strawberries and the best dachshunds, and he has convinced Mrs. Taft about the strawberries from samples which he continually sends to her at the White House, so that she has permitted herself to become interested in the dog problem too, and so we are going to inspect his kennel this afternoon.

I have just an hour between luncheon and the hour set

for the motor trip, so instead of sleeping I am putting in the time writing to you. I find that if I delay writing when I have something in mind to write, the time and place never return to do it just in the same way. It is the same thing when one is looking for old pieces of furniture. If you fail to purchase when you find what you want, thinking to get something else later, you never do it. China and Japan are filled with bric-à-brac which I passed by, thinking another opportunity would come to get them, and I see empty places in my cabinet and on my table, whenever I look at them, in consequence.

Good-bye.
ARCHIE.

May 16, 1910.

Played golf with the President, General Edwards, and Secretary Meyer yesterday afternoon. The President was in better form than he had been this season, and when the game was finished it was found that the Secretary and I had defeated the President and General Edwards two down, but that the President had the best individual score by eight points.

"I could not play Saturday," he said, "for I could not put my mind on it. I was thinking about that damned scoundrelly stenographer who sold himself to betray the private correspondence of the man he was working for. It would have been bad enough had his affidavit contained the truth, but when it consisted of a lie, or to say the least a perversion of the facts, it seems to me that there was no excuse for his offense. However, I got him off my mind by ordering Ballinger to dismiss him to-day, and so with a clean conscience I can buckle down to this game. The beauty of golf to me is that you cannot play if you permit yourself to think of anything else."

To-night the Preston Gibsons are giving an Indian

party at their country place down near Alexandria. Everyone has to go in an Indian costume, and the fête is to be on
the lawn.

The entire spring has been so chilly continuously that
many think that the comet is drawing the heat rays of the
sun away from the earth. Certainly we have no record of
such a cold season before. Before the comet appeared last
March we had extremely hot weather, and it was thought
that there would be a general exodus from the city in May.
Most of the houses have relighted their furnace fires. They
have done so at the White House, which I think is a mistake, for every room has an open fireplace in it, and the
wood logs are much more healthful at this season of the
year than furnace heat.

I am going to wear at the Gibsons' to-night the full cow-
boy costume which was presented to President Roosevelt
by the people of Wyoming, and which he gave to me the
last month he was President. It is made entirely of skins
and is a wonderful work of art. This and the Navajo saddle
blanket which he used on his sixty-mile ride in Wyoming
on the famous horse presented to him by the state and
named after it are the most valuable mementoes I have
of my former chief. I must not forget the spurs which he
gave me, but these I keep in my cabinet. Apart from
having been given to me by him, they are of great interest
as a relic of the earliest Spanish days in the Far West.

Tuesday, 17, 1910.

The Indian lawn fête was a great success. It was exceedingly well done. There was no one there who was not in
costume. Dinner was served under tents, and here happened the only disagreeable incident of the evening. A
band of Sioux Indians who had been asked by Gibson to
attend and execute a war dance, came in full war parapher-
nalia, and when supper was announced they stolidly went

into the tent and sat themselves at one of the tables. They were members of Buffalo Bill's Wild West Show, and they were not supposed to be up in all the small points in etiquette. They simply saw food coming and they prepared for it. However, there were not seats enough for the make-believe Indians, and so the real redskins were invited to leave the table and tent, and they got in a huff and left the grounds, not returning at all. Everyone felt keenly the insult which Preston had laid on these people, but it was too late to do anything, and so the party went on, uproarious in its merriment and madness.

After dinner a monstrous bonfire was lighted on the grounds and the revelers danced around it with tomahawks and occasionally let off firearms, while others sat in groups around, watching the scene, and added to the picture themselves. I wore the buckskin and chamois suit of Mr. Roosevelt and styled myself a squaw man.

I returned rather early, bringing Nick Longworth back with me. We went to the Metropolitan, where he and I ordered sausages and scrambled eggs and talked until two in the morning.

The Roosevelts believe that the Tafts are in the White House solely as a result of their father's predetermination to put him there. The President agrees to this, and he thinks he has done everything in his power to pay that debt, and feeling as I do toward both men, I think he has done so. From his standpoint he has shown every honor to Alice and Nick, and in Mrs. Taft's condition it was not possible for her to do more in the way of entertaining them. The President has written to Mrs. Roosevelt on both her sailings to Europe, and he has dined with Alice and the De Chambruns several times.

If I were a judge on the bench, I could not decide as to which of the two men has acted the lesser part in the matter of courtesy and proper conduct. They have both been marvels in self-restraint and fairness up to the present time, and it will be a public calamity to have such splendid examples of honesty and fair dealing marred now by petty personal jealousies.

Well, I think this enough for one day, don't you?

With love,

ARCHIE.

CHAPTER XXXVIII

HE HEARS FROM CATHOLICS AND TALKS TO METHODISTS!

[Washington, D. C.,]
May 21, 1910.

DEAR CLARA:

The President has worked in the afternoons now for several days, and except on the days of the stupid garden parties we have been able to get in eighteen holes. Yesterday he and General Edwards and I played again, doing most of the holes in misty rain. He made a wonderful score, making the eighteen holes in ninety-two, defeating the best ball of Clarence and me by one. I made a splendid score, coming back in forty-four. He told me yesterday that he wanted me to go to New York and meet Mr. Roosevelt and take a letter from him. He is going to invite the ex-President to come to Washington to visit him, and my prediction is that he will come.

The President is getting a great many letters from priests and bishops all over the country on one subject or another, but their real purport is to pledge themselves to him, and, as far as they can do so, their congregations. Carpenter says it is surprising the number of such letters which have come in since the episode in Rome. The President does not underrate this influence. He told me yesterday—that is why I mention it to you to-day—that the feeling among the clergy in the Church against Mr. Roosevelt was very intense, and he did not think he would be able to overcome it for the reason that the Church felt that the Vatican had lost prestige by the incident, and I confess it has done so. I feel it myself. My only hope is that it will not manifest itself in any way in the reception in New York.

I think the President looks for the Church to be a powerful factor in his renomination, and he, of course, has the brains to take advantage of the mistakes of others. But whether Mr. Roosevelt will not be able to overcome this feeling on his return, or else take another tack and utilize the hostility of the Church to his advantage, providing, of course, that he will have any desire to try again for the Presidency, remains to be seen. There seems to be no doubt in the President's mind that Garfield, Pinchot, and the magazines will go to any limit to force the nomination of Mr. Roosevelt next time. My own opinion is that he himself will be the main obstacle. I have certainly seen no reason so far to change my opinion that he will refuse to permit his name to be used for the overthrow of the President in the next convention—the allies, Nick, all others, to the contrary.

Night before last the President addressed ten thousand Methodists at a Sunday-school convention and made a remarkably fine address. I went for him just after dinner and found that Mrs. Taft wanted to go also. She had on an evening gown, and I did not think it was a nice costume for such a strait-laced meeting and said so. The President agreed with me, but thought she might keep on a wrap. Her wrap was a light pink satin and had slits down the back. When she got there and went on the stand, she saw, and so did the President, that her dress was entirely inappropriate, and she spent most of the time dragging at her wrap to keep the flesh underneath from peeping out at the bishops. The convention, when it heard that she was there, kept calling for her, until the President took her by the hand and led her to the stand. She looked very sweet and bowed gracefully, and I thought she made a good impression in spite of the ungodly raiment she had on. The President presented her as the real President of the United States, which was greeted with great applause.

ARCHIE.

A Rebuff for Secretary MacVeagh

[Washington, D. C.,]
Saturday night, May 21, 1910.

When I went for the President this afternoon to go to the golf links, he was closeted with Secretary MacVeagh. However, we got away by three and started for Chevy Chase, Mr. Charlie Taft being with us. We were to meet General Edwards out there, which we did, and the game ended by Clarence and I defeating the President two down, he playing our best ball.

Going out, the President said he feared that MacVeagh was getting himself in hot water. The Secretary of the Treasury had come to him to plead with him for Beveridge and to get the Administration to help the latter in his fight for reëlection. Ever since the President had his frank talk with the Indianian and told him what he thought of it, Beveridge, he said, had not been near him, but he had secured MacVeagh's assistance. It seems that the Secretary is a connection in some way of Beveridge's wife and,

"More than that," said the President to his brother, "MacVeagh is a little tinged with insurgent doctrines. MacVeagh tells me that he has got into a most embarrassing situation regarding Indiana and Beveridge, and has pledged to them his support. I told him frankly I would do anything to aid the Republicans of Indiana, but I would do nothing for Beveridge, and if MacVeagh has got himself into an embarrassing situation he must get himself out of it, for I will not permit him to compromise the Administration. If I do anything for Beveridge, Watson and Cannon and their friends will do nothing to aid me to secure the legislation which I want, which they do not want, but which they are willing to assist me to obtain, and I know that if their support is withdrawn my bills are defeated. If MacVeagh expects me to sacrifice my legislation for Beveridge, he is mistaken. I am putting these bills over all personality and politics."

"Do you think MacVeagh contemplates threatening you?" asked his brother.

"I think he would if Mrs. MacVeagh did not like official life as much as she does. Even this may not deter him from going to extremes," said the President, "but I have decided on my line of action, and he must acquiesce or—— If MacVeagh would quit the Administration for Beveridge, then he is at liberty to do so. That is all I have got to say."

ARCHIBALD.

Taft's View of Sunday Card Playing

[Washington, D. C.]
May 23, 1910.

DEAR CLARA:

After luncheon we tramped over the gardens and ate cherries and strawberries *ad libitum*, and I suppose most of the party got the stomach ache. The President and I did not, for almost immediately we went for a ride on horseback and met a pouring rain before we returned, and so the body had little time to think of such lesser evils as cherries and berries. He had ordered his riding togs sent out, and we made the start from the Glovers'. It began to rain just as we left, but we refused to turn back. While we were in the woods a heavy thunderstorm came up, and this always makes me a little nervous, for I invariably remember every case I ever heard of where people have been killed by lightning while out riding. I don't feel that way unless I am with him. I find that having a President on one's hands so continuously makes one conscious of the responsibility.

Mr. Charlie Taft is spending two days at the White House and met us at the door with a good laugh when he saw his big brother soaked but steaming like a big bake oven. I went back for dinner, and we got General Edwards, and the four of us played auction bridge while the President read Omar Khayyám. Mr. Charlie Taft made some comment on bridge playing on Sunday, and the President agreed with him that from a purely puritanical point of view it was wicked.

"I abstain on account of public sentiment, but I don't think it is one whit as wicked as spending one's evening reading Omar," the President said, laughing.

"Nor as tiresome," said Mrs. Taft, and so glibly that we all began to laugh.

After Mrs. Taft left the room Mr. Charlie Taft said seriously to his brother that he hoped it would not become known that cards were ever played at the White House on Sunday.

"I don't care if it does, old man, I see no harm in it, and moreover I will not forbid anything which gives Mrs. Taft any amusement and takes her mind off her troubles. I should not like it to become known, because I do not think anyone, especially one trusted by the people with office, has the right to violate any of the prejudices of the people; but for any effect it would have on my own fortunes, I do not think I care. I am going through this administration and do what I deem to be right irrespective of what people may think. I am prepared to take my hammering, and I have also made up my mind not to let it make me unhappy, as it did Cleveland and Harrison."

"That's right, old man," said his brother, laughing cheerily and slapping him on the back, "and I will stand by you whether right or wrong."

"I know that, Charlie," said the President, giving the elder man an affectionate hug. "No one could accuse you of ever being a fair-weather brother."

Good-night.

ARCHIE.

A Poor Golfer Has His Day

Sunday, May 29, 1910.

DEAR CLARA:

Several other important things have taken place within the past few days. The President told me last night that he had written a long letter to Mr. Roosevelt telling him what he had accomplished during the past year, what he had hoped to be accomplished, and the reasons for his failures where he had failed. At first he said he thought he ought not to write at all; then he felt that possibly this silence would be misunderstood, for after all he owed Mr. Roosevelt a debt of gratitude which he had to acknowledge, and silence at this time might be construed by him as an evidence that he was trying to evade it. I am glad he wrote, for, as I told him, President Roosevelt would have done so had the situations been reversed. It gives the latter one less reason to assume a hostile attitude toward him, if that is in his mind at all.

Mrs. Taft has gone on a visit to her home, and the President is entirely by himself. He and I and Secretary Dickinson played golf yesterday afternoon. The President wanted the Vice President and Secretary Meyer, but both had gone out of town, and so I suggested Secretary

Dickinson. The latter had ridden out in the car one day with him, and coming back he had asked me on the sly to suggest him sometime for golf. When I told him yesterday the President wanted him, the old war horse looked frightened for the first time and began to make all sorts of excuses, but as he had got me into it I did not let him off. He played an awful game, making each hole in anywhere from ten to sixteen, besides paying no heed to the etiquette of the game, but kept walking and talking on the putting greens and driving out of turn, etc.

Last night I dined with the President. He had Judge Wright and Representative Austin and the Postmaster General to settle some political matters down in Tennessee. He said to me as he came downstairs:

"Archie, the next time you ask a cabinet officer to play golf with me, be sure that he knows something about the game. Poor old Mack! I felt more sorry for him than I did for you or me, for he hates to show himself deficient in anything, and even he could see that he knew nothing about the game. However, I'll bet anything he will begin to take some lessons, and the next time he offers to play he will be up on the game, and will, before he quits, play as well as any of us, if he does not become an expert."

Dwight, the whip of the House, came in late and sat with the President until near midnight. I heard him tell the President that he had the satisfaction of cursing out Representative Fish of New York and daring him to slap his face when that New York statesman threatened to do so. The President urged him to keep his temper when dealing with insurgents, but Dwight, deprecating what he had done, still claimed that he had great provocation and regretted that Fish had not seen it to be his duty to resent his language.

"My dear old man," the President said to Dwight, "the first duty of a party whip is to get votes, and you cannot get them by threats of personal violence. I am not placing too much blame on you, for I know, and no one better, how aggravating an insurgent can be, but always remember that you can catch more flies with molasses than on a club."

We leave to-night for New York to review the Veterans in New York to-morrow. I got him to send wreaths of flowers to the graves of Lawton and Liscomb and leave off sending them to Cook and Carroll. McKinley began sending flowers to the latter two generals for personal reasons, but there is no reason for the President to continue the custom, whereas Lawton and Liscomb do mean something to him.

ARCHIBALD.

After a Trip to New York

[Washington, D. C.,]
Tuesday, May 31, 1910.

DEAR CLARA:

We returned from New York last night at nine o'clock. The trip going and coming was very tiresome and the day in New York was as hard a one as I have yet experienced. We were up before seven and had breakfast with the Harry Tafts and then were taken in charge by the committee of old veterans and conducted by a perfectly absurd looking troop of cavalry, made up, as I understand, of society men, to the reviewing stand on Riverside Drive.

To see those old veterans march by makes the best of us feel like tin soldiers, but when I think of the troop which escorted us, mounted on docked-tailed horses and poor specimens at that, and the riders bedecked in light blues and gilt with grenadier caps and all the equipment which goes with the fancy parade volunteer, I had more respect for the uniform I wore and an actual veneration for that worn by the old vets.

I am glad I reviewed this parade with the President. The term G. A. R. does not mean much to us in the South, and I fear we have little respect for the old fellows. Even in the North it has become the fashion to sneer somewhat at them. I seemed to see them in a new light yesterday for the first time, to get them in proper proportion. The tottering thin line was a visual touch in history to me. In some organizations there were only two left, and they marched by holding to each other for support. For the first time in my life I was able to look upon them without some feeling of bitterness welling in my heart. The resentment I have always felt toward them and which I attributed to prenatal influences, was not there.

The President stood for three hours and was pretty well fagged out when it was over. We walked to the Soldiers' and Sailors' Monument, where some memorial exercises were held. Fortunately a downpour of rain cut the exercises short, and we were permitted to scurry away without much leave taking.

Cornelius Vanderbilt called on the President just after lunch by appointment, but remained only a few minutes. The President said:

"I bet you can't guess in a hundred times what it was Vanderbilt wanted to see me about."

"The home-coming of Mr. Roosevelt," I said.

"No, he wants to be special ambassador to the Coronation. I was very frank with him and told him I left those matters largely to Knox. I would not mind having Mrs. Cornelius to represent us at that time, but I hardly think the husband has either the presence or the importance for such a mission."

I made no comment other than it was pretty hard for a man burdened with the name of Vanderbilt to live it down. I will do what I can, for here is a Vanderbilt anxious to represent something else than mere money and he gets no encouragement at all. Yesterday he rode in the parade as an aide to General Roe's staff. He is a modest, retiring fellow, ambitious to be a man of affairs.

Good-bye. With love to the old man, as ever, your affectionate brother,

ARCHIE.

Captain Butt Forecasts Interest in His Letters

Bryn Mawr, Penn.,
June 2, 1910.

DEAR CLARA:

We left Washington at seven this morning. In order to make the train we had to arise at six. I slept at the White House, the second time since I have been on duty there. The last time, I went to bed at eleven and was called by President Roosevelt at three o'clock or a little after to start on our memorable ride to Warrington. In spite of the fact that I was to have a fair night's rest, I did not sleep much better than on this former occasion. I think there is something about the White House which occasions wakefulness until one gets accustomed to the surroundings.

I had spent the early part of the evening calling on General and Mrs. Perry and later on the Wetmores. Norton, the President's new secretary, took dinner at the White House, and when I returned there I found the President still working on the speech which he delivered at Bryn Mawr to-day. I had all the guest rooms to choose from, but chose the suite in the southeast corner, as I wanted to get the view of the Mall and the Speedway with the Monument faintly outlined in the semi-darkness. I put out the lights and had sat for a few minutes at the southern window, when, apparently overcome by sleep, I crawled into the big, old-fashioned four poster and thought to be asleep in a minute. Whether it was the perfect stillness or that the imaginative sense was awakened by the memories of the place, I do not know, but I lay awake a very long time, while scene after scene passed before me, and I thought of almost every President who had lived there. It was mostly their troubles which came uppermost in my mind.

Miss Wetmore had just been telling me of the first night which President Pierce spent in the White House. She had thought of this in connection with old Mr. Sidney West Webster, who was Pierce's private secretary, who died in Newport yesterday. He must have been a very interesting man, from what she said. He married a Fish, and on account of his death the Kanes and the Fish connections will all go into mourning. She remembered his telling her once of the first night Pierce spent in the White House. She could but compare it with the form and ceremony which is in vogue there to-day, and it was the memory of this incident, I think, which set me to thinking as I got into this delightful, luxurious bed.

Webster said that there was no one but a few colored servants in the house when he and the President decided to go to bed. He related how there was no one to show them to their rooms. Illness or something had kept the other members of the family from coming to the inauguration. After the departure of the last guest, who was the Secretary of State (and so ignorant was she and so ignorant am I that I do not even know who he was), the President suggested that they turn in. They had nothing but a candle, and they wandered around the second floor and went from bedroom to bedroom, all being in a general state of disorder. At last Pierce said:

"Sidney, you had better turn in here, and I will find a bed across the hall."

What a pity men such as Mr. Webster did not preserve such memories! When I think what might have been preserved in those simple old days I can but think that the letters I am writing to you must have some historic value some of these days. And yet, I suppose it will be from the incorrect reports of the newspapers of to-day, and the imaginative stories in them, that the permanent reports will be gathered.

ARCHIBALD.

CHAPTER XXXIX

NOT A LINE FROM MR. ROOSEVELT!

Nearing Harrisburg,
June 5, 1910.

DEAR CLARA:

Nothing of any special interest has occurred during this trip, except possibly the fact which the President made known to me for the first time, that Mr. Roosevelt has never written him a line since he has been away and not even answered the letter he sent him by me when he left for Africa, and has never thanked him for the present he sent him on that occasion. Mr. Roosevelt told me he intended to answer it on his way across the ocean, but if he did, the letter never reached Washington, and the President feels the oversight more deeply than appears on the surface.

"There is no doubt that he received it?" the President asked me.

"None whatever," I said. "I gave it to him, and he held it up for the press men to see and sent his thanks by me and said he would answer it on his way over."

"I simply do not understand it," said the President.

I repeated this conversation to Jimmy Sloan, the Fidus Achates of us all. He said: "It is just what I have been telling you all along, Captain. These men had split in spirit long before the inauguration, and you will see that when the Big Chief comes back he will follow the same course he has done all along, simply ignore this administration and act as if it did not exist."

The time, however, is nearing when we shall see who is right and who is wrong, and what all this silence means.

ARCHIE.

The President Gets a New Secretary

Monday, June 6, 1910.

DEAR CLARA:

There was quite a buzz of excitement about the White House this morning. The new Secretary [Charles D. Norton] was sworn in and promptly began to attend his duties in a masterful and able way. I believe that the President has found the right man for the place. My only hope is that the press will let me get along happily with him.

The New York *Times* yesterday morning had a long article in its supplement in which it naïvely remarked that no secretary to the President could be a success as long as Captain Butt was in the confidential position he is with the President. I cut it out and sent it to Norton with the comment: "Darn them, we will learn them yet."

He joined us last night in Baltimore and came to Washington with the President. The President told him he was going to take him traveling with him in the future. I do not know whether that means he will take me with him less or not, but it will not be unwelcome if he does. Another such trip as the last one and I shall be done up, to use a slangy expression. He kept his car crowded all the time, and there was hardly a place to rest. He ought to have his secretary along with him, but our duties are so divergent that there should be no clash whatever. If he is as interested in his chief as I am, there will never be, and I think he is. To what extent the love of power and authority will creep into him I do not know, but it is embedded in all of us, I imagine, and one has to be constantly on the watch to keep it at least in the background.

It is a beautiful day for golf, but the President is to meet a number of railroad presidents this afternoon with a view to reaching some understanding regarding the injunction he has got to prevent the roads from raising their freight rates. Everything on the stock market is up in the air, and the financiers pretend to think that we are on the eve of a panic on account of the injunction proceedings of the Administration. I saw Mr. Glover of the Riggs National Bank this morning, and he says that the whole financial world looks upon Wickersham as the greatest traitor since Benedict Arnold. Strange how these corporation lawyers become the most radical advocates for the control of corporations as soon as they enter the office of the Attorney General! Wickersham is the most radical man who has held that office for years.

There is a growing excitement in administration circles as the hour approaches for the arrival of Mr. Roosevelt. The President is not free from anxiety any more than the rest of us are. My anxiety has a very personal touch to it for I am exceedingly anxious to go to New York and meet Mr. Roosevelt. I had hoped the President would send a letter by me as he said he would, but I fear he has abandoned that idea since he wrote to him in Europe. With a little tact now, I still think the situation could be saved.

I had a long talk with Cal O'Laughlin this morning. He was First Assistant Secretary of State for a minute or two under President Roosevelt and is now on the Chicago *Tribune*. He is one of the most influential writers of the daily press, and, you may remember, he gained considerable notoriety by being with Mr. Roosevelt in Rome and becoming a party to the Vatican incident. On his return to Washington, after leaving Mr. Roosevelt in Europe, he came to the White House and called on the President.

I had heard the President's description of that call, but never O'Laughlin's side of it until to-day. The President laughingly told Edwards and myself how O'Laughlin had called at the office, and again at the White House by appointment, and how he had evidently expected him to discuss Mr. Roosevelt with him. He was rather funny as he told of the interview, in which he never asked O'Laughlin any questions about the ex-President, and the blank expression which finally overcame the ex-Assistant Secretary of State. At the time it sounded plausible enough for the President to refuse to take O'Laughlin into his confidence, but O'Laughlin's version of the silence on the part of the President gives importance to it as it relates to Mr. Roosevelt.

He told me of the interview and said he wanted to tell the President how the Colonel was looking and something of the trip; instead of which, he said, the President never even asked after the Colonel's health. In writing he had told Mr. Roosevelt of the interview and expressed regret that President Taft had never even asked concerning him. O'Laughlin, of course, does not know that the President has written to Mr. Roosevelt. He said that Mr. Roosevelt did not understand why he did not receive some word of welcome from the President as he came out of the desert into Khartoum, nor could I explain to him that President Roosevelt had never answered the President's letter, nor acknowledged the gift he sent to him by me on the day of his departure from the United States.

If I go to meet Mr. Roosevelt I shall certainly let him know of this, for it may be that he did write and gave the letter to someone to mail, and that it was purloined as a souvenir or for other purposes. His lecture to the British in his Guild Hall speech is still discussed with heat here. The President told me that he had had a talk with Henry White who went to England with Mr. Roosevelt, and that his utterance on the Egyptian matter was at the request of Grey, the Secretary of Foreign Affairs under the Liberal Government.

The President is perfectly well aware that his Cabinet do not approve of his traveling as he does and especially of attending insignificant commencements, but the President loves it. He said so last evening, coming from Baltimore, when he asked Senator Burrows if he thought it was not right for him to travel. The Senator had only that morning deplored to me the fact of the President's continuous absence from Washington, but when asked outright he had not the heart to say what he really thought, and said he felt that possibly it might do the party good.

"The fact of the matter is," said the President, "I want to go so much that it is easy for me to persuade myself that it is a good thing to do. I am somewhat of a tramp by nature, and," then he laughed that contagious laugh of his and said, "I want to get in as much traveling as I can during these four years, for after they are over I do not know when I will ever get another opportunity to do so."

And I believe that is the milk in the coconut.

A. W. B.

A Visiting Prince and a Grand Dinner

[Washington, D. C.,]
Tuesday, June 8, 1910.

DEAR CLARA:

Everybody seems happier to-day, the President and his official advisers because the railroads have withdrawn their increased rates, and the railroad men because the government has stopped its injunction, and the people because stocks are going up and there is less likelihood of a panic. The President is quite free from care, apparently. His railroad bill has gone to conference, and the House decided this afternoon to bring in a rule for the consideration of the Postal Savings Bank bills. He feels that he has easy seas ahead of him for a while.

Norton is still handing out good advice to the press and Senators and Representatives, and these weather-beaten veterans in politics are somewhat inclined to smile at the enthusiasm of the neophyte. The President told Norton to-day that he wanted me always to travel with him and to ride with him in the same automobile or carriage, and he also wanted Norton with him too. I have an idea that Norton would have preferred it to be otherwise, but he said nothing; so we will in the future star the country as a double header to the President.

The President, Miss Helen, and myself went horseback riding this afternoon. They seemed to enjoy themselves. I certainly did not. It is bad enough to look out for one of them, without being the guardian for both.

At eight o'clock I, with Chandler Hale and Captain Potts of the navy, went to the station to meet the Japanese Prince and Princess Fushimi. Chandler Hale represented the State Department, Captain Potts the navy, for the Prince is an admiral, and I represented the President. The Prince is a second cousin to the Mikado and is a tall soldierly looking fellow, less marked like an Oriental than most of his race, while she looks all the world like a little Japanese doll with French clothes. The entire embassy was there, and as the young couple stepped from their car I never saw such bowing and scraping. The women all courtesied low, as they do before the Queen of England. The men bowed very low, dipping one knee, and appeared to be holding one hand over the heart. This ceremony was scarcely fitted to a public station, but no part of it was left out, and whenever the Prince or Princess would speak the Orientals all began to bow and courtesy all over again. I felt they would never cease, so finally I stepped forward and was presented by the Ambassador, when I brought my heels together with a clang of spurs and bid their Imperial Highnesses welcome in the name of the President.

I headed the procession out of the station, passing through the President's private reception room, and bowed their highnesses into the limousine. We reached the Willard Hotel ahead of the party, and when the others finally entered the room where we were, the same bowing and scraping was resumed. I slipped away finally, after being bowed and kowtowed to myself as the representative of the President, and reported all these things to the President very much as I have told them to you here. He laughed heartily over the description, but seemed quite pleased that everything had been done for them. The Prince's father had entertained them in Japan on two occasions and had presented Mrs. Taft with a large solid silver punch bowl.

The President thought it would be nice to take a motor ride, so he and Mrs. Taft bundled up in heavy wraps, which will give you some idea how unseasonable it is here still, and we spent an hour or more in the park and on the roads in Maryland.

The President thought that more naval people should be invited, to the coming state dinner, and Mrs. Taft objected. I suggested Captain Potts, and the President wanted the Wainwrights also, but Mrs. Taft was so positive against increasing the number for the dinner that the President finally asked her what she had against the navy. She finally confessed that she had nothing against the navy, but that she had ordered only so many squab chickens, and she did not propose to order any more.

"Then we will invite them, and the family can hold back and not eat chicken," said the President, laughing, "or else we can invite the comet," he said, pointing to

Halley's visitor, which is still visible, "which does not have to be fed chicken."

This got Mrs. Taft laughing also and she finally agreed to have the Wainwrights. When we got back to the White House the President said to me:

"Come to the office to-morrow early and we will arrange things."

And quick as a flash Mrs. Taft said:

"I know that you and Captain Butt are going to do as you please, but I swear I will order no more chickens."

"Then we will order crow for them to eat," and, putting his arm about Mrs. Taft, he entered the White House.

Of course she should have nothing to say as to who will or will not come to these state dinners, but as the housekeeper she says a good deal, and while the President and I usually get whom we want in the long run, we generally have a fight before getting them. She feels that we played some sort of a trick on her concerning this dinner, as we sent out the invitations while she was absent. She does not understand it wholly, but her guess is pretty near correct. He got very angry when I told him that Chandler Hale would present the Prince and his suite at quarter before eight o'clock, immediately before the dinner. Huntington Wilson, the Assistant Secretary who is coming to the dinner, would not do it. I frankly told him I had asked the same question, but learned that Wilson thought this duty a little beneath him and so had detailed Hale to come with the Japs.

"I would just like to sit on Wilson once and mash him flat. What Knox sees in him I do not see. I won't have Chandler Hale hanging about when he is not coming to dinner. So remind me to send an order for him to present the Japs himself to-morrow evening."

There is some talk about the Secretary of State running for Governor, and if he does he had better provide for

Wilson before he leaves the State Department, for it would not take the President long to find a successor for him. Well, it is after midnight, and I will close. I am glad I had not gone to bed, for the doorbell has just rung, and it was a telegram from Tim Murphy, thanking me for his appointment as Postmaster of Augusta.

ARCHIE.

Postscript.

June 8, 1910.

The seating of the table brought up the question of rank of the secretary to the President. Norton had told me yesterday that the President said his place was immediately next to the Cabinet, and I so placed him at the table. But when I took in the plate of the table for the President to see and called his attention to the fact that I had placed Norton next the Cabinet, he said that he certainly should not be placed above Senators. Forster came in and said that the official place for the name of the secretary on all official lists was between the Cabinet and the Senate. I recalled the fact that at all state dinners at the White House, when Loeb was a guest, he invariably sat next to me at the end of the table, and Forster said that the President had done this for the reason that he regarded Loeb as a part host at the White House and therefore sat him below other officials. The President looked at me and began to laugh and said finally:

"Well, I prefer to give Norton a higher place at table and not divide my prerogatives as host with him. Place him just below the Senators and above Representatives and assistant secretaries. Senators claim rank as ambassadors from the sovereign state to the nation, and I am willing to accept this bit of fiction and recognize them accordingly."

So we got that settled at any rate.

ARCHIE.

CHAPTER XL

A DAY OF GOLFING AND FEASTING

[Washington, D. C.]
June 9, 1910.

DEAR CLARA:

The day started out very stupidly yesterday, but ended most pleasantly. In the afternoon the President and Walter Travis played golf against Clarence Edwards and myself and defeated us badly. We are to have another try at it this afternoon. The President asked Travis to remain over another day especially for that purpose. I am ashamed to confess it, but they gave us a handicap of a stroke a hole on match play and also a stroke a hole on medal play. Travis is a Scotchman, and, therefore, while on pleasure bent his frugal mind was not idle, so he got permission to have a photographer follow the foursome around the course. Instead of one photographer, he had two women photographers with small cameras and one man with an instrument which looked for all the world like a disappearing gun. The photographs are to adorn the pages of Travis's golf magazine and to illustrate the article he is to write. The President consented to the photographers, a thing he will never permit, in order to help out Travis financially.

Travis plays too well to have his game injured by snap-shooters, and both the President and myself are too accustomed to them to be terrified by them, but they got horribly on the nerves of the General; if they did not cause his exceedingly bad game, they at least gave him an excuse for it. All photographers will be barred this afternoon, and the game will be lost or won on its merits.

We had little time to dress between the arrival home

and the presentation of the Imperial party of Japanese. I left the White House at twelve minutes past seven and was under the portico at half-past seven. That time included a shave, but I confess I had to forego the bath. It was a very pretty ceremony. Their highnesses the Prince and Princess Fushimi with their entire suite, and the ambassador and his wife, Baroness Uchida, were shown into the Blue Room. The President kept them waiting a few minutes, as is his wont, for he is never exactly on time, and then he entered the room, coming down to the flurries and the "Star-Spangled Banner," preceded by Lieutenant Commander Palmer and myself, and the presentations were made.

As the other dinner guests arrived, some forty of them, they were shown into the Green Room. Miss Helen, who was to take her mother's place, came in later to the Blue Room and was presented by her father. She looked very sweet and girlish in white. She has quite an air about her when she has to go through official ordeals. I was very much struck with her manner and appearance throughout the evening.

When the Secretary of State arrived I showed him into the Blue Room also. The Secretary of State and I are getting to be great friends—for the reason, I think, that I always watch carefully to preserve his dignity and status.

When all the guests had arrived I got the President to take his position at the door leading into the Blue Room from the Green Room and placed Miss Helen next to him, and with his consent the Prince and Princess next to them. The President laughingly said:

"I suppose, Prince, you understand that we have managers here the same as in Japan."

The Prince and Princess speak English very well and so understood the point of the reference, and he replied:

"It is only on ship I know what to do without being told."

I then entered the Green Room and announced to the Meyers that the President was ready to receive their guests, and they filed through just as they used to do in the Roosevelt time.

I know your woman's soul wants to know if there were enough chickens. There were. Hoover was in a terrible stew for fear there would not be enough to eat. It is too funny the way Hoover takes everything to heart that goes wrong about the White House. He said sometimes it was just as bad in the Roosevelt administration. Mrs. Roosevelt, he said, would order a light lunch for two, and the President would come over with three or four more and there would be no time to add to the menu.

"I have seen people come out of the dining room hungry sometimes. Mr. LaFarge once came out here and said to his friend: 'Let's go to the hotel and get something to eat. Liver and bacon are cheap enough to give enough of it, at least.'"

Hoover said on such occasions he felt mortified, but the Roosevelts felt that they had done enough when they asked people to have what they themselves had.

This will go to show you that even a ménage like the White House is not always ready for emergencies. The Roosevelts always had the simplest home food at lunch time, as Mrs. Roosevelt believed her husband's digestion would be permanently impaired if she did not keep him to the kind of meals they had when they lived in private life. It was seldom, however, that Alice, the black cook now relegated to scullery maid, was caught napping, and the lunches at the White House during the Roosevelt time will always stand out as one of the features of that administration.

Well, where was I when I got rambling back in the

Roosevelts' time? The Roosevelts are rather uppermost in my mind to-day, for the President told me last night that he was going to send me to New York to meet the ex-President and was going to send a letter by me. He has also directed Secretary Meyer and Secretary Wilson, the two overlapping cabinet officers, to go; and he has ordered the Secretary of the Navy to take our party down the bay to meet the Hunter and convey him up the harbor to the dock on the S. S. *Dolphin.*

What a meeting it will be! Mrs. Meyer and I fairly hugged one another last evening when the secretary confirmed this bit of news. But what a splendid thing for the President to do! It seems to me he always does the right thing at the right time. I have never seen him fail in matters of good manners or good taste. It was not agreeable to read in the *Post* of this morning, which I have just finished doing, "Two cabinet officers to accompany Captain Butt down the bay to meet Roosevelt." As the representative of the President, or the conveyor of the letter, I may be supposed to take precedence even of cabinet officers, but it looks rather startling in print and is not conducive to good feeling.

After dinner the President took the men to his study to smoke, and the women remained in the East Room for coffee. The President got me to see if Mrs. Taft was strong enough to receive the Prince and Princess in the upper corridor, and she said she was, so I went below to bring the Princess. I found her sitting in the midst of some twenty women quietly smoking a cigarette. The only other person smoking was Mrs. Townsend. As the Princess started across the room on my arm, the Baroness Uchida arose and took from her fingers the lighted cigarette.

Mrs. Taft was very sweet and gracious to them and talked, I thought, very well. She wore a lovely gown and looked quite the Grande Dame.

I heard Mrs. Townsend telling the President of the cigarette incident, which he seemed to enjoy greatly. She said that when the cigarettes were passed the Princess took one and everyone else refused, leaving the guest of honor the sole person to smoke. Seeing this, Mrs. Townsend called to the waiter and took one also. She said the Princess smoked three during the evening, and that was too much for her. She gave me a wink as she said this, for she knew that I knew she was fibbing. It is a matter of constant controversy between us, as I am one of those old-fashioned persons who, as you have had occasion to know, disapprove most heartily of women smoking.

Good-bye.
Archie.

Mr. Taft Punishes His Foes

[Washington, D. C.]
Friday, June 10, 1910.

Dear Clara:

Yesterday at the White House office some of us were reminded of the other administration and the days when things hummed and buzzed about the executive offices. The President, in refusing to receive Burton Harrison, has given rise to much criticism, the general consensus of opinion being that the Chief Executive of the nation should not decline to receive any public official in his office, no matter how objectionable that official might be to him. But Harrison had practically accused the President of equivocating and intentional deception, and it was in perfect accord with the President's character to resent this implication just as he did, for his honor is his sensitive point, and any reflection on that arouses him as nothing else does.

President Roosevelt never declined to see anyone at his office. When he wanted to cut a man, he did so by ignoring him at the receptions at the White House. He might have an out-and-out row with an enemy in his office, but he felt that he had no right to refuse to see a member of Congress coming to transact business for his constituency.

After the President had told Norton that he would not see Harrison, his secretary said to him that he thought he was making a mistake. I think the President should have seen the New York Congressman and possibly a friend might have been made instead of an implacable enemy.

I had the same problem put up to me last week at Monroe, Mich., when I saw Colonel Mann, the editor of *Town Topics*, standing among the veterans of Custer's brigade. *Town Topics* has always vilified the Tafts, even from the old days in Manila when Mrs. Taft refused to receive Mrs. Dean, then writing under the nom de plume of "the Widow" from those Islands. But the nasty sheet has been rather decent since Mrs. Taft's illness, owing solely to the fact that I once did "the Widow" a kindness and appealed to her to protect the White House at the present period. When I saw Colonel Mann, I motioned to him to come forward to meet the President, who was sitting immediately in front of me on the reviewing stand. As he came forward, I leaned over and whispered to the President that Colonel Mann was desirous of paying him his respects.

"I don't want to see him," said the President. "He has no respect for anyone, certainly none for me."

He got to smiling over his own wit, and taking advantage of it I said:

"He is here, Mr. President," and then I presented him, and the President reached back and shook hands and then became interested in something going on in front of us. I thought his reception a little chilly, but I was glad he did not actually repulse him. However, the result is that only yesterday I received a two-page typewritten letter from old Mann overflowing with gratitude for my kindness and overwhelming in his praise of the gracious manner in which the President received him. There followed later in the day a copy of the paper, with a whole page devoted to Monroe, in which the President was praised in every sentence.

Harrison intends to make a bitter attack on the President from the floor of the House to-morrow, and Miss Edythe Wetmore and I are going to the Capitol to hear him.

The President and Travis and General Edwards and I played off our second game of golf yesterday in a driving rainstorm. There were no camera fiends present, it is needless to say. Our game, while slightly better, did not reach perfection by any means, and we were defeated four down by our two distinguished opponents.

When we returned to the White House, the President wrote out three names and gave them to me, telling me to see to it that none of them nor any member of their families were ever invited to the White House again. They were Representatives John A. Martin of Colorado, Burton Harrison of New York, and Henry T. Rainy of Illinois. I could not help but recall what the President said to me on one occasion before his inauguration, when he was telling me what his hopes were for the White House. He said he did not propose to use the White House to punish or discipline members of Congress. He believed, he said, that the Democrats and Republicans should be entertained alike at the White House and that political attacks should not debar public men from its entertainments. I confess that he has been very consistent up to the present time. Indeed, it has seemed to me at times that he has entertained more Democrats than Republicans at entertainments of a purely personal character.

When I told President Roosevelt of his successor's determination, he laughed, and said:

"I will give him one year to change his mind on that subject."

It has taken him a little more than a year, but he has changed it completely.

Good-bye.

ARCHIE.

CHAPTER XLI

AT DINNER WITH CONVIVIAL SENATORS

[Washington, D. C.]
Sunday, June 12, 1910.

DEAR CLARA:

I am feeling rather rocky and seedy this morning. I went to dinner last evening at Senator Frank Brandegee's and did not even sleep at home last night, but spent the night with Nick Longworth, returning at luncheon time to my own home in evening clothes, much to the consternation of my Filipino boy and to my own humiliation. I found that several people had called me up, and to each one he had said that I had not come home at all. Can you surpass that in innocence? I hated to instruct him in other ways, but I finally got him to understand that, when his master did not come home, he must say that I was sleeping and could not be disturbed. As I was innocent of all offense last night, save that of good fellowship and bibulous conviviality, I could the better instruct him in the art of subterfuge.

Brandegee is famous as a host, but he quite surpassed himself last night. There were some forty guests present, and Nick and McClung and I were the only persons present not members of the Senate. There were no insurgents there, but the rest were present, even to Senator Wetmore and Senator Aldrich. It was a thorough Republican gathering. The dinner itself was excellent. It has to be to hold the epicurean attention of a Senator of the first class. Brandegee makes a specialty of Smithfield hams. The one last night was a poem, as Senator Elkins remarked in the course of the dinner.

I sat between Senator Buckley of Connecticut and Senator Gallinger of New Hampshire. The former is as disingenuous and real as the latter is crafty and sinister. There were two large tables, Senator Aldrich sitting at the head of one, and Tom Carter of Montana sitting at the head of the other. . . .

As the dinner waxed, the Senators became more communicative, and finally Tom Carter declared himself toastmaster, and from that time it was really a Lucullian feast, if that term means wit, wisdom, and humor intermingled with a semi-serious discussion of passing events of moment. In his introductions Carter would place his finger on the weak spot of each speaker as that weakness was known in the cloakrooms of the Senate. Each reference was greeted with shouts of laughter by the other persons present, and even the victim of the toastmaster enjoyed the passing references, as he knew that at the next moment someone else would be griddled.

I got quite a new light on some of the men present. Hepburn, for instance, whom I had always thought of as a crabbed, disagreeable partisan, developed a wit that was amazing, while Senator Bradley's stories, even while broad and suggestive in the extreme, were so well told as to come within the limitations established for a smutty story by Henry Watterson. The old editor said in my presence once that a smutty story was only permissible in polite society when the wit outweighed the vulgarity.

Senator Elkins was introduced as "smooth Steve Elkins, the friend of the people, who did not know what the people needed but was always trying to find out through a process of elimination."

The one serious note in the speeches was a sincere regret

that Senator Aldrich was to retire from the Senate; and it developed, as the evening progressed, that the Senator's proclamation that he was to retire was not considered final by his confrères; in other words, that this refusal to stand for election again was securely fastened with a string.

Finally, in the course of the evening, Nick Longworth was reached, and he made quite a hit by lecturing the Senate. Then it came my turn. I was short and to the point. I said that had I known that I was to have met the majority of the majority of the Senate, I should have come prepared with a bill giving the personal aide of the President the pay and the rank of a full colonel. I then said laughingly that I appeared the one discordant note in an otherwise harmonious dinner, and someone asked why. I said I could better explain by telling of the incident which happened in Chicago when the Reverend Ernest Stires had been asked to open with prayer the Democratic Convention, the one which first nominated Bryan. Chairman Harrity of the National Committee, doubting whether a rector of a fashionable Episcopal Church could be a Democrat, asked: "Mr. Stires, may I ask if you are a Democrat?" To which Stires promptly replied: "I am a gentleman, sir, and was born in Virginia."

Having taken this way to let these old fellows know that there was at least one Democrat present, I proceeded to plagiarize the speech I made at Tom Walsh's dinner, when I had been called on to answer to the toast of the "Playmate of two Presidents." None of them had heard it, and so I made a palpable hit with the toast I offered.

I reminded the Senators that it was the duty of an aide to be discreet and never to talk. I would say this much, however, that I had been most fortunate in having served President Roosevelt, whom I regarded as the greatest man who ever lived. As very few of those present thought this, there was an ominous silence, for no one knew just what sort of break I was going to make. I filled my glass and continued:

"I am also fortunate in serving President Taft, who is the greatest man possibly who ever will live, and therefore I ask the company to rise and drink to the health of both."

There was a perfect roar of laughter and applause from these old fellows, and so we stood and drank the health of the two men. Tom Carter said that if, after making that speech, I would change my bill from a colonel to that of an ambassador, the Senate would be willing to pass it unanimously. We did not leave the house until after one o'clock, and then Nick and I wandered about town in his motor, finally ending up at his house, where we talked for another hour. . . .

I am rather undecided whether to wear my uniform when I go to meet Mr. Roosevelt. I should not hesitate for a minute but for Mrs. Roosevelt. I know that she will begin to laugh as soon as she sees me, for she was always wont to say that "you Georgians"—referring to the ex-President and myself—"are such peacocks." This was at the time when her husband was uncertain whether to take a full dress uniform of a colonel of cavalry with him when he went to Africa. I am going in as purely official a capacity as it is possible to go and I think it will look too casual, if indeed not too intimate, to go in jaunty citizen clothes. I think I shall let the President decide. We ride this afternoon, and to-night I am dining with the Pattens, if I am not bid to the White House at the last moment.

Nick told me this morning that he had received the assurance from his father-in-law that he would give him the first twenty-four hours of his return to America.

"My advice may not be the wisest in the world, but he will at least get an unbiased statement of the political situation as it appears to me."

I was lying in bed reading the *Star*, and Nick was sitting

near reading the *Post*. I saw that Pinchot was making speeches in the West and talking about the uplift.

"Nick," I asked, "can you reconcile all the things which Pinchot is doing now with the Pinchot we knew during the last administration? I can't."

"That is one of the things I want to steer the President right on," he said more emphatically than grammatically.

I told him of a conversation I had with President Roosevelt one morning while he was posing for DeCamp for a portrait. I may have told you of it at the time, for I set down most things which I think of any interest to you, but in case I have not it is well worth telling now, especially in view of more recent developments. President Roosevelt had been talking about Fitz Lee and myself and then suddenly began to talk about Gifford Pinchot. He said that with Fitz and me he felt at home and that we were of his fiber and courage (how I wish it were true!).

"Now there is Gifford Pinchot," he said. "We have literally nothing in common, yet he has a sort of fetish worship for me. He thinks that if we were cast away somewhere together and we were both hungry, I would kill him and eat him. AND I WOULD TOO," he said, turning to me, grinning and showing his teeth in the semi-humorous yet ferocious way he had when he wanted to say something seriously, yet in a half Pickwickian vein.

Nick laughed until he said his side ached.

> Good-bye.
> ARCHIE.

"Colonel" or "Mr." Theodore Roosevelt?

> [Washington, D. C.]
> June 14, 1910.

DEAR CLARA:

Leaving to-night for Marietta and returning again on Wednesday evening. I shall go to New York to meet the ex-President Thursday night so as to have the whole of Friday there to enjoy the crowds. Belle Hagner is going over at the same time, and we will simply make it a holiday. Possibly after Saturday we may all get dragged into different camps and be forced against our wills to line up on one side or another. Still, I do not anticipate this dénouement, certainly not for the present. At any rate, none of the old crowd will permit any anticipation of coming separation to dim the pleasure we anticipate in the return of Colonel Roosevelt.

I must stop calling him "Mr. President." I understand that Mrs. Roosevelt really gets angry when people do so. But none of us seems to know just how to address him just yet.

Yesterday morning I wrote out the order directing me to proceed to New York, meet the *Kaiserin Auguste Victoria*, and deliver the letter entrusted to my care to "Colonel Theodore Roosevelt." I made the order most specific, detailing just what I was to do and how to proceed. Norton, before signing it, took it in to the President and the President read it, and the only change he made was to have the "Colonel" taken out and "Mr." Roosevelt take its place. Before doing so, however, he sent for me and asked what was my judgment. I expressed the belief that he would prefer to be called Colonel Roosevelt. The President thought otherwise and so ordered that change made in the order.

Clarence Edwards still seems to be vindictive toward Secretary Dickinson. In spite of the fact that he is going to the Philippines with the secretary and has accomplished what he wanted in the matter, he never lets an occasion go by without detailing some little insignificant shortcomings of Mr. Dickinson to the President. He tells me the secretary does not like him, and I presume he is trying to forestall any complaints the secretary may make of him to the President. Yesterday was the first time his complaints seemed to have borne any fruit. After telling the President several times that no one was permitted to do anything at the War Department without convincing the secretary of the necessity, and how different was this method from the great Root and Taft administrations of the same office, he elicited this remark from the President: "I fear Dickinson is not as elastic as I thought he was. He also seems much older than I thought, somehow."

What hurts me is to see the President's mind being poisoned about the great strong man he has in the War Department, whose administration of that office is thorough, far more thorough than that of Secretary Taft, who did leave most of the details to his subordinates and thereby permitted the department to accumulate a dozen different heads and factions, whereas there should have been but one. I have to keep my hands out of it entirely, but I never fail to repeat the words of praise I hear others speak of Mr. Dickinson when I am by myself with the President, in order to let him know that the opinion of General Edwards is not the general opinion of all the chiefs of bureaus in the department.

Good-bye.
ARCHIE.

CHAPTER XLII

REDRAFTING A LETTER TO COLONEL ROOSEVELT

[Washington, D. C.]
June 16, 1910.

DEAR CLARA:

We returned this morning from Marietta, having left Tuesday night at midnight. We are all fagged out, and Norton, the new secretary, is completely done up. He is a very delightful fellow, but I fear a little casual with the President. When he came into the car the other evening he threw himself on the sofa and stretched himself out while proceeding to discuss some matter with the President. The President raised his eyebrows just the breadth of a line, but they remained fixed. It gave a complete shock to the secret service men and others as they passed through the car. Finally Norton said:

"Mr. President, you don't mind my resting here."

"Guess you are pretty tired," the President said, and in a few minutes Norton righted himself, and I never saw him lie down again on the trip.

At breakfast the next morning he said to me: "Is the President one of those domestic tyrants who expects everyone to be up when he is? I noticed you had me called very early."

"I fear he is," I said. "He likes everyone ready when he comes out."

I rather expected him to contradict me, but he remained silent. Mrs. Norton fears her husband is not going to stand the strain, but he enjoys meeting people, and this little dash into politics is invigorating to him. He is greatly impressed by the most trivial discussion in politics at present and interpolates over the simplest statements of facts, "That's very important."

After dinner last night with Carmi Thompson, who wants to be nominated for governor in place of Longworth, Norton said to me: "That was all very interesting, wasn't it?"

Candidly I did not think so, and so told him why. The conversation related to local politics in Ohio, and Thompson was trying to persuade the President that Governor Harmon had no chance to be reëlected. It seemed to me that every statement he made was misleading, and I thought, moreover, that the President thought so too.

So I told Norton that it was difficult to get at the truth of a situation from a statement of the situation to the President, for it was my experience that people seldom speak the whole truth to a President. Norton has a keen mind and a most engaging manner, and I believe the President will find great comfort in him.

After dinner I tried to teach him some bridge, so that he can play with the President on these trips. He knows little about the game, and so I fear will not be an acceptable fourth for some time to come.

I was glad to see that there was no disposition on his part to reach over into my territory. It is going to take some tact to get along with Norton, but I am sure he thinks the same thing about me, so we are both putting our best foot forward, and we may turn out to be great friends. He made a very good start yesterday when he presented me with two of the first coins struck from the St. Gaudens dies of our new twenty-dollar and ten-dollar gold pieces. They were among those which were called in because it was found that the bas relief was so great that the money could not be stacked without wabbling. One cannot get them for love or money, though Norton thinks that he may be able to replace those he gave me. He told me when he gave them to me that he wanted to show in some way his appreciation of what I had done for him while the matter of appointment was pending and for the great help I had been to him since.

I liked his acknowledgment of the debt, but I hope he does not feel that he has paid it off with the St. Gaudens coins. I think he relies a good deal on my judgment. He told me he wanted me to read the letter the President had written to Mr. Roosevelt, which I was to take. He had a copy of it with him. It begins:

"I am sending this letter to you by Archie Butt."

Then he rather jokes about the strain on his digestive

organs and how worn out he must be. It is not until the close of the letter that he invites the President to visit the White House, and he makes no reference to Mrs. Roosevelt.

I insisted that the jocular portion of the letter should be eliminated and that in its place the President should give an open, frank, and generous invitation to both the ex-President and Mrs. Roosevelt to visit the White House at the present time, regretting that Mrs. Taft was leaving for the summer home at once and would be unable, therefore, to welcome them herself; but that should they come again in the fall or at any time to visit their "old home," both he and Mrs. Taft would give them a hearty welcome. I frankly told Norton that this letter was no place to joke or to become casual. He took it to the President and asked to be allowed to rehash the letter on lines suggested by me. The President said he had no objection, only he must not commit him to anything which would look like fawning or seeking favors at the hand of the ex-President:

"For I am charged with the dignity of the Executive, and I will say or do nothing that will put a momentary slight even on that great office. After all, I am determined to paddle my own canoe, and I do not want to say anything at first which might mislead Roosevelt into thinking that I expect or desire advice. I think, moreover, that he will appreciate this feeling in me and would be the first one to resent the slightest subordination of the office of President to any man."

I felt that this was a clear statement of the case, and he said it without any animosity or bitterness, only he wanted his side to be thoroughly understood. I still thought, and so said, that the jocular part of the letter should be eliminated, and so Norton got to work to interpolate my suggestion, and the result will be seen to-day, whether the President prefers our draft of the letter to his own. The letter begins, "My dear Theodore," and is written in such a vein as to offer no suggestion that there has come the slightest rift in their old friendship.

The day at Marietta was very tiresome. The President made several speeches to crowds which were large, but which seemed to be without enthusiasm. But I think the Ohio people are rather a cold and calculating lot and not given to much spontaneity. One incident happened at the Unitarian Church which I think might interest you. He agreed to go by this edifice and show himself, but when he got in the conventicle, he made a speech and quite a long one too. He said several things about religion which I did not altogether approve of, and I thought it rather unwise for him so to frankly endorse Unitarianism. I never get quite accustomed to his faith that he and the world in general can be saved through some mental process.

However, as no one had expected him to make a speech, his stenographer, Mr. Michler, had not entered the church, and came in only to catch the closing paragraphs. When he got back to the car he came to my room where I was lying down and in great perturbation of mind told me that he did not have the President's speech and was afraid to have the President know it, and thought if Norton found it out he would get a very prejudiced view of his work. I told him I could make the same speech, and proceeded by some trick of memory to speak it very much as he had done, and, moreover, I softened down very much that part which I thought was a reflection on our more conventional beliefs. What I dictated made several pages on the typewriter, and when it was shown to Norton he did not recognize that it was not the speech the President had delivered, and, moreover, when the President reviewed it, a thing he always does before his speeches are given out, he made only one correction, that being in the closing sentence, which had been taken down verbatim. Michler said the President read it carefully and did not give one indication that he suspected it might have been changed in any way.

At the luncheon at the charming old home of Mr. Mills, the President of the First National Bank of Marietta, we met a number of the "has beens" of the McKinley and Roosevelt administrations, prominently among whom were Charlie Dawes and Loomis, former Assistant Secretary of State.

We visited the original office of the Ohio company which had been purchased and renovated by the Colonial Dames of Ohio. Miss Putnam told me that it was the only excuse the Colonial Dames had for existence in Ohio. I suggested a work for them if they wanted something to work for. It was to have a portrait of Mrs. Taft painted for the White House. Mrs. Taft being a Colonial Dame and from Ohio, it might be a nice and interesting thing for the society to do.

Good-bye. When I write again I will have seen Mr. Roosevelt.

ARCHIE.

Mrs. Taft Writes to Mrs. Roosevelt

[Washington, D. C.]
Tuesday evening
June 16, 1910.

DEAR CLARA:

Just a line, before starting, to say that the President has changed his letter according to my suggestions and invited both Mr. and Mrs. Roosevelt in the name of both Mrs. Taft and himself. I went to say good-bye to him in his study late this afternoon, when he told me of the changes he had made. I made bold to ask if Mrs. Taft had written to Mrs. Roosevelt, and he said she had not and then asked if I thought she ought to do so.

"I think so, Mr. President. If she does that, then you and Mrs. Taft have left nothing undone, and it can never be charged in the future that there was the slightest discourtesy toward Mr. or Mrs. Roosevelt from the White House. If either now feels aggrieved that more attention has not been shown to the children, not understanding Mrs. Taft's condition of health, I think a note of invitation from Mrs. Taft will set this right."

The President thought for a few minutes and then said he thought I was right, and to come back during the evening and he would have a note to Mrs. Roosevelt from Mrs. Taft. When I returned after dinner the Ellises were there and Miss Helen. I sat for a few minutes when the President said:

"Nellie, will you go and do that for me, dear?"

She went upstairs, wrote the note, and brought it down to me. I don't know that it will be altogether welcomed, for when women get at cross purposes it is hard to get them straightened out again. But I am sure it was the thing to do, and I am sure it will be appreciated by Mr. Roosevelt.

If the families are unable to get together in the future, it will not be the fault of either at this time, for everything has been done which should have been done. I, at least, have done what I could to keep them in accord, and I am sufficiently fond of both to hope that my efforts will result in some little good to each.

I feel like Sentimental Tommy to-night, wondering what people would think of my good thoughts and deeds if they were known. Did you ever read *Sentimental Tommy?* He has delightful mental attitudes at all crises.

Good-night. I'm off.

A. W. B.

CHAPTER XLIII

ROOSEVELT'S TRIUMPHANT RETURN TO NEW YORK

[Washington, D. C.]
June 19, 1910.

DEAR CLARA:

All the morning I have been trying to begin this letter to you with a view of setting down some things of interest which happened yesterday during the welcome to Mr. Roosevelt in New York, but the task frightened me away from the effort and I have been listlessly lying on the lounge waiting for something to happen, but what to happen I do not know—only something which would give me a starting point. So much did happen there that I am bewildered when I look back on it, and when I read the papers I am surprised that none of them seems to rise to the occasion and see the thing as it appeared to me. Bert Patchin, the correspondent of the New York *Herald* in Ottawa, Canada, ran in to see me for a minute this morning and found me literally surrounded by sheets of the Sunday papers.

"Reading about yourself?" asked Pat, as he sat down all aglow with the race upstairs.

"No," I replied, "but I have been reading the accounts of the New York reporters, and I am surprised to see how much they wrote and how little of interest they really tell. For instance, no one mentioned the fact that Pinchot was not on one of the boats to go down the bay, and not one saw that Garfield was on the *Manhattan* and looked pale and ill as if expecting to be snubbed, and that, in fact, most people seemed to avoid him. Every one of the men who did this work for the New York papers expended columns of energy on faking imaginary conversation between the President and those whom he greeted, but none commented on the fact that this great outpouring of people, this wonderful enthusiasm seen on all sides, was just to see one man pass, to see him lift his hat, and to hear him address them as fellow citizens."

They had stood in the heat for hours for this, and they would have stood just as long in the rain. Nothing could have daunted their spirits yesterday. He was back, that was enough for them. And now where it is going to end is a matter for the future—not for the present. The chapter has been written in the lives of both Taft and Roosevelt and in the history of American politics.

I was interested to see that the record of the man I serve now was straight and that the man I served in the past was equally clear on this home-coming occasion. The President has done all he could have done to add dignity to the welcome and to extend a warm personal greeting to his predecessor, and whatever may happen now must be the result of something else than ingratitude or discourtesy.

I did not arrive in Washington until this morning, and as soon as I had had a cup of coffee, I went to the White House, where I found the President at his breakfast. I gave him an account of all that happened and brought back the thanks and the sincere good wishes of Mr. Roosevelt to him.

"And," I added, "he asked me to say to you that nothing touched him more than that you should have chosen me as the bearer of your welcome."

He then said:

"Archie, this is one of those incidents which come into our lives which require great tact and good taste to carry through. It would have been so easy to have made a mistake or to have touched a jarring chord, and I feel it is due largely to you that yesterday has passed off as it has, for I have largely followed your suggestions and your advice, and I want you to know that I am grateful."

This he said as he rose from the table and he only turned round to say:

"Let us ride this afternoon and I will then get you to tell me further what happened. I am having most of Congress to see, it seems to me, this morning but I will be ready by four o'clock."

I was greatly touched by this acknowledgment, for, as you know, I seldom expect much praise from him, and when he gives it I am usually speechless from surprise. I went by the office to see Forster there and to give him the ex-President's love, and I told him what the President had just said to me and he said:

"He only said what was true, but I am glad he was willing to say it."

He then showed me the letter which had come from Mr. Roosevelt only yesterday in answer to the one which the President had written to him in London, the duplicate of which I took with me to New York, but which I did not deliver when I learned that he had received the original and answered it.

But I am getting away ahead of the procession. Suffice it to say in reference to this letter that it was short but kindly and courteous; that it began "My dear Mr. President" (not "My dear Will"), and that it contained this one important, the only important, sentence in the letter:

"I shall make no speeches nor say anything for two months, but I shall keep my mind as open as I keep my mouth shut."

Now to New York. I shall only tell you what occurred wherein I took part and let you have the glimpse of him that I had. The press has carried columns of the crowd enthusiasm, the water pageant, even of the Alexander luncheon, and of the fact that he visited the home of his future daughter-in-law, to see her wedding presents, but the press only followed him as far as the doors. I went with him everywhere, for he asked me to stay by him and he used me on shipboard, on the revenue cutter, at the Alexanders', just as he was wont to use me when he was President and I was his aide. It was so natural to say while walking ahead of him:

"Will you kindly let the President pass?" or, "The President desires this," or "The President will not be able to see you," etc.

He was just the same in manner, in appearance, in expression, yet there was something different. We, all of us who had been closely associated with him in the past, felt it. I spoke of it. Senator Lodge spoke of it. Secretary Meyer, who is not keen to see much, he even spoke of it; and so did Nick. Loeb and I, for we rode together in the procession, talked almost entirely of him and each of us felt that there was a change in him. Mr. Meyer thought he had grown older, but it wasn't that. Loeb, Senator Lodge, and I figured it out to be simply an enlarged personality. To me he had ceased to be an American, but had become a world citizen. His horizon seemed to be greater, his mental scope more encompassing. I don't think this was in our imaginations alone, yet if you were to ask me to give you an incident to illustrate what I mean I should fail to find one, or if I should find one it would fail to mean anything to you. But it is there. He is bigger, broader, capable of greater good or greater evil, I don't know which, than when he left; and he is in splendid health and has a long time to live. What a horoscope to cast if one could cast it!

I went over Thursday at midnight, carrying the letters with me. I left them in the safe at the Waldorf. Then I spent the day with Belle Hagner. The White Company put a motor at my disposal and we went from the Battery to the Bronx. We went just where the spirit moved us to go. We shopped—and, by the way, I bought a dozen pair of silk socks at a dollar a pair. Did you ever hear of anything so cheap?

I called on Mrs. Robinson, and it broke my heart to see her. They have just returned from a trip around the world. She is the saddest woman I ever looked upon. It is just as if someone had picked her up and broken her. Belle left the room for a few minutes. She took my hand and the tears flowed freely. I could not comfort her. I know what it is to have lost the one loved person in the world. I was saddened at the sight of her suffering, but I was overwhelmed the following day with my own memories when Mrs. Roosevelt rushed down the gangway and took Archie in her arms, calling his name, just as Mother was accustomed to greet me when we had been separated. In the midst of the hurrah and confusion and the interest, my mind was absolutely with her at that moment and I left it all to go below to be with these thoughts alone. Well, this is not the place for my sorrow and my memories.

I took dinner at Sherry's that evening with Teddy and several of the Robinson family, but I could not linger with them long, as I had to be aboard the *Dolphin* at half-past nine. The Secretary of the Navy and Mrs. Meyer, the Secretary of Agriculture, Mr. Wilson, Senator Lodge, and Nick came aboard a little later, and the secretary ordered the captain to take us down the bay and anchor off quarantine. Loeb was to leave at daylight and had agreed to take our party aboard the *Kaiserin Auguste Victoria* before anyone else. In anticipation and excitement none of us slept well, and we were roused at half-past six o'clock. Loeb was not in sight nor any of the committee's boats, so we took the launch and circled the steamer, hailing the health officer who had gone aboard. At last they gave us permission to come on board if we could scale the ladder.

We all thought we could do so, except Mrs. Meyer, who scoffed at the suggestion. I slipped the letters down my boot leg and went up last. The secretary went first, as he had the right, and then Senator Lodge, which he did not have the right to do, and then Secretary Wilson, then Nick and myself. Secretary Wilson is nearly eighty, I think, and for a few minutes everyone who was watching feared he would not make it, and had he fallen it would have been the end of him, for the scow was moored immediately under the ladder.

We shook hands in the order we had gone up the ladder. We found Mr. Roosevelt in his sitting room.

"Hello, Cabot. How are you, George? And how is Tamer Jim?" to Secretary Wilson, and to Nick:

"Ah, Nick, it is good to see you."

And then, when he caught sight of me, he seized my hand and said:

"Oh, Archie, but this is fine."

I saluted and said:

"Mr. President, I have a letter from the President, which I am charged to deliver at once, and a duplicate of the one he wrote to you in London, if you had not already received it."

"I did receive it and have answered it," taking the other letter which I handed to him. He tore it open and then began to read. He read it through and said:

"Please say to the President that I greatly appreciate this letter and that I shall answer it later; also say to him that I am deeply touched that he has chosen to send it by you."

I then said:

"Mr. President, I have a hundred messages intrusted to my care for you, but I have sifted them down to two; one is from Jimmy Sloan and the other from Mrs. Richard Townsend."

"Good. You could not have shown better discernment."

Then, turning to the others, he said:

"To you and to the casual observer, these two might seem to be very far apart, but the truth is, as Archie and I know, they are pretty close together."

He meant that Jimmy, the secret service man, and Mrs. Townsend, the leader of fashion in the Capitol, were alike in loyalty, devotion, and soundness at heart.

"How is good old Jimmy? Give him my love and also give my love to Mrs. Townsend."

He then began to talk with Senator Lodge at one side. Mrs. Roosevelt came in, and I gave her Mrs. Taft's letter. After her came Alice, then dear old Kermit, looking just as he did before he went away. Mrs. Roosevelt said then:

"Archie, come let us see if we can see the children on any of the boats."

We went to the railing and saw, far below, Belle Hagner, Mrs. Robinson, Mrs. Cowles, Archie, Quentin, Teddy and his bride-to-be, and a lot of connections. It was a long time before we could get them to look up, and when Mrs. Roosevelt saw Archie she looked as if she wanted to jump overboard.

"Think; for the first time in nearly two years I have them all within reach!"

She went back to the cabin and called to Mr. Roosevelt:

"Come here, Theodore, and see your children. They are of far greater importance than politics or anything else."

After that we went on board the *Manhattan*, where only the family were permitted. Later the President, Loeb, the two secretaries, and I went on the *Androscoggin*, which contained Cornelius Vanderbilt and the committee of one hundred, who were to take charge of him. He shook hands with everyone on board, and then Vanderbilt, Loeb, and the President's party went to the bridge, where he watched the formation of the line of ships and steamers and simply crowed with delight when he saw the *South Carolina* take her place at the head, or near the head, of the column.

For the next hour there was a perfect pandemonium of sound. Every craft which could float was out, and each was yelling its steam whistle hoarse. The fleet went as high as Twenty-fourth Street and then turned back to the Battery. Just as we were reaching the pier he said he wanted to go below to speak to the engineers and asked me to go with him. While there, Captain Arthur Crosby, a Rough Rider, began to show him some documents and to ask him to fill certain dates with the members of his old regiment. The whistles were blowing and we were near the landing, so, stepping up, I said:

"Mr. President, you have not got the time to look at anything now, sir. You ought to be on the bridge."

He dropped what he was doing and when he reached the bridge such a shout went up from the shore as to waken the stones. Then ashore—and you have read, of course, the short pithy address of welcome of Mayor Gaynor and the nervous energetic reply of the President. He had written it on the steamer and read it from the manuscript. It was very short. In a few sentences he rose to some lofty heights.

It took a half hour to form the line of carriages. The ex-President, the mayor, and Cornelius Vanderbilt rode in the first carriage, while Secretary Wilson, Judge Gary, Loeb, and I rode in the second. Secretary Meyer rode in the carriage behind us, for the reason that he wanted to ride with Senator Lodge, and Senator Lodge could not ride ahead of us. Rather curious, wasn't it, that I should be placed ahead of Lodge? I might have felt some embarrassment had it been anyone else.

The drive up Broadway and Fifth Avenue was one continuous heartfelt ovation. I have never witnessed anything like it, and when, as I said in the beginning, it was to see just one man in a frock suit it was simply marvelous. Not even the band was allowed in line, though every band in the city offered its services gratis. They were permitted to stand on the line of march and play, which they did. Everything was donated. There was no expense for anything but the printing and the postage. Even I came in for some of the results of this enthusiasm. I had engaged a room at the Waldorf by wire, but when I got there I found a beautiful suite of four rooms at my disposal. I had signed for all the meals I took there Friday and Saturday, and when I asked for my bill I was told there was no bill, and when I questioned further I was shown a note on the margin of the ledger that the courtesies of the house were to be extended to me.

Well, I will end this, for I am now getting prolix. I went to a vacant home at Fifth Avenue where Mrs. Alexander was giving a lunch and where the Roosevelt family witnessed the parade. The President made a speech to the Rough Riders and then he returned there for lunch also. One dish appealed to him as strongly as it did to me. It consisted of boiled rice and creamed chicken. When he had tasted it he said:

"They must have some Georgia blood in their veins, or else Mrs. Alexander knew she would have a goodly contingent of Georgians as her guests."

While the President was finishing his luncheon, Alice, Nick, and I went to the Vanderbilts', where we had coffee and cigars with their guests. August Belmont, Mayor Gaynor, and Creighton Webb fell to my lot to talk to chiefly, and later I had a few words in confidence with Mrs. Neily and pledged my support to Cornelius for special ambassador at the coronation. I spoke of it to her, and she said she had wanted to talk to me, but would have cut her arm off before she would have broached the subject first, as she feared I might have misunderstood her friendship for me in the past.

I then went to the Alexander home, where I had several opportunities to talk with Mr. Roosevelt alone. I told him frankly about Mrs. Taft's illness and how she dreaded to see anyone whom she had known in the past. He made no comment either then or at any time. He told me, however, that he had heard much that had distressed him, but he would not be led into any criticism or comment and did not propose to utter a word on politics for at least two months. He repeated what he said to me on the boat.

"I wish you could tell the President that his letter was doubly welcome because he sent it by you, but I fear he might think that rather uncomplimentary, don't you?" he said, laughing. "It's just bully to see you, Archie," he said again, "and nothing I have done has been better than that ride we took together to Warrenton. Wasn't that bully?"

We went to the room where the presents were, and I showed him the pitcher the President had sent.

While we were at the Alexanders' the most frightful storm came up, and the papers this morning say that seventeen persons were killed. I never saw such a storm in New York before. It had rained up to the night before and then cleared, and the morning hours were beautiful and clear. Everyone began talking about Roosevelt luck. The only bright hours of the day were those during his celebration.

Senator Lodge and Secretary Meyer went to Oyster Bay with the Roosevelts. They asked me to go, but I thought it better taste to decline, as much as I hated to do so.

Alice and Nick and I had quite a long chat together.

She told him that she and her father had such fun laughing at the advice and at the fears of himself and Senator Lodge. It seems that Nick wrote a long letter over, urging Mr. Roosevelt to make a statement in regard to an advertisement appearing in *Collier's Weekly* calling upon readers of that paper to cut out a coupon in the advertisement, to fill it out and mail to the *Outlook*. The coupon contained a lot of questions relative to the present administration, to its policies, and some were very searching and all reflected on the President. It was to discountenance this that Nick had written to Mr. Roosevelt. He did make some statement, but it was a rather noncommittal one and evidently was not what Nick thought it should have been, so he cabled Alice that neither he nor Senator Lodge thought it equal to the occasion, and it was this cable which Alice said made her father and her laugh very much, Mr. Roosevelt even calling them children in the game of politics. Nick rather flushed up when Alice said this to him, but he said nothing.

I don't think Nick has the lightest inkling what his father-in-law intends to do—and I don't think anyone else has either. I was with him most of the day, and he never said a word that could be construed one way or the other. I was at his side when he was talking with Lodge and Meyer, and they did a lot of talking, but he kept silent, only asking a few questions now and then. His old associate, Secretary Wilson, had quite a long talk with him. He repeated it to me word for word when we got to the hotel where we were both stopping, and he thought that the silence of Mr. Roosevelt was most ominous. He said that he told his former chief that the present administration was in perfect accord with his own and that the President had carried into legislative form nearly every policy advocated by Mr. Roosevelt during the past four years. He said Mr. Roosevelt listened and then said:

"Wilson, you must expect no comment from me. These things may be so, but I will make no comment or criticism for at least two months."

The secretary read in this silence, or rather Mr. Roosevelt's refusal to make any comment to him, a hostile attitude toward the President, but I thought not and so told him, for the reason that he had said the same thing to every person who had approached him.

When we got back to Washington this morning, the old man and I came down from the station together. He asked me to say to Mr. Taft that he would like to see him and make this report to him. When I saw the President at breakfast, I told him this and also the tenor of what Mr. Roosevelt had said to Mr. Wilson, and that I saw nothing in it to justify the secretary's fears. He agreed with me and said to telephone the secretary that he would see him in the course of business Monday or Tuesday. One thing the secretary said to me that interested me much was:

"Captain, Taft is a mighty big man and a good man, and it will not do for Theodore to reckon too much on swaying the people against him. I have served Roosevelt seven years and I am deeply attached to him, but between the two men I could not repudiate Taft for the other, and I think it would be so with most of us who know them. Roosevelt can split the Republican party wide open now if he chooses and bring it to certain defeat, but I doubt if he could unite it on himself sufficiently to secure the Presidency another term, for there is a very strong feeling against the third-term idea."

Well, enough of politics and forecasting. Let me tell you a funny incident on Alice; one that Loeb told me driving up Fifth Avenue. He said that he wrote Mr. Roosevelt after his appointment as special ambassador that he was now entitled to the courtesies of the port both for himself and his immediate family. When Mr. Roosevelt got this letter he read it to Alice and she promptly sent this cable:

LOEB

NEW YORK

PIG

ALICE

But it was not delivered for twenty-four hours, for it seems that the banking or brokerage firm of Kuhn & Loeb have "Loeb" as their cable address, and so it was sent to them. They spent hours, so one of the firm told Loeb, looking through codes to see what "Pig Alice" meant. They thought it was a tip to buy or sell pig iron, but they could find nothing which would extricate them from their difficulties, so they finally cabled back to their house in London asking the meaning of the strange cipher, and the firm there was as much puzzled as the house in New York had been, but finally got at the truth and sent word that the cable had been sent by Mrs. Longworth, and so the cable was then sent to the Custom House. Later I heard Mr. Roosevelt telling of the same incident. He said that he had cabled later that he would not accept the courtesies of the port, as he thought he should pay his duties and not take advantage of the technicality of the law, as it clearly was not meant to apply to cases such as his.

This is a long letter, and I have done. It may interest you or it may bore you. The writing of it has tired me extremely.

With love,

ARCHIE.

Monday

June 20, 1910.

The President and I went horseback riding in the park yesterday afternoon. We started from the Newlands'. We had a very good ride, getting back late. He asked me to come back to dinner, and I hastened home to dress and forgot in the rush that I had promised to dine with Mrs. Townsend and tell her about her hero. However, I got away from the Executive presence about half-past ten and went out to Massachusetts Avenue. Mary Patten and Mrs. Corbin were there, and also the Rianos.

After our ride this afternoon, while we were coming back in the motor, we got talking about Mr. Roosevelt again; what he intended to do and so on. I said:

"Anyhow, Mr. President, your record is straight, and whatever comes up now must be based on anything else rather than on any resentment for any slight you may have put on him. Of course, he may decide to make the effort to become President again. This will evidently come into his mind, and he alone can settle that issue. Should the line be drawn, the friends of you two will not have to discuss the question of whether you did the right thing now or not."

"You have hit it exactly right, Archie. I wanted to do all that was proper at this time, so that whatever happens this time will not become any issue. Whether he has any ambition to be President again, I don't know either. He will have to fight that out by himself, for there is no way that a discussion of it can ever come up between us."

A. W. B.

CHAPTER XLIV

NORTON WORKS AGAINST BALLINGER

[Washington, D. C.]
June 22, 1910.

DEAR CLARA:

Mrs. Taft left this morning, and the President and I will leave as soon as Congress adjourns. The insurgents are filibustering against the Postal Savings Bank bill, but the President thinks that it cannot last and that Friday or Saturday will see the end of it. He may stay for a couple of days after the adjournment, or he may pull out at once. If the weather remains as it has been for the past three days, I think he will get out the first moment he can do so.

We were to have gone to New Haven last Monday and then again yesterday, but the situation in Congress is such that he believes he had better remain and fight it out. It is a great disappointment to him not to be present at Bob's graduation, but there was such a protest against his leaving while the postal bill was in the shape it is that he abandoned the trip, much to the relief of each of us who are compelled to go with him. We go riding every afternoon, just he and I.

Norton is very anxious to get into his pastimes and play with us, but he is not made for sportive tricks, I fear. He acknowledges that he is as afraid as death of a horse, and although the Secretary of War left him his horse to ride this summer, he has not mounted him so far, and got me to give him a trial to reassure him. The animal is as gentle as a cat, but I don't believe Norton will ever bring himself to get on him. If I were he, I would confine myself to the job of secretary and try to make good at that and not run the risk of boring the President with wanting to do things for which one is not fitted by nature.

Norton is intent on getting rid of Ballinger. He asked me yesterday to help him make the President see that Ballinger must go.

Up to the present time the President has shown no inclination to let Ballinger out, but since he yielded in the matter of Carpenter, I would not be surprised to see him weaken on Ballinger and possibly choose me as an emissary to give the hint. I confess that the rôle of official bouncer is not a pleasant one to me, and should he delegate that task to me I should decline to do it. We met Ballinger on horseback in the park day before yesterday, and the secretary rode with us a little distance and then turned back. As he left, I remarked how ill he was looking. The President said:

"Yes. There was never a man more persecuted and so unjustly persecuted as Ballinger. He is as high-minded a man as I have ever known, and I propose to stand by him."

Let us see if he will make these words good. If he should yield to Norton and the others, who are urging him to ask for Ballinger's resignation after this, I should feel like asking to be relieved myself, for I could not have the same respect for him as I ought to have for one whom I serve as I do the President. Secretary Ballinger was riding President Roosevelt's blooded horse, Rosswell. He bought him from DeNaigue for four hundred dollars. I wonder what Mr. Roosevelt would think if he knew that his favorite horse was owned by Ballinger, the man whom Pinchot and Garfield and all the uplift crowd believe to have horns.

An Evening with "Alice and Nick"

June 23, 1910.

I dined with Alice and Nick last evening. The former was most enthusiastic over her experiences in Paris. The Rockhills and the Winthrops were there at dinner also. We were all much amused with Alice's description of the Guildhall speech and the luncheon that followed it. She went to Paris, and on her return Ambassador Reid said he did not see how she had much of a time as she was there only two days.

"Ah, but I was there three nights, and it is the nights which count in Paris," she said, much to the amusement of the Bishop of London, who was sitting near her.

Alice said when was she in Paris last, she had a husband

and no latch key. This time she had the latch key and no husband.

The President and I rode yesterday afternoon. It was the hottest day of the season, and both he and his horse were nearly prostrated from the excessive heat. Before attempting to enter the swampy part of the island, I suggested to him to turn back, which he was very glad to do. He asked me to invite Alice to dinner on Friday evening. "Tell her to bring Nick and her cigarettes."

Just before going to ride yesterday Norton came to the White House to tell the President that the Postal Savings Bank bill had passed. The President was greatly delighted and congratulated his secretary on the part he had played in getting the bill through. This closes practically the legislative program, and Congress will adjourn possibly Saturday. While riding, the President told me he doubted if he could get away until Tuesday of next week, as he intended to veto the river-and-harbor bill, as it was full of corruption and log-rolling schemes, and that possibly Congress might try to pass it over his veto.

Good-bye. With love,

ARCHIE.

CHAPTER XLV

FORMAL LETTER FROM ROOSEVELT

[Washington, D. C.]
June 24, 1910.

DEAR CLARA:

The President has little time for riding or golfing; in fact, little time for anything save the matters which are now pending before Congress. He is holding conferences hourly with Senators or Representatives, and last night he was busy until a quarter past twelve. He had asked me to come by for him with the motor car at ten o'clock, which I did, and found him in conference with an Ohio quartette. They were urging him to name the candidate for the governor of that state, and he was trying to get them to unite on someone with whom he thought they might win.

There was Senator Dick, who learned his politics in the Hanna school; Wade Ellis, considered a marvel in politics by some; Walter Brown of Toledo, and a Mr. Boland, a boss of Columbus. These are the four men who have come to settle the fate of the Ohio governorship and incidentally to kill off Harmon in that state. If they do, they think it will eliminate him as a Presidential factor. That is the fight now, and that is why the President is so much interested. Harmon has grown so strong recently as to impair the chances of President Taft's success in Ohio. It is now anything to defeat Harmon.

They talked until after twelve o'clock. It seems that Boss Cox of Cincinnati wants Britt Brown, and the President has set his face against the nomination for the reason that the state will not elect a man whom Cox endorses. The other candidates are Harding and Carmi Thompson. These names mean nothing to me except that each one has a certain following and each one is opposed by the President. He is inclined to Judge Kincaid of Toledo. When the conference broke up, the matter stood that way. The bosses were to let the names of Harding, Brown, and Thompson go before the convention, and then were to unite on a second ballot on Kincaid. They are all afraid of Cox, as they think he may be setting up the cards himself, and when the hands are shown that he will have the winning one.

The President has heard from Mr. Roosevelt in answer to the letter I carried to him. He told Norton to let me see it, which he did this morning. I read it over most carefully, and it seemed to me rather noncommittal. He addressed the President as "My dear Mr. President" and not as "Dear Will." He thanked him for sending the letter by me and then declined to accept the President's invitation to visit the White House. He told the President that he was opposed to the idea of ex-Presidents visiting Washington, and would, therefore, never come to Washington while any of the political people were here. He said he would be compelled to come here to look over some of the skins from Africa, but that he would time his visit when everyone was out of the city.

The letter was almost too frank to please me, for, after all, ex-Presidents have come to Washington and quite frequently too, and there is no reason why Mr. Roosevelt should not come except for some ulterior reason that does not show in the letter itself. I think the President was somewhat disappointed at its tone.

Norton told me that while I was in New York the New York *World* sent over to get some expression from the President on the arrival of his predecessor. Norton took the request in to the President and advised him to make some statement complimentary to the hunter, and he says the President showed irritation and said he would not do it.

He had done all he could do, and it may have been a momentary spell of irritation, which I should think was justifiable in one way, and yet wholly unjustifiable in another. For, after all, Mr. Roosevelt has played the game to the limit, and he cannot help the remarkable enthusiasm displayed over his return, nor does he seem to be able to do anything to check the growth of his popularity.

June 24, 1910.

Dined at the White House last night on the terrace. Alice, Nick, and Norton and I were there, and it was a very delightful evening. The only thing of importance which transpired was the fact that the President is now uncertain whether to sign or veto the river-and-harbor bill. He told us last night that Senator Crane, Tawney, and most of the leaders in both houses are most anxious for him to sign it, but he feels that he should veto it. They predict that it will have a most disastrous effect politically if he vetoes it, and Nick begged him while making up his mind to keep the necessity of carrying the counties on the Ohio River next fall in his mind. He is very much at sea. If he has the nerve to veto it, I believe that it will have a bad effect on some of the politicians who helped to pass it, but I believe it will have a splendid political effect on the whole country. It will be a guarantee of good faith from the President that he will do what he thinks right whether it is injurious to his party or not.

ARCHIE.

Mr. Taft Signs the Last Minute Bills

[Washington, D. C.]
Sunday, June 26, 1910.

MY DEAR CLARA:

I went with the President last night to the Senate, where he signed all the remaining bills. Congress was to adjourn at eleven, and all bills must be signed before adjournment to become law. This makes the President's journey from the White House to the Capitol always one of ceremony and interest. There is something a little spectacular in it, and therefore it always pleases the Executives to perform this duty. It is a little out of the ordinary, and if they happen to have any dramatic sense, it appeals to it. Last night Norton, Mr. Bowers, and the Solicitor General and I accompanied the President. Mr. Bowers went in the absence of the Attorney General to cast a hasty glance over the bills, so that the President might feel reasonably assured that Congress in its last hour was not hoodwinking him with some joker in legislative form.

We reached the Capitol at ten, and for the next hour the President was kept busy signing bills and resolutions and shaking hands with the leaders in the Senate and the House who came at different times to pay their respects. Most of them handed him some pet measure, and each wanted the pen with which the President approved the measure.

Even Senator Wetmore, heavy and dull and pretentious, did not scorn asking for the pen which the President used in signing some bill in which he was interested. I do not know what the bill was, but I can reasonably guess that it carried some appropriation for Rhode Island somewhere in its paragraphs. On some bills Mr. Taft used two pens, in order that conflicting claims might be adjusted in the matter of the pens. These public men are like so many children looking for souvenirs. The other day, in approving the Postal Savings Bank bill, he used three pens, and I think he used six in affixing his signature to the bill admitting Arizona and New Mexico as states into the Union. I can see some day conflicting claims of museums as to which was the pen he actually used in signing the statehood bills.

Promptly at eleven we left the Senate, and with very little ceremony. I was surprised that there was not more, but I presume that most of the Senators were anxious to get to their homes, and many possibly had already left the Capitol before the hour of adjournment. When we left there were not more than two Senators in the room or corridor to say good-bye.

Instead of going to the White House direct, the President said he wanted to take a joy ride. We went humming through the Soldiers' Home and down through the park. I think the only incident which marred the closing hours of Congress to him was the fact that not one of the so-called insurgent Senators came in to pay his respects or to say good-bye. He hates not to be able to pacify those whom he hits, and somehow their evident resentment toward him saddened him somewhat. Not one of them, not even Beveridge or Dixon, to say nothing of Dolliver, Cummins, La Follette, and that type, came near him. Senator Borah came into the room, spoke to someone else there, and went out without addressing a remark to the President. He spoke of this with seeming resentment as we were riding, and said:

"Bowers, did you notice the utter absence of the insurgent Senators in my room to-night? I don't give a damn. If they can get along without me, I presume I can do the same without them."

But I could see that he wished it had been otherwise. He spoke freely as to his act in signing the river-and-harbor bill. He told Mr. Bowers that he possibly ought to have vetoed it, but Congress had done so much for him that he had not the heart to veto it.

"Crane and Aldrich, I am sure, used that measure to gain over a number of votes for my bills, and it would have greatly embarrassed them to have had me veto the bill. They did not confess this much to me, however, for if they had I might have felt constrained to veto it on this very account. I accompanied my approval with a message warning them not to send me another such bill while I was in the White House."

I did not see the message, but I heard Senator Nelson say it was a fine message and he was coming to the White House Monday to see what it means.

Perhaps some interesting things may occur [at Beverly]; if so you may be sure you will get the news of them, but the President said last night that he wanted complete rest and to remain as quiet as possible and let what little good has been accomplished work its way to the top. He is a little worried over the reports that Mr. Roosevelt is determined upon Governor Hughes's resigning from the Supreme Bench and making the race for the governorship. He does not think the governor will consider the possibility of such a thing, but until he knows that Mr. Roosevelt's hypnotism has failed in this respect, he will feel some uneasiness. As much as he wants the Republican party to succeed in New York this fall, he wants still more to have Hughes on the bench. He did not say so much in so many words, but from what he said on the matter to Mr. Bowers, I gathered such were his sentiments.

I have packed up the skins, the curtains, and the rugs, and the house looks lovely with the bright-colored Filipino mats which now cover the floors. I have sent the dogs to the country. Diana, who is going to have puppies again, I have persuaded Palmer to take up to his mother's home in New Jersey. I am sorry for the Palmers, but Diana always takes the most inconvenient time to produce, and she is never satisfied with having one or two puppies. Nothing under eleven seems to satisfy her.

God bless you.

ARCHIE.

Friction with Roosevelt Seems Likely

[Washington, D. C.]
Monday, June 27, 1910.

DEAR CLARA:

I went over to the White House very early this morning and found the President at breakfast, and Norton with him with the mail. He had just seen in the morning papers a report that Mr. Roosevelt and Governor Hughes were coming to see him at Beverly in the near future. He thought it only a newspaper report and was not inclined to put any credence in it at all.

"The fact of the matter is," said the President, "I hope he will not come. He can scarcely do so without my inviting him, and I don't propose to do that. I invited him to the White House and he declined to come, giving some good reasons from his point of view possibly, but not from mine, so I am not in a position to ask him again. In fact, I do not want to see him until he has had plenty of opportunity to think the situation over and has made up his mind definitely what course he wishes to pursue, because I cannot argue my case with him or before him. He says he will keep silent for at least two months. I don't care if he keeps silent forever. Certainly the longer he remains silent, the better it will please me."

This last he said with a laugh, but there was a serious undertone to it nevertheless. Norton thinks he is preparing himself for a break of some kind with him. At least he says he does not wish to be in a position to seem to be seeking his favor. We had a long talk afterward about it, and what he said above is more than he has ever said to me before, and Norton says it is more than he has ever admitted to him.

I think the President is a little nettled over the visits of Garfield and Pinchot to Oyster Bay. He says they could have gone there without invitation, but they could not have stayed over night and remained next day playing tennis without one.

I had not thought to write again, but I thought this important as simply one more link in the chain.

Good-bye,
ARCHIE.

Monday afternoon,
June 27, 1910.
The President told me coming back [from Chevy Chase] that the Ohio situation bothered him; that Cox had sent

him word that Britt Brown would be nominated unless he, the President, interferred, and that he would not dare to interfere.

"I would like to show that political tyrant that I am not afraid of him, and while I do not want to further complicate the situation by a needless controversy with him, yet if he attempts to force the nomination of his man I will sweep him aside (that is, if I can). He is puffed up with success [so] that he thinks no one dares to tackle him. The state is lost if we accept any man of his dictation; if it has to be lost, it had better be over such equipment as he than by carrying the load."

Good-night.
A. W. B.

CHAPTER XLVI

Roosevelt's Visit to the President

[Beverly, Mass.]
Friday, June 30, 1910.

My dear Clara:

Mr. Roosevelt has come and gone, and the press and public are completely nonplussed over what occurred. I never saw as much interest manifested over any one event in the administration of either man. The President had asked me to be there when the colonel arrived, and I was considerably in doubt what to do after the two had met. The President was in his office with his secretary and assistant secretary, and I remained on the porch with Jimmy Sloan watching for the arrival of our former chief. I had just been saying what a splendid thing this meeting was for the President; that it would give the lie to all the false reports of the enmity between the two men. Jimmy said in his stoical way:

"It does not mean anything."

And when I expressed my surprise at this statement, Jimmy laconically answered:

"I know this man better than you do. He will come to see the President to-day and bite his leg off to-morrow."

Jimmy, however, has always believed that they would split and had already come to loggerheads, so I felt his judgment was biased, and said nothing more.

We both felt a quiver of excitement when we saw a big motor car turn into the roadway leading to the house, and recognized a minute later Senator Lodge and the ex-President. I notified the President that his predecessor was coming and he came on the porch just in time to meet him as he stepped from the machine. The President stretched out both hands and exclaimed:

"Ah, Theodore, it is good to see you," and Mr. Roosevelt said impulsively:

"How are you, Mr. President? This is simply bully."

"See here now, drop the 'Mr. President,'" said the President, hitting Mr. Roosevelt on the shoulder, but the latter said:

"Not at all. You must be Mr. President and I am Theodore. It must be that way."

The President did not address him as Theodore again and always spoke to him as Mr. President, and when the latter complained later on, as the two got more accustomed to the situation, the President said:

"The force of habit is very strong in me. I can never think of you save as Mr. President."

He shook hands with Norton, and when he saw Forster, his old assistant secretary, he said, his whole face lighting up:

"This is simply splendid. I must tell Mrs. Roosevelt I have seen you and how well you look."

Then, catching a glimpse of me, he sprang toward me

and, giving me a friendly punch, which is very characteristic of him, shook my hand and asked:

"How is Georgia?"

"She's lame. I wrote Mrs. Roosevelt."

"Hang it, Archie, I meant the state not the horse."

The President put his arm through that of Mr. Roosevelt and led him around the corner of the veranda, and we all sat down. There were present then only the President, the ex-President, Senator Lodge, Mr. Norton, and I. I thought both were a little strained at first. I was a little embarrassed whether to stay or to leave, and I looked at the President for some sign, but his face was a blank when he caught my eye. The butler came out and the President asked us what we would like to drink. No one took anything, but Mr. Roosevelt, and he said he needed rather than wanted a Scotch and soda. Senator Lodge and I took cigars, and as the wind was blowing rather high, Senator Lodge went round to the sea side to strike a match. I took that opportunity to say to him:

"Do you think they want to be left alone? If so, I will arrange to have the others leave and to delay the coming of Mrs. Taft and Miss Helen."

The Senator told me that he had asked Mr. Roosevelt that very question coming over, and that he had asked him to remain during the visit, that he wanted it to be like any other social call and not to be left alone with the President. So when we went back to the others, I sent word to Miss Helen that the President wanted her and her mother to come down to meet Mr. Roosevelt.

The President started the subject of New York politics, which was the ostensible reason for this meeting. I don't think it was the real reason at all, but it simply furnished to Mr. Roosevelt an excuse to call. I am sure Senator Lodge advised the ex-President to pay this visit, and Mr. Roosevelt thought it would be the wisest thing to do. I don't think it was altogether altruistic on the part of Lodge either, for he wants the aid of both in the fight he is making in his state for reëlection.

The talk between them on the subject of New York politics was of the most desultory character. The President said merely that he was willing to do all in his power to assist Hughes to pass the primary bill as amended by Cobb, and the ex-President said he was not only willing, but as a citizen of New York thought it to be his duty to do it. While they were talking, Norton was called to the long-distance telephone. When he came back, he said he had just been talking to Lloyd Griscom in New York, and the latter had asked him to say to the President and Mr. Roosevelt that there was not the ghost of a chance to elect the next governor, that every member of the committee looked upon the fight as a hopeless one. The President said he would continue to send messages to those in the New York Senate whom he might influence and dictated one to Norton saying that he hoped So and So would vote for the bill, for without it there was little chance to elect the Republican ticket this fall. The wiliness of Senator Lodge became apparent, and he said:

"Can't you get him on the telephone? It is always dangerous to put things in writing."

"Oh," said the President, "if that can hurt us we are ruined already, for I have already sent a dozen far more incriminating than this one."

They all agreed that the situation looked pretty hopeless, and Senator Lodge turned to me and said *sotto voce:*

"I wish they had both remained out of it, for it cannot do either of them any good and they are certain to be defeated."

Just here Mrs. Taft and Miss Helen came on the scene, and Mr. Roosevelt greeted both most kindly, but he had evidently been primed not to ask Mrs. Taft any questions, so he did the talking, which put her very much at her ease.

President Taft then said:

"Now, Mr. President, tell me about cabbages and kings."

"Ah, I see you remember *Alice in Wonderland*," said Mr. Roosevelt, and forthwith launched into a description of his experiences in Europe which lasted over an hour. He was in his best vein, and I never heard him more witty, more humorous, and more incisive than on this occasion. The President told Norton, who had never met him before, that he had seen him and heard him in his very best vein.

When he reached the Kaiser—I put this first because it was the most important thing which happened at the conference—the President asked:

"Is he intent on war with England?"

"No, I don't think so," said Mr. Roosevelt, "but William is no longer the German people. He is not as big a man in Germany, Mr. President, as he is out of Germany. I must say that on the whole I was disappointed with him. I found him vain as a peacock. He would rather ride at the head of a procession than govern an empire. That is what has contributed mostly to his downfall, for he certainly has had a downfall."

"You mean his comb has been cut?" asked the President.

"Yes, and cut close to the head at that," continued Mr. Roosevelt. "I asked him the blank question if he contemplated war with England, and he assured me that there was nothing further from his mind or that of the German people. In fact, he told me that he loved England next to Germany, and then in a sort of whimsical way, almost leerish, I thought, he told me the British did not treat him kindly when he visited there. That is what hurts him. He wants the English to make a fuss over him and they don't do it. He told me, and this I say in the utmost confidence, that his chief ambition was to unite with the United States and England and form a compact to guarantee the peace of the world. He was not altogether sincere in this, for he said the same thing in the utmost secrecy to Pichon, the French ambassador. But even if he could get England to agree to cease building ships and to enter some such agreement, the German people would not consent to it. The Kaiser no longer represents them, and they have got the whip hand, and they know it, and there is not the slightest chance of their ever relinquishing it again. If William had been content to govern Germany wisely, they would have put up with a lot, but he not only wanted to be a ruler, he wanted the world to recognize in him a despotic ruler. He wanted to parade his power before the world, and so they undid him. But he is a strong man; don't let me give you the wrong impression about him. If he were in New York politics, he would have his following vote largely as he wished. He might even pass this primary bill for Hughes."

"You don't think he would consider the proposition to cease to build ships?" asked the President.

"If he would, the German people would not," said Mr. Roosevelt.

"Then you don't look for much advance in the universal-peace plan?" asked the President.

"No, I don't," said Mr. Roosevelt, "and I know what you are leading up to also, and I say don't do it, that is all."

"Yes, you are right," said the President. "That is what I am leading to. I had decided to consult with you, and if you think there is any chance of the next peace conference accomplishing anything of importance, to ask you to head the mission and to choose your own confrères, but if you don't think the conference is going to amount to much, then to appoint on it a lot of cranks and let it go at that."

"No, no, I wouldn't take it," said Mr. Roosevelt, "but I feel flattered at the offer. I would not feel justified in throwing so much of myself away, for that is what it would amount to. I think the conference will do a good many useful things, but that it will accomplish anything like what the real peace lovers want, I doubt. In fact, as long as Germany builds ships, England will continue to do so. Germany says she wants as many as England, and England says she must, on account of her colonies, keep just so far ahead of Germany, and there you are."

"Then you think bankruptcy is the only cure?" asked the President.

"I think Germany may get tired before that comes; but if she does not, then bankruptcy must call a halt."

"Well, I am sorry for this, for I had hoped to have you head that commission. I suppose I must begin to look for cranks."

Said Mr. Roosevelt: "You might find some men who would carry some weight and represent us fairly well. Another reason why I would hesitate to go on it is that it might look like betraying those who have entertained me so royally, for I would go there burdened with a good many state secrets." Then with a laugh: "Why not name Carnegie? He would certainly finance the commission, and if you could seal his mouth so that he would not be talking about what we think and so on, he might do fairly well."

"I don't think Mr. Carnegie would do at all," said Mrs. Taft. It was the first time she had said anything.

Senator Lodge said: "I agree with you, Mrs. Taft. He would simply get us into world trouble with his officiousness." And the President nodded his approval of the veto.

"Yet that old fox there," said Mr. Roosevelt, pointing

to Lodge, "almost got us in a worse muddle than this would be, by trying to force Eliot on us as Ambassador to Great Britain."

"Yes," said the President, "both of you got me to offer the embassy to Eliot, and had he accepted it I would have died of mortification."

"I know, I know," said Mr. Roosevelt, "but Lodge got me into it. Can't you see old Eliot delivering a Guildhall speech, saying that he could not endorse the British being in Egypt for the reason that he disapproved of his country's remaining in the Philippines?"

They all laughed, and Lodge said he must have been suffering from aberration of the mind when he saw only Eliot for this mission.

The President then asked Mr. Roosevelt what he thought of the King of Italy.

"He is the strongest man in Europe, that is my opinion. He is a stronger man than the German Emperor, but whether George will grow stronger than them all remains as yet to be seen. The Italian King has greater insight than any man I met on a throne. Unfortunately, he lacks confidence in himself. He is undersized, and it is always uppermost in his mind. If he is standing he wants to sit down at once so that his height will not be so apparent, and when he sits he always chooses a high chair and his little feet hardly touch the floor. If I were in his place, I would not care a hang about my height. If he had his ability and Knox's assurance, he would be one of the most dominant figures in the world to-day."

They all laughed at this reference to Knox.

"Yes," said the President, "there is no lack of confidence in Knox. I have found out that much."

Mr. Roosevelt gave a very funny description of his meeting with the Secretary of War in Austria. He said he was asked confidentially by him if he intended to touch on the subject of disarmament while in Germany, and he said he did not expect to do so, though he would like to sound the German people on the subject; yet it would be a most delicate thing to do, and to him an impossible one.

"These people would write letters from king to king as I passed them en route," said Mr. Roosevelt, "and tell the one ahead what sort of barbarian I was and what I might say. In fact, I think each ruler screwed his throne down a little tighter as I approached. When I reached Berlin I learned that my conversation with the Austrian secretary of war had been transmitted to the foreign office and that it had leaked from there, and the press was sounding the alarm and advising me what bad taste it would be to come there as a guest and discuss their policies of state. I told the Emperor what I thought of this and said that I had been in politics myself, and that while I expected what I had said in confidence to be repeated to Germany, still I had expected to have it correctly repeated. He looked perfectly wooden and denied all knowledge of it, and then I had to tell him that he must have known it and suggested, as mildly as I might, if he must lie not to lie so blunderingly.

"However, we got along famously, and I thanked him for all those execrable presents he had sent me while I was President—the bust of himself, which is now over at the Corcoran Art Gallery; the books on religion, of which he knows little; the work on art, of which I found he knows nothing, and the hideous vase with nymphs for handles. This I hope to give to the Harvard Museum some day. The nymphs are built after the German *hausfrau* order and are clumsily thrown against the sides of the vase and look as if they are too fat to hang there another minute. But what I did appreciate was a copy of the *Nibelungenlied*, which I saw in the German collection at the St. Louis exhibition. I made him present this to me. He did not want to do it, so I value it as anything else which I may have secured through craft or valor."

The President amused us all with a description of the dinner the night before the funeral of the late King. He said it was a regular wake.

"Everyone went to the table with his face wreathed and distorted into grief. Before the first course was over, we had all forgotten the real cause of our presence in London. I have never attended a more hilarious banquet in my life. I never saw quite so many knights. I had them on every side. They ran one or two false ones on me, and each had some special story of sorrow to pour into my ear. Finally when I met a little bewizened person known as the King of Greece, he fairly wept out his troubles to me. He insisted I must make a speech on the subject of Crete.

"'But I can't speak on Crete,' I insisted.

"'Then you must write me what you think of Crete. You know that Europe is acting abominably toward Crete,' he tearfully said.

"'I cannot discuss Crete even with you,' I said.

"'You must mention Crete in some of your speeches,' he at last yelped.

"Finally I simply walked away from him while he was pitifully muttering and spluttering Crete to me."

Mr. Roosevelt said he was much impressed with Alfonso. He thinks him quite a man. One thing he said he told him, which he thought very significant.

"I had a chat with him at this wake I was telling you about. He said to me that I must know that he did not like anarchists, but as much as he hated anarchists, he hated the clericals more.

"'I hate them and I fear them more,' said the little fellow—and if ever it takes his word to put down the power of the Church in Spain, you can depend on it that he will exercise it."

He gave an account of the funeral and the way in which the special ambassador from France, Monsieur Pichon, resented having the Orleans princes and the Chinese put ahead of himself and Mr. Roosevelt in the line of march.

"I did not care a hang where they put me," said Mr. Roosevelt. "I remembered too vividly the trouble I used to have with Cannon, Frye, and Dewey, ever to make myself ridiculous about rank. When I left the White House, I resolved to stay put wherever I was placed and never to raise a question. Archie, don't you remember what a time we used to have with those three old peacocks at the White House, when each one thought he should be above the other two, no matter which was placed first? I can see Cannon sulking now and glowering over his dinner because he thought he ought to be ahead of someone else, and Dewey went always with his credentials in his pocket to prove to me that more guns were fired for him than for even the Secretary of the Navy."

"It will amuse you to know that I have given George Meyer as many guns as Dewey is entitled to," said the President.

"Then I bet he has never been in the White House since," said Mr. Roosevelt.

The President looked at me and I said he had declined every dinner this winter.

"Well, Pichon was just of that type," said Mr. Roosevelt. "He fairly leaned on me for support. I always told him I did not care where they put me. He came to me once and with tears in his eyes, tears of anger, said did not I notice that the other guests had scarlet livery and that ours was black? I told him I had not noticed, but I would not have cared if ours had been yellow and green. My French, while fluent, is never very clear, and it took me another half hour to get it out of his mind that I was not protesting because my livery was not green and yellow.

He wanted me to enter a protest with him, and I declined
to do so and finally sidetracked him. Finally, when the
Persian prince was put into our carriage, I laughed until I
almost cried. I saw Pichon jump into the carriage, and
I naturally thought it was for fear I would take the right-
hand seat. But it was not so. He jumped in and then
hauled me in after him, giving me the seat of honor. He
really thought the poor little Persian would take possession
of the back seat. Nothing was further from his mind. He
was frightened to death as it was, and looked as if he would
rather die than enter the carriage at all. He did not dare to
look at Pichon and apologized to me when he had to
address some remark to one of us.

"Finally Pichon seized my arm and pointed to the
representatives of Portugal walking ahead of us, and
threatened to jump out and disrupt the funeral procession.
I had to literally hold him in his seat. I said to him:

"'My dear Mr. Pichon, will France and the United
States be any smaller to-morrow or Portugal any larger
because those little fellows are walking ahead of us? For
heaven's sake,' I begged him, 'be quiet. This is a funeral
and we are in deep grief for a great and good friend there.
Wait until another king dies and then settle it beforehand.'

"I really felt superior to Pichon, and I feel ever-
lastingly grateful to Cannon, Frye, and Dewey for giving
me an object lesson in this matter of wrangling after rank,
for without it I might have been led into all sorts of pitfalls
by my friend Pichon."

Mr. Roosevelt started to leave, and the President said:
"Wait just one moment longer. I want you to tell me
about George and just what you think of him."

"I like him," said Mr. Roosevelt. "I like him thoroughly. He is a strong man. He is going to make himself
felt, not only in England, but in the world, and he will keep
well within the constitutional limitations. I don't think

he has the tact of Edward, from what I hear; but that may come. But he struck me as one who has a thorough hold on himself and thorough knowledge of the people he is to rule.

"I like the little I saw of his family life. Mrs. Roosevelt and I dined with them alone one evening." Here Mr. Roosevelt began to laugh. "After dinner he permitted the three older children to come into the room. They had heard of my romping with the little boy, son of the King of Denmark, and they rather expected me to romp with them, I think. But it was hardly the place to do it. In the hall, as I was leaving the King and Queen of Denmark, I met the little tot. I took him in my arms and swung him over my head, and just then the Dowager Empress of Russia popped her head out of a door. Seeing me hesitate, the little fellow said: 'You aren't going to stop playing just for her, are you?' So I laughed and swung him once or twice more. This incident had evidently been talked of in the family circles, and so George's children had the expectant air of being thrown over my head. The King told me that as a rule they were well behaved, and I found them so, but he said his younger son John was very disobedient. He had not as yet appeared.

"'When he comes in,' his father said to me, 'he will pay no one any attention. Last night was his birthday, and so we had him to dinner, and on the sideboard there is the remnant of his cake. He will go there and nibble and not mind who is in the room.'

"Sure enough, when John came into the room, his father motioned to remain silent, and the little rascal went to the cake and put both hands in it."

"It must have reminded you," said the President, "of that luncheon when there were only six chocolate éclairs on the table and Quentin had three on his plate."

"Worse than that," laughed Mr. Roosevelt, "he had

already bitten into two of them and had the third in his hand when I asked him if he wanted all the chocolate éclairs. Biting into the third so that no one else would want it, he said No, he thought three would be enough for him."

Everyone laughed over this incident.

"Well, to continue," said Mr. Roosevelt. "King George said, as any one of us might, 'John, come here.' 'I'm coming,' he growled, and went on eating his cake. 'Come here,' said his father. 'Oh, I'm coming, Father, if you don't hurry me so.' As he passed a dog on his way to his father's seat, he stopped and patted him on the back and rubbed his head. ''Appy is 'airy, hawfully 'airy, Father.' 'Good Lord,' said his father, 'he's worse than usual.' 'It is his nurse,' said his mother, Queen Mary. 'He talks just like her.' Nothing would content John but that I should pat Happy, for that was the dog's name—and we got to be great friends."

Well, there is a lot more that I might write, but I am pretty well tuckered out with this much. It was all so interesting and so different from anything which the public seemed to think really took place that I thought it worth while to put into form. I have quoted Mr. Roosevelt, but I have not misquoted him. Some of his witty parentheses I have not added, and a good deal of the wit and verve of his anecdotes are missing, but on the whole I have quoted fairly accurately. Certainly what I have written is a true account of what took place.

They made mention of Burton, and both the President and Mr. Roosevelt gave a slap at him. Mr. Roosevelt said: "Thank heaven I was never followed by Burton."

As Mr. Roosevelt got up to leave, Senator Lodge said: "It may be just as well for you to decide what will be given out as to this meeting, for when we came in there were at least two hundred newspaper men at the gates and almost as many cameras."

Mr. Roosevelt said if the President had no objection he would stop a minute and say that he had simply paid a personal call and that they had each spent a most delightful afternoon.

"Which is true as far as I am concerned," said the colonel.

"And more than true as far as I am concerned," said the President. "This has taken me back to some of those dear old afternoons when I was Will and you were Mr. President."

So they parted, and the papers this morning simply have nothing on which to hang a story. I never saw the imaginations of the reporters so utterly at sea before. They did not have a clue to go on. Wisely, for a wonder, they remained absolutely silent, not even attempting to manufacture a line.

Mrs. Taft and Helen went upstairs to get on their motor veils. Norton went to the gate to assure the newspaper men that nothing would be given out as to the conference, and the President and I were left alone.

He looked up, smiled, and said:

"Well, Archie, that is another corner turned."

I told him what Senator Lodge had said to me when I asked if he thought Mr. Roosevelt wanted to see him alone. He said:

"I think he felt just as I did, that it was best to have simply a social personal visit and not give any opportunity for confidences which might be embarrassing."

Love to Lewis and with much to yourself, I am as ever,

Your affectionate brother,

ARCHIE.